The Practitioner's Guide to

Interest Rate
Risk Management

Bernard Manson

Graham & Trotman
A member of Wolters Kluwer Academic Publishers
LONDON/DORDRECHT/BOSTON

Graham & Trotman Limited
Sterling House
66 Wilton Road
London SW1V 1DE
UK

Kluwer Academic Publishers Group
101 Philip Drive
Assinippi Park
Norwell, MA 02061
USA

British Library and Library of Congress Cataloguing-in-Publication Data is available
upon request.

ISBN 1 85333 741 2 (book)
ISBN 1 85333 765 X (book & disk)
ISBN 1 85333 766 8 (disk only)

Computer typeset in Garamond by The Orbital Press Ltd, Letchworth, Hertfordshire
Printed and bound in Great Britain by Athenæum Press Ltd, Newcastle upon Tyne

To the memory of my father, Dr Joseph Manson,
who always wanted to understand what I did for a living.

Contents

Acknowledgements

No book is an island. My knowledge of the subject matter came originally from learning on the job while working for Brian Crowe at The Chase Manhattan Bank, but the book itself grew out of notes I prepared for a course which I gave at BRI Financial Training on the invitation of Alan MacDougall.

I could not have completed this book without the assistance of the many people who answered questions, sparked ideas, or read drafts of various chapters; these include Kaveh Alamouti, Steve Bloch, Paul Broder, Lee Frewin, Bob Johns, Brian Kettell, Kevin Liddy, Fiona Mann, Claire Meikle, Peter Ng, Bibi Qureshi, Simon Ramsden, Nick Robinson, and David Setters.

Ken Tregidgo read a next-to-last draft of the manuscript and checked the equations and the numbers; he also made some useful suggestions on improving the text. Any remaining – or new – errors are my responsibility. Ken also tested the spreadsheets which are being marketed to accompany this book.

I am grateful to The Chase Manhattan Bank, N.A. for permission to print the information in Table 3.1 and to Futures and Options World (a division of Metal Bulletin plc) for permission to print the material in Appendix C. In chapters 10 and 11 on options I have followed closely the usage of *Options Markets* (see bibliography), which is a standard textbook on the subject; I hope that my treatment will assist readers in understanding some of the more difficult sections of that work. The references to original papers in Part V are taken from *Options Markets*. The formula in Chapter 11 for calculating the normal distribution function is developed from a formula in *Numerical Recipes in C – The Art of Scientific Computing* (see bibliography), and is used with the kind permission of the Cambridge University Press.

My wife Sarah has contributed doubly to this book; not only has she run a home and raised a family single handedly while I was hunched over the word processor, but she has also found time to read and improve key sections of the text. Lastly, I should mention my children, without whom this book would probably have appeared earlier but with less joy to its author.

Introduction

Interest rate risk management is the process of controlling the risks to the profitability and net worth of an organisation or portfolio due to the possibility of changes in interest rates. This is a vast subject, and to keep this book to manageable dimensions it is tightly focused on practical techniques and on the most commonly used instruments. Working through the material should teach you to understand, identify, measure, report, and account for interest rate risk, and to price and use Forward Rate Agreements, interest rate swaps, Eurodeposit futures, caps, swaptions, foreign exchange swaps, and other instruments to manage the risks identified. The primary concern is market risk, although other risks and costs are identified and discussed.

The magnitude of a risk is approximately the sensitivity of the organisation to changes in rates multiplied by the expected change in rates over a period; the book develops a more precise definition. Since short-term interest rates in any currency typically change by 1% or more over a year, a useful rule of thumb is to test the materiality of interest rate risk by multiplying the net debt portfolio by 1% times the number of years within the organisation's planning horizon. (The book develops the analysis needed to give an accurate figure; meanwhile, this rule can give an imprecise but useful estimate.) Thus a company funded by US$100 million of debt will make or lose about US$1 million per year for each 1% change in rates, and an investor or a bank with a net US$100 million portfolio of interest rate instruments will face a similar magnitude of profit or loss. If the risk is material, then the organisation should consider implementing risk management techniques.

The book is addressed primarily to interest rate risk management practitioners. For the most part, these will be people employed by organisations incurring interest rate risk. Such organisations can be split into three general classes: corporations, investors, and financial intermediaries. Corporations tend to be net borrowers, giving them risk on their funding cost, but they may also have interest rate risk from other sources such as fixed price contracts or from a correlation between high interest rates and low turnover. Investors tend to have their risk exposure concentrated into an investment portfolio; this may make identifying risk easier, but it may also mean that more accurate management is expected. Financial intermediaries such as banks will have risk from borrowing and lending, as well as from entering into risk management transactions with their customers with the intention of making spread and trading income.

All three types of organisation encounter the same problems and need to understand the same techniques and to use the same instruments; this book should therefore be of use to all of them. However, since the most prolific buyers and sellers of interest rate risk tend to be banks, and since banks therefore have the problem of managing trading portfolios as well as simply hedging existing risk, this book is written specifically from the point of view of the banker. It therefore includes a detailed analysis of the costs imposed by the regulatory environment on banks, and attempts to establish a practical framework for banks to price and market interest rate risk management transactions.

It is hoped that the material which is specific to banks will be of some interest to corporate and investor readers on the principle of 'know your enemy'. This material may also be of interest to the academic community, who appear to fight shy of analysing the management of a bank at a level of detail which allows the specification of operational guidelines.

The logic of this book is that interest rate risk management is an integrated subject. It therefore starts by developing a theory which defines interest rate risk and shows how it can be measured, reported, and managed, and only then does it consider individual instruments; enough detail is given to enable the reader to calculate price, market risk, and credit risk for each common instrument. The ultimate goal is to present a framework for integrating interest rate risk management into the overall management of an organisation.

In order to give the fullest value as a study text and as a source of reference, there are worked examples throughout, and at the end of each part there is a comprehensive set of self-study questions with full answers.

Incorporating all of this has meant excluding other material. In particular, the book does not cover cash and liquidity management, tax, and legal issues. The next paragraphs briefly comment on these exclusions.

Cash management is concerned with finding the most effective way of using cash balances, and liquidity management is concerned with ensuring that an organisation always has access to adequate short-term funding. The demands of cash and liquidity management may interact with each other and with the process of managing interest rate risk; within an organisation there should be some integration of the three activities. The use of the word 'liquidity' in the book will generally refer to its other meaning of the cost of closing out a market position. It is probably no exaggeration to say that the two most important concerns in finance are liquidity and liquidity, and it is unfortunate that the one word has to suffice for both concepts.

Tax is important in risk management for two reasons. First, there is a need to consider the tax implications of proposed transactions on your own organisation, and secondly, a bank which can identify tax-driven opportunities for its customers can greatly increase its earnings in the risk management and capital market areas. Unfortunately, it is not practical for a book such as this to give even a cursory review of the tax treatment for all the instruments covered in all the possible jurisdictions; on the principle that a little knowledge is a dangerous thing, no explanation of tax treatment has been included. The large accountancy firms are a good source of current information on the taxation of these instruments.

As for tax, so for legal issues. It is important for an organisation entering into a transaction to check that it has the legal power to do so and that its counterparty also has the legal power to do so. The UK local authorities swaps fiasco of the late 1980s demonstrated that transactions entered into in good faith could be judged *ultra vires*. Banks also have to contend with a complex regulatory environment, and they need to ensure that all of their activities comply with the regulations. Most large organisations will have their own legal or compliance departments which can clarify these issues.

Other material not covered includes contemporary practice in the capital markets, portfolio theory, and the prediction of interest rates through econometric forecasting. A select bibliography suggests further reading in these and other related areas.

The book is divided into seven parts, which are subdivided into a total of eighteen chapters. There are five product parts covering Forward Rate Agreements and Eurodeposit futures, interest rate swaps, basis risk, options, and cross currency risk; these are sandwiched between two more general parts which define a framework for analysing, reporting, and managing interest rate risk.

The book is designed to be read from Chapter 1 through to Chapter 18, but you can skip certain chapters or even parts without affecting your understanding of subsequent material. In particular, missing out Chapter 5 on Eurodeposit futures will affect only that section of Part V which relates to exchange-traded options and that small portion of Part IV relating to futures on government bonds. Similarly, missing out Chapters 7 and 8 on complex interest rate swaps will not affect any of the subsequent material, except for the discussion of the cost of capital and credit in Part VI. You can miss out Parts IV, V, or VI, without affecting your understanding of the subsequent material, except for references in Part VII to basis, volatility, and cross currency risks respectively.

Except in one chapter, the level of mathematical sophistication required is not high; algebra and calculus are used sparingly, and, where calculus is used, a fairly basic knowledge should suffice.

Unfortunately, it is not possible to derive the risk characteristics of options without using partial derivatives, and so readers with a limited knowledge of calculus will have to take most of the results of Chapter 14 on trust. However, care is taken to ensure that even if you cannot understand in detail the derivation of some results, you should still be able to appreciate the factors which are important in the derivations and the assumptions which are being made, and you should still be able to use the results in calculations.

The absence of complex mathematics does not mean an absence of complex calculations. In order to get full value from the book you should work through as many of the worked examples and self-study questions as possible. This will require the use of a calculator; in order to encourage you to use the industry standard HP12c or its later versions, some worked examples are given showing how to use the capabilities of this particular calculator. Even better, you can use a spreadsheet, which will be particularly useful in checking the calculations to be found in Part V on options. A disk containing spreadsheets which perform many of the more complex calculations described in the text is available from the publishers. It should be emphasised that an aim of the book is to let you calculate numerical answers as a step towards executing live transactions or taking risk management decisions; if you do not follow through the calculations you will be in the same position as a learner trying to drive on his own on the basis of skimming through an instruction manual.

The convention adopted for rounding is that answers are calculated to a number of decimal places which seems reasonable; no consistency is claimed in the number of decimal places chosen. Where no intermediate result is given, the final answer should be accurate to the number of decimal places given, but where an intermediate result is quoted then that result will be used in the subsequent calculation. This means, for example, that $1.6 * 1.6 * 1.6 * 1.6$ equals 6.6; however, if an intermediate result is quoted, then you might have:

$(1.6 * 1.6) * (1.6 * 1.6)$ equals $2.6 * 2.6$, which equals 6.8.

Forewarned, you should not be confused.

One stylistic point deserves mention. The use of 'he' and 'she' has been addressed by using them in different places, so that readers of either sex can feel themselves represented. This usage has the advantage of intermittently jarring the reader into paying some attention to the text.

Since markets and theories change, you should apply the techniques explained in this book only when you have understood them and checked their applicability. In particular, you should identify and resolve legal, regulatory, and tax issues specific to your organisation or to a proposed transaction. It is worth repeating the warning above that liquidity is perhaps the most important concern in evaluating market risk; remember that liquidity can vary widely between markets and over time. There is no substitute for knowing the market, knowing the counterparty, and knowing the instrument.

PART I

THEORETICAL STRUCTURE

Part I defines a framework for measuring interest rate risk; it thus lays the foundation on which the rest of the book is built.

The first two chapters cover the basic ideas of *present valuing*, first where interest rates are unvarying, and then, more realistically, where interest rates may vary with the tenor of the underlying period. As an aid to calculation, present values are developed in terms of *scaling factors*, which are presented as being more fundamental than interest rates. The concepts of scaling factors and present value are central to the remainder of the book.

Chapter 3 is devoted to the idea of risk management and to its application to interest rates. The risk of a series of future fixed cashflows turns out to be the variability of the present value of the cashflows under likely changes in interest rates. Since there are many different interest rates, depending on the tenor of the period in question, a simplifying model is developed to allow quantification of risk.

This part derives a theoretical structure for interest rate risk management and Parts II–VI show how the various types of risk management instrument fit into the theory; it is left to Part VII to show how to use the theory and the instruments to set and achieve goals. You must keep in mind that it is the ultimate goals which justify the whole process.

CHAPTER 1

Present valuing

This chapter develops the concepts of present valuing future cashflows in a world of constant interest rates. The basic analysis tool is the *scaling factor*, which turns out to be a more fundamental concept than interest rates themselves. *Zero coupon interest rates* are then introduced as a method for recording scaling factors over different periods.

With these concepts defined, it would be possible to go straight on to Chapter 2 to examine present valuing when interest rates are not constant. Instead, in an extended digression, the last section of this chapter is devoted to the important practical question of converting an interest rate corresponding to one payment frequency into the equivalent rate for a different frequency. The techniques developed in this section will prove useful in estimating and in checking results for reasonableness, but it is emphasised that the conversions will be only approximate if rates are not constant. An exact technique for converting interest rates from one frequency to another is developed at the end of Part III.

In this chapter, and throughout Parts I–V, it is assumed that only one currency is being dealt with. For variety, different points are illustrated with examples using different currencies, but you should realise that the techniques apply to only one currency at a time. If you are responsible for interest rate risk across different currencies, it is possible to manage each currency separately; however, there are additional instruments and techniques for handling such cross currency risks, as will be discussed in Part VI.

1.1 THE TIME VALUE OF MONEY

The starting point of the analysis is an observation of the time value of money, which can be expressed:

'Given the choice of receiving £1 today or £1 in a year's time – or after any other period – the rational person would choose £1 today.'

Why? Because £1 received today can be spent today or spent in a year's time, whereas £1 received in a year's time cannot be spent today. The statement of the time value of money can be made stronger:

'The rational person would generally choose to receive £1 today rather than some significantly higher sum in a year, say £1.11; however, there will be a higher amount, say £1.13, which she would choose to receive in a year rather than to receive £1.11 today.'

Why? Because of the investment opportunities available over the course of the year, you would expect to be able to turn £1 today into, say, £1.12 in a year's time. Therefore you would prefer £1 today to £1.11 in one year, but you would prefer £1.13 in one year to £1 today. You would be *indifferent* whether you received £1 today or £1.12 in a year. (If there were *no* investment opportunities then you would prefer any sum greater than £1 in a year's time to £1 today, but presumably you would still prefer £1 today to £1 in a year, since receiving it today would give you additional freedom as to when you spent it.)

In this context, inflation acts as a type of investment opportunity, since given, say, 5 per cent inflation, a basket of goods bought at £1 today could in principle be sold for £1.05 in a year. Thus inflation can give a lower bound to the time value of money. However, in practice it would be difficult to buy goods which were guaranteed to match inflation, which did not require any expenditure for maintenance, storage, or insurance, and whose purchase and resale did not involve extensive transaction costs; inflation may thus be understood to act on the time value of money by influencing expectations or by affecting macroeconomic factors such as the total supply of money in the economy, rather than by giving a direct return.

It is important to note that the time value of money is, in general, different in different currencies; thus the same rational person who is indifferent between £1 today and £1.12 in a year may at the same time be indifferent between US$1 today and US$1.08 in a year.

1.2 SCALING FACTOR

Assume that our rational people have all agreed that £1 today is equal in value to £1.12 in one year. Ignoring the question of credit risk and the need for financial intermediaries to earn income in the form of a bid-offer spread (as will be done throughout the rest of this chapter), banks will lend or borrow £1 today and receive back or pay out £1.12 in a year's time.

If a bank wanted to receive back only £1.11 on a £1 loan it would be swamped by rational people borrowing £1, investing it elsewhere to make £1.12, repaying £1.11 and making a £0.01 profit. Conversely, a bank giving back £1.13 on deposits of £1 would be swamped by people making a riskfree round trip in the opposite direction. Thus, the general agreement as to the time value of money constrains the rate at which banks can borrow or lend.

The easiest way to describe this rate is by a *scaling factor*. The scaling factor for a period is the ratio of cash sums at the end and beginning of the period which are equal in value. In the example above, the scaling factor is £1.12 over £1, which is 1.12, for a period of 1 year. It is important to recognise that the scaling factor is the fundamental description of the time value of money, and that in general financial arithmetic is easiest when done in terms of scaling factors. Note, for example, that the statements of the time value of money in section 1.1 can be simply expressed as: 'For any period, the scaling factor is greater than 1.'

Throughout this chapter it is assumed that the time value of money depends only on the tenor of the underlying period, that is, if you are indifferent between £1 today and £1.12 in one year, then you will be indifferent between £1 at any future time and £1.12 one year later. For reasons which will be explained in Chapter 2, this is described as assuming 'a flat yield curve'.

If there is a flat yield curve and you are indifferent between £1 today and £1.12 in a year's time, what sum would you be indifferent about receiving in 2 years' time instead of £1 today? The answer can be obtained by noting that the scaling factor from year 1 to year 2 is the same as the scaling factor from today to year 1, which equals 1.12, since the tenor of both periods is 1 year. This means that you would be indifferent between £1.12 in a year and £1.2544 (£1.12 ∗ 1.12) in 2 years. But since you are indifferent between £1.12 in 1 year and £1 today, you should be indifferent between £1 today and £1.2544 in 2 years.

This means that the scaling factor for 2 years is £1.2544/£1, which equals 1.2544. An examination of the argument used to derive this result should convince you of the truth of:

Result 1.1 If the yield curve is flat and the scaling factor for a period is s, then the total scaling factor over n consecutive periods is s^n.

A schematic proof is shown below:

What would the scaling factor be for 6 months? In this case we have to resort to some algebra. Assume the answer is s. The scaling factor for any 6-month period must be the same, because of the assumption of a flat yield curve, and so, by Result 1.1, the 1-year scaling factor of 1.12 equals s^2. This gives:

$s = 1.12^{1/2}$, which equals 1.0583.

The argument used here can again be generalised, giving:

Result 1.2   If the yield curve is flat and the scaling factor for a period of length t years is S, then the scaling factor for a period of length t/n years, where n is a whole number, is $S^{1/n}$.

The diagram used to illustrate the proof of Result 1.1 will also serve to illustrate the proof of this result; if you call the n period scaling factor S, you recover the relationship $s^n = S$, which gives $s = S^{1/n}$. Putting together Results 1.1 and 1.2 gives:

Result 1.3   If the yield curve is flat and the scaling factor for a period of length t years is S, then the scaling factor for a period of length $(p/q) * t$ years, where p and q are whole numbers, is $S^{p/q}$.

The proof of this is simple. The scaling factor for a period of (t/q) years must be $S^{1/q}$ by Result 1.2. Then, by Result 1.1, the scaling factor for $p * (t/q)$ years must be $(S^{1/q})^p$, which equals $S^{p/q}$. But $p * (t/q)$ equals $(p/q) * t$, and so the result is proved.

As an example of the use of this result, if the scaling factor for 8 months is 1.08, what is the scaling factor for a year? Here the period is of length two-thirds of a year, so that t equals 2/3. In order to determine the scaling factor for a year, set p equal to 3 and q equal to 2. This gives that the scaling factor for a year is the 8-month scaling factor to the power 3/2, which is $1.08^{3/2}$ which equals 1.122369.

The scaling factor for a 1-year period corresponding to the scaling factor for another period under the assumption of a flat yield curve, will be given the special name of the *annualised scaling factor*; the annualised scaling factor will normally be represented by the symbol r.

(In some books you will see the annualised scaling factor written as e^r, where e is the basis of natural logarithms and equals 2.718281828459...; this makes explicit the fact that the scaling factor is an exponential function of time, since the scaling factor for a period of t years is e^{rt}. You can recover agreement between this notation and the notation used here by replacing every occurrence of e^r by r; thus, for example, you would replace e^{rt} by r^t.)

Result 1.3 can be extended to cover the case where p and q are not whole numbers:

Result 1.4   If the yield curve is flat and the scaling factor for a period of length t years is s, then the scaling factor for a period of length $x * t$ years, where x is any positive real number, is s^x.

A mathematical proof would involve taking a series of terms (p/q) such that each successive term was closer and closer to x, and applying a limiting procedure to $s^{p/q}$. The technicalities of such a proof are beyond the scope of this book, and so you are requested to accept the result as reasonable. Since x can be greater than or less than one, this result lets you calculate the scaling factor for a period of any length.

Revisiting the last example using Result 1.4, if the scaling factor for 8 months is 1.08, then, since a year is 1.5 times 8 months, the scaling factor for a year is $1.08^{1.5}$, which again equals 1.122369. The use of Result 1.4 allows us to obtain the same result while skipping finicky details.

You can check that it is simple to derive Results 1.1, 1.2, and 1.3 from Result 1.4. Result 1.4 will therefore be the main tool for manipulating scaling factors below.

Since the time value of money can differ between currencies, scaling factors for the same period will generally be different for different currencies.

1.3 INTEREST

Although the scaling factor is the most useful way of looking at the time value of money, convention dictates that we must talk about *interest rates*.

If you borrow £p for a period of t years you will have to repay a total of more than £p, since the lender would prefer £p today to £p in the future. If the loan is to be repaid in one lump sum at time t, then, if the scaling factor for the period is s, the total loan repayment should be $s * $ £p. This is deemed to be a repayment of the principal £p together with a payment of interest $(s - 1) * $ £p. Thus, if the period is 6 months, the scaling factor is 1.05, and the principal is £200, then the interest will be £10 and the total repayment will be £210. This example illustrates that the scaling factor for a period uniquely defines the interest rate for a loan over the period with interest paid at the end; running the calculation in reverse shows also that this interest rate uniquely defines the scaling factor.

Interest may be paid on a succession of intermediate payment dates during the period of the loan, instead of all being paid at the end. Thus, for example, if the loan period is one year and the principal is US$500, then the interest payments might be US$10 at the end of months 3, 6, 9, and 12, with the principal also being repaid at month 12. The cashflows in this case, from the viewpoint of the borrower, would be:

Year 0	+500
Year 0.25	−10
Year 0.5	−10
Year 0.75	−10
Year 1	−510.

Note the convention that cashflows in have a plus sign while cashflows out have a negative sign; this convention will be used consistently below.

Typically, where interest is paid on intermediate dates, the dates are on a regular frequency and the end date of the period is also an interest payment date; the period from the start of the loan to the first interest payment is the first *calculation period*, the period from the first payment date to the second is the second calculation period, and so on. The interest amounts would usually be calculated from an *interest rate* which is quoted as an annualised percentage; the convention used in this book for calculating the interest amount is:

Definition 1.1   If a loan on £p has interest payable at the end of a calculation period of t years at an interest rate of i%, then the interest payable is £$p * t * i/100$.

This definition is adopted to simplify formulae and to remove extraneous detail from calculations. Real-life conventions for quoting rates generally involve actual number of days, rather than assuming that all periods are given as fractions of a year. Appendix A at the end of Part I gives the most common conventions for quoting interest rates; these are known as interest bases. The self-study questions at the end of Part I include a calculation of interest amounts in different bases, and conversion of an interest rate quoted in one basis into another. You will have to be aware of the necessity of converting the formulae derived in the book – often by multiplying or dividing by a factor of 365/360 – in order to cope with the different conventions used for quoting rates.

To convince yourself that scaling factors are more fundamental than interest rates, try to express Result 1.4 in terms of interest rates. Your answer should look something like:

If a loan at i% payable after t years is *compounded* for $x * t$ years, that is, if interest is payable only at the end of the $x * t$ year period, then the net interest rate over the $x * t$ years is:

$$\frac{100}{x * t} * \left(\left(1 + \left(\frac{i * t}{100}\right)\right)^{x} - 1\right)$$

You should enjoy proving this, using the definitions given above.

1.4 ZERO COUPON RATES

A *bond* is a certificate which evidences that the holder has lent money to an organisation, and entitles him to receive repayments of interest and principal. A *coupon* is a tear-off section of a bond which the holder hands in to receive each interest payment. If a bond has no coupons, then it repays all its principal and interest at maturity with no intermediate payments, and it is referred to as a *zero coupon bond*. A *zero coupon interest rate* is an interest rate appropriate for a zero coupon bond.

In practice, if a zero coupon bond with a maturity of t years is quoted at an interest rate of $i\%$ on an initial principal of £p, it means that the interest at the end will be as in Definition 1.1:

£$p * t * i/100$, at the end of the t years.

Zero coupon rates defined this way turn out to be complicated to use, and, since the definition of interest rates is purely a convention, we are free to choose a convention which makes life easy. The useful definition is:

Definition 1.2   If a zero coupon rate for a period of t years on a principal of £p is quoted as $Z\%$, then the interest at the end will be: $(((1 + (Z/100))^t) - 1) * £p$.

This seemingly peculiar definition has the advantage of making zero coupon rates relate closely to scaling factors, as will now be demonstrated. Suppose the annualised scaling factor is r; then the scaling factor for t years is r^t. An initial deposit of £p would have a final value of £$p * r^t$. Of this, £p is principal and the rest is interest, and so the interest is $(r^t - 1) * £p$. Equating this expression for the interest with the expression in Definition 1.2 gives

r equals $(1 + (Z/100))$

and so it can be seen that zero coupon rates defined in this way equate directly to the annualised scaling factor.

Zero coupon rates prove to be a convenient way of recording and comparing scaling factors for different periods, and they are used extensively throughout the book. The relationship between the zero coupon rate and the annualised scaling factor is important enough to be recorded as:

Result 1.5   If the zero coupon rate for a period of length t years is $Z\%$, then the annualised scaling factor is $(1 + (Z/100))$ and the scaling factor for the period is $(1 + (Z/100))^t$.

This result applies whether or not the yield curve is flat, since it is based on Definition 1.2 which does not require a flat yield curve.

Unfortunately, the difference between the convention for quoting loan interest rates given in Definition 1.1 and the convention for quoting zero coupon interest rates in Definition 1.2 gives scope for confusion. For example, if the yield curve is flat and the zero coupon rate is 10%, then the annualised scaling factor is 1.1, and the scaling factor for 6 months is $1.1^{0.5}$, which equals 1.048809; this means that the appropriate interest rate for a 6-month loan is 9.7618%, since this is the interest rate which will give interest of 0.048809 on a principal of 1 to recover a scaling factor of 1.048809 for 6 months. The 6-months loan interest rate is thus different from the 6-months zero coupon rate of 10%. If you examine this example closely you will see that there is, in fact, no contradiction; the two different rates describe the same underlying scaling factor. You should make sure that you understand this problem and that you take care to use the correct convention in the correct calculation.

The usual reminder applies, in that zero coupon rates will generally differ between currencies.

1.5 PRESENT VALUING FIXED CASHFLOWS

If our rational person is indifferent between £1 today and £1.12 in a year, we can express this by saying that the *present value* of a cashflow of £1.12 in a year's time is £1, and that the rational person will be indifferent between cashflows with the same present value. The concept of present value is important enough to be recorded as:

Definition 1.3 The present value of a future cashflow is the cashflow today which a rational person would be indifferent in exchanging for the future cashflow.

If the scaling factor for a period of t years from today is s, then the present value of a cashflow of c at t years is c/s. For example, if the annualised scaling factor is 1.12, the present value of a cashflow of £2.5088 in 2 years' time is £2.5088/1.12^2, which equals £2. The sign convention which we are using is that minus signifies a payment and plus signifies a receipt. The sign of the present value will clearly be the same as the sign of the cashflow itself; thus the present value of a cashflow of -£2.5088 in two years is -£2.

The concept of present value can be extended to:

Definition 1.4 The (net) present value of a *cashstream* (a set of future cashflows) is the cashflow today which a rational person would be indifferent in exchanging for the future cashstream.

The key property of present values is that they are *additive*, that is, the present value of two cashflows equals the sum of the present values of the individual cashflows. To see this, remember that present value is defined in terms of indifference. If the two future cashflows are c_1 at time t_1 and c_2 at time t_2, then you should be indifferent between c_1 in the future and its present value PV_1 today, and separately you should be indifferent between c_2 in the future and its present value PV_2 today. You should thus be indifferent between future payments of c_1 and c_2 *together* and their present values PV_1 and PV_2 today. But you should certainly be indifferent between the two separate cashflows PV_1 and PV_2 today and their sum PV_1 plus PV_2 today, and thus the result is proved.

Extending the argument to an indefinite number of cashflows gives:

Result 1.6 The present value of a cashstream equals the sum of the present values of its individual cashflows.

As an example, consider the following cashstream:

−£3 today
+£1 in 6 months
+£1 in 1 year
+£1 in 2 years
+£1 in 3 years

Assuming a flat yield curve with an annualised scaling factor of 1.12, the present value of each of these cashflows is:

−£3
£0.9449   £1 in 6 months has present value £1 divided by the 6-months scaling factor. This is £1 divided by $1.12^{0.5}$, which equals £0.9449
£0.8929   £1 divided by 1.12^{1}
£0.7972   £1 divided by 1.12^{2}
£0.7118   £1 divided by 1.12^{3}

The net present value of the cashstream is thus £0.3468.

Note that the calculation of present values is often referred to as 'discounting', and the scaling factor used in each calculation is often referred to as a 'discount factor'.

The same procedure can be used to present value *any* cashstream; most of the calculations in the rest of this book involve calculating and comparing present values of cashstreams in some guise. As well as calculating present values, scaling factors can be used to equate the value of a cashstream to the value of a single cashflow on a given future date; this is known as *future valuing*, and it can be a powerful calculation technique in its own right. However, any problem which can be solved by future valuing can also be solved, possibly more longwindedly, by present valuing and so there is no need to develop a separate theory for future values.

All the machinery is now in place to consider scaling factors, zero coupon rates, and present valuing, when the yield curve is not flat. However, there is an important practical problem which often faces participants in the money markets and capital markets, which is converting an interest rate for a loan or bond on one payment frequency and basis into an equivalent interest rate for a different basis or frequency. An exact solution of this problem will be given at the end of Part III, but it is possible to use the techniques of present valuing and the assumption of a flat yield curve to find a solution which will be reasonably accurate in most cases. Section 1.6 below is therefore devoted to carrying out the conversion on the assumption of a flat yield curve; since the HP12c calculator is widely used by participants in financial markets, it is shown how to carry out the conversion using this calculator. If this section is not relevant to you, then it can be skipped without impeding your understanding of the rest of the book.

1.6 CONVERTING INTEREST RATES BETWEEN BASES AND FREQUENCIES

Suppose a bond pays interest every 6 months at 10% and matures in 1 year. What interest rate would you want to receive on a bond paying interest annually in order to be indifferent between the two bonds? The yield curve is flat with the zero coupon rate 12%.

You will be indifferent between two bonds if they have the same present value; so start by assuming that the interest rate on the annual bond is $x\%$ and calculate the two present values.

On the semiannual bond, for a £1 principal the cashflows are:

£0.05 at 6 months and
£1.05 at 1 year

giving present value £0.04725 plus £0.93750, which equals £0.98475.

On the annual bond the cashflow is £1 plus £x/100 at 1 year, giving a present value of £0.89286 plus ((£x/100) over 1.12).

Equating the two present values gives:

$$0.98475 \ = \ 0.89286 + \frac{x/100}{1.12}, \text{ giving}$$

$$0.09189 \ = \ \frac{x/100}{1.12}, \text{ giving}$$

$$x/100 \ = \ (0.09189 * 1.12), \text{ giving}$$

$$x \ = \ 10.292, \text{ so that the annual bond rate is } 10.292\%.$$

You can check the present value of the annual bond at 10.292%; the cashflow at 1 year is £1.10292 which has a present value of £1.10292 divided by 1.12, which equals £0.98475, which agrees with the present value of the semiannual bond.

Alternatively you can use an HP12c calculator to check the two present values.

For the semiannual bond set:

$$n \ = \ 2$$
$$i \ = \ 5.83$$

The interest entered as i must be:

(the scaling factor for an individual period − 1) * 100.

This will differ from the zero coupon rate unless the periods are exactly one year.

PMT =   0.05
FV =   1
Press PV to get the value -0.98475.

For the annual bond set:

n =   1
i =   12
PMT =   0.10292
FV =   1.
Again PV calculates as -0.98475.

Instead of equating the present values manually you can use the calculator to find the interest rate on an annual bond which has a present value of -0.98475. Set:

n =   1
PV =   -0.98475
i =   12
FV =   1

Press PMT to get the value 0.10292, which means that the interest payment must be 10.292% of the principal repayment of 1.

Yet another way to look at this example is to consider the difference between the cashflows on the two bonds. The semiannual bond pays an extra £0.05 at 6 months, and the annual bond pays an extra $((£x/100)$ minus £0.05) at 1 year. The value of the 6-month £0.05 at 1 year is £0.05 times the 6-month scaling factor, which equals £0.05 times 1.0583, which is £0.05292. Thus valuing all cashflows at 1 year (*future valuing* instead of present valuing) gives:

$((£x/100) - £0.05) = £0.05292$, giving
$(£x/100) = £0.10292$, giving again
$x = 10.292.$

Note that the logic of this approach shows that a 2-year semiannual bond at 10% will also have the same present value as a 2-year annual bond paying 10.292%; you should check this yourself to show that you understand the calculations. The same result will hold for 3-year bonds, or for bonds with maturity any *whole* number of years. (If the period is not an exact number of years the answer will be slightly different, but it can still be obtained by equating present values.) This result can be expressed as:

'If the yield curve is flat with the zero coupon rate 12%, a bond paying 10% interest semiannually for a whole number of years and principal at maturity is equivalent to a bond paying 10.292% annually.'

A similar conversion exercise can be done between any two interest frequencies. As another example, convert a bond paying 12% quarterly to a semiannual rate, when the constant zero coupon rate is 10%. Again assume that the total period is a whole number of years.

Because the pattern repeats itself every 6 months, you need equate present values for the differential cashflow over only the first 6 months. Call the unknown semiannual interest $x\%$, and work on a principal of £1. Then the differential cashflow is:

£0.03 at 3 months and
$((£x * 0.5/100) - £0.03)$ at 6 months.

Present valuing gives:

£0.0292936 $= ((£x/200) - £0.03)/1.04881$, giving
$((x/200)/1.04881) = 0.0578975$ giving
$x = 12.1447$

which means that the semiannual rate is 12.1447%.

The same result can be calculated using the HP12c by first working out the present value of the cashflows on the quarterly bond, and then determining the interest rate on the semiannual bond which gives the same present value. Set:

n	=	2
i	=	2.4114 (the quarterly interest rate equating to an annual rate of 10%)
PMT	=	0.03
FV	=	1

Press PV to give the present value as -1.011359.

Now set:

n	=	1
i	=	4.8809 (the semiannual interest rate)

and, leaving PV unchanged at -1.011359 and FV unchanged at 1, press PMT to give the semiannual interest as 0.060723, which corresponds to an interest rate on the semiannual bond of 12.1446% on the principal of 1. This agrees to within a rounding error with the interest rate calculated above.

Alternatively you can equate the present values of two bonds each maturing in 6 months (or equivalently each maturing in any whole number of 6-month periods), remembering to include the final payment of principal for both bonds, or you can equate future values of the differential cashflows at 6 months. All of these methods should give the same answer.

These techniques are fully accurate only when the yield curve is flat. When the yield curve is not flat then they should still provide reasonable approximations in normal circumstances, provided that a sensible estimate of the average zero coupon rate is used to generate the scaling factors; the interest rate on an annual-payment bond over the period might provide such an estimate. Remember, however, that the techniques apply only when the bonds have a series of calculation periods all of the same length. If there is a short period then you will have to use a more complex calculation to convert the interest rate; such a calculation is explained in Part III.

Where interest rates are expressed on a day basis rather than on a year basis, they should be converted to a year basis, if necessary with a slight approximation, and then treated as above. The most common bases are described in Appendix A at the end of Part I.

For example, if a financial instrument pays principal at maturity, plus interest annually at 10%, calculated on an actual/360 basis, then the interest is:

$$\frac{10 * \text{principal} * \text{actual days between payments}}{100 * 360}$$

Then, if the number of days in a year is 365 (this is not exact because of weekends, holidays, and leap years), this is equivalent to paying (365/360) ∗ 10% per year, which equals 10.139% per year. 10% on an actual/360 basis is thus closely equivalent to 10.139% on a year basis.

This is a good approximation for converting the interest rate into an equivalent rate in another basis; for an exact equivalent, you should equate present values for exact cashflows. A general method for this is again given at the end of Part III.

The self-study questions at the end of Part I include further examples on the conversion of interest rates between bases and frequencies.

SUMMARY

Starting with the concept of the time value of money, this chapter has built a theory of present valuing in a world of constant interest rates. The machinery derived here of scaling factors, annualised scaling factors, and zero coupon rates, will be further developed in the next chapter for use where interest rates depend on the underlying period. Most market interest rates are quoted as deposit rates; care must be taken in converting between deposit and zero coupon rates.

CHAPTER 2

The term structure of interest rates

In Chapter 1 the annualised scaling factor, and hence the zero coupon rate, was assumed to be independent of the underlying period; unfortunately, life is not that simple, and the zero rate generally depends on the period in question. This variation is referred to as the *term structure* and this chapter considers the implications of the existence of such a structure.

Note that we are still working within a *static* picture, considering scaling factors for different periods as they are today; a discussion of how scaling factors vary *dynamically* as time passes will have to await Chapter 3.

The main theme of the chapter is the calculation of market zero coupon rates. This is approached by demonstrating that the prices of market instruments imply a *par yield curve*; the par rates imply zero coupon rates to each maturity. The theoretical model then has to be expanded to allow for *bid-offer spreads* and credit risk. It is necessary to define *arbitrage* to allow the inclusion of bid-offer spreads; analysis of the possibility of arbitrage shows which market instruments should be used to build the yield curve. The problem of incorporating credit risk is analysed and resolved by making a distinction between the *riskfree zero coupon curve* applicable to the present valuing of cashflows linked to government debt, and the *interbank zero coupon yield curve* applicable to the present valuing of cashflows carrying the risk of the banking system. The final step is to develop an explicit formula for calculating the zero coupon rates from the market par yield curve. The chapter proper concludes by revisiting present valuing with a varying yield curve; this process will be the mainstay of calculations throughout the book.

The final section is really a postscript, reviewing the concept of *internal rate of return*; this is included because many readers will have used the internal rate of return, and may wonder how it fits into the theoretical model developed here. You can skip this section without affecting your understanding of subsequent material.

You may wonder *why* yield curves in general should not be flat. The answer to this lies in macroeconomic theory, and is outside the microeconomic mainstream of the book. However, to satisfy your curiosity, or to whet your appetite, a brief introduction to the economic theory of the determination of interest rates is given in Appendix B at the end of Part I.

2.1 MARKET INSTRUMENT PRICES IMPLY SCALING FACTORS

Zero coupon rates prevailing in the market are not quoted directly, but must be deduced from the market price of financial instruments; the goal of this section is to demonstrate that market rates do uniquely determine zero coupon rates. Credit risks and bid-offer spreads are still assumed to be zero; when we have developed a treatment of bid-offer spreads and of credit risks, it will be possible, in section 2.5 below, to repeat the derivation of zero coupon rates using more realistic assumptions, and to obtain an explicit formula for the zero rates.

For ease of exposition, this section concentrates on the period from 1 to 10 years, although the treatment could be extended to any period for which market instruments are available.

The simplest market instruments in these maturities whose value is determined by the scaling factor are bonds. The bonds for which a market price is readily available tend to have straightforward structures, paying interest on a regular frequency with the principal being repaid in full at maturity; all the bonds dealt with in this chapter will have this structure.

The underlying principal of a bond is known as its *face value*. A bond with a price equal to its face value is said to trade *at par*; a bond with price greater than its face value is trading *at a premium* and a bond with a price lower than its face value is trading *at a discount*. It is assumed here that there is a wide variety of bonds, so that in each maturity some are trading at a premium, some at a discount, and some at par.

It is simple to prove:

Result 2.1   If credit risks and bid-offer spreads are zero, two bonds, paying interest on the same frequency and having the same maturity and the same price, must both have the same interest rate.

This can be proved by considering the differential cashflow between the two bonds. If they have a different interest rate, then you will have a non-zero net cashflow from buying, say, £100 face value of the bond with the higher interest rate and selling £100 face value of the other. The initial payment will match the initial receipt, and the final receipt of principal on the bond purchased will match the final receipt of principal on the bond sold. However, each periodic receipt of interest will be greater than each periodic payment of interest, and so you will have a net positive cash flow on each payment date, giving you a positive net present value of future cashflows, for no risk. But market pricing which allows you to make a profit for no risk is inherently unstable, since everyone in the market will want to buy the cheap bond and sell the expensive bond, and so prices will quickly adjust so that the price of the two bonds is the same. Thus in the circumstances given, the two bonds must have the same interest rate.

Now select a set of bonds paying interest on the same frequency and trading at par, with maturities 1 year, 2 years, ..., 10 years. By Result 2.1, the interest rates on these ten bonds are uniquely determined by the state of the market, and they define a *par yield curve*. ('Yield' is a measure of the effective interest rate to an investor holding a bond.) There is a different par yield curve for each payment frequency; for example, a par 2-year bond paying interest annually will have a higher interest rate than a par 2-year bond paying interest semiannually. Figure 2.1 illustrates the relationship between annual and semiannual par yield curves for representative market rates.

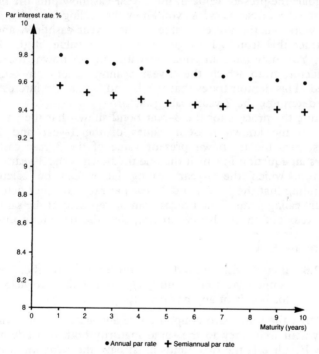

Figure 2.1 The par yield curve is a series of points rather than a connected line. The value for each maturity depends on the frequency of interest payments on the underlying instrument as well as on market rates.

The key result is that these par rates will uniquely define the scaling factor to each maturity and hence will uniquely define the zero coupon rates to each maturity – the *zero coupon yield curve*. This is important enough to be recorded as:

Result 2.2   The par yield curve, consisting of the interest rates on par bonds with the same payment frequency to each maturity, uniquely determines the scaling factor to each maturity and hence determines the zero coupon yield curve, which records the zero coupon rate to each maturity.

The proof is given for bonds paying interest annually, but it can be amended to cope with bonds paying on any frequency. Consider £1 principal value of the 1-year par bond. Its only future cashflow is £1 principal plus $(£m_1/100)$ interest at 1 year, where $m_1\%$ is the 1-year par interest rate. This cashflow has a present value of £1, and hence the ratio between $(£1$ plus $(£m_1/100))$ and £1 defines the scaling factor for 1 year. The 1-year par rate can thus be seen to determine the 1-year scaling factor.

Now consider the 2-year bond. Assume its interest rate is $m_2\%$. It has two cashflows, $£m_2/100$ interest at 1 year, and £1 principal plus $£m_2/100$ interest at 2 years. The present value of the bond is £1, which equals the present value of the 1-year cashflow plus the present value of the 2-year cashflow. As you know the scaling factor for 1 year you can work out the present value of the 1-year cashflow, and you can subtract this from £1 to give the present value of the 2-year cashflow. You now have an equation with one unknown, the 2-year scaling factor, from which the 2-year scaling factor can hence be calculated. This demonstrates that the 1- and 2-year par interest rates together determine the 2-year scaling factor.

Repeating the process for the 3-year bond shows that the par value is equal to the known present values of the 1-year and 2-year cashflows, plus the unknown present value of the 3-year cashflow. This gives an equation in which the one unknown is the 3-year scaling factor, from which the 3-year scaling factor can be calculated, demonstrating that the 1-, 2-, and 3-year par rates together determine the 3-year scaling factor. The process can be repeated in the same way for each year out to 10, hence proving that the par curve uniquely defines the zero curve.

It is easy to show:

Result 2.3   If credit risk and bid-offer spreads are zero, then the zero coupon yield curve uniquely defines the par yield curve for bonds of any payment frequency.

Suppose that the same zero coupon curve allows two bonds with the same payment frequency to the same maturity both to trade at par. Then, by Result 2.1, the two bonds must have the same interest rate. But the definition of the par yield to a maturity is the interest paid on a bond trading at par, and hence the par yield curve is uniquely defined.

This result leads to:

Result 2.4 The par yield curve for bonds of one frequency uniquely determines the par yield curve for bonds of any other frequency.

This is proved using Result 2.2 to show that the par yield curve uniquely determines the zero coupon yield curve, and using Result 2.3 to show that the zero coupon yield curve uniquely determines the par yield curve for any payment frequency.

The following result represents a digression here, but will be useful later.

Result 2.5 A flat zero coupon curve implies a flat par curve at the same interest rate for bonds paying annual interest, and vice versa.

First it is proved that a flat zero curve implies a flat par curve. The proof uses mathematical induction; the result is proved for 1 year, and then it is demonstrated that if the result is true for n years then it is also true for $n + 1$ years. Thus it can be seen that the result will also hold for 2, 3, ..., 10 years.

If the zero curve is flat at, say, 10%, a 1-year bond paying 10% annually will have one cashflow of 110% at 1 year with a present value of 100%, and thus will trade at par. This demonstrates that the result does hold for a maturity of 1 year.

Now consider the differential cashflows between an n year 10% bond and an $n + 1$ year 10% bond. These are:

100% in year n (no principal on $n + 1$ year bond in year n)

110% in year $n + 1$ (no payment on n year bond in year $n + 1$)

Since the annualised scaling factor is constant at 1.1, the future value of the two cashflows at year n is the same at 100%, and hence their present value is also the same, and so the n year bond has the same present value as the $n + 1$ year bond. Thus if the n year bond trades at par, then so does the $n + 1$ year bond. This demonstrates that the inductive step holds, and thus proves that a zero curve flat at 10% implies a par curve flat at 10%. Clearly the argument can be generalised for any constant interest rate, to show that a flat zero curve implies a flat par curve at the same interest rate.

Now, suppose that there is a flat par curve at, say, $Z\%$. From Results 2.2 and 2.3, the par curve uniquely defines the zero curve and the zero curve uniquely defines the par curve. Therefore, there cannot be two zero curves which both give a par curve flat at $Z\%$. But the first part of the proof of Result 2.4 shows that a zero curve flat at $Z\%$ gives a par curve flat at $Z\%$, and hence a par curve flat at $Z\%$ must give a zero curve flat at $Z\%$. This completes the proof of Result 2.5.

This result can be extended to:

Result 2.6 A flat zero curve implies a flat par curve for bonds of any payment frequency.

The proof that a flat par curve implies a flat zero curve again relies on induction. Consider a semiannual payment frequency, and again assume that the zero curve is flat at 10% giving an annualised scaling factor of 1.1. Then, if the 1-year par bond has interest rate $m\%$, its cashflows are

Year 0.5 $m\%/2$
Year 1 $100\% + (m\%/2)$.

Since the bond trades at par, the present value of these cashflows must be 100%, and since this gives an equation in which $m\%$ is the only variable, $m\%$ is uniquely determined.

The differential cashflows between an n year bond and an $n + 1$ year bond, both paying $m\%$ interest semiannually, are:

100% in year n	(no principal on $n+1$ year bond in year n)
$m\%/2$ in year $n+0.5$	(no interest on n year bond in year $n+0.5$)
$100\%+(m\%/2)$ in year $n+1$	(no payment on n year bond in year $n+1$).

But, since the zero curve is flat, future valuing the last two payments to year n must give the same as present valuing the year 0.5 and year 1 cashflows above, which is 100%. Thus if the n year bond trades at par then so does the $n + 1$ year bond. This proves the inductive step and thus demonstrates that the par curve is flat at $m\%$ for years 1, 2, ..., 10.

The proof that a flat par curve implies a flat zero coupon curve is the same as that given for Result 2.5 above.

To progress further in determining market zero coupon rates, it is necessary to modify the unrealistic assumptions of zero spreads and credit risks. The next section deals with the effect of spreads in allowing different instruments to be priced slightly differently, and the following section incorporates credit risk into the theoretical model.

2.2 ARBITRAGE

The dictionary definition of arbitrage is 'buying in the cheapest market', but among traders arbitrage has a tighter definition of 'buying in one market and simultaneously selling in another to realise a riskfree profit'. In general, if such an opportunity exists, the increased demand in the first market will tend to increase the price there, and the increased supply in the second market will tend to reduce the price there, and eventually (sooner rather than later in an efficient market) the price differential making the arbitrage possible will vanish.

Exceptions to this tend to be arbitrages driven by government-imposed regulatory or tax asymmetries; certain arbitrages of this nature can persist for a long time, with the taxpayer or inflation footing the bill.

Before analysing arbitrage in more detail, it is worth a brief digression to give a clear definition of a bid-offer spread. A market participant who wishes to buy a commodity will quote the *bid* price at which he will buy; a participant who wishes to sell will quote the *offer* price at which he will sell. (In American usage, 'offer' becomes 'ask'.) Some participants, known as *market makers*, will in principle quote a *two-way price* at any time, that is, they will quote a bid and an offer rate simultaneously. A quote of this nature is typically written as, for example, 'DEM104/105', meaning that the market maker will buy at DEM104 and will sell at DEM105; the bid is conventionally on the left hand side.

Since a market maker commits to buy at her bid price or sell at her offer price, it is clear that her bid cannot be greater than her offer, since otherwise she would find herself selling the commodity and immediately buying it back at a loss. Moreover, since the market maker wishes to make a profit, her bid cannot be the same as her offer, since otherwise she would receive no compensation for the risk and transaction costs of buying and selling. It is thus clear that the market maker must quote a bid and offer price separated by a *spread*; this bid-offer spread must be enough to compensate her for her risk and expenses. Indeed, it is the possibility of earning spread income which makes being a market maker worthwhile.

The possibility of arbitrage will act to keep the prices quoted by different market makers in line with each other. It will not keep prices identical, because of bid-offer spreads, credit risks, and transaction costs.

For example, if in London a market maker buys gold at US$350 an ounce and sells at US$351, and in Tokyo a market maker buys at US$450 and sells at US$451, then you will definitely make money if you buy gold in London and fly it out to Tokyo to sell it. However, if the Tokyo price is US$353/354, then the transaction costs may be too great to enable you to make money, despite the price differential.

You should be aware of the limitations of the assumption that arbitrage will at all times keep the prices in different markets exactly in line. Not only can two market makers quote differing prices with overlapping bid-offer spreads which do not allow arbitrage, but they can quote different prices with non-overlapping bid-offer spreads, which in theory do allow arbitrage; a potential arbitrage cannot be realised if the potential income is exceeded by transaction costs and risks. However, *large* potential arbitrages can exist only temporarily, since they will be realised, and this will act to adjust prices.

Figure 2.2 illustrates these three possibilities. It shows three pairs of market makers' quotes; within each pair the commodity being quoted is the same. In the first pair the bid-offer spreads overlap and there is no arbitrage. In the second pair the offer by one market maker is slightly less than the bid by the second, but the arbitrage is smaller than the transaction costs and so it will not be exercised. In the third pair, the arbitrage is large and will be exercised by market participants; this will force the market makers to move their prices closer to each other.

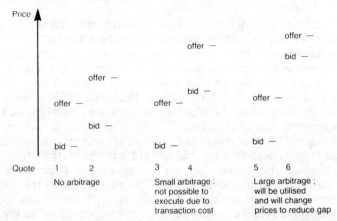

Figure 2.2 Possible price quotations for the same product. Within each pair of quotes, the commodity is the same. You can enter into a transaction with a market maker either by paying his offer to buy or by selling to him at his bid.

Bonds are traded in the same way as other commodities, with the bid and offer prices quoted being subject to the arbitrage relations discussed above. However, other interest rate instruments are traded by market participants quoting buy or sell interest rates, rather than prices.

For example, a 1-year interbank placing has two cashflows: minus the principal today, and plus the principal plus the interest in one year. Banks wishing to make placings will quote their *offer interest rate* at which they will place funds and *receive* interest, and banks wishing to receive placings will quote their *bid interest rate* at which they will take funds and *pay* interest.

On such interest rate instruments, some banks will choose to be market makers and will quote bid and offer rates. The same arguments as above show that the offer rate must be higher than the bid by a suitable spread, and that the bid-offer spreads of two market makers cannot be widely separated without allowing arbitrage. Figure 2.2, with the vertical axis relabelled 'interest rate', would also illustrate the properties of arbitrage for these instruments.

In the same way that prices of bonds uniquely imply zero coupon rates, the market interest rates on other instruments also imply and are implied by the zero coupon yield curve. Combinations of different instruments can be used to create the same result in terms of cashflows; consequently, the possibility of arbitrage ensures that the market rates on different instruments will not get so far out of line that they imply widely different zero coupon curves. However, arbitrage cannot prevent different instruments being priced off a slightly different zero curve.

The bid-offer spread on an instrument must be wide enough at least to compensate a market maker for the risk and expense of entering into two offsetting transactions. Therefore, if the width between the quotes of two market makers becomes greater than the spread itself, then exercising the arbitrage should become economic. (Generally an arbitrage would become economic before this point was reached.) Therefore, it seems plausible that the narrower the spread on an instrument, the less the possible difference in quotes between market makers.

Since it is easier to exercise arbitrages involving instruments with narrower spreads, such instruments would also tend to be mispriced less relative to the market zero coupon curve. It this therefore these instruments which are identified in section 2.4 below for use in constructing the par curve from which the market zero curve will be calculated.

2.3 CREDIT RISK

There is a problem present valuing future cashflows involving credit risk. The effect of the credit risk is to make the future cashflows uncertain, and the theory developed in Chapter 1 dealt only with certain future cashflows. Only government debt provides reasonably certain cashflows; any other future receipt will be to some extent uncertain.

Intuitively, you might believe that if you had, say, a 90 per cent chance of receiving a future cashflow and a 10 per cent chance of not receiving it, then you should be indifferent between the chance of the future cashflow and receiving 90 per cent of the present value of the cashflow today. It seems logical that on a portfolio basis your gains would cancel your losses, and that you would end up equally well off by taking the appropriate percentage of the present value for each such uncertain future cashflow.

Unfortunately, intuition in this case turns out to be wrong. In particular, if there is a positive correlation between the chances of all the different future cashflows not arising, then you will have a risk which you cannot diversify. Since you would expect to receive a premium for taking a risk, you should expect to pay a premium to remove a risk, and hence you should accept a riskfree payment today lower than the appropriate percentage of the present value of the future cashflows.

The treatment of present valuing uncertain future cashflows is the subject of *Modern Portfolio Theory*, and the simplest predictions of this theory are expressed in the *Capital Assets Pricing Model*. This model gives a structure for analysing the present value of future cashflows generated by assets such as bonds and shares, by stipulating that risk-free cashflows are present valued at the market zero coupon interest rate, while a progressively higher zero coupon rate should be used for cashflows with progressively higher *systematic risk*.

Systematic risk is risk which cannot be diversified by holding a portfolio of assets. For example, in a particular stock market it is likely that the price of all shares is positively correlated with the stock market index and that, therefore, regardless of what diversified portfolio of stocks you hold, your future cashflows will still have a positive correlation with the stock market index and hence will incorporate risk.

Portfolio theory and the Capital Asset Pricing Model are beyond the scope of this book; however, they have an important relationship with interest rate risk management, and references are given in the bibliography to encourage you to investigate them further.

Luckily, given the small number of defaults of major banks in developed countries in recent years, it is not unreasonable to make:

Assumption 2.1 Any systematic risk in bank debt is small enough to ignore. That is, although banks may default on debts or on other financial instruments, there will be no material correlation between the value of such bank instruments and the value of assets in general.

It is likely that there is, in fact, some small correlation between bank defaults and, say, the stock market index. For example, if the stock market index plummets to 10 per cent of its value it is probable that knock-on effects would include bank defaults, and it is hard to imagine the stock market index doubling while banks default. However, in normal circumstances, Assumption 2.1 does seem to hold, if only because the number of major bank defaults is too small to allow proper statistical analysis.

The advantage of Assumption 2.1 is that it simplifies the development of the theory below. Without such an assumption, it would be necessary to calculate the systematic risk of bank debt in order to develop a consistent theory of present valuing. If, as seems likely, this systematic risk is very small, then the effort involved in incorporating it into the theory would not be worthwhile. The development of the theory below will therefore rely on Assumption 2.1, although a more sophisticated theory would not necessarily produce materially different results.

(Note that Assumption 2.1 relates to bank *debt*; the price of bank shares is strongly correlated to stock market indices, and thus bank shares incorporate material systematic risk.)

Suppose that a 1-year government bond paying all principal and interest at maturity trades at par and pays an interest rate of 10%; then the riskfree zero coupon rate is 10%. Suppose further that on average one bank out of 101 is expected to default in any year, and that in the event of such default there would be no repayment on outstanding debt. What should the interest rate be on a 1-year interbank deposit?

If a bank makes a 1-year interbank deposit it expects to receive back the full principal plus interest 100 times out of 101, and to receive back zero the other time. In order for it to be indifferent between this deposit and the government debt, it must therefore receive 101/100 times as much on the deposit; that is, the total interest and principal must be 110% times 101/100, which equals 111.1%, giving an interest rate of 11.1% on the interbank deposit.

(In fact, this analysis is flawed, since it does not take into account the attraction of government bonds as traded instruments. Market participants are willing to pay a premium for the flexibility of holding an instrument which can be resold at the cost of a small bid-offer spread, and therefore the spread of interbank rates over government bond rates is partly due to the *liquidity premium* of the government bonds. This does not invalidate the conclusion below that interbank zero coupon rates should be used to present value bank debt, but it adds an extra dimension of risk to the spread of interbank interest rates over riskfree rates. This *spread risk* will be discussed further in Part IV.)

It can be seen that the appropriate rate to use for discounting 1-year cashflows relating to interbank debt is the zero coupon rate of 11.1% derived from the 1-year Libor rate, since this is the rate which will give a present value of the deposit principal. Moreover, the analysis can be extended to show that zero coupon rates derived from the market prices of interbank instruments should be used in present valuing cashflows relating to bank debt in any maturity. This *interbank zero coupon yield curve* will be different from the *riskfree zero coupon yield curve* discussed above, and in fact it can be seen to be higher in every maturity, since it will incorporate the price of bank credit risk. Since we now have two distinct zero coupon curves, it is important to record:

Result 2.7 The riskfree zero coupon curve should be used to present value cashflows relating to government debt, while the interbank zero coupon curve should be used to present value cashflows relating to bank debt.

Except in very specific circumstances, it is financial transactions with the banking system which are available for banks, corporations, and institutions to shift cashflows between maturities; moreover, such organisations are generally net borrowers of funds. It is thus reasonable to make:

Assumption 2.2 The correct zero coupon curve to use in present valuing certain cashstreams within a bank, corporation, or institution, is the interbank zero coupon curve.

The logic of this assumption is that an organisation could, in principle, borrow funds against a positive future cashstream, and could net off such existing borrowing against a negative future cashstream. The riskfree yield curve is not accessible to an organisation for such purposes, and therefore the interbank yield curve should be used for present valuing.

Assumption 2.2 is not strictly compatible with the Capital Asset Pricing Model, but it seems to represent a better approximation to the realities of the market. Luckily, the question of the exact discount rate to use can be regarded here as academic, since the analysis of Chapter 3 will show that a consistent small difference in the rates used for discounting will have a fairly immaterial effect on the measurement of risk.

The assumption holds only for certain cashstreams. If the cashstream has risk which is not systematic, then it must be present valued using the same credit analysis which was developed above for bank debt; this is investigated further in section 2.6 below.

Management of cashflows incorporating systematic risk, such as the cashflows from a portfolio of shares, will require the use of Portfolio Theory and of the Capital Asset Pricing Model, and is therefore beyond the scope of this book.

2.4 CREATING A PAR YIELD CURVE

There are, fundamentally, two classes of interbank interest rate instruments: *on balance sheet* and *off balance sheet*.

On-balance-sheet products are instruments such as loans or bonds, where a principal amount is paid by one counterparty to another today, and repaid with interest at some time in the future; such products usually involve a substantial credit risk. They are called 'on balance sheet' because they appear as assets or liabilities on the balance sheets of the two counterparties. Where a bank holds an asset of this nature it typically has to allocate a certain amount of its own capital for regulatory purposes; this represents an opportunity cost to the bank and acts to widen bid-offer spreads.

Off-balance-sheet products are typically *contracts for differences*, where one party pays to the other the difference between two interest amounts calculated on different bases; such contracts usually involve far lower credit risk, and they do not appear on either counterparty's balance sheet. These products are often *derivative products*, that is, they are priced with reference to other products such as interbank placings. Banks have to allocate capital for off-balance-sheet products also, but the amount is usually relatively small with a limited impact on bid-offer spreads.

Following the analysis of section 2.2 above, in constructing an interbank zero yield curve from a set of par instruments we should select off-balance-sheet instruments, since these will have a minimum bid-offer spread and will thus be priced most correctly off the market zero curve.

In fact we cannot achieve this for all maturities, since the only available instruments with a short maturity are interbank placings. There is a liquid market in London for short-term interbank placings in many currencies, and this defines short-term rates in these currencies. The interest rate quoted in this market for a bank offering funds in a particular currency to a particular maturity is referred to as the London Interbank Offered Rate, abbreviated to *Libor*. To construct a yield curve with points from 1 to 10 years, the starting point should therefore be the 1-year zero rate implied by the 1-year Libor rate. (It might be marginally better to take, say, 6-month Libor to define the 6-month zero rate, and then to use off-balance-sheet instruments to calculate the implied zero rates beyond 6 months; this is discussed further in Part VII.)

For years 2-10 the market instrument with the smallest bid-offer spread is the *single currency interest rate swap*. The mechanics of these instruments will be explained in Part III; it is sufficient to anticipate here the result that the par rate for a swap is an off-balance-sheet equivalent of the par rate for a bond, and can be manipulated arithmetically in the same way. Consequently the analysis above indicates that the 1-year Libor rate together with the 2-, 3-, ..., 10-year swap rates will uniquely define the zero curve to 10 years.

A more sophisticated approach would be to take more points on the par curve, particularly in the shorter maturities where the zero curve is more likely to have fine structure. For example we might add overnight, 1-week, 1-month, 3-month, and 6-month Libor, together with points between 1 and 2 years to give more detail to the structure of the zero curve. This is pursued in Part VII.

For the riskfree yield curve these complications do not arise, and it is possible to construct the curve simply by using the interest rate on par government bonds to each maturity. (In practice there may be no government bonds trading at par, and then the zero curve must be deduced from bonds trading at a premium or a discount; this is considered further in Part IV.)

2.5 CALCULATING ZERO COUPON RATES

It was demonstrated in section 2.1 above that the par curve uniquely determines the zero coupon curve, and it has now been shown which market instruments to select to determine the par yield curves; this section will calculate the zero curve explicitly. For simplicity, the calculation is shown for interbank rates only; the calculation for the riskfree zero curve from par rates would be effectively identical.

Suppose that the par rates for swaps paying annual interest for 1-10 years are $m_1\%$, ..., $m_{10}\%$, and that the zero coupon rates for these years, which we are going to calculate, are $Z_1\%$, ..., $Z_{10}\%$. It will simplify the notation if we call the scaling factors for each year s_1, ..., s_{10}, so that, for example:

$$s_{10} = (1 + (Z_{10}/100))^{10}.$$

Then Z_1 equals m_1 (since the 1-year placing is the same as a 1-year bond as far as the present value calculation is concerned). Now consider the 2-year swap. As mentioned above, for the purpose of present value calculations we can treat the swap as though it were a bond, and so its par value of 100% is the present value of the following cashflows:

$m_2\%$ at 1 year
$(m_2\% + 100\%)$ at 2 years

and thus:

$100\% = (m_2\%/s_1) + ((m_2\% + 100\%)/s_2)$, which gives
$100 - (m_2/s_1) = (m_2 + 100)/s_2$

so that

$$s_2 = (m_2 + 100)/(100 - (m_2/s_1))$$

where

$$Z_2 = 100 * (s_2^{1/2} - 1)$$

Similarly, considering the 3-year swap gives:

$100 = (m_3/s_1) + (m_3/s_2) + ((m_3 + 100)/s_3)$, so that
$s_3 = (m_3 + 100)/(100 - (m_3/s_1) - (m_3/s_2))$ and
$Z_3 = 100 * (s_3^{1/3} - 1)$

Continuing the same calculation gives:

$s_4 = (m_4 + 100)/(100 - (m_4/s_1) - (m_4/s_2) - (m_4/s_3))$ and
$Z_4 = 100 * (s_4^{1/4} - 1)$

We can simplify the calculation by introducing a new set of variables, $A_1, ..., A_{10}$, where:

$A_1 = 0$
$A_2 = 1/s_1$
$A_3 = (1/s_1) + (1/s_2)$ and in general
$A_{n+1} = A_n + (1/s_n)$

Using A we can express the results above as:

$s_1 = (m_1 + 100)/(100 - (m_1 * A_1))$
$s_2 = (m_2 + 100)/(100 - (m_2 * A_2))$
$s_3 = (m_3 + 100)/(100 - (m_3 * A_3))$
$s_4 = (m_4 + 100)/(100 - (m_4 * A_4))$

and a brief inspection of the way in which these formulae are derived should convince you that we can continue the sequence all the way out to

$s_{10} = (m_{10} + 100)/(100 - (m_{10} * A_{10}))$
$Z_{10} = 100 * (s_{10}^{1/10} - 1)$

or even further, if we have par rates going out further.

To test your understanding of the above formulae, calculate zero rates for par rates equivalent to bonds paying annual interest:

m_1 10.0%
m_2 10.2%
m_3 10.3%
m_4 10.4%
m_5 10.5%
m_6 10.6%
m_7 10.7%
m_8 10.8%
m_9 10.9%
m_{10} 11.0% (Try yourself before looking at the answer.)

The calculation is best laid out as shown in Table 2.1.

TABLE 2.1 CALCULATING ZERO COUPON RATES

Year	m	A	s	Z
1	10	0	1.1	10
2	10.2	0.9091	1.2146	10.210
3	10.3	1.7324	1.3426	10.318
4	10.4	2.4772	1.4871	10.430
5	10.5	3.1497	1.6510	10.548
6	10.6	3.7554	1.8374	10.671
7	10.7	4.2996	2.0502	10.801
8	10.8	4.7874	2.2942	10.937
9	10.9	5.2232	2.5751	11.082
10	11.0	5.6116	2.9002	11.236

The order of calculation is A_1, s_1, Z_1, A_2, s_2, Z_2, etc.

Figure 2.3 shows the par and zero coupon curves graphically.

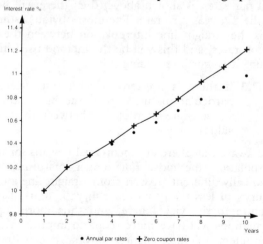

Figure 2.3   Par yield curve and generated zero coupon yield curve.

The advantages of using a spreadsheet for this calculation should be apparent. For full accuracy, the exact days and cashflows of each instrument should be used in the calculation; it is straightforward to incorporate this in a spreadsheet.

Note that this example illustrates:

Result 2.8 A rising par curve leads to a more steeply rising zero curve, and a falling par curve leads to a more steeply falling zero curve.

A proof requires more space than is appropriate here; you are therefore requested to take the result on trust, and to experiment with different values for the par curve to convince yourself that the result does hold in general.

The analysis above covers the period beyond 1 year. For maturities less than 1 year, the zero coupon rate can be calculated directly from the Libor rate. The main problem is the possibility of confusion between the Libor interest rate quoted according to the loan convention of Definition 1.1, and the zero coupon rate quoted according to the zero coupon convention of Definition 1.2.

This can be clarified by a simple example. If 6-month Libor is 10%, what is the 6-month zero coupon rate? From Definition 1.1, the interest on a 6-month deposit of £100 is £100 $*$ 0.5 $*$ 10/100, which equals £5. The 6-month scaling factor is thus £105/£100, which equals 1.05. From Result 1.4, the annualised scaling factor is thus 1.05^2, which equals 1.1025, and the zero coupon rate is thus 10.25%. The same conversion can be made for Libor rates of any maturity.

Where a zero coupon rate is required for an intermediate maturity, it will have to be interpolated from the known points on the yield curve. For example, if the zero coupon curve has been calculated from the ten annual par rates as shown above, then there will be no value calculated for the $2\frac{1}{4}$-year zero rate. The most obvious estimate of the $2\frac{1}{4}$-year rate is the straight line interpolation between the 2- and 3-year zero coupon rates, and this will be the method used in this book for interpolation. It is worth recording this as:

Assumption 2.3 If there is no zero coupon rate calculated to a particular maturity, then the best estimate is the straight-line interpolation between the two adjacent values.

You should be aware that there are theoretical reasons for using more complex interpolation methods. For longer maturities these will seldom give radically different answers from straight line interpolation, but for a maturity of less than two years there is more likely to be a complex structure to the yield curve, and thus more sophisticated interpolation methods will have more scope to improve accuracy. To reduce the problem of interpolation errors it can therefore be worthwhile to take extra points on the par curve; Libor rates can give extra points out to one year and Forward Rate Agreements (FRAs), which are explained in Part II, can be combined with placings to give points on the par curve out to two years. This is discussed further in Part VII.

2.6 VALUING FUTURE CASHFLOWS

We now have all the machinery to present value future cashflows when the yield curve is not flat. The results of section 1.6 still hold when yield curves are not flat, that is, the present value of a cashstream equals the sum of the present values of its individual cashflows, and the present value of a cashflow c at time t, with annualised scaling factor r, is c/r^t.

Following the analysis of section 2.3, the scaling factor to be used in the above formula is the riskfree scaling factor if the cashflow is linked to government debt and the interbank scaling factor if the cashflows are linked to bank debt or are certain cashflows within an organisation. The analysis of interest rate risk in Chapter 3 and the analysis of the various instruments throughout the remainder of the book will generally assume that the interbank zero curve is the appropriate curve to use for present valuing.

However, where cashflows carry non-systematic risk very different from the risk of the banking system, it will be necessary to use a different strategy for present valuing, following the analysis used to value bank debt in section 2.3. The key extra information is the chance of a default and the likely payout after a default. For example, suppose you own a 2-year bond carrying no systematic risk, which pays 10% annually on a principal of £100; you estimate that there is 3% chance that the bond will default in year 1, and a 4% chance that the bond will default in year 2, with the likelihood of a 60% payout in the event of default. You can present value the bond by calculating the probabilities of the cashflows as:

Year 1 £10   97%
        £66   3%   (If there is a default, the principal repayment
                      is accelerated; you thus receive 60% of £110)
Year 2 £0   3%   (when there was a default in year 1)
        £110 93.12% (96% of the remaining 97% of the time)
        £66   3.88%   (4% of the remaining 97% of the time)

The present value of each of these cashflows, using the riskfree zero coupon rates, times the probability of each cashflow occurring, gives a good estimate of the value of the bond.

This calculation is not wholly consistent with Assumption 2.2. Also, a more sophisticated calculation would add a premium or discount for the market valuation of the *liquidity* of the bond, that is, the effective bid-offer spread in buying and selling it. However, as will be shown in the next chapter, although such considerations affect value, to a good approximation they do not affect *risk*.

2.7 INTERNAL RATE OF RETURN

You may have wondered why up to now there has been no mention of the *internal rate of return* (IRR) of a cashstream. Traditionally, financial analysis, particularly of investments, involved working out the constant discount rate at which the future cashflows had the same positive present value as the original investment; this rate is known as the IRR, and the exercise is intended to show that the investment will be worthwhile if the IRR is above some hurdle rate.

Now that you understand that the present valuing calculation has to use the appropriate zero coupon rate to the date of each cashflow, you can see that the IRR calculation is at best an approximation. It is also worth noting that if an investment involves systematic risk a higher rate of return should be required; this necessitates a further complication of the IRR model. For these reasons, this book does not use IRR as an analysis tool.

Despite the approximation involved it is often a useful exercise to work out an IRR to *check* the reasonableness of a more sophisticated calculation involving zero coupon discounting.

As an aside, even in a world of flat yield curves and no systematic risk it would still be dangerous to rely on the analysis of IRRs in order to make investment decisions. For a discussion of this, see any modern textbook on corporate finance.

SUMMARY

This chapter has extended the model developed in Chapter 1 to cope with the term structure of interest rates. The machinery of scaling factors and zero coupon rates is still used for present valuing, but now the zero coupon rate depends on the underlying period. In practice, zero coupon rates are not given but have to be deduced from the market rates for par instruments. Considerations of bid-offer spreads and credit risk lead to the use of off-balance-sheet instruments in the par yield curve from which the interbank zero coupon yield curve is to be calculated; this curve should be used for present valuing cashflows carrying the risk of the banking system. Separately, government bond prices define the riskfree zero coupon yield curve used for present valuing cashflows relating to government debt. The model still assumes a static yield curve; the next chapter will consider the effect of changing interest rates.

CHAPTER 3

Interest rate risk

This chapter uses the framework of zero coupon rates and present valuing to analyse the interest rate risk inherent in fixed future cashflows. The starting point is a definition of *risk* in general and *interest rate risk* in particular. The measurement of interest rate risk is then addressed. This involves three steps: creating a simplifying model of the yield curve, analysing historic rates in order to predict the likely magnitude of future yield curve movements, and reporting the sensitivity of present values to these expected movements. It is then shown that using a yield curve shifted by a small amount does not greatly affect the risk measured, provided that the shift is stable; this is a justification for not having taken more time in Chapter 2 to develop a fully consistent methodology for present valuing. With the machinery of risk measurement and reporting in place, the chapter closes with a discussion of *hedging*, that is, active management to reduce risk.

3.1 RISK AND UNCERTAINTY

This book is concerned with *risk management*, and it is about time that this term was defined. The basic distinction to be made is between risk and uncertainty. A reasonable attempt at defining the difference would be:

Definition 3.1 Risk is the impact on the value of a firm or of a portfolio of future events whose occurrence is predictable but whose exact form is unpredictable, while uncertainty is the impact of completely unpredictable future events.

A formal definition of risk itself will come later, but even without this it is possible to make:

Definition 3.2 Risk management is the process of monitoring risks and taking steps to minimise their impact.

To put some flesh on this, consider what might happen to the environment in which your organisation operates over, say, the next five years. Obviously you cannot predict the future, but you can imagine types of events which would impact the profitability or even the survival of the organisation. For example:

- accidental damage to premises or production capacity;
- customers becoming insolvent while owing you money;
- changes in financial market prices;
- key employees dying or defrauding you;
- theft;
- change in customer preferences;
- strikes;
- recession or boom in different markets;
- actions by competitors;
- changes in regulations;
- technological change;
- civil unrest.

As a generalisation, events near the top represent risk, while events near the bottom represent uncertainty. You can manage certain types of risk by taking out a policy with an insurance company; for example, you can insure against your premises burning down or against employees defrauding you. It is up to you to determine in each case whether the cost of the insurance outweighs the reduction in risk.

You can manage other types of risk by constraining the way in which you run your business. For example, you may give up possibilities of expansion in order to keep a relatively low amount of debt, so that in the event of a recession the business will survive. Again you should carry out a cost-benefit analysis before making a decision such as this.

A cost-benefit analysis demands some calculation of the potential cost of the risk under consideration. The economic theory of the firm asserts that the goal of the firm's management should be to maximise the firm's present value, and therefore risk should be measured in terms of the possible change in this value.

Consider, for example, the risk factor of customers becoming insolvent. Suppose that the firm can insure against credit losses at a premium of *expected* losses plus 20%, where expected has the technical sense of arithmetic mean. By analysing past experience, it should be possible to make a statistical prediction of credit losses over the next year. Assume this gives you a probability of credit loss over the next year of:

£0	5%
£300	10%
£500	20%
£700	30%
£900	20%
£1,100	10%
£1,400	5%.

Multiplying each possible loss by the probability of its occurrence gives you an expected loss of £700. Since the expected loss is £700, credit insurance would cost £840, and hence, if the loss were known with certainty, there would be no point in buying insurance cover. The management could still consider steps to reduce credit losses by, for example, changing its credit policies, but this would be a form of cost reduction and not risk management.

Given that the loss is not known with certainty, how should the management plan? There are basically two strategies: insure or accept the loss. If the firm insures, the cost will be £840, while if it accepts the loss the expected loss will be £700, while the worst case loss will be £1,400. Management could therefore calculate on the basis that not insuring could save £140 on average but would cost an extra £560 in a worst case.

In this example, the worst case loss is given definitively as £1,400, but a closer investigation of the derivation of this figure would probably show that more extreme assumptions would predict an even higher loss. The full spread theoretically possible might, for example, go up to £1,000,000, with the extreme figure having a probability of, say, 0.0000001%. It is generally not practical to plan on the basis of such unlikely events, and therefore, in order for management to make rational decisions, it will be necessary to choose some *confidence level* beyond which losses caused by a particular risk will be assumed not to go. For example, the 97.7% confidence level for a particular risk factor would be the loss caused by that factor which would be exceeded only 2.3% of the time. In the above example, a 97.7% confidence level might give a credit loss of £1,600. It might be appropriate to take such a confidence level for all risk factors, on the basis that there will be a portfolio effect among different factors so that when one happens to exceed its confidence level the others will tend to be within theirs. The usual warning about portfolios applies: when risks are correlated with each other they should be analysed jointly and not separately.

In order to calculate a particular confidence level for a risk factor it is necessary to have some sort of description of the likely distribution of values of that factor. Many risk factors can be assumed, to a reasonable approximation, to be distributed as a *normal distribution*. A normal distribution of a random variable has the familiar shape of a bell-shaped curve, as illustrated in Figure 3.1. The distribution is symmetric about its midpoint, which is also the mean value, and the distance from the midpoint to the kink in the curve is the *standard deviation*[1] of the distribution; the mean and standard deviation uniquely define the distribution, with the standard deviation measuring the expected dispersion around the mean. The probability of the value of the variable

---

[1]The standard deviation of a random variable x is defined as the squareroot of the *variance*, which is the expected value of $(x - \text{mean}_x)^2$, where mean_x is the expected value of x. The standard deviation is thus the 'root mean square deviation' of x.

being between x and x' is the shaded area above the x axis and under the curve; the total area under the curve is one, since at any time the variable must have one (and only one) value. Note that although the curve gets closer and closer to the x axis as it gets further and further to the left or right it never actually touches, and therefore there is always some small probability of the value of the variable being beyond any given distance from the mean. Therefore, if a variable can never be negative, it cannot be precisely normally distributed, although a normal distribution may still give a very good approximation to its behaviour. All of these properties of the normal distribution will be explained in detail in any elementary book on statistics.

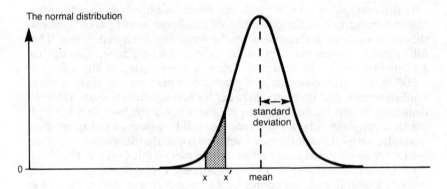

Figure 3.1   The normal distribution.

A key theorem in statistics is that a random variable whose value is the sum of a large number of uncorrelated random variables will itself be very close to normally distributed, given certain very broad assumptions about the distribution of the underlying variables. Since many movements in risk factors result from movements in a large number of uncorrelated variables, it is reasonable to make the splendidly vague:

Assumption 3.1   Risk factors are usually normally distributed.

The reasonableness of this assumption will have to be checked for each risk factor considered.

Since the normal distribution is uniquely determined by its mean and standard deviation, it is possible to give confidence levels for normally distributed variables knowing just these two pieces of information. In particular, if a risk factor has a negative effect on present value when it is high and a positive effect when it is low, then a value which will be exceeded only 2.3% of the time is the mean plus twice the standard deviation; this value will give the 97.7% confidence level. For other confidence levels, or for circumstances where both high and low values of the risk factor have a negative effect, a different multiple of the standard deviation must be added to the mean to give the value for calculating the confidence level; these multiples are available from tables.

Putting all of this together gives:

Definition 3.3 Risk is the maximum expected negative change in the present value of a firm or portfolio, due to a particular risk factor for a given confidence level.

The size of the risk is thus dependent on the confidence level required; the greater the confidence level, the greater the stated risk. If the change in present value due to the risk factor is normally distributed, then the risk will be a fixed multiple of the standard deviation of the distribution, where the multiple depends on the confidence level; working with standard deviations simplifies computation of risk. There is an implicit assumption that the mean of the distribution is zero, or that, if it is not zero, then it represents an expense or income which is being managed separately from the associated risk.

Returning to the main thread of the argument; once the management has chosen its confidence levels, then, in theory at least, it should eliminate risk only when the cost of doing so is less than the resultant increase in the present value of the firm's future cashflows. (In practice it may be difficult to identify the costs and benefits of eliminating risk, and management will set other criteria for defining acceptable levels of risk.)

A key point is that there are often asymmetries in factors such as tax or cost of funding between profitable and unprofitable firms, and therefore reduction of risk may increase expected future *net* cashflows even though it does not increase expected future *operating* cashflows. For example, if a firm has a 50% chance of having an operating cashflow in 1 year's time of $+£500$ and a 50% chance of having a cashflow of $-£100$, then the expected value of the operating cashflow in 1 year is $(50\% * £500)$ $-(50\% * £100)$, which is $£200$. Assume that there is no systematic risk involved throughout, so that present values will be based on interbank zero coupon rates. Suppose that the firm can take some action to reduce the spread of its 1-year cashflows, so that the possible cashflows become $+£300$ and $+£100$, each with probability 50%. Then the expected value of the 1-year operating cashflow is unchanged, and so its present value is also unchanged.

However, if the firm pays tax at 35% on profits and has no tax losses carried forward, then its original after-tax cashflows will be $+£335$ or $-£100$, each with 50% probability. This gives an expected after-tax 1-year cashflow of $£117.50$. (A complication is that an after-tax cashflow should be present valued using an after-tax zero coupon rate; this difficulty is finessed here by leaving the cashflows future valued. For a discussion of this point see *Principles of Corporate Finance*, which is listed in the bibliography.) If the firm takes avoiding action so that its possible 1-year cashflows become +£100 and +£300, then the after-tax cashflows become +£65 and +£195, and the expected after-tax 1-year cashflow will be +£130.

Thus reducing the variability of cashflows in this example does not change expected operating cashflows, but it does increase expected after-tax cashflows. Reduction of variability of cashflows can also increase 'bottom line' cashflows through other mechanisms such as reduced funding costs, avoidance of the expenses of financial distress, and improvements in planning achievable when cashflows are more predictable.

In general you would not expect to eliminate all risk and still increase the firm's value, since the price of insuring against risks which are more and more specific to one firm will go up and up. At some cutoff point therefore, you will decide that you will live with certain risks and manage them as efficiently as you can. For example, a car manufacturer will live with the risk that customers will not like his next model; he will manage that risk internally by doing market research, employing good designers and engineers, and so on. The manufacturer has made the decision that it can manage this risk more cheaply itself than by, say, paying a premium to an insurance company to insure against selling less than 100,000 cars a year. Looked at this way, risk management is a large part of what businesses do.

This book is on interest rate risk. As mentioned above, interest rates go up and down; it is worth noting that this movement tends to be fairly continuous and unpredictable. If changing interest rates will impact an organisation's 'bottom line', then the organisation should consider managing that risk, either through entering into financial contracts with banks or other counterparties, or through other means, provided that the benefits of so doing outweigh the costs.

3.2 COMPONENTS OF INTEREST RATE RISK

Interest rate risk is the impact of changes in interest rates on the value of a firm or portfolio. This impact can happen in two ways, *transaction risk* and *economic risk*. Transaction risk results from changes in the value of financial instruments or of fixed future cashflows arising from the business, whereas economic risk results from changes in the level or profitability of future business.

An example of economic risk would be the downturn in demand experienced by a housebuilder when interest rates increase. A discussion of economic risk will be postponed until Part VII; meanwhile we concentrate on transaction risk, which is more amenable to a quantitative treatment.

(The impact of rising rates on the cost of floating rate borrowing does not affect the present value of future cashflows, since the discount rate rises in line with the borrowing rate; therefore it does not contribute to interest rate risk on the above definition. Nevertheless, as will be discussed in Part VII, the techniques of interest rate risk management can be extended to manage the cost of funding.)

Suppose a firm has certain future cashflows. Then its value is the sum of the present values of each future flow. As interest rates change, each of these present values will change and the value of the firm will fluctuate. To find the expected size of the fluctuation it is necessary to have some measure of how large interest rate movements are likely to be; according to the discussion following Definition 3.3, the required measure is a multiple of the standard deviation of the expected distribution. A statistically valid way of finding the standard deviation would be to revalue the firm, say, 250 times, using the yield curves existing at close of business over the last 250 business days. This would give 250 valuations, which would be expected to approximate a normal distribution; the standard deviation of this distribution would give the required measure of interest rate risk. Critical to the logic of this approach is:

Assumption 3.2 Future fluctuations in rates will be similar in size to past fluctuations.

Some such assumption is necessary in any analysis of risk.

Unfortunately, the approach discussed above would be expensive computationally and would not give guidance on how to manage any risk detected. It is therefore necessary to move away from mathematical precision and to adopt an approach based on relating risk more directly to expected changes in the yield curve. To give an idea of expected changes, Table 3.1 shows representative past fluctuations of zero coupon rates:

TABLE 3.1 HISTORIC FLUCTUATIONS IN ZERO COUPON RATES

Currency	3 month	6 month	2 year	7 year
BEF	4.6	5.0	4.5	3.6
CAD	9.4	8.0	8.0	7.3
CHF	6.4	5.1	4.0	2.9
DEM	4.5	4.3	3.1	3.4
DKK	6.9	5.7	3.6	5.7
ESP	10.3	8.0	5.4	5.4
FRF	5.4	5.1	4.3	4.5
£	6.1	6.7	5.7	5.7
ITL	11.3	8.9	4.2	4.2
JPY	3.2	4.0	3.9	3.7
NLG	3.8	3.6	3.1	3.3
US$	6.1	5.7	5.1	4.9
XEU	4.8	5.1	3.8	4.0

(Information supplied by The Chase Manhattan Bank, N.A.)

Daily changes in zero coupon rates analysed between trading days in period 1 March 1990 to 30 September 1991, covering 317 changes. Each figure shown is the mean absolute change trading day to trading day in hundredths of a per cent. The zero curves were generated from Libor and the offer side of the swap curve.

The basic problem with using such fluctuations in individual zero coupon rates as a starting point is that changes in the yield curve can happen in an infinite number of dimensions. Given the finite time available, it is necessary to make a fairly drastic assumption about the shape and movement of yield curves in order to reduce the dimensionality of the problem; the approach adopted here will reduce the number of dimensions to three. (In addition to this, it will be necessary to look briefly at *short-term repricing risk*.)

The assumption, which is broadly borne out by statistical analysis, is that the zero curve can be reasonably approximated by two straight lines, one from 0 to 1 year and one from 1 to 10 years, which on a day-to-day basis move rigidly up or down or rotate about the 1-year point (or do a bit of both). The two straight lines are chosen as the lines intersecting at 1 year (not necessarily at the 1-year zero coupon rate) which give the minimum sum of the squares of the distance from each of the zero curve points. (A more sophisticated approach would adjust the sum to be minimised to take into account the different number of points in each line segment.) This is referred to as the *best hinged-line fit*.

Any movement from day to day can thus be defined by three numbers, the change in absolute level and the two rotations; the rotations can be recorded as the movement of the 10-year rate relative to the 1-year rate and the movement of the overnight rate relative to the 1-year rate. This is illustrated in Figure 3.2.

It is assumed here that there is no correlation between movements in the different variables; however, in real life there generally will be some correlation, which will add some complexity to the model.

Note that this is only a model aiming to approximate the measurement of risk; it is not guaranteed to be the best approach in any particular circumstances, and it certainly does not capture all of the possible risks. In particular, even if you want to keep just three variables you might find a better fit by moving the hinge point from 1 year to, say, 2 years, and you might find that there is a material correlation between some of the variables. These considerations should not detract from the basic approach being described here.

For the particular currency in which you are working, you should carry out a statistical analysis for, say, the past 250 days, to confirm whether the model explains a satisfyingly high percentage of interest rate movements from day to day, and to obtain standard deviations for the daily movement in rates. For example, you might discover that in sterling the model explains 83 per cent of the movement in rates and that the daily standard deviations measured in *basis points*, that is, in hundredths of a per cent, are:

Level   7 basis points;
0–1 year rotation   3 basis points; and
1–10 year rotation   4 basis points.

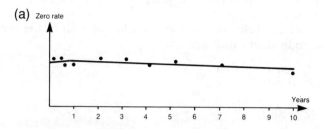

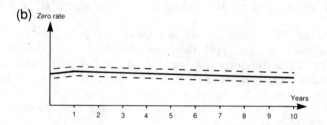

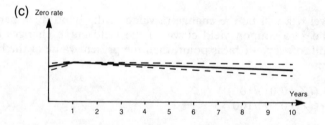

Figure 3.2 Best hinged-line fit of zero coupon yield curve. (a) Best hinged-line fit of zero coupon yield curve. (b) Plus and minus envelope showing standard deviations of daily level shift. (c) Plus and minus envelope showing standard deviations of daily rotation.

This would probably encourage you to use the model for risk management; you would quantify risks based on the standard deviations of present values, as detailed in the next section.

The management of short-term repricing risk will be discussed separately, in Part II, after a treatment of Forward Rate Agreements (FRAs) which introduces some necessary concepts.

3.3 MEASURING INTEREST RATE RISK

Suppose you own a bond with a series of future cashflows, c_1 at year 1, c_2 at year 2, ..., c_{10} at year 10. You can construct a yield curve to calculate the zero coupon rates for years 1-10, and as before we shall call these $Z_1\%$, $Z_2\%$, ..., $Z_{10}\%$.

Then the present value of the bond will be the sum of the present value of the individual cashflows:

$$c_1/(1 + (Z_1/100))^1 \qquad +$$
$$c_2/(1 + (Z_2/100))^2 \qquad +$$
$$... \qquad +$$
$$c_{10}/(1 + (Z_{10}/100))^{10}$$

The measure of the interest rate risk will be the change in value for the expected change in interest rates. Using the three variable model described above, you should calculate the risk separately for each variable.

For ease of illustration we are not using any points on the yield curve less than 1 year, and therefore we shall not calculate the component of risk relating to a rotation of the 0-1 year yield curve. The calculation given below for rotation of the 1-10 year curve could be followed through for rotation of the 0-1 year curve, and there would be no improvement in explanation in going through effectively the same calculation twice.

Let us therefore calculate the level risk and the 1-10 year rotation risk.

The level risk will be the change in value of the bond for a parallel shift in the zero coupon yield curve. If the yield curve changes by a parallel shift of, say, +1 basis point, then the present value of the bond will become:

$$c_1/(1 + ((Z_1+0.01)/100))^1 \qquad +$$
$$c_2/(1 + ((Z_2+0.01)/100))^2 \qquad +$$
$$... \qquad +$$
$$c_{10}/(1 + ((Z_{10}+0.01)/100))^{10}$$

The change in value, and hence the risk for a +1 basis point movement in the yield curve level, will be the difference between this new value and the old value calculated above. This will be referred to as 'the value of a 1 basis point shift'.

Note that the analysis in section 3.4 below shows that the calculation of the *change* in value of the bond, and hence of the interest rate risk, will be reasonably accurate, even if the credit risk on the bond means that its cashflows should be present valued using a zero coupon curve significantly different from the interbank curve, provided that the difference between the two curves is stable.

A mathematical analysis will show that the change in value for a -1 basis point shift will be close to minus the value of a +1 basis point shift, and, in general, the change in value for an n basis point shift will be approximately n times the value of a 1 basis point shift, with the accuracy being better the lower the value of n.

To quantify the risk in terms of the expected overnight movement, you might measure the risk for a shift in level of two standard deviations, giving a 97.7% confidence level of capturing the worst case movement. Assuming that the standard deviation of the level is 7 basis points, this represents the change in value of a 14 basis point shift, which is approximately 14 times the value of a 1 basis point shift; let us call this the *daily level risk*.

As noted above, this will be an approximation. For full accuracy you should explicitly repeat the valuation of the bond for the zero curve 14 basis points above and below the original curve. This will be particularly relevant for more complex cashflows where the value of a 1 basis point shift is zero. Part VII will show how the reporting could be extended to include *convexity* in order to give a more accurate result for larger yield curve shifts, but for our purposes here we can assume that simply multiplying the value of the 1 basis point shift will provide enough accuracy.

You have calculated the daily level risk. Following the calculations and assumptions through, this represents the overnight change in value of the bond which you would expect to see exceeded on only 4.6% of days. (The move would be positive 2.3% of the time, and negative 2.3% of the time.) A similar calculation could be done to produce a weekly or a monthly level risk. Assuming that there are 5 business days in a week and 21 business days in a month, the weekly level risk should be (the squareroot of 5) times the daily level risk, and the monthly level risk should be (the squareroot of 21) times the daily level risk. This follows from properties of the standard deviation of a normal distribution; a statistical check should be made to ensure that the rate movements do follow a normal distribution, since if they do not the weekly and monthly risks may have to be calculated explicitly by the same process as for the daily risk.

The choice of over which period to measure the risk will depend on how you intend to manage your business. If you are prepared to look at the position every day, then the daily risk is appropriate, whereas if you want to put the bond away for a month at a time then you ought to consider the possible risk over a month. This book concentrates on the daily risk, but you should remember that the magnitude of a risk depends on how actively you intend to manage it.

In concentrating on the daily risk there is an implicit assumption that you can close out an unwanted position within a day. If market liquidity means that it will take, say, a week to close out a position, then the risk you are running is the possible change in value over a week. This consideration will be most important in less liquid currencies, or in positions with unusually long maturities, or in *option* positions; the last of these is discussed in Part V.

You can measure the rotation risk in a similar way to level risk. Calculate the value of the bond after a 0.111 basis point change in the 2-year rate $Z_2\%$, a 0.222 basis point change in the 3-year rate $Z_3\%$, ..., up to a 1 basis point change in the 10-year rate $Z_{10}\%$. This will be:

$$c_1/(1 + (Z_1/100))^1 \qquad\qquad +$$
$$c_2/(1 + ((Z_2+0.00111)/100))^2 \qquad +$$
$$\ldots \qquad\qquad\qquad\qquad\qquad\qquad +$$
$$c_{10}/(1 + ((Z_{10}+0.01)/100))^{10}$$

The change in value, and hence the risk for a +1 basis point rotation of the yield curve, will be the difference between this new value and the original value calculated above. This will be referred to as 'the value of a 1 basis point rotation in the 1-10 year'. A similar definition would give 'the value of a 1 basis point rotation in the 0-1 year'.

As before, the daily rotation risk can be quantified as being twice the daily standard deviation of the rotation times the value of a 1 basis point rotation. The interpretation of this, the approximations involved, and the calculation of risk for other periods, follow through as for level risk.

If you assume that the three risks are exhaustive and uncorrelated, then the total daily risk will be the square root of the sum of the squares of the individual risks, that is, the square root of:

((level risk squared)   +
(0-1 year rotation risk squared)   +
(1-10 year rotation risk squared)).

This follows from the fundamental result in statistics that the variance of the sum of uncorrelated random variables is the sum of the individual variances.

If you make the most conservative assumption that individual risks are correlated 'optimally badly', then the total risk should be taken as the sum of the three individual risks, that is:

(level risk)   +
(0-1 year rotation risk)   +
(1-10 year rotation risk).

In either case, the interpretation of the total daily risk is that it is the amount which you would expect the daily movement in the bond's present value to exceed on only 4.6% of days, with the movement being negative on half of these days.

We have carried out the risk analysis for a single bond, but exactly the same analysis would work for a portfolio of bonds or for *any* fixed cashflows. This section has, therefore, defined a general formula for the calculation of interest rate risk.

The section concludes with a numerical example. Assume that there are future cashflows:

-£1 at 1 year
£2 at 3 years and
£1 at 5 years

and that the zero curve is

year 1   9%
year 2   9.2%
year 3   9.3%
year 4   9.2%
year 5   9.1%.

Assume further that the standard deviation of the daily level movement is 6 basis points, and of the 1-10 rotation is 3 basis points, and that two standard deviations will again give the confidence level. Calculate the daily level risk and 1-10 year rotation risk.

Try to work through the example yourself rather than just auditing the answer.

Year	Cash	Zero	PV	Level shift Zero	PV	Rotation Zero	PV
1	-1	9.0	-0.91743	9.01	-0.91735	9.00	-0.91743
3	2	9.3	1.53169	9.31	1.53126	9.30222	1.53159
5	1	9.1	0.64696	9.11	0.64666	9.10444	0.64683
Total PV			1.26121		1.26058		1.26099

The value of a 1 basis point shift is therefore -£0.00063, and the value of a 1 basis point rotation is -£0.00023. Multiplying by twice the standard deviations gives:

daily level risk   £0.00756 and
daily rotation risk £0.00138; and summing these gives
total daily risk   £0.00894.

Note that risk is always taken as positive.
This calculation incorporates:

Assumption 3.3 If interest rates are normally distributed then the present value of future cashflows will be normally distributed.

This is a good approximation except for very large movements in rates, and even then the resultant inaccuracies are likely to be relatively small, in the context of the risk management process. Assumption 3.3 will be used consistently below.

If you assume zero correlation, so that risks are added by taking the squareroot of the sum of their squares, then the total risk becomes £0.00768.

The method of calculating interest rate risk demonstrated above will be referred to as the *discrete cash gaps* methodology. This is a powerful and accurate technique, but it will be argued in Part VII that it is best suited to the close management of individual risk positions, that is, *micro hedging*, and that other, less accurate, methodologies may prove more practical for managing the risk of a portfolio of positions or of an entire organisation; managing such global risks is referred to as *macro hedging*.

An organisation partly funded by debt will be interested in minimising the cost of that debt. This is an example of a key point made in the introduction to Part I: the critical decision in managing risk is to decide on the ultimate objective. Part VII will discuss setting such objectives and managing towards them; in particular it will look at reducing the cost of funding.

3.4 RISK MEASUREMENT USING
A DISPLACED ZERO CURVE

The purpose of this section is to demonstrate that measuring interest rate risk using the interbank yield curve gives close to the correct answer, even if a materially different yield curve should be used for present valuing the cashflows, provided that the difference between the two yield curves is stable. This justifies the general use of the interbank zero curve in Chapter 2.

Rather than give a comprehensive proof incorporating complex mathematics, the calculation of risk of section 3.3 above is repeated with a shifted yield curve. This illustrates that in this case the change in risk is very small, even for a substantial movement in the yield curve, and you are then asked to take the general result on trust.

Assume that the zero curve is shifted by:

year 1	+1%
year 3	+0.6%
year 5	+0.7%

Recalculating the risk gives:

Year	Cash	Zero	PV	Level shift Zero	PV	Rotation Zero	PV
1	-1	10.0	-0.90909	10.01	-0.90900	10.00000	-0.90909
3	2	9.9	1.50674	9.91	1.50632	9.90222	1.50664
5	1	9.8	0.62660	9.81	0.62631	9.80444	0.62647
Total PV			1.22424		1.22363		1.22402

This gives values of 1 basis point shifts of -0.00061 for level and -0.00022 for rotation, compared with -0.00063 and -0.00023, thus demonstrating that the fractional change in the risk calculated is very small, even for a substantial change in the yield curve used.

This confirms that calculating interest rate risk using the interbank zero coupon curve gives close to the correct answer, even if a different yield curve should be used to present value the cashflows, *provided* that the difference between the correct yield curve and the interbank zero curve is stable. If the difference is not stable, as would, for example, be the case where the cashflows should be discounted using the riskfree yield curve, then there will be an additional spread risk dependent on the relative movement of the two yield curves; spread risk will be discussed in Part IV.

3.5 HEDGING AND RISK TAKING

Once you have calculated the risk of your future cashflows, you can decide if you want to do anything to reduce it. The act of entering into financial contracts or restructuring business activities in order to reduce risk is known as *hedging*.

Before taking any action to reduce risk you will have to decide how far out you want to predict cashflows – the *hedging horizon* – and what change in value is material for your business. As mentioned above, you will also have to decide how actively you wish to manage your positions, so that you will know over which period to measure your risk. You should ascertain management's risk appetite, and should have a view of likely movements of rates. You should also compare the costs and benefits of collecting information on future cashflows; it might be cheaper to sack the treasurer than to hedge.

Assuming that all this information is to hand, you can decide which risks to hedge. For example, if you manage your positions daily and the daily level risk is £1,000, you might decide to take no action, whereas if the risk were £1,000,000 you might wish to hedge all or part of it.

In the definition of hedging at the start of this section it was pointed out that there are two ways of hedging, restructuring the business or entering into financial contracts.

Restructuring a business is at best a slow and complex process, and it is not always practicable; it could involve, for example, changing standard terms of sale or entering into a new business area which is contracyclical to existing areas. Where such restructuring is practical, it can represent a powerful method of reducing risk in a cost-effective way. Restructuring as a hedge will not be treated further in this book, but you should be aware of the possibility.

The use of financial contracts as a hedge is relatively straightforward. The steps are:

- decide what risks you wish to hedge;
- identify a collection of portfolios of financial contracts which have equal and opposite risks to the ones you are hedging; and
- enter into the portfolio of contracts with the lowest cost.

For example, suppose you wish to hedge cashflows with a value of a 1 basis point level shift of +US$100,000, and a value of a 1 basis point rotation in the 1-10 years of -US$20,000. You would then wish to enter into a portfolio of financial contracts with a value of a 1 basis point shift of -US$100,000, and a value of a 1 basis point rotation of +US$20,000.

You would examine which combinations of instruments gave you this exposure, and enter into the cheapest combination. However, when deciding which combination is cheapest you should take into account the points in the next three paragraphs.

You should consider that most financial contracts involve some credit risk, and that this should be included when calculating costs. If you are hedging for a bank, it will have to maintain capital for most contracts which it enters into, and this involves an opportunity cost. There will, in addition, be expenses involved in administering each contract; if you have a large number of contracts, these expenses can be substantial. All these costs will be discussed in more detail in Parts II-VI, which cover individual products.

Also you should not stretch the risk model further than necessary. We assumed that the yield curve between 1 and 10 years was rigid, but this does not mean that you should try to hedge cashflows in, say, 9 and 10 years, with cashflows in, say, 3 and 4 years. You should be aware that the correlation of changes in value between the original cashflows and the hedging contracts will be greater if the hedging contracts have cashflows in approximately the same maturities as the original cashflows.

Finally, you should remember that hedging cashflows today does not mean that they will stay hedged tomorrow. The behaviour of the risk of the hedge over time may differ from the behaviour of the risk of the original cashflows. Since there will be transaction costs every time that you have to adjust the hedge, you should try to put on a hedge which will continue to be effective for as long as is necessary or practical; for the same reason you should use the most liquid instruments available, that is, the instruments with the smallest bid-offer spread.

The discussion above concentrates on hedging. If you have a particular market view you may wish to take risk rather than hedge. The same analysis will let you take a position which incorporates the correct risk/profit relationship. For example, if you believe that the long end of the yield curve will rise while the short end will fall, you will wish to be neutral on level risk, positive on 1-10 year rotation risk, and negative on 0-1 year rotation risk; the size of your positions will depend on factors such as your appetite for risk, the cost of closing out positions, and the strength of your convictions of your market view.

You now have enough theory about the use of interest rate risk management instruments, and it is time to turn to the instruments themselves.

SUMMARY

Risk is the change in present value of a portfolio of transactions or of a firm due to the maximum likely change in a particular risk factor over a future period; the greater the confidence level required the larger is the measured risk. Transaction risk arises from changes in the present value of existing cashflows; economic risk arises from changes in the cashflows generated by future business.

Interest rate risk is the sensitivity of the present value to changes in the zero curve multiplied by the expected magnitude of the movement in the zero curve. The discrete cash gaps methodology can calculate the sensitivity, and a statistical analysis of historic rate movements can estimate the magnitude of future movements. Since the zero curve can change in many different ways, a simplifying model was developed to represent the zero curve using only three variables; the strengths and limitations of this model were emphasised. Hedging and risk taking are two sides of the same coin; each involves entering into financial contracts to achieve a particular risk profile.

APPENDIX A

Interest bases

There are several different conventions for quoting interest rates, of which the most common are:

Actual/365 fixed Interest is calculated as the principal times the interest rate times the days in the period over 36,500. For example, interest at 10% on £200 for the period 24 February 1992 to 24 August 1992, would be

$$\frac{£200 * 10 * 182}{36,500}$$

which equals £9.97.

This basis is commonly used for all sterling interest rates, including Libor; it is also used for Belgian franc Libor. Actual/365 fixed is sometimes confused with Actual/365, which is defined below.

Actual/360 Interest is calculated as the principal times the interest rate times the days in the period over 36,000. For example, interest on a 3-month deposit at 10% on XEU500 for the period 1 May 1992 to 3 August 1992, would be

$$\frac{XEU500 * 10 * 94}{36,000}$$

which equals XEU13.06.

This basis is commonly used for all Eurocurrency[2] Libor rates, except for sterling and Belgian francs.

---

[2]A *Eurocurrency* transaction is a transaction in a currency outside its domestic banking system; it will therefore not be subject to the regulation of the domestic central bank, although it will be regulated in the country in which it takes place. As governments standardise tax and regulation, the distinction between domestic currency and Eurocurrency becomes less important.

Actual/365 or
Actual/actual

Interest is calculated as the principal times the interest rate times

((days in the period in a normal year over 36,500) plus

(days in the period in a leap year over 36,600)).

The day from 31 December to 1 January is assumed to fall in the earlier year.

For example, interest on a 7% coupon US$1,000 Treasury bond for the period 2 November 1991 to 2 May 1992 would be

$$\frac{US\$1000 * 7 * 60}{36,500} + \frac{US\$1000 * 7 * 122}{36,600}$$

which equals US$38.84.

This basis is commonly used for US Treasury bonds and for some US$ interest rate swaps.

Fixed coupon

It is assumed that the period is exactly a half year or exactly a year, even though there may be a few days difference due to weekends or holidays; interest is calculated as the principal times the interest rate times the number of years in the period over 100.

Thus, for example, if a bond pays 10% on a fixed coupon basis on a principal of DEM10,000,000 with semiannual payments, then the interest for a period running from 22 June to 24 December would be

$$\frac{DEM10,000,000 * 10 * 0.5}{100}$$

which is exactly DEM500,000.

This basis is commonly used for Eurobonds.

Bond basis
or **30/360**
or **30E/360**

Confusingly, this is generally not used for bonds, except for calculating *accrued interest*, that is, the compensatory payment made for interest in the current payment period when a bond is purchased in the middle of a period.

There are two variants of bond basis: 30/360 (also known as 360/360) and 30E/360: the difference is defined below.

Under bond basis, interest is calculated as the principal times the interest rate times the number of days in the period *as defined below* over 36,000.

The number of days in the period is calculated as if every month had 30 days; thus, for example, the period 1 May to 11 September would have 130 days. For 30E/360 *only*, the 30-day-in-a-month rule is reinforced by assuming that any period beginning or ending on the 31st of a month actually begins or ends on the 30th. Thus the period 1 January to 31 January would have 29 days under 30E/360 and 30 days under 30/360. This complication exists only for periods beginning or ending on the last day of a 31 day month; for all other periods the two bases give the same number of days. Note in particular that the period 1 February to 28 February would be 27 days in both bases, with the period 1 February to 1 March being 30 days.

As an example of the calculation of interest under bond basis, a US$1,000 bond with a coupon of 8%, sold for delivery on 17 May when its last interest payment was on 3 February, would have accrued interest

$$\frac{US\$1,000 * 8 * 104}{36,000}$$

which equals US$23.11.

The 30/360 basis is used primarily for calculating accrued interest on domestic US bonds, while 30E/360 is used for calculating accrued interest on Eurobonds. You can deduce from this that the 'E' stands for 'European', and, indeed, the 30E/360 basis is sometimes referred to as the Eurobond basis. Many European currency interest rate swaps use one of the bond bases for calculating their fixed interest side.

In addition to ensuring that you know the interest basis when you enter into a transaction, you should also ensure that you know the other conventions of the particular market, such as the movement of dates which fall on a holiday and the treatment of interest if a date is so moved.

APPENDIX B

Economic theory

The focus of this book is microeconomic. However, interest rates clearly reflect macroeconomic forces, and so this appendix exists as a brief introduction to – it would be an exaggeration to say a review of – the macroeconomic theory of interest rates. The intention is to draw your attention to three basic questions in economics, all of which are different facets of the same question: 'How can I best predict rate movements?' Sadly, no satisfactory answer will be given here to any of these questions, and the reader is directed to the literature for further enlightenment.

The three questions are:

1 What determines the broad level of rates over a period of months or years?
2 What determines the term structure of interest rates?
3 How do rates move over a period of days or weeks?

Contrary to the well-known jibe that any three economists will have 4.9 opinions on a given question[3], there is unanimity that the level of interest rates is determined by the balance of supply and demand for *money* in the economy. Unfortunately, unanimity quickly breaks down when you try to get a clear definition of 'money'. Roughly speaking, money is cash or cash substitutes that are available for immediate spending. There are different measures of the amount of money in the economy – the *money supply* – depending on how broad a definition you wish to take; hence you will see M0, M1, M2, and so on, each of which measures a progressively broader definition of the money supply. A distinction is usually made between the *nominal* interest rate, which is the interest rate as normally quoted, and the *real* interest rate, which is the excess of the nominal interest rate over inflation; needless to say, the treatment of inflation is also subject to controversy.

Although there are many different schools of economists, notably Keynesians and Monetarists, it is only fair to point out that the

---

[3]This is not an exact integer due to rounding error.

theories of each school tend to be self-consistent, and the controversy lies with the interpretation of real-life data. In this, economics suffers with other social sciences in the difficulty of obtaining clean data and the impossibility of carrying out controlled experiments.

The money supply and the demand for money will be affected by factors in the economy such as the levels of production, consumption, investment, saving, imports, and exports, all of which will also be interdependent; the interdependencies will depend on your choice of theory. As these factors change, the general level of interest rates will change. In principle this could be predicted by a detailed model of the economy, but in practice neither the data nor the theory has proved satisfactory for much accurate prediction. Within Europe the situation is further complicated by the decision to merge the currencies of the European Community countries on a fixed timetable; any economic model somehow has to incorporate the impact of this.

There is no general agreement as to why and how interest rates should vary along the yield curve, and we are left looking at three competing theories.

The *expectations* theory emphasises expected values today of what the yield curve will look like in the future. For example, if you think that in 1 year's time the 1-year zero rate will be 12%, and you know that the 1-year zero rate is 10% today, then you will price a 2-year zero coupon bond at around 11% interest (ignoring compounding effects). More accurately, you will price a long-term bond so that your return on holding it to maturity is equal to your expectations of the return on repeated investment in a strip of short-term bonds to the same maturity. Expectations of future returns could be based on the econometric models mentioned above.

The *liquidity preference* theory emphasises that risk aversion by investors will make them less willing to tie up their money in long-term assets, whereas borrowers, who have to ensure that they can renew loans at maturity, will tend to want loans fixed for longer periods; this will increase the demand for long-term money relative to the supply, and therefore long-term rates should be systematically greater than short-term rates. This prediction can be tested empirically, but the results seem to be inconclusive.

The *preferred habitat* theory emphasises that different groups of users have strong preferences for instruments within different maturity ranges. For example, pension funds are typically keen to buy bonds with a maturity from 15 to 30 years, since this will match the maturity of their liabilities, whereas bank loans to corporate customers tend to have a maximum tenor of about 10 years. Provided the yields to adjacent maturity ranges do not differ by a large amount, market supply and demand may make a substantial total difference across the full range of maturities.

This brings us to question (3) to which the usual answer is that interest rates are set in an *efficient market*, that is, in a market in which prices incorporate all available information. Therefore, except for small movements due to 'random noise', rates should move only following the announcement of some new information, such as a money supply figure or an inflation rate. If an individual figure is unpredictable, the trick then becomes working out in advance how the market would respond to the various possible values, and dealing appropriately as soon as the figure is released. (A related area for obtaining a trading advantage, ruthless as it may seem, is to work out in advance a strategy to apply in the event of such relatively foreseeable natural disasters as an earthquake in Tokyo or in San Francisco.) The predictions of the efficient market hypothesis can be checked against real life data, and it does seem plausible that the hypothesis is reasonably valid; however, almost all tests have been made against end-of-day rates, and so there remains the possibility that intraday rates do not immediately incorporate all available information, thus leaving space for efficient operators to make profitable deals.

The moral of all of this is that it seems difficult – or impossible – to predict interest rate movements, and therefore you should carefully identify and manage the risk that rate movements give you.

Self-study questions

Unless otherwise stated, all interest is quoted on an annual basis, and each month should be considered to be an exact twelfth of a year.

1.1 If the scaling factor for 1 year is 1.09, what is the zero coupon rate?

   If the yield curve is flat, what is the scaling factor for 3 years?

   What is the scaling factor for 3 months?

1.2 If the scaling factor for 2 years is 1.15, what is the zero coupon rate?

1.3 If the zero coupon rate is 6%, what is the scaling factor for 18 months?

1.4 If the zero coupon rate is 8% for all maturities, what is the present value of a cashflow of $-£10$ in 2 years and 6 months?

   What is the present value of the cashstream:

Year 0	$-£10$
Year 1	$+£20$
Year 1.5	$-£30$
Year 2	$+£25$

   What is the future value of the same cashstream at 3 months?

1.5 A bond with an exact number of years to maturity pays annually at 10% when the zero coupon rate is 7% to all maturities. What minimum quarterly interest rate should you be willing to receive on another bond in exchange?

1.6 Convert an interest rate of 10% on an actual/360 basis to an equivalent interest rate on an actual/365 fixed basis.

1.7 Convert an interest rate of 5% on a bond basis to an approximately equivalent interest rate on an actual/360 basis.

   If the period is 23 May to 25 November, convert an interest rate of 5% on a bond basis exactly to an equivalent interest rate on an actual/360 basis.

1.8   If the 1-year zero coupon rate is 10% and a 2-year par bond pays annual interest at 9.8%, will the 2-year zero coupon rate be lower than, higher than, or equal to 9.8%?

Calculate the 2-year zero coupon rate.

What is your best estimate of the 21-month zero coupon rate?

1.9   If the 6-month zero coupon rate is 7%, and the 1-year zero coupon rate is 7.1%, and a 2-year par bond pays interest semi-annually at 7%, then, making reasonable assumptions, work out:

The rate for a 1-year par bond paying semiannually.

The rate for an 18-month par bond paying semiannually.

The zero coupon rate for 18 months.

The zero coupon rate for 2 years.

1.10 What is the present value of a 5-year bond paying interest semiannually at 8% if the zero coupon yield curve is:

Year 0	6%
Year 1	6.5%
Year 2	6.8%
Year 3	7.0%
Year 4	7.1%
Year 5	7.2%.

1.11 A company pays tax at 30% on its profits; losses can only be offset against future years' profits.

Case A
If the company's interest rate risk means that, before tax, it has a 50% chance of making £100 and a 50% chance of making £200 this year, what is its expected pre-tax profit, and what is its expected post-tax profit?

Case B
If its interest rate risk means that, before tax, it has a 50% chance of making £500 and a 50% chance of losing £200 this year, what is its expected pre-tax profit and what is its expected post-tax profit?

Without further information, would you advise the company to hedge its interest rate risk in either case?

1.12 The zero coupon yield curve is:

Year 1	10%
Year 2	10.3%
Year 3	10.5%
Year 4	10.6%
Year 5	10.6%

What is the level risk, calculated for a 1 basis point movement of the yield curve, for a 5-year bond paying 10% interest annually on a principal of £100,000.

What would the risk be if the bond paid 3% interest annually?

What is the ratio of risk to present value in each case?

1.13 With the zero coupon curve as in question 1.12, work out the sensitivity of the value of the 10% 5-year bond to a rotation of the yield curve about the 1-year point, where the 5-year point moves by plus 10 basis points.

Repeat the calculation for the 5-year point moving minus 10 basis points.

What is the corresponding sensitivity for the 3% bond?

1.14 If you have issued £100,000 face value of the 10% bond, what value of the 3% bond must you buy to hedge the level risk?

What residual rotation sensitivity do you have?

PART II

FRAs AND EURODEPOSIT FUTURES

Part II defines and analyses two of the most common interest rate risk management instruments, *Forward Rate Agreements* (FRAs) and *Eurodeposit futures contracts*. The common thread is that each of these is relatively short term and is related to the value of a single future interest rate.

Each instrument has a chapter to itself. The focus is how market needs drive the form of each instrument, and how the form of each instrument causes its present value to change in response to changing interest rates. This provides a framework for a comparison of the *risk profile* of the two instruments and a discussion of the circumstances in which each is appropriate.

As a useful reference, Appendix C at the end of the module lists the futures and *options* exchanges round the world which have contracts based on interest rates; although options are not introduced until Part V, it is convenient to position this appendix here to demonstrate the variety of interest rate futures contracts available.

CHAPTER 4

Forward rate agreements (FRAs)

This chapter considers Forward Rate Agreements (FRAs). First a hedging need is demonstrated and then, to meet this need, a hedging instrument is specified. It is then shown that this hedging instrument, with minor adjustments, is the same as a standard FRA contract. A rigorous definition of the standard FRA contract is then given, together with an overview of the FRA market. Most of the rest of the chapter concentrates on the *risk profile* of FRAs, that is, on the change in their present value under changing interest rates, and on their performance as hedging instruments. It is demonstrated that, under certain assumptions, any interest rate risk position can be hedged using some combination of FRAs, and using a worked example it is shown that the costs of using FRAs are not excessive in a real-life hedge. With the techniques developed to analyse risk it is then simple to show how to calculate the market value of an FRA; this will be needed for managing and accounting for a portfolio of FRAs. The final section analyses *short-term repricing risk*, using the concepts developed in this chapter.

4.1 CREATING A HEDGE CONTRACT

It would be possible to give a bald statement of the mechanics of FRAs, but it should help you to understand them better by going through the process of 'inventing' them, through creating a contract to meet a hedging need.

Consider a company with only one source of interest rate risk: it has to pay £10 million to a supplier in 3 months' time and will not receive payment of £10,291,262 from a customer until 3 months later. (The sales price is chosen in order to simplify the working later on.) The risk can be calculated by the process detailed in Part I, but it can be more simply expressed by observing that the company will wish to borrow £10 million for 3 months in 3 months' time, with the interest rate at that time being currently unknown. Consequently, if interest rates go down the company will save money, but if rates go up it will lose money.

The company could hedge this risk by agreeing today to borrow £10 million from a bank in 3 months' time, at an interest rate fixed today. A bank will certainly quote a price on this, but its price will include a higher cost of credit than if the company were borrowing today for 3 months (since the credit risk is on a 6-month instead of a 3-month horizon) and also a higher cost of capital (since bank capital rules involve maintaining capital for commitments). Also, from the company's point of view, such a *forward loan* is inflexible as it will lock it in to a particular funding arrangement and stop it shopping around in 3 months' time.

What the company really needs to lock in today is not the loan but the interest rate. Therefore, what it needs to agree with its bank is that if interest rates go up then the bank will pay the company money; the bank will require some compensation for this arrangement, and the most obvious way to provide this is to agree that if interest rates go down the company should pay money to the bank. On the assumption that interest rates are as likely to rise as to fall, such an agreement will be fair to both parties.

The above discussion avoids the important point of the base rate for comparison. Assume for the moment zero bid-offer spreads, no cost of credit or of capital, and no transaction costs. (This example will be reexamined later, with more realistic assumptions.) Suppose that the 3-month scaling factor is 1.03, and the 6-month scaling factor is 1.06. Then the implied 3-month scaling factor 3 months forward will be 1.06/1.03, which equals 1.0291262.

To prove this, consider borrowing £1 for 3 months or 6 months; you would have to repay £1.03 or £1.06. Conversely, if you borrowed £1 for 3 months and then borrowed the repayment amount for another 3 months, *at a rate locked in today*, then you should also have to repay £1.06 at 6 months, or else there would be a possibility of arbitrage. Consequently the 3-month scaling factor, 1.03, times the 3-month forward scaling factor for 3 months, should equal the 6-month scaling factor, 1.06. Dividing both sides of this equality by 1.03 gives the expression for the forward scaling factor quoted above.

Generalising the above proof gives the following result for the forward rates implied by the zero curve:

Result 4.1 If the scaling factor to t_1 years is s_1, and to t_2 years is s_2, then s, the implied forward scaling factor from t_1 to t_2, is:

$$\frac{s_2}{s_1}$$

Using the forward scaling factor of 1.0291262 calculated above, it can be seen that future valuing the 6-month receipt from the customer to the 3-month date gives a value of $+£10$ million; this exactly offsets the payment to the supplier on that day, giving a net future value of zero. The net present value is therefore also zero. Eliminating interest rate risk in this example, therefore, means ensuring that the present value of the company's future cashflows remains at zero, regardless of what happens to interest rates.

What are the 3- and 6-month scaling factors calculated from? As shown in Part I, the short end of the zero curve is calculated from Libor rates, which are the market offer rates quoted for interbank placings. The 3-month factor of 1.03 is calculated from 3-month sterling Libor, and the 6-month factor of 1.06 is calculated from 6-month sterling Libor.

Working the other way, you can calculate the Libors from these scaling factors. The 3-month scaling factor is 1.03; this means that $£1$ invested today will repay $£1.03$ in 3 months. Of this $£1$ will be principal and $£0.03$ will be interest, and so the market Libor rate $L\%$ should therefore also give interest of $£0.03$. The formula for interest for a 3-month period is:

$$\frac{\text{principal} * \text{interest rate} * 0.25}{100}$$

and equating this to $£0.03$ gives the 3-month Libor as 12%.

Generalising this argument gives:

Result 4.2 If the scaling factor for a period of t years is s, then $L\%$, the implied Libor rate for the period, is:

$$\frac{(s - 1) * 100}{t}$$

Using this result shows that 6-month Libor is also 12%.

Putting Results 4.1 and 4.2 together gives:

Result 4.3 If the scaling factor to t_1 years is s_1 and to t_2 years is s_2, then $L\%$, the implied Libor rate for the period t_1 to t_2 is:

$$\frac{((s_2/s_1) - 1) * 100}{t_2 - t_1}$$

What is the implied 3-month Libor 3 months forward? The scaling factor for the appropriate period is 1.0291262 and Result 4.2 gives the Libor rate, sensibly rounded, as 11.65%; the same value can be obtained directly from the original scaling factors by using Result 4.3. Note the unobvious result that 3- and 6-month Libors both equal to 12% imply a forward Libor less than 12%; it should help your understanding of what is going on if you compound all the rates involved to give annualised scaling factors, and then compare them.

Call the 3-month Libor which is actually set in 3 months $L\%$. The company wishes to reduce its risk that $L\%$ will differ from 11.65%,

with the company losing or making the interest differential on the
3-month loan on £10 million. Since there are no spread or transaction
costs, both the company and the bank could lock in a forward rate of
11.65% today, and hence a fair contract would be:

- If L is greater than 11.65, then the bank will pay the company
  interest calculated at ($L\%$ -11.65%) on £10 million for 3 months.
- If L is less than 11.65, then the company will pay the bank interest
  calculated at (11.65% - $L\%$) on £10 million for 3 months.
- If L equals 11.65, nobody will pay anything.

Any interest is paid, as usual, at the end of the period; in this case it
will be paid at the 6-month date.

Let us check that this contract actually achieves the aim of giving
the company a perfect hedge for its risk. Remember bid-offer spreads
are assumed to be zero, so that the company can always borrow or
invest funds at the appropriate Libor for the period involved. Its
cashflows, on the purchase, sale, loan, and hedge contracts, in
£ million, are:

At 3 months -10	(payment to supplier)
10	(loan principal)
At 6 months 10.291262	(receipt from customer)
-10	(loan principal)
$-10 * L\% * 0.25$	(loan interest at $L\%$)
$10 * (L\% - 11.65\%) * 0.25$	(hedge)

Clearly, at the 3-month date the net cashflow is zero. At 6 months,
the flow relating to the hedge can be expressed as:

$$(10 * L\% * 0.25) - (10 * 11.65\% * 0.25)$$

The first of these expressions nets with the loan interest to give zero,
and the second is equivalent to -0.29125; netted with the receipt from
the customer and the loan principal this gives £12, which can be
treated as zero to within a rounding error. Thus the net future
cashflows on each date are effectively zero, and so the company has
successfully hedged its risk.

The contract which the company has agreed with the bank is almost
an FRA; a small adjustment will make it equivalent to one. Currently,
the contract involves a 6-month credit risk, albeit on the difference
between two interest rates rather than on a principal amount. This
aspect of the contract can be improved by stating that any settlement
payment will be made at the 3-month date at the then present value of
the differential interest. How should the scaling factor to discount the
payment from 6 months to 3 months at the 3-month date be
calculated? It should be based on the then prevailing 3-month Libor,
which is denoted in the contract by $L\%$. Explicitly, it will be:

$$1 + (L * 0.25/100).$$

Since a payment at the 6-month date is being replaced by a payment with the same present value at the 3-month date, the net present value of the future cashflows does not change, and thus the company will still have a perfect hedge, regardless of movements in interest rates up to the 3-month date. The improved contract has also achieved the goal of reducing from 6 to 3 months the period during which credit is extended; this enables banks to charge a slightly lower bid-offer spread for this type of contract, since their credit and capital costs are lower.

Note that unless $L\%$ turns out to be exactly 11.65%, the company will have a residual interest rate risk from 3 to 6 months, since the cashflows will no longer exactly net out on each of these days; however, this will be considerably smaller than the original risk, and it can be hedged, if required, by slightly increasing or decreasing the amount of the loan.

We have now invented a contract which is, in fact, identical to an FRA; for ease of reference it would be helpful to write down the full contract terms:

Any interest payable under this contract will be paid at the 3-month date, and will be the interest defined below discounted at a discount rate corresponding to the then prevailing 3-month Libor of $L\%$.

That is, the amount calculated by the formula

$$\frac{\text{principal} * \text{interest} * \text{fraction of year}}{100}$$

will be divided by $1 + (L * 0.25/100)$.

- If L is greater than 11.65, then the bank will pay the company interest calculated at $(L\% - 11.65\%)$ on £10 million for 3 months.
- If L is less than 11.65, then the company will pay the bank interest calculated at $(11.65\% - L\%)$ on £10 million for 3 months.
- If L equals 11.65, nobody will pay anything.

You can compare this contract with the standard form of an FRA, given in the next section.

4.2 FRA CONTRACT TERMS

Recasting the contract terms of the previous section into standard market terminology gives:

Definition 4.1 A Forward Rate Agreement (FRA) is a contract in which two counterparties exchange interest rate risk positions as follows:

The *fixed payer* contracts to pay interest at the agreed *contract rate* on a principal of the *contract amount* over a future *contract period*. The *floating payer* contracts to pay interest on the same principal and period at the *reference rate* prevailing at the start of the contract period. The reference rate will be a variable rate set in the market; usually it will be the Libor for the contract period and the currency of the contract amount. The reference rate prevailing at the start of the contract period is referred to as the *settlement rate*. A particular source will be specified for the settlement rate; a standard source is the British Bankers' Association Libor rates collated at 11.00 each morning from a panel of banks and listed on Telerate pages 3740 and 3750.

The two interest payments are settled net at the start of the contract period, according to the following formula:

Settlement =
Interest differential divided by *Discount factor*

where

Interest differential =

$$\frac{(\text{settlement rate - contract rate}) * \text{contract amount} * \text{fraction}}{100}$$

where fraction is the fraction of a year in the contract period.

$$\text{Discount factor} = 1 + \frac{\text{settlement rate} * \text{fraction}}{100}$$

(Although the payment is referred to as 'interest', in many jurisdictions it is technically not interest for tax purposes; this is also the case for other contracts for differences such as swaps.)

Note that the fraction referred to in the settlement formula above is normally calculated as:

(actual days in contract period) divided by 360

since the convention in the interbank placing market, in almost all currencies, is to quote interest rates on a 360-day year. The main exception is sterling, where Libor is quoted on a 365-day year, and the fraction would be:

(actual days in contract period) divided by 365.

This real-life practice does not detract from the logic of the approach here, and so for simplicity it will continue to be assumed that interest rates and settlements are quoted on exact fractions of a year.

To test your understanding, express the hedge contract of section 4.1 in standard FRA language.

The company is the *fixed payer*, and the bank is the *floating payer*. The *contract amount* is £10 million, and the *contract period* is 3 months from today to 6 months from today. The *contract rate* is 11.65%, and the *reference rate* is 3-month sterling Libor.

You should check that these specifications inserted into the FRA terms above give the same contract as the original hedge.

4.3 TRADING FRAs

This section is a brief review of the FRA marketplace, together with an explanation of terms you will hear used in the market.

Prices for FRAs under standard contract terms are quoted by many banks. The FRA market is most liquid in US dollar, sterling, and Deutschemark, but quotes are generally available in other major currencies, albeit at a wider bid-offer spread. The market is most liquid in shorter maturities, with the majority of contract periods ending within 1 year and almost all ending within 2 years; 3- or 6-month contract periods are the most common. Typical contract amounts would be between US$5 million and US$100 million; amounts tend to be smaller outside the major currencies.

A bank can use FRAs as an asset-liability management tool to reduce its own interest rate risk, or it can use the instrument to trade interest rate risk with the aim of making trading profits. Some banks make a market in FRAs, that is, they quote two-way prices for FRAs in certain currencies and maturities; their intention is to earn a *spread income* by entering into offsetting deals on either side of the bid-offer spread. Corporations, institutions, government bodies, and supranationals use FRAs to hedge their interest rate risk. In some cases, often against written policy, they use FRAs or other instruments to *take* risk, in the belief that a favourable market movement will occur.

Brokers collate the prices which banks are quoting and attempt to find another counterparty to agree a deal at the quoted price; the broker will take a commission on such deals.

All these participants in the FRA market constantly compare FRA rates with rates available through other instruments, with the aim of identifying favourable transactions. This incessant activity tends to keep FRA bid-offer spreads low, and tends to prevent arbitrages existing for long.

In a two-way quote on an FRA rate, the lower rate is the bid, at which the market maker will pay fixed interest and receive Libor, and the higher rate is the offer, at which the market maker will receive fixed interest. By analogy with other markets, where a market maker will buy at his bid *price* and sell at his offer *price*, entering into an FRA where you pay fixed interest is referred to as *buying an FRA*, and entering into an FRA where you receive fixed interest is referred to as *selling an FRA*. Also by analogy with other markets, if you buy an FRA you are *long funded*, since you will benefit if interest rates go up; if you sell an FRA you are *short funded* and will benefit if rates go down.

The opposite of a fixed rate is a *floating rate*, so that if you buy an FRA you will *pay fixed* and *receive floating*, while if you sell an FRA you *receive fixed* and *pay floating*. This terminology is also used for other instruments, particularly swaps.

Many FRAs are traded for contract periods of an exact number of months starting an exact number of months in the future. These are described as, for example, a '3 v 6' (or a '3 versus 6' or a '3 against 6') for a contract period starting 3 months from today and ending 6 months from today. If an FRA has a contract period of an exact number of months but does not start an exact number of months in the future, then it will be described as, for example, a '5 v 8 over the 23rd', for a contract period starting on the first 23rd of a month more than 5 months from today, and lasting for exactly 3 months. Thus, if today is 15 January, then a 5 v 8 over the 23rd has contract period 23 June to 23 September, while if today is 30 January the contract period is 23 July to 23 October.

The start of the contract period is often referred to as the *value day*, and the end of the contract period is often referred to as the *maturity day*. The date that the FRA contract is agreed is the *deal day* or the *transaction day*.

It should be noted that in all *Eurocurrencies* (that is, effectively, currencies used outside their own country), it is the convention to make financial market transactions relate to the *spot date*, that is, 2 business days after the date the transaction is agreed. This convention is current in the FRA market, and most FRAs for currencies other than sterling are dealt for the spot date. This means, for example, that a 6 v 9 JPY FRA dealt on 5 January will have contract period 7 July to 7 October. The settlement under the FRA contract will still be made on the first day of the contract period, in this case on 7 July, but the settlement rate will be the reference rate set on 5 July, since that is the date on which spot is 7 July.

Many FRAs, particularly those dealt by London banks, are dealt under the 'FRABBA' terms specified by the British Bankers' Association. These define a settlement formula which looks different from the formula in section 4.2, but which reduces to the same numeric answer. A reference for 'FRABBA' terms is given in the bibliography.

4.4 RISK PROFILE

Part I defined interest rate risk in terms of fixed cashflows; now we have met our first hedging instrument, it turns out to contain a floating cashflow. How can FRAs be included within the risk management structure?

One way to analyse the problem is to consider that the FRA derived in section 4.1 must have an equal and opposite risk profile to the cashflows which it sets out to hedge. The proof of this is that the combined cashflows have zero risk, and thus any change in value of the FRA for a particular movement in interest rates must be matched by an equal and opposite change in value of the original cashflows. The original cashflows were:

- the company pays £10 million at 3 months; and
- the company receives £10 million plus 3 months' interest at the FRA fixed rate at 6 months.

The risk profile of the hedge, where the company pays fixed on a 3 versus 6 FRA with a contract amount of £10 million, must therefore be the same as the risk profile of the following fixed cashflows:

- the company receives £10 million at 3 months; and
- the company pays £10 million plus 3 months interest at the FRA fixed rate at 6 months.

This analysis can be generalised to give:

Result 4.4 The risk of an FRA where you pay fixed against Libor, and where the settlement rate has not yet been set, is the same as the risk of the following fixed cashflows:

- you receive at the value date the contract amount; and
- you pay at the maturity date the contract amount plus interest calculated at the contract rate on the contract amount for the contract period.

The risk of an FRA where you receive fixed against Libor, and where the settlement rate has not yet been set, is the same as the risk of the following fixed cashflows:

- you pay at the value date the contract amount; and
- you receive at the maturity date the contract amount plus interest calculated at the contract rate on the contract amount for the contract period.

The risk of an FRA where the settlement rate has been set is zero if the value date is today or in the past, and is the same as the risk of a single cashflow of the settlement amount on the value date, if the value date is in the future.

Another way to obtain this result starts with the observation that the risk of an FRA would be unchanged if it were settled as an undiscounted interest differential on the maturity date; indeed this was the initial structure proposed for a hedging contract above. Suppose you are paying fixed on such an FRA. Although you will settle net, your risk is the same as if you were actually paying a fixed interest amount and receiving a floating interest amount at the

maturity date. You can add two pairs of equal and opposite cashflows
to the contract without changing the risk:

- at the value date, you receive and pay the contract principal; and
- at maturity, you also receive and pay the contract principal.

You now have six cashflows which between them have net risk equal
to the original FRA. Group them into two subgroups as follows:

(a)   On the value date you receive the contract amount; and
      on maturity you pay the contract amount plus fixed interest.

(b)   On the value date you pay the contract amount; and
      on maturity you receive the contract amount plus floating
      interest.

The cashflows in (a) are the cashflows of a forward loan at a fixed
rate, and those in (b) are the cashflows of a forward deposit at a
floating rate. Provided that the floating rate is the Libor for the
contract period, the present value of the cashflows in (b) will be zero,
since the zero curve is defined from Libor, and hence cashflows at
maturity are discounted to value date at a scaling factor which scales
principal plus Libor interest to principal. Therefore, the present value
of the original cashflows of the FRA equals the present value of the
cashflows in (a) alone, and hence we recover Result 4.4 for the risk of
a pay-fixed FRA. The result for a receive-fixed FRA follows similarly.

If the floating rate is not the Libor for the contract period and
currency, then the above analysis does not work, and the formula for
the fixed cashflows equivalent in risk to an FRA is more complex; this
type of complication is treated in Part IV on basis risk. (This is not, in
fact, an important consideration for FRAs, since the vast majority of
these do have the appropriate Libor as a floating rate.)

The risk profile of an FRA can be seen from Result 4.4 to be
symmetric, that is, if you gain from an increase in interest rates you
will lose a similar amount from an equal decrease in rates, and if you
gain from a decrease in rates you will lose from an increase in rates.
This is what you would expect from the derivation of the FRA
contract.

The risk profile can be illustrated by a *payoff diagram* which shows
the value of the FRA contract as a function of the settlement rate.
Figure 4.1 shows a payoff diagram for an FRA on which you pay
fixed; the diagram for a receive fixed FRA would be identical except
that the plus values would become minus and the minus plus. The
diagram is exactly symmetric only when future value at the FRA
maturity date is considered. When values are taken at the FRA value
date, then the effect of the higher discount factor for higher settlement
rates is to curve the payoff diagram and to increase the negative value
of low settlement rates relative to the positive value of high settlement
rates; this effect is exaggerated in the figure to make it more visible.

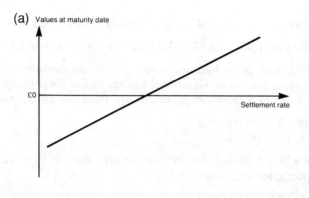

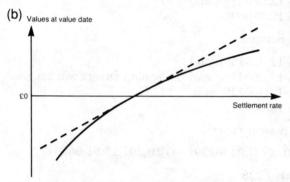

Figure 4.1 Payoffs for an FRA paying fixed; valued at maturity date and at value date. The curvature of the continuous value line is exaggerated for clarity.

Figure 4.1 (a) with its diagonal straight line is the standard payoff diagram for a *forward contract*, that is, a contract where one party agrees to buy a commodity at a future date at a price fixed today. Figure 4.1 (b) is a curved line because of the effect of present valuing at different settlement interest rates, but essentially it has the same shape as the forward. In Part V on options you will meet payoff diagrams with a notably different profile.

Armed with this analysis, we can now calculate the interest rate risk of the pay-fixed FRA in our worked example. The relevant rates from the company's viewpoint are:

Contract amount £10 million;
Contract rate 11.65%;
FRA equivalent fixed cashflows: +£10,000,000 at 3 months; and
                                  −£10,291,250 at 6 months.
3-month Libor 12%;
6-month Libor 12%;
3-month scaling factor 1.03; and
6-month scaling factor 1.06.

The present value of the FRA equivalent fixed cashflows is:

(£10,000,000/1.03) - (£10,291,250/1.06) which equals £11.

(It would be zero, if we had not resorted to an approximation earlier, to avoid having too many significant figures in the FRA rate.)
The zero coupon rates can be calculated from the Libors as:

3 month 12.55088%; and
6 month 12.36000%.

If there is a plus 1 basis point shift in the zero coupon yield curve, the zero coupon rates will become:

3 month 12.56088%; and
6 month 12.37000%.

Libors will become:

3 month 12.00915%; and
6 month 12.00943%; and the scaling factors will become:
3 month 1.0300229; and
6 month 1.0600472.

This gives present value

(£10,000,000/1.0300229) - (£10,291,250/1.0600472)

which equals £228.
   Thus the risk for a plus 1 basis point move in the zero coupon yield curve level is £228 minus £11, which equals £217.
   If there is a plus 1 basis point rotation of the 0–1 year zero curve, there will be a plus 0.75 basis point change in the 3-month rate and a plus 0.5 basis point change in the 6-month rate; this will give zero coupon rates of:

3 month 12.55838%; and
6 month 12.36500%, and scaling factors:
3 month 1.0300172; and
6 month 1.0600236.

This gives present value
   (£10,000,000/1.0300172) - (£10,291,250/1.0600236)

which equals £65.
   Thus the risk for a plus 1 basis point rotation of the 0–1 year yield curve is £65 minus £11, which equals £54.

Assuming:

- the company's statistical analysis has given confidence levels of 1.5% for level movements and 0.3% for 0–1 rotation movements in sterling on a 3-month horizon; and

- it will decide to hedge either when it does its original deal or not at all;

then its decision to hedge should involve the materiality to it of the expected 3-month changes in value of:

- level risk £217 times 150, which equals £32,550; and
- rotation risk £54 times 30, which equals £1,620.

4.5 FRAs AS A GENERAL HEDGE

The FRA contract has been developed above as a hedge for a very specific type of interest rate risk. However, it turns out that, within the three variable model of interest rate risk developed in Part I, FRAs, if available in the appropriate maturities, can be used to hedge *any* interest rate risk.

To see this, concentrate first on the period out to 1 year. According to the model, interest rate risk relating to cashflows in this period can be described by two amounts: the level risk, and the 0–1 year rotation risk.

Consider a 3 v 6 FRA and a 9 v 12 FRA, both pay-fixed and both with the same contract amount. Each of these will have a level risk and a rotation risk, but in general the ratio of these will be different for the two FRAs. (If the ratio turns out to be the same, then you can pick two other suitable FRAs where the ratio is different.) Call the risks for the two FRAs:

	3 v 6	9 v 12
level	$L_{3 v 6}$	$L_{9 v 12}$
rotation	$R_{3 v 6}$	$R_{9 v 12}$

Then if you pay fixed on the 3 v 6 FRA and receive fixed on $R_{3 v 6}/R_{9 v 12}$ of the contract amount of the 9 v 12 FRA, you will find that the net rotation risk of the two FRAs is zero, and you are left with a pure level risk. Some multiple of this portfolio of two FRAs will provide an exact hedge for your existing level risk.

Similarly, if you pay fixed on the 3 v 6 FRA and receive fixed on $L_{3 v 6}/L_{9 v 12}$ of the contract amount of the 9 v 12 FRA, then the level risk vanishes and you are left with a pure rotation risk. Again some multiple of this portfolio will be an exact hedge for the rotation risk of your existing position.

It can thus be seen that combinations of FRAs can be chosen to give pure level risk or pure rotation risk. Since the same procedure will give a combination of FRAs with a pure 1-10 year rotation risk, we have proved:

Result 4.5 Within the framework of the three variable model of interest rate risk, any risk can be exactly hedged by some combination of FRAs.

A practical difficulty is that FRAs do not exist for all currencies in all maturities. Moreover, since the three variable model is not exact, there is scope for the exercise of judgement in choosing the appropriate combination of FRA contracts to act as a hedge; it is unlikely that you would wish to follow the mechanical procedure outlined above.

Recasting all this in terms of the process explained in Part I would give the following procedure for identifying the best FRA hedge for a particular position:

- evaluate the risks of your current cashflows, in terms of level risk, 0–1 year rotation risk, and 1–10 year rotation risk;
- decide on the materiality of hedging; and
- choose the cheapest combination of FRAs which has the equal and opposite risks.

The analysis leading to Result 4.5 should be used as a tool in identifying combinations of FRAs which have the correct risk profile.

If you wish to use FRAs to *take* risk, the same analysis will let you identify the best combination of FRAs to achieve a particular risk profile.

4.6 EVALUATING A HEDGE WITH REAL-LIFE CASHFLOWS

The numerical example used so far in this chapter makes some rather unrealistic assumptions; in particular there are no bid-offer spreads on FRAs, the company is able to borrow exactly at Libor, and there are no transaction costs. In order to check that FRAs are useful in the real world as well, the example can be revisited with the following more realistic assumptions:

- In addition to the payment at 6 months, the customer pays £50,000 today as a deposit. (A real-life transaction would involve some profit.)
- The bank quotes a 3 v 6 FRA rate of 11.62%/11.68%. This means it will buy an FRA (pay fixed) at a contract rate of 11.62%, and sell an FRA (receive fixed) at a contract rate of 11.68%.
- The company can borrow £10 million at Libor plus 50 basis points.
- The company estimates its cost of administering an FRA as £150.

The company will now pay fixed at 11.68% rather than 11.65%, the interest on its loan will be Libor plus 0.5% instead of Libor, and it will have a cost of £150 if it enters into the FRA contract.

If the company does not enter into the FRA, its cashflows in £ million are:

Today	0.05	(receipt from customer)
At 3 months	-10	(payment to supplier)
	10	(loan)
At 6 months	10.291262	(receipt from customer)
	-10	(loan principal)
	-10 * $(L + 0.5)$ * 0.25/100	(interest)

The expected value of $L\%$, which is the value of 3-month Libor at the 3-month date, is the midpoint FRA rate of 11.65%. Assuming that $L\%$ does have this value, the present value of the cashflows, discounting at the Libor yield curve, will be the present value of the £50,000 receipt today plus the 50 basis point spread interest at 6 months, since the remaining flows net to zero, as demonstrated previously. The present value of the 50 basis point spread interest is:

$$(\text{£}10 \text{ million} * 0.5\% * 0.25)/1.06 = -\text{£}11,792.$$

The net present value of the cashflows is therefore this sum plus £50,000, which equals £38,208.

Note that since the company's cost of funds is Libor plus 50 basis points, then, if this transaction is typical, the company should theoretically calculate present values using a zero coupon curve 50 basis points above the Libor curve. This complication is ignored here, since, as discussed in Part I, although the exact yield curve used affects the present value, provided that its difference from the interbank curve is stable it will not materially affect the calculation of risk.

This figure of £38,208 represents the present value of the *expected* profit on the deal, but, as we have seen, the interest rate risk is of the order of £32,550 plus £1,620. If the company therefore decides to hedge and enters into the FRA, the cashflows become:

Today	0.05	(receipt from customer)
At 3 months	-10	(payment to supplier)
	10	(loan)
	$\dfrac{10 * (L - 11.68) * 0.25/100}{1+(L * 0.25/100)}$	(FRA)
At 6 months	10.291262	(receipt from customer)
	-10	(loan principal)
	-10 * $(L + 0.5)$ * 0.25/100	(interest)

As before, the FRA payment at three months can be replaced, for risk management purposes, by the equivalent undiscounted payment at 6 months, that is, by

$$10 * (L - 11.68) * 0.25/100.$$

Making this replacement, the 3-month cashflows net out, and the 6-month cashflows become:

10.291262	(receipt from customer)
-10	(loan principal)
$-10 * L * 0.25/100$	(loan interest Libor)
$-10 * 0.5 * 0.25/100$	(loan interest spread)
$10 * L * 0.25/100$	(FRA)
$-10 * 11.68 * 0.25/100$	(FRA).

The variable cashflows involving $L\%$ net out, leaving a fixed net cashflow of -£13,238, which has a present value of -£12,489.

Adding this to the £50,000 receipt today gives a present value of £37,511. From this should be subtracted the transaction cost of £150, to give a net present value of £37,361. (This figure involves a small residual risk on the discount rate used to present value the net £12,489 payment at 6 months.) Since the FRA removes almost all dependence of the present value on future rates, it achieves the aim of hedging the original cashflows.

It can be seen that the unhedged cashflows have an expected present value of £38,208 with a great deal of variability, while the hedged cashflows have an expected present value of £37,361 with almost zero variability. The 'cost of hedging' in this example is thus the difference in expected present values of £847.

This should demonstrate that FRAs can be useful, even in real life, but it should also concentrate your minds on the costs and complications involved.

4.7 MARKING AN FRA TO MARKET

Establishing the market value of an instrument or portfolio is known as *marking to market* the instruments. Where financial accounts are made up on the basis of market values, it is clearly important to have a well-defined methodology for establishing these values; there is also a need for the values to be accurate to allow dealers and management to evaluate performance.

Where an instrument involves purely fixed cashflows then its market value can be established by taking the net present value of the future cashflows. As discussed in Part I, the zero coupon curve used in discounting should reflect the systematic risk of the future cashflows. Choosing an exact yield curve for general cashflows is beyond the scope of this book, and so it is necessary to make:

Assumption 4.1 Using the midmarket interbank zero coupon yield curve as a basis for discounting will give a reasonable approximation to the present value of future cashstreams involved in the instruments discussed in this book.

This assumes that the risk of the cashflows is equivalent to the risk of the banking system. For a portfolio of instruments most pay positions will be offset by receive positions, and little accuracy would be gained by using some 'more correct' discount curve closer to the zero curve generated by market bid or offer rates. For short-term instruments such as FRAs, credit risks and other costs are generally small, but for longer-term instruments such as swaps, the risk of credit losses and the cost of administration (and for banks also the cost of capital) become material, and so a deduction should be made from the net present value of the cashflows to give a better estimate of market value; this is discussed in the appropriate chapter for each product.

Remember that despite the unsatisfactory nature of these approximations, the effect on the calculation of *risk* of using a marginally incorrect yield curve will be small. Also, as time passes and cashflows come into value, the mark to market will become completely accurate; the choice of a discount curve can therefore affect the timing of income recognition, but it cannot affect the total income.

The analysis of risk in section 4.4 above showed that an FRA can be replaced for risk purposes by two fixed cashflows:

- at value date minus the contract amount, and
- at maturity plus the contract amount plus interest at the contract rate.

The same analysis carried through will show that the market value of the FRA equals the market value of these two cashflows, that is, their net present value using the midmarket interbank zero curve to discount.

As an example, consider the hedging FRA of section 4.6, where the company pays fixed on a 3 v 6 FRA with contract amount £10 million and contract rate 11.68%.

From Result 4.4 this FRA will be represented by the two cashflows:

3 months	+£10,000,000 and
6 months	−£10,292,000.

Initially the scaling factors to the two dates are 1.03 and 1.06, giving a mark-to-market value of (£10,000,000/1.03) - (£10,292,000/1.06), which equals -£696. (You would expect the value to be slightly negative since the company is paying higher than the midmarket rate.) If, after a few days, the scaling factors become 1.028 and 1.059, then the mark-to-market value will become:

$$(£10,000,000/1.028) - (£10,292,000/1.059) = +£9,024.$$

The value has become positive since the implied 3-month Libor at the 3-month date is now 12.06% (you can check this using Result 4.3), and so the cost of the company's loan will go up and consequently the value of the hedge must become more positive to compensate.

This explanation for the change in value leads to an equivalent method for marking an FRA to market. The value of the FRA can be locked in by entering into an opposite FRA at the current market rate. Grossing up the cashflows of the two FRAs so that each is equivalent to a placing and taking, as in the discussion following the statement of Result 4.4 above, all the principal and floating interest payments net out, leaving only the two fixed interest payments. The value of an FRA is thus the present value of the difference between interest on the contract amount for the contract period

(a) at the contract rate, and
(b) at the current market rate.

Using the example above, the contract rate is 11.68% and the new FRA market rate is 12.06%. The difference of 0.38% on £10 million for 3 months is £9,500; present valuing with a scaling factor of 1.059 gives £8,970. The difference from the value of £9,024 calculated above is due to the rounding of the market FRA rate from 12.062257% to 12.06%.

Here the two methods give identical values within rounding error; if market FRA rates differ slightly from the rates implied by the Libors, then there may be a small difference between the two values. Since any differences will be small, it makes sense to choose the method which you find easier and more meaningful.

It was mentioned above that the credit risk on FRAs is generally low. In Part III a model will be developed for calculating credit risk on swaps; this model will also work for FRAs and using it will allow you to confirm that the risk is small.

4.8 SHORT-TERM REPRICING RISK

The model developed in Part I for the management of interest rate risk involved carrying out a statistical analysis to determine confidence levels for day-to-day rate movements. A problem is that, regardless of the level of confidence, rates do occasionally jump substantially from one day to the next. This can be because of central bank intervention, or period end money shortage, or some political event, or just a sudden change in market sentiment, such as in October 1987.

Therefore, even if your risk is low according to the risk model, you may be exposed to *short-term repricing risk* if you have substantial cashflows on a particular day in the near future involving, for example, fixing a large Libor-based loan; if Libor spikes by 0.25% on that particular day, it might prove far more expensive than the risk indicated by the model.

It is appropriate to discuss this risk here, since you have now covered the concepts involved in dealing with Libor-based instruments.

The way to manage short-term repricing risk is to keep track of the net amount of floating rate fixings which you will have to make on each day over the next few months. If the amount on a particular day is high, but is not reflected by high risk in the risk model, you should consider using FRAs or some other instrument to hedge the fixing, thus eliminating the risk from a dramatic movement of the floating rate on the day.

It is difficult to give a more exact theoretical framework, and so this risk and its management is illustrated here by a concrete example.

Suppose the mortgage subsidiary of an insurance company is financed by a floating rate note with a principal of £180 million, on which it pays interest at 3-month Libor set at the end of each quarter. The assets of the subsidiary are floating rate mortgages, where the floating rate can be changed from time to time in accordance with the average rate set by mortgage providers, which in turn will move with the average value of 3-month Libor over a period.

The subsidiary pays interest set on a particular date, and receives interest, in effect, averaged over a period. It is thus at risk if interest rates spike at the end of the quarter. One way to hedge this risk would be for the subsidiary to enter into a series of FRAs during each quarter, to hedge a portion of its repricing. On each FRA it would pay fixed with a contract period from the end of the current quarter to the end of the next quarter. Thus on 31 January it might enter into an FRA with a contract amount of £60 million and contract period 31 March to 30 June, and on 28 February it might enter into a second FRA with the same contract amount and period. By entering into these two FRAs it would reduce its exposure to short-term rate movements around 31 March to one-third of its original value.

This would not necessarily be the most effective way to hedge this particular risk, but it serves to illustrate the point.

It should be noted that the problem of short-term repricing risk shades into issues of funding and cash management which are outside the scope of this book.

SUMMARY

This chapter has defined FRAs and shown how they meet a natural hedging need. The risk profile of an FRA can be represented in the cash gaps methodology as the cashflows of a fixed deposit: principal on the value date, and principal plus fixed interest on the maturity date. A future deposit to be fixed at the then prevailing Libor carries no interest rate risk. An FRA can be marked to market by present valuing the cashflows of the equivalent fixed deposit or by comparing it with a market FRA for the same dates and amount. To within the limits of arbitrage, today's zero coupon curve implies the FRA rate for any period.

Short-term repricing risk must be managed outside the framework of cash gaps; a simple report listing net Libor repricing by day for the next few months could form the basis for identifying and managing this risk.

CHAPTER 5

Eurodeposit futures

In the previous chapter it was demonstrated that, in principle, FRAs can meet all interest rate hedging needs. Therefore, in order to justify the rest of the book, this chapter starts with a discussion of some of the shortcomings of FRAs; in the light of these shortcomings it becomes appropriate to consider other hedging instruments. A definition is then given of *futures contracts* in general and Eurodeposit futures in particular. Considerable trouble is then taken to show that the risk profile of the Eurodeposit futures contract is similar to the risk profile of an FRA. A detailed discussion of the subtle effects involved in using futures then leads into a comparison of futures and FRAs; the unsurprising conclusion is that each is useful in different circumstances. The chapter ends with a brief survey of the trading of futures contracts.

5.1 IMPROVING FRAs

The investigation of FRAs in Chapter 4 started with the invention of a hedge contract for a specific interest rate risk, and progressed by adjusting the terms of the contract until it became an FRA. A similar process could be carried out to produce a Eurodeposit futures contract, but that would prove to be a long exercise involving much repetition of the analysis already done for FRAs. Instead, this section proceeds by reviewing some potential areas in which the FRA contract could be improved, and the next section defines a Eurodeposit futures contract, which, it will then be demonstrated, does achieve certain improvements over the FRA contract.

The starting point will be the FRA contract. What are the shortcomings of FRAs from the point of view of risk management? An FRA exactly meets hedging needs, but it does so at the cost of a bid-offer spread and with a certain credit risk. It also has a transaction cost which could be material for organisations entering into large numbers of FRAs. Each of these areas in turn is examined below.

In a perfect market, the bid-offer spread on an instrument will be squeezed to the point at which it just covers the expenses and risks of the market makers. (If the spread is wider, more participants will enter the market, and if it is narrower some participants will leave.) The FRA market is not perfect, if only because banks cannot analyse their costs accurately and therefore sometimes cannot identify whether they are making or losing money in a particular activity. However, it has enough of the attributes of a perfect market, such as low entry barriers and good information flow, for the spread to be a reasonable estimate of the costs and risks of participation. These include the fixed costs of maintaining dealers and a back office, variable costs such as sending confirmations and making settlements, the opportunity cost of the capital used, and *liquidity risk* (discussed below), position risk, and credit risk. In order to reduce the bid-offer spread of a comparable instrument, some of these costs or risks would have to be reduced.

Liquidity risk is the risk that entering into a contract will involve paying more or receiving less than the theoretical market rate for that contract. In general, a market maker enters into FRAs where customers come to her, and she pays fixed at the bid side of the market or receives fixed at the (higher) offer side of the market. If the market maker wishes to enter into a *specific* FRA, then she may have to go to another market maker and pay that market maker's bid rate or receive his offer rate. The total cost of doing this will be the bid-offer spread times the number of times that she has to go to another market maker.

Related to this is the cost of terminating an FRA position. If both counterparties agree to terminate an FRA, then one will pay the other a fee, the FRA will be cancelled, and neither counterparty will have subsequent transaction costs or credit risk. However, if one counterparty is unwilling to terminate, then the other counterparty will have to negate its risk position by entering into an equal and opposite FRA position in the market, and will thus end up with two sets of transaction costs and credit risk.

The cost of administering an FRA includes the cost of recording the deal, of confirming it, of agreeing the settlement amount, and of making the settlement payment. In addition there are administrative costs associated with the credit process.

The credit risk on an FRA is small compared to the principal involved. Typically, the maximum expected interest rate movement between the deal day and the value day would be far less than, say, 5%, even for a 12 v 24 FRA, and therefore the settlement amount will generally be far less than 5% of principal. However, there is an administration cost to a bank in extending any credit, and therefore banks tend to deal FRAs with a customer only if the expected volume is very great or if other business with that customer justifies the expense of maintaining a credit line. Thus certain classes of organisation, and most individuals, will find themselves excluded from the FRA market.

5.2 FUTURES CONTRACTS

Eurocurrency deposit futures contracts are one of many types of *futures contracts*. In essence, a futures contract, often referred to simply as a 'future', is an agreement between two counterparties, a *buyer* and a *seller*, that the seller will deliver on a fixed future date a determined amount of a particular commodity, for which the buyer will pay an agreed fixed price. Such a contract has the effect of transferring risk between the two counterparties, since the buyer will benefit if the price of the commodity rises and the seller will benefit if the price falls.

The special feature of futures contracts, in distinction to *over-the-counter* forward contracts, is that they have standardised terms and are traded on a *futures exchange*. A futures exchange is an institution set up to provide the following functions:

- definition of standard specifications for futures contracts;
- a physical marketplace for trading futures;
- confirmation and settlement services;
- supervision of market activities;
- acting as a principal in every contract; and
- holding cash collateral from counterparties to contracts.

The last two of these functions need further explanation. Both are aimed at reducing the credit risk of dealing in futures. First, whenever two counterparties agree a futures contract they notify the exchange, and thereafter each of them automatically has a contract with the exchange instead of with the other counterparty. This replaces the counterparty credit risk with the credit risk of the exchange. The credit risk of the exchange is minimised by ensuring that all counterparties to futures contracts put up cash collateral with the exchange; this is adjusted daily to ensure that each morning it is worth more than the current market value of the contract. Thus, even if a counterparty to a futures contract defaults, the exchange should not lose more than one day's price movement. (In extreme circumstances where a contract becomes totally illiquid the loss could in fact be greater.) The creditworthiness of the exchange is further enhanced by making sure that it is adequately capitalised, that its powers are strictly limited, and that its members are liable, within limits, to make good any cash shortfalls. (The members of the exchange are the only organisations which are allowed to trade in the exchange.)

In some exchanges, government securities can be used as collateral in place of cash.

The existence of the exchange allows the credit risk on a futures contract to be close to zero for a member dealing with the exchange. For a non-member, dealing a futures contract involves using a member as a broker. The non-member will have a contract directly with the exchange, but it will transfer collateral through the member; the credit risk of this can be reduced by ensuring that the member uses a segregated account for such funds. The credit risk to the non-member is thus again effectively zero, and any credit risk to the member in its capacity as a broker can be reduced, if necessary, by it requiring the non-member to put up a higher collateral.

Different futures contracts traded on different exchanges are used in management of a wide variety of risks; for example, there are contracts on various exchanges which relate to the price of coffee, foreign currencies, or oil. The main types of futures contract relating to interest rate risk are futures on government bonds and futures on Eurocurrency deposits. The Eurodeposit future is described here, since this is the contract which, it will be demonstrated, has a similar risk profile to an FRA. The framework for other futures contracts is very similar.

The definition of a Eurocurrency deposit future will use the US dollar as a sample currency and the contract traded at the Chicago Mercantile Exchange as a sample contract. After the contract is defined, the next section will show that its risk profile is similar, but not identical, to an FRA with a US$1 million contract amount and a 3-month calculation period.

The contract is called the '3-month Eurodollar Time Deposit Futures' contract. There are four different contracts defined for each calendar year, with *underlying periods* starting on a particular date in March, June, September, or December, and ending 3 months later. The 'price' of each contract is the price agreed between the buyer and the seller; it is quoted as a number under 100 with two digits after the decimal point, for example 91.99. This does not mean that you pay over US$91.99 when you buy a contract; rather, settlement is calculated relative to this price. The minimum price movement of US$0.01 is referred to as an *01* (pronounced 'oh one') or as a *tick*.

The initial two counterparties to each contract are a *buyer* and a *seller*. When you enter into a contract you do so with another market participant, but thereafter each of you automatically has a contract with the exchange rather than with the other. This has the advantage that there is perfect netting when you buy or sell and subsequently *close out* (sell or buy) the same contract. Each contract must be closed out by its *expiry date*, which is two working days before the start of the underlying period; contracts which are not closed out then will automatically be closed out by the exchange at a closing price based on the prevailing 3-month dollar Libor rate as defined by the average of a representative group of banks. The formula for the closeout price in these circumstances is:

The price equals 100 minus the 3-month Libor rate.

It will be demonstrated below that this closeout formula acts as the link between the contract price and Libor for the underlying period, and ensures that at all times:

Result 5.1 The price of a Eurodeposit future will be close to 100 minus the expected 3-month Libor rate at the expiry date, where the expected Libor is given by the market FRA rate for the underlying period of the future.

This type of closeout arrangement is called *cash settlement*, in contrast to other futures which specify that if the contract remains open at the expiry date then the seller has to make *physical delivery* of the underlying commodity to the buyer.

When you buy *or* sell one contract you must pay an *initial margin* of US\$750 to the exchange. Thereafter, every day that the contract remains open it is marked to market at the price prevailing at the close of business, and a *variation margin* is paid by you to the exchange or by the exchange to you. If you have bought a contract then the calculation of the variation margin is as follows:

If today's closing price is higher than yesterday's closing price then the exchange will pay you US\$25 for every 01 increase in the price; if today's price is lower than yesterday's price then you will pay the exchange US\$25 for every 01.

This is expressed as the price of the contract being 'US\$25 for an 01'.

On the day on which you buy the contract the variation margin is calculated against your purchase price, and on the day on which you close out the contract the variation margin is calculated against your selling price. When you close out a contract, the exchange returns your initial margin.

The calculation of variation margin for the seller of a contract is equal and opposite to the calculation for the purchaser.

It is not immediately obvious that a contract so defined is similar in interest rate risk to an FRA, so the next section is devoted to a careful explanation.

5.3 RISK PROFILE OF A EURODEPOSIT FUTURE

This section is based on the Chicago Eurodollar deposit future, which is defined above. For simplicity, concentrate on the June contract, and assume that the underlying period from, say, 22 June to 22 September, is exactly a quarter of a year. Suppose you have just bought a contract at 91.99. Consider an FRA with contract amount US\$1 million, calculation period the same as the underlying period, and contract rate 8.01%. In order to make the comparison work, this amended FRA is going to have an unusual feature in that its settlement formula will not involve dividing by the discount factor; explicitly, the settlement formula will be:

US$1 million ∗ (contract rate - reference rate) ∗ 0.25/100.

The settlement date will be 22 June, as for a standard FRA. In order to have the same risk profile as buying the future you will have to sell the FRA; this is an unfortunate accident of market terminology which you will just have to learn to live with.

You should remember that, in real life, dollar FRA rates are quoted on the basis of a 360-day year and on the basis of the exact number of days in the calculation period; therefore, to recover the agreement discussed here between the FRA and the futures contract, in place of 0.25 the settlement formula would have to use

(number of days in calculation period)/360.

After the equivalence between the futures contract and this amended FRA is demonstrated, a separate comparison of the FRA to a standard FRA will show how the difference in risk profile should be interpreted.

Consider your net cashflows if you hold the futures contract to the expiry date of 20 June. For simplicity the time value of money is ignored here, and later on it is proved that the resultant error in the calculation is relatively small. Suppose 3-month Libor on 20 June is 7%, so that the closeout price is 93.00. When you buy the contract you have to pay the initial margin of US$750, but you get that back when the contract is closed out on 20 June, and so the net cashflow effect of the initial margin is zero. With regard to the variation margin, you do not know the precise amount paid each day, but you do know that you must receive a total of 101 times US$25, which is US$2,525, since each day the exchange pays you US$25 for each 01 increase in price since the previous day, and the net increase in price over the holding period is 1.01. If the price decreases one day so that you have to pay the exchange US$25 per 01, then you will subsequently receive back US$25 per 01 when the price rises again. Therefore the net cashflow will not be altered by the path which the price takes to reach 93.00 on 20 June, although the present value of the variation margin payments will be path dependent.

This can be summarised as:

Result 5.2 If you buy a futures contract at price B and sell it at price S, then, if S is greater than B you will receive a net variation margin of $S - B$, and if S is less than B then you will pay a net variation margin of $B - S$. In either case the path which the price takes from B to S will not affect the net payment, but it will change the present value of the payment.

An equivalent result could be given for the case where you sell and then buy a futures contract.

What will the settlement be on the FRA? Since the settlement rate is 7%, you will receive on 22 June:

US$1 million $* (8.01 - 7) * 0.25/100 =$ US$2,525.

This shows that the futures contract will have the same risk profile as this FRA, provided that the market FRA rate was 8.01% at the time when you bought the future. Because of the possibility of arbitrage, it can be shown that the FRA rate implied by the futures contract price cannot be too dissimilar to the market FRA rate. To see this, suppose, for example, that the future is trading at 90 when the FRA rate is about 9%. You can buy a future at 90 and buy an FRA at about 9% and hold both to the expiry date. Suppose that the settlement rate is 8%. You will receive net US$5,000 variation margin on the future (200 times US$25) and pay US$2,500 on the settlement of the FRA. You have thus made US$2,500 less opportunity cost of the initial margin less any bid-offer spread on the FRA rate. You can check that you would make the same profit for any settlement rate. If the FRA rate had been 11% you could have obtained a riskfree profit similarly by selling a future and selling an FRA. An extension of this argument shows that an arbitrage will be possible unless the interest rate implied by the futures price is close to the FRA rate.

This proves Result 5.1 for the contract rate of the amended FRA; it will be shown below that the rate on the amended FRA will be close to that on a standard FRA, which will complete the proof of Result 5.1.

The argument so far shows that the futures contract will have a similar risk profile to an amended FRA if you ignore the time value of money with respect to margin payments. It is now necessary to show that the effect of the time value of money on margin payments is relatively small, and that the amended FRA is similar in risk profile to a standard FRA. When these two results are proved we shall have shown that the Eurodollar future has the risk profile of an FRA, and that Result 5.1 holds for the standard FRA contract rate.

Let us start with the effect of the time value of money on the cost of a futures contract. It is necessary to assume some values in order to be able to come up with numeric answers, and so let us assume that interest rates are around 10% and that you buy and hold the futures contract for six months. The initial margin of US$750 will thus have a financing cost of US$37.5 for the half year. US$37.5 represents 1.5 basis points per annum on the future's underlying principal of US$1 million for the underlying period of three months; equivalently it is the variation margin cost on 1.5 01s. Since both the buyer and seller have this opportunity cost, the effective bid-offer spread on the future is thus increased by 3 basis points per annum.

It is important to note that the effective bid-offer spread will be lower if the future is held for a shorter time or if interest rates are lower; for example, if the future were held for only one month then the effective increase in the bid-offer spread would be only 0.5 basis points.

It is more complex to analyse the financing effect of the variation margin, since this will be dependent on the exact path on which the futures price moves. Since the best estimate of the closeout price is the current price, you would expect that on average you will be a net receiver of variation margin half the time and a net payer half the time. You have bought the future, and so you will be a net receiver when interest rates go down, and a net payer when interest rates go up. Therefore, when you are a net receiver you will receive reinvestment income at a lower interest rate than you will pay to borrow when you are a net payer. (There is an implicit assumption that the slope of the short-term yield curve remains constant.) Making the extreme assumption that interest rates will be 1% higher than the initial rate for 3 months and then 1% lower for 3 months, your net reinvestment cost in the first 3 months will be:

$$\frac{US\$25 * 100 * 11 * 0.25}{100}$$

and the net reinvestment income in the second 3 months will be:

$$\frac{US\$25 * 100 * 9 * 0.25}{100.}$$

Ignoring second order effects, the net cost will be:

$$\frac{US\$25 * 100 * 2 * 0.25}{100}$$

which equals US$12.50. Thus, even an assumption about future rates considerably more violent than would be predicted from historic movements gives a net reinvestment cost of the variation margin of only US$12.50. This equals only half of an 01 on the price of the futures contract. Moreover, since the seller of the contract has an equal and opposite variation margin, she must have a corresponding income of US$12.50. Therefore it can be seen that the opportunity cost of the variation margin should shift the futures contract price very slightly and should have no effect on its bid-offer spread.

Now consider the amended FRA defined above compared with a standard FRA. The contract rate on the amended FRA was 8.01%. This means that on a standard FRA, at the deal date, the expected discount factor to be used in calculating the settlement amount would be:

$$1 + (8.01 * 0.25/100) = 1.020025.$$

Consequently, any settlement amount on the standard FRA would be expected to be $1/1.020025$ times the settlement amount on the amended FRA. It is more fruitful to look at this the other way round, and to say that the amended FRA with contract amount US$1 million has the same expected settlement amount as a standard FRA with contract amount US$1,020,025. However, this amount would be paid on the FRA value date, and equating it with the payment of variation margin on the future paid today involves present valuing the FRA settlement amount by dividing by the scaling factor to the value date. Suppose the value date is in about 6 months with scaling factor 1.04. Then having an FRA with the same present value settlement amount as the future involves multiplying the US$1,020,025 contract amount by a further 1.04, giving US$1,060,826. This shows that the futures contract has the same risk profile as a standard FRA with contract amount US$1,060,826, provided that rate movements are small.

Following through the calculation above will show that in general, provided interest rate changes are small, the following result holds:

Result 5.3 A futures contract has the same risk profile as a standard FRA with a contract amount equal to US$1 million multiplied by the discount factor for FRA settlement multiplied by the scaling factor to the FRA value date. The discount factor equals

$$(1 + (\text{FRA contract rate}/400))$$

and the scaling factor equals

$$(1 + (\text{zero rate}/100))^{\text{years to value date}}$$

Most futures are traded with underlying periods starting within a year, and so 'years to value date' will usually be a fraction less than one. Note that by Result 4.1, the product of the two discount factors should be the scaling factor to the FRA maturity date, giving:

Result 5.4 A futures contract has the same risk profile as a standard FRA with a contract amount equal to US$1 million multiplied by the scaling factor from today to the FRA maturity date.

The discussion above also shows that the contract rate on the amended FRA must at all times be close to the contract rate on the corresponding standard FRA; this is the promised completion of the proof of Result 5.1.

Since the risk of a Eurodeposit future is equivalent to the risk of a particular FRA, it can be represented in the discrete cash gaps methodology in the same way as that FRA. It is thus straightforward to manage futures positions using cash gaps.

The discussion so far has dealt with small movements in the FRA contract rate; the next section examines what happens when FRA rates shift substantially.

To summarise: the price of a Eurodeposit futures contract will at all times be close to 100 minus the FRA rate, for the FRA with calculation period equal to the underlying period of the future. The risk profile of the future for small price movements will be the same as the risk profile of an FRA with a contract amount slightly greater than the underlying US$1 million contract amount of the future; explicitly, the FRA contract amount will be

US$1 million ∗ (scaling factor to FRA maturity date).

This relationship should be corrected for an exact day count. The effect of the opportunity cost of the margining on the future will be relatively small; for example, in the example discussed above, the effective widening of the bid-offer spread is 3 basis points when the future is held for 6 months and only 0.5 basis points when the future is held for 1 month.

5.4 TECHNICAL ASPECTS OF THE USE OF FUTURES

This somewhat clumsily named section covers two main topics: the risk profile of a Eurodeposit future when the price shifts substantially during the holding period, and the use of futures to replace FRAs which do not have calculation periods identical with the underlying period of a particular futures contract. After these points you will be ready for the next section, which addresses whether the futures contract succeeds in improving on FRAs.

Before these main topics, it is worthwhile recording some observations about futures contracts. First, the Libor rate used by the Chicago exchange to close out contracts on the expiry date is the average of Libors quoted by a group of banks at 11am Chicago time. This will in general be different from the rate calculated from a different group of banks at 11am London time which is used by the British Bankers' Association to calculate its Libor rates, which are the rates most frequently used as reference rates in FRA and swap contracts. There is therefore a *basis risk* that the future closeout rate will not exactly equal the rate of the corresponding FRA, although usually any difference should not exceed a few basis points. The Eurodeposit future dealt in the London International Financial Futures Exchange (LIFFE) is closed out at a rate set at 11am London time, thus reducing this basis risk.

A greater source of basis risk during the life of a futures contract is that the futures rate will not move exactly with the FRA rate; as we have seen, the possibility of arbitrage will keep the two rates close but cannot keep them identical. The difference at any time should not be more than a few basis points, but this may be material in particular circumstances. The management of basis risk is discussed in Part IV.

The last observation is that the tax treatment of futures may differ from the tax treatment of FRAs; this may sometimes act as an incentive or a disincentive to the use of futures contracts.

Now let us look at the first of the main topics, the risk profile of a futures contract under a large movement in price. Suppose you hedge a risk position by buying 100 June contracts at a price of 92.00 when the scaling factor to the start date of the underlying period is 1.03. By Result 5.3, for small rate movements this has the same risk profile as selling an FRA with a contract amount of US$105.06 million.

Suppose now the price of the contract goes to 88.00 while the scaling factor remains unchanged. (An unrealistically large movement is used to demonstrate the effects as clearly as possible.) You have lost US$1 million on the futures, but on the FRA you would have lost, present valued:

$$\frac{\text{US\$105.06 million} * 4 * 0.25}{100 * 1.03} \Big/ 1.03$$

which equals US$990,291. For this large price movement you have thus lost US$9,709 more on the futures than you would have on the FRA.

What would happen if the price had gone instead to 96.00? You would have made US$1 million profit on the futures, while on the FRA you would have made, present valued:

$$\frac{\text{US\$105.06 million} * 4 * 0.25}{100 * 1.01} \Big/ 1.03$$

which equals US$1,009,901. Again you would have been better off with the FRA, and by a similar amount.

If you follow through the situation where the hedge consists of selling futures, you will discover that the futures always do better than the FRA. The amounts involved here, of a difference of about US$10,000, may be considered fairly immaterial in the context of a total settlement of about US$1 million, but it is important to be aware of the phenomenon, especially if your hedging needs would make you always the same way round in the futures market.

Moreover, you should note that we have made the unrealistic assumption that the scaling factor will remain the same when the FRA rate changes, whereas in practice the scaling factor will tend to move with the FRA rate, exacerbating the above effect.

Taking this example of buying 100 contracts further, consider what you should do with the futures you have bought when the price does go to 88.00. Your 100 contracts now have the same risk profile as an FRA with a contract amount of US$106.09 million, since the FRA rate used to calculate the equivalence has changed to 12%. Therefore, if you had a perfect hedge before, you should sell one of the futures contracts to restore your risk profile to that of an FRA with a contract amount of approximately US$105 million. (In fact the equivalent amount will be US$105.03 million; this reflects the discrete nature of futures contracts, which is discussed later in this section.)

From this you can see that hedges involving futures must, in principle, be adjusted dynamically when rates change, in order to ensure that the risk profile of the futures continues to equal the risk profile of the position being hedged. However, even if rates do not change, the hedge will need to be adjusted as time passes and the scaling factor decreases from 1.03 to 1. The effect will be material in this case, requiring you to increase your futures holding from 100 to 103. In general, all hedges involving futures will have to be adjusted dynamically in this way. This is not a problem which is unique to futures; however, it may be exacerbated for futures because of the effect discussed below.

When you sell one contract at 88.00 you lock in a loss on the hedge of US$10,000. Suppose now that the futures price returns to 92.00; you should now buy another contract at 92.00 to restore your hedge, but you find that although you have come back to where you started you have lost US$10,000 in the process. You might think that had the price gone up instead of down you would have gained instead of lost, so follow through what happens if the price had gone to 96.00 instead of 88.00. At 96.00 the 100 contracts will hedge an FRA with a contract amount of US$104.03 million, and so you need to buy an extra futures contract; when the price returns to 92.00 you will have to sell this extra contract to maintain your hedge, and you again find yourself back where you started with a loss of US$10,000! If instead you follow through the same process for selling futures instead of buying them, you discover that every time you go through a loop of this nature you make US$10,000 instead of losing it. In the language of options, when you buy a future as a hedge you are 'selling volatility' and stand to lose if prices fluctuate violently, whereas if you sell a future you are 'buying volatility' and gain from price fluctuations.

This effect is material only if you hold a large number of futures contracts and if prices move substantially, but again you should be aware of it if you intend to use futures regularly.

The examples above also illustrate that, since futures come in exact millions of dollars, it is not always possible to create an exact hedge using futures or to maintain an exact hedge when market rates change. Since a futures contract has an underlying principal of US$1 million, you could find yourself in the worst case US$0.5 million away from a perfect hedge. If you expect a maximum rate movement of, say, 1% between putting on a hedge and the expiry of the position, then in the worst case you could lose 100 times US$25 times 0.5, which equals US$1,250. Since this is a worst case and the average would be close to zero, this consideration is unlikely to be material except in a very small real-life hedge.

A more serious problem is how you can use futures to hedge a position which is equivalent to an FRA with a calculation period from, say, 22 May to 22 August. The answer is that you cannot do so exactly, but you can do so approximately.

Let us follow the example through, taking the FRA to have a contract amount of US$100 million. For simplicity, the exposition below takes a futures contact to have the same risk profile as an FRA of exactly US$1 million rather than a slightly larger amount; it also ignores again the complication caused by the quotation of real-life FRA rates on an exact number of days over a 360-day year. You should take these factors into account to build a wholly accurate model.

Suppose it is in January when the hedging problem arises. There is one futures contract with an underlying period starting on, say, 22 March, and another starting on 22 June. We shall make the basic assumption in accordance with our standard risk model that the zero curve between March and September is a straight line. (If you have grounds for making a different assumption about the shape of the zero curve, then you can adjust the calculation accordingly.) To proceed further you need:

Result 5.5 If the zero curve moves as a straight line, then, to a good approximation, the curve of 3-month FRA contract rates moves as a straight line also. The approximation will be better for level shifts than for rotations, and it will also be better when the zero curve is flatter.

The same result holds for 6-month FRAs or for FRAs of any other contract period.

A proof would be excessively mathematical, and so you are requested to take this result on trust as being reasonable. However, it would not hurt to try a little experimentation with rates to convince yourself that the result does seem to hold in normal circumstances.

This result implies that, to a good approximation, the curve of 3-month FRA rates implied by the zero curve is a straight line from March to June. In that case, if you buy 33 March contracts and 67 June contacts, then you will be close to perfectly hedged. The number of each contract is calculated as follows:

If the zero curve has a parallel shift of 1 basis point, then all the FRA rates will shift by (almost exactly) 1 basis point; the FRA position which you are trying to hedge will thus change in value by 0.01 times US$100 million times 0.25 over 100 (ignoring the discount factor), which equals US$2,500. To achieve the same change in value for a shift of one 01 would require 100 futures contracts. So we have that M plus J equals 100, where M is the number of March contracts needed and J is the number of June contracts.

Suppose now that the June v September FRA rate stays constant, but the May v August rate changes by one basis point. Since the curve is a straight line, and the ratio of the 3-month period June to March over the 1-month period June to May is 3 to 1, the

March v June rate must change by 3 basis points. The change in
value of the FRA will be US$2,500 as above, and M should be
picked to make the change in value of the March futures in this
circumstance also equal to US$2,500. This gives:

$M * 3 * US\$25 = US\$2,500$ so that
$M = 33.33$.

Since we are restricted to whole numbers of futures we take M
equal to 33, which gives $\mathcal{J}$ equal to 67, thus proving the figures
above.

If you are suspicious of the mathematics involved, you should check
what happens when the March rate stays the same and the May rate
moves by 1 basis point. By the same ratio argument as above, the June
rate will move by 1.5 basis points. The change in value of the FRA
will be US$2,500 as before, and the change in value of the futures will
be 67 times 1.5 times US$25, which equals US$2,512.50, which is
close enough.

You can see the complications and approximations necessary in this
exercise, but it gets worse if you wait another two months until
22 March. The March contract has now expired, and the only
available hedge is the June contract. The best you can do is to buy
100 June contracts and hope that the movement in the May rate will
be close to the movement in the June rate; this is equivalent to hoping
that the rotation in the 0–1 year yield curve will be small.

The statistical analysis described in Part I should be able to give a
confidence level for the expected rotation, and you can then derive the
expected risk from hedging this position using futures. More
accurately, you could use the original rates database to analyse the risk
which you would have run historically by following this hedging
strategy.

Hedging FRA positions based on, say, 6-month Libor can also be
done through futures, using similar strategies based on similar
approximations.

What this section should have shown you is:

(a) The use of futures generally involves slight over or under hedging.
(b) Hedges using futures must be adjusted dynamically, either with
     movements in rates or with the passage of time.
(c) There may be a hidden cost or income in the dynamic adjustment
     of a hedge using futures.
(d) Since most hedging requirements do not match the exact
     underlying period of a futures contract, hedging using futures
     generally involves complex calculation together with major
     approximations.
(e) There is a small basis risk in the use of futures compared to
     FRAs.
(f) The tax treatment of futures and FRAs may differ in particular
     jurisdictions.

Given these features, the next section discusses whether and in what circumstances futures represent an improvement over FRAs.

5.5 ADVANTAGES OF FUTURES OVER FRAs

Section 5.1 identified the following disadvantages of FRAs:

- liquidity;
- credit risk; and
- transaction cost.

It is fair to say that Eurodeposit futures are more liquid than FRAs, provided that they are held for relatively short periods; for example, the nominal bid-offer spread quoted for Eurodollar deposit futures in the 'near contracts', that is the contracts with underlying periods in the next few months, tends to be one 01, and the daily number of these contracts traded will be in the thousands. However, it is not necessarily the case that a future held for longer than, say, 6 months will have a lower bid-offer spread when the opportunity cost of the margining is taken into account.

It is also true that futures involve practically zero credit risk. However, the credit risk on most FRAs is relatively small and short-term, and for many counterparties credit is not a major restriction on their ability to deal in the FRA market.

It is difficult to compare the transaction costs of futures and FRAs. The costs of using futures include brokerage fees, internal systems and operational costs, and the cost of transferring margin payments. The cost of transferring margins can be reduced by agreeing a threshold with the broker, such that margin payments are only made when the threshold is exceeded; however, increasing the average margin in this way can increase the interest cost of margining. Brokerage fees per contract will tend to be lower for an organisation which is dealing regularly; such an organisation will also have a lower cost per contract for margin payments. In principle, the internal operational costs of managing positions in futures should be less than the corresponding costs for managing FRAs, since for futures the number of variables to record is far fewer, and there is no requirement to maintain complex legal documentation with a large number of counterparties.

Note that, in contrast to the situation for FRAs, there is little operational overhead in marking to market a portfolio of futures since an exchange will publish a market price every day.

Section 5.4 identified the following disadvantages of futures:

- inability to hedge exactly; and
- need for complex analysis.

FRAs do not have either of these disadvantages, since you can hedge any dates and amount with an FRA, and, as explained in the derivation of the rationale for the FRA contract, an FRA is the natural hedge for the most common short-term interest rate risk.

Given the advantages and disadvantages on both sides, a tentative summary might be as follows.

Futures are most appropriate for:

(a) organisations or individuals who cannot access the FRA market;
(b) organisations whose hedging needs change rapidly and which will benefit from the liquidity of futures held for short periods; and
(c) risk takers (speculators) entering into short-term trading positions.

FRAs are most appropriate for:

(a) organisations hedging relatively static positions; and
(b) organisations micro-hedging a series of positions.

You should use your judgement in recommending futures or FRAs in specific circumstances; for example, the tax treatment might be a relevant factor in particular cases.

It is worth noting that FRAs are relatively uncommon in the USA, and that futures are used there for applications which the above analysis would suggest were more suited to FRAs.

5.6 TRADING FUTURES

The marketplace for futures contracts is the relevant futures exchange. Access to trading on an exchange is through *futures brokers*. These are members of the exchange who will execute contracts and handle margining and settlement.

Within an exchange, trading in a particular contract will be allowed only at particular times; all contracts traded must be notified to the exchange authorities almost immediately, and the exchange will then publicise the price and number of contracts traded through information vendors such as Telerate. This immediate reporting of market information is a powerful method of ensuring a fair market where outsiders cannot be easily misled by insiders; it contrasts with the relative lack of transparency in over-the-counter markets such as FRAs and swaps.

Trading on an exchange is typically by some variety of open outcry; a large number of brokers will sit or stand in a small area, often called a pit, and will bid or offer futures on behalf of their clients on the basis of orders arriving via their assistants around the pit. Some of the participants in the pit may also be trading on their own account.

Although futures have been presented as a hedging instrument, they are also used by various varieties of speculator as a convenient means of taking a risk position. Such speculation has the beneficial effect of adding liquidity to the futures market.

The liquidity of the Eurodollar deposit future discussed above is typically very high, with a bid-offer spread of one 01 in the near contracts. The liquidity of Eurodeposit futures in other currencies traded on other exchanges may be lower than this with substantially wider bid-offer spreads; you should check market conditions before deciding on using futures as part of your risk management strategy. You should also check that the margining conditions described above are still current.

Apart from Eurodeposit futures there is a wide variety of other interest rate futures contracts traded at different exchanges. Before using such contracts you should carefully check their risk profile, liquidity, and margining requirements. You should also consider the credit risks of dealing in particular countries. As a useful reference, Appendix C following this chapter lists interest rate futures contracts currently traded worldwide.

SUMMARY

This chapter has explained how the Eurodeposit futures contract is similar in risk profile to an FRA. The futures contract has advantages in liquidity and accessibility, but it also has disadvantages. In particular, a futures contract can be only for one of four dates in any year, reducing the accuracy of any hedge; also, the exact risk profile of a future is subtly different to that of an FRA, requiring careful analysis and management.

Futures and options exchanges and contracts

This appendix lists all the futures and options exchanges round the world which currently have contracts based on interest rates. Note that futures were introduced above, exchange-traded options are discussed in Part V, and futures on government bonds are discussed briefly in Part IV.

The information is taken from the *International Futures & Options Databook*, published by Futures and Options World, a division of Metal Bulletin plc, Park House, Park Terrace, Worcester Park, Surrey KT4 7HY, UK, telephone +44 (81) 330 4311. The January 1992 update of the databook was used.

The type and name of each contract is given; 'F' stands for futures, 'O' for option, and 'FO' for futures and option. Further information on each contract is available from the databook mentioned above, from futures and options brokers, and from the exchanges themselves.

Before using a futures contract or exchange-traded option you should obtain full information about the contract and you should check current market conditions, particularly the number of contracts traded each day and the bid-offer spread quoted by brokers. You should also make sure that you understand fully the risk characteristics of the contract.

Africa

South African Futures Exchange	F	Long bond
32 Diagonal Street	F	Short term interest
Johannesburg		
2001		
South Africa		

Tel +27 (11) 836 3311

America

Bolsa de Mercadorias & Futuros	F	1-day interbanking deposits
Praça Antonio Prado 48	F	30-day interbanking deposits
São Paulo		
SP 01010		
Brazil		

Tel +55 (11) 239 5511

Chicago Board of Trade	FO	US Treasury bonds
141 West Jackson Boulevard	FO	US Treasury notes
Chicago	FO	5-year T-notes
IL 60604	F	2-year T-notes
USA	FO	Mortgage backed securities
	FO	Japanese Government Bond
Tel +1 (312) 435 3500	FO	Municipal Bond Index
	F	30 day interest rates
	FO	3-Year interest rate swap
	FO	5-Year interest rate swap

Chicago Board Options Exchange	O	Short Term Interest Rate
400 South LaSalle	O	Long Term Interest Rate
Chicago		
IL 60605		
USA		

Tel +1 (312) 786 5600

Chicago Mercantile Exchange	FO	US Treasury bills
30 South Wacker Drive	FO	Libor
Chicago	FO	Eurodollar
IL 60606		
USA		

Tel +1 (312) 930 1000

FINEX	F	Treasury Auction 5-Year
4 World Trade Center		Note
New York	F	Treasury Auction 2-Year
NY 10048		Note
USA		

Tel +1 (212) 938 2629

MidAmerica Commodity Exchange 141 West Jackson Boulevard Chicago IL 60604 USA	FO US Treasury bonds F US Treasury bills F US Treasury notes

Tel +1 (312) 341 3000

Montreal Exchange The Stock Exchange Tower 800 Victoria Square PO Box 61, 4th floor Montreal Quebec H4Z 1A9 Canada	F 3-month Canadian Bankers' Acceptances FO 10-year Government of Canada bonds O Canadian T-bonds

Tel +1 (514) 871 2424

New York Futures Exchange 20 Broad Street New York NY 10005 USA	F UST - bonds

Tel +1 (212) 656 4949

Asia

Hong Kong Futures Exchange Ltd Room 911, 9/F New World Tower 16-18 Queen's Road Central Hong Kong	F 3-month Hibor

Tel +852 525 1005

Manila International Futures Exchange 7th Floor, Producers Bank Centre Paseo de Roxas Makati Metro Manila Philippines	F Interest rate

Tel +63 (2) 818 54 96

Singapore International Monetary Exchange 1 Raffles Place 07-00 OUB Centre Singapore 0104 Tel +65 535 7382	FO FO F	Eurodollar Euroyen Euromark
Tokyo International Financial Futures Exchange 2-2 Otemachi 2-chome Chiyoda-ku Tokyo 100 Japan Tel +81 (3) 3275 2111	FO F	3-month Euroyen 3-month Eurodollar
Tokyo Stock Exchange 2-1 Nihombashi-Kabuto cho Chuo-Ku Tokyo 103 Japan Tel +81 (3) 3666 0141	FO F F	10-yr Government bond future 20-yr Government bond future UST-bond future

Australasia

New Zealand Futures & Options Exchange PO Box 6734 Wellesley Street Aukland New Zealand Tel +64 (9) 309 8308	FO FO FO FO	90 day Bank Bills NZ 5 year government stock NZ 3 year government stock NZ 10 year government stock
Sydney Futures Exchange Ltd 30-32 Grosvenor Street Sydney New South Wales 2000 Australia Tel +61 (2) 256 0555	FO FO FO	90 Day Bank accepted bills 10-year T-bond 3-year T-bond

Europe

Belgian Futures & Options Exchange Palais de la Bourse Rue Henri Maus 2 1000 Brussels Belgium Tel +32 (2) 512 80 40	F	Belgian Notional Government Bond

DTB Deutsche Terminboerse Grueneburgweg 102 D-6000 Frankfurt am Main 1 Germany Tel +49 (69) 153 030	O FO	Medium-term notional bond DTB Bund
European Options Exchange Optiebeurs NV PO Box 19164 1000 GD Amsterdam Netherlands Tel +31 (20) 550 4550	O O F	Government bonds Guilder bond Notional bond
Irish Futures & Options Exchange Segrave House Earlsfort Terrace Dublin 2 Irish Republic Tel +353 (1) 767 413	F F	Long Gilt Short Gilt
Guarantee Fund for Danish Options and Futures Kompagnistraede 15 Box 2017 DK-1012 Copenhagen K Denmark Tel +45 (33) 93 33 11	FO FO	9% 2006 Mortgage Bonds Danish Government Bonds
London International Financial Futures Exchange (LIFFE) Royal Exchange London EC3V 3PJ UK Tel +44 (71) 623 0444	FO FO FO F FO FO F F F FO FO	US Treasury bond 3-month Eurodollar 3-month Sterling Japanese Government Bond German Government Bond 3 month Euromark 3 month Ecu 3 month Euro Swiss Franc Interest Rate Ecu Bond Italian Government Bond Long Gilt
Matif SA 176 Rue Montmartre 75002 Paris France Tel +33 (1) 40 28 82 82	FO FO FO FO	Ecu bond Notional bond 3-month Pibor Italian Bond

Mercado de Futuros Financieros	F	3 year notional bond
Via Laietana, 60-62	F	5 year notional bond
08003 Barcelona	F	90 day Mibor
Spain		

Tel + 34 (3) 412 1128

OM Stockholm FK AB	O	Interest rate options
Box 16305		
S-103 26 Stockholm		
Sweden		

Tel +46 (8) 700 06 00

Swiss Options & Financial	F	3-month Euro Swiss
Futures Exchange		Franc Interest Rate
Neumattstrasse 7	F	5-year Swiss Franc
CH-8953 Dietikon		Interest Rate
Zurich		
Switzerland		

Tel +41 (1) 740 3020

The Spanish Options Market	O	Notional Bond 10% (3 year)
Torre Picasso	O	Notional Bond 10% (5 year)
Planta 26	O	MIBOR 90
28020 Madrid		
Spain		

Tel +34 (1) 585 0800

PART II

Self-study questions

Unless otherwise stated, all interest is quoted on an annual basis, and each month should be considered to be an exact twelfth of a year.

2.1　If zero coupon rates are 7% to 6 months and 7.1% to 9 months, then assuming no bid-offer spreads or transaction costs, what is the implied 3-month Libor in 6 months' time?

2.2　If zero coupon rates are 8% to 1 year and 7.8% to 18 months, again assuming no spreads or transaction costs, what is the implied 6-month Libor in 1 year's time?

2.3　You agree a contract with your bank whereby in 3 months' time:

if 6-month Libor is greater than 12% you will pay the bank interest calculated as Libor - 12%, and
if 6-month Libor is less than 12% the bank will pay you interest calculated as 12% - Libor,

where in each case interest is calculated on £123,456,789 for 6 months and is settled at the 3-month date discounted by the prevailing 6-month scaling factor.

Express this contract in standard FRA terms.

Fixed payer:

Floating payer:

Contract amount:

Contract period:

Contract rate:

Reference rate:

Who is 'buying the FRA'?

2.4   If today is Friday, 23 January, what is the contract period for a 6 v 9
      FRA in sterling, and what would the contract period be if the spot
      date convention were used? What is the contract period for a 3 v 6
      FRA over the 15th?

2.5   US$ Libor is quoted on an actual/360 basis and is therefore
      calculated using an exact day count.

      On 1 February, what is the cash gaps equivalent of an FRA where
      you pay fixed at 6% on US$10,000,000 on a contract period 25
      April to 25 October?

      On 1 February, what is the cash gaps equivalent of an FRA where
      you receive fixed at 8% on US$20,000,000 on a contract period
      12 June to 12 September? What is the equivalent on 11 June, if
      3-month Libor on 10 June is 7%?

2.6   Today is 1 March, and Libor is 9% to 1 June and 9.1% to
      1 September; you pay fixed at a contract rate of 10% on a
      £10,000,000 3 v 6 FRA. What is the sensitivity of the value of
      the FRA to a 1 basis point parallel shift in the yield curve and to a
      1 basis point rotation in the 0–1 year yield curve? Use an exact
      day count.

      If the daily standard deviation level shift is 7 basis points, and the
      daily standard deviation rotation is 3 basis points, what is the one
      standard deviation movement in the FRA value due to level risk and
      rotation risk over 25 days?

      If the bid-offer spread on the FRA is 8 basis points per annum, what
      does this represent as a present value cost?

2.7   A company is funded by a floating rate loan of £100,000,000; the
      loan rolls every 31 March, 30 June, 30 September, and
      31 December, and reprices at the prevailing 3-month Libor plus
      1%. The company's net income after dividends but before interest
      expense exactly matches its current funding cost and is not sensitive
      to the level of interest rates.

      What is the cost to the company of a 10 basis point per annum
      movement on 3-month Libor on a repricing date when Libor is
      about 12%?

      The company estimates that it can enter into a sterling FRA at an
      effective spread of 2.5 basis points per annum from the theoretical
      midmarket rate. What would the cost of this spread be if it hedges
      the full loan for, say, the June roll? Future value your answer to
      30 June.

All the following questions assume a 3-month Eurodollar deposit futures contract with an underlying principal of US$1 million, an underlying period of 3 months, a price quoted as 100 minus the implied interest rate, an initial margin of US$750, and a settlement of US$25 per 01 price movement.

2.8   If you buy a June future at 93.80, and the closing price that day is 93.78, what total margin payment must you make?

The following day, the closing price is 93.81; what margin payment is made?

On the following day you sell a June future at 93.82; what total margin payment do you receive?

What is your net profit? Ignoring compounding, if overnight interest is 6.2% on an actual/365 basis, what is your total funding cost?

2.9   A market maker buys a 6 v 9 FRA on 22 March, for a contract amount of US$25,000,000 at a contract rate of 6.37% on an actual/360 day basis; there are 91 days in the contract period.

The market maker decides to hedge his position through the futures market, where the price for a September future, which has underlying period starting 22 September, is 93.61/93.62. The market maker has to take the price of the futures market. Will he buy or sell futures, and what price will he pay?

The zero coupon yield curve is flat at 6.5238%; using an exact day count, how many futures contracts will there be in the hedge? If the market maker expects the futures price to change by about fifty 01s over the few days he holds the position, what is the unhedged risk? If the futures price and the FRA price would typically move half an 01 apart or together over the same period, what is the magnitude of the basis risk?

2.10 Assume that the zero coupon yield curve is fairly flat at about 7%. In March of this year you sell futures for September of next year to hedge a position equivalent to an 18 v 21 FRA with a contract amount of US$100 million; how many futures do you sell?

If the zero coupon curve does not alter, how long is it before you have to adjust your hedge? How far would the 21-month zero coupon rate have to decrease to make you alter your hedge immediately?

2.11 On 21 January you wish to hedge a 3 v 6 FRA for US$100 million using futures; you have to sell the futures. Assume that the March future has underlying period starting on 21 March, that the June future has underlying period starting on 21 June, and that the zero coupon rate to July is 6.8%. What futures should you sell?

PART III

SINGLE CURRENCY
INTEREST RATE SWAPS

Part III deals exclusively with one instrument, the single currency interest rate swap. The importance of this instrument, and the reason for its widespread use, is that it allows liquidity in risk management beyond the maturity limits of FRAs or Eurodeposit futures.

Chapter 6 covers the mechanics of single currency swaps and examines the use of simple swaps as a hedging instrument. The following two chapters build on this material to establish a pricing structure for more complex swaps; this incorporates an analysis of costing and transfer pricing within a bank.

CHAPTER 6

Interest rate swaps

The definition of a new instrument, in this case the interest rate swap, is again approached by recognising a hedging need and going on to 'invent' the new instrument to meet this need. This approach is not as direct as starting with the definition of a swap, but the lost time should be more than compensated by the gain in understanding.

The chapter starts with a section identifying another shortcoming of FRAs which prevents them meeting a particular hedging need. In this case the shortcoming is the illiquidity of FRAs at longer maturities, and so the following section examines how to design a hedging instrument which would be more liquid at these maturities. This approach bears fruit in section 6.3, where the swap contract emerges naturally as the necessary instrument.

A rigorous definition of the swap contract is then given, together with an overview of the swaps marketplace. It is then possible to examine the risk profile of a swap and to work through a numeric hedging example. The chapter closes with an examination of how to mark swaps to market.

6.1 LIMITATIONS OF FRAs AT LONGER MATURITIES

As described in Results 4.1 and 4.3 of Part II, FRAs are priced off a zero coupon curve with no bid-offer spread as follows: where the calculation period is from t_1 years to t_2 years, and the scaling factors to the two dates are s_1 and s_2, the implied scaling factor for the calculation period is s, which equals s_2/s_1, and the FRA contract rate, $m\%$, equals

$$\frac{((s_2/s_1) - 1) * 100}{(t_2 - t_1)}$$

Where there is a bid-offer spread on the zero curve, it is necessary to incorporate it into the calculation, and this will give a bid-offer spread for the FRA rate. To show how this works, the derivation of the implied scaling factor is repeated, this time including bid-offer spreads.

Suppose that the 3-month scaling factor is 1.03/1.0301, and the 6-month factor is 1.06/1.0602. This means that if you deposit £1 with a market maker you will receive back £1.03 in 3 months, but if you borrow £1 you will have to repay £1.0301. For 6 months you would receive £1.06 on a deposit but pay £1.0602 on a loan.

Suppose now you want to arrange to deposit £1 in 3 months for 3 months at a rate fixed today. You can do this by borrowing funds today for 3 months and depositing funds today for 6 months. Explicitly, you borrow £0.97078 today and repay £1 in 3 months, and you deposit £0.97078 today and receive back £1.02903 in 6 months. Your net cashflows are:

3 months -£1
6 months   £1.02903

and the implied 3 v 6 bid scaling factor is thus £1.02903 divided by £1, which equals 1.02903.

To calculate the offer factor, you can work out the cashflows if you borrow for 6 months and deposit for 3 months. This involves borrowing and depositing £0.97087, with net cashflows

3 months   £1
6 months -£1.02932

giving an offer scaling factor of 1.02932. Converting the scaling factors gives an FRA rate of 11.61%/11.73%.

In short maturities FRAs are very liquid, and a 3 v 6 FRA would trade with a narrower bid-offer spread than implied by the above analysis. However for longer maturities, say beyond 2 years, there is no liquid FRA market, largely because there are relatively few organisations needing to hedge individual forward loans or deposits at these maturities. Therefore, a market maker quoting on an FRA beyond 2 years will do so at a rate he can derive from other instruments. To discuss how he will do this requires:

Definition 6.1 The bid zero coupon curve is the zero coupon curve calculated from the bid interest rates on market instruments along the maturity spectrum.

The offer zero coupon curve is the zero coupon curve calculated from the offer interest rates on market instruments along the maturity spectrum.

The midmarket zero coupon curve is the zero coupon curve calculated from the mean of the bid and offer market interest rates along the maturity spectrum.

In all three cases, the derivation of the zero rates follows the calculation laid out in Part I.

Just as the cashflows of a 3 v 6 FRA can, in principle, be synthesised from a 3-month placing and a 6-month taking, so a longer term FRA, say a 36 v 42, can be synthesised from a zero coupon 3-year placing and $3\frac{1}{2}$-year taking. In practice, a market maker would not enter into the 3- and $3\frac{1}{2}$-year placing and taking to create a hedge for a 36 v 42 FRA, but would use the prices of these instruments only to imply the price of the FRA, and would then hedge through more liquid instruments. Therefore, the market maker would use, not the true price of the placings and takings, but an estimate of the price incorporating a narrower bid-offer spread to reflect the lower bid-offer spread in off-balance-sheet instruments. This is the rationale for pricing such an FRA off the 3-year bid zero coupon rate and the $3\frac{1}{2}$-year offer zero coupon rate, even though, as will be demonstrated in Part VI, the bid-offer spread on long-term zero coupon placings and takings will be well outside the spread of the bid and offer zero coupon curves.

Even using the narrower spread incorporated in the bid and offer zero coupon curves, the resultant FRA rate incorporates a much wider bid-offer spread than the underlying yield curve. This can be demonstrated with some figures. Suppose the 3-year zero coupon rate is 10.00%/10.05% and the $3\frac{1}{2}$-year rate is 10.10%/10.15%. Then the scaling factors are

1.3310/1.3328 and
1.4004/1.4026

giving implied forward scaling factors 1.0507/1.0538, which gives FRA rates

10.14%/10.76%.

Such an FRA would be hopelessly illiquid as a hedge, and there is thus a need for another instrument which has similar characteristics to an FRA but can trade liquidly to longer maturities.

6.2 ACHIEVING LIQUIDITY AT LONGER MATURITIES

Risk exposure to movements in long-term rates comes from long-term fixed cashflows. Companies may have such cashflows from fixed-rate debt or from long-term projects; investors who buy bonds will have equal and opposite long-term cashflows to the issuers.

Typically, a long-term fixed-rate loan involves borrowing a principal amount at the value date, paying fixed interest regularly, say every 6 months, and repaying the principal amount in full at maturity with the last interest payment. Such an arrangement is known as a *bullet loan*, in contrast to an *amortising loan*, where the principal amount is repaid in tranches, so that the outstanding principal decreases with time. A bullet

loan in the form of a bond is a *bullet bond*. The discussion which follows
will assume that there are a large number of bonds in existence, and
that there are fixed-rate bullet bonds which are trading at par to each
maturity.

The cashflow on a project may be more irregular, but typically it will
occur on or close to a regular frequency. A cashstream which involves
cashflows on a regular frequency is said to be *on even dates*; for example

    £2 today
    -£1 at 1 year
     £1 at 2 years
    -£2 at 3 years

is on even dates, despite the cashflows themselves being irregular.

Suppose we want to invent a hedging instrument which will enable us
to hedge any fixed cashflow on even dates. In order to make the
instrument liquid, it should come in as few varieties as possible. Luckily it
is possible to prove:

Result 6.1 You can duplicate *any* fixed future cashstream on even dates
by buying or issuing a set of par bullet bonds, and hence for a
hedging instrument for cashflows on even dates to be
generally applicable it need cope only with par bullet bonds.

To prove this, suppose you have a set of cashflows on an annual frequency
out to 10 years; call them $c_1, c_2, \ldots, c_{10}$. Let the bid for the fixed rate on the
annual interest bullet bonds trading at par for the 10 years be $b_1\%, \ldots,$
$b_{10}\%$, and let the offer be $o_1\%, \ldots, o_{10}\%$.

The proof proceeds by showing that you can buy or issue a 10-year
bond which will have a 10-year cashflow matching c_{10}. The other
cashflows of the bond will not in general match c_1 to c_9, but the argument
can be repeated to show that you can buy or issue a 9-year bond, which
will have no cashflow in year 10, to match the residual cashflow in year 9.
Similarly an 8-year bond will then match the residual cashflow in year 8,
and you can continue the process until you have bought or issued a 1-year
bond and matched the residual 1-year cashflow. The net cashflow of the
bonds will then be c_1 to c_{10}, together with a single cashflow today
representing the net cost or proceeds of all the bonds.

There are two cases, depending on whether c_{10} is positive or negative.
Start with it being positive. You then want to receive cash at year 10, so
you must buy principal amount p of the 10-year bond today; this will have
interest rate $b_{10}\%$. Its cashflow in year 10 will be:

$$p + (p * b_{10}/100) = p * (1 + (b_{10}/100)).$$

Choosing p to be:

$$\frac{c_{10}}{1 + (b_{10}/100)}$$

gives a cashflow at year 10 of precisely c_{10}.

Taking the other case, with c_{10} negative, you will want to pay cash at year 10, and so today you must issue a 10-year bond with principal p. The bond will have interest rate $o_{10}\%$, and hence the cashflow in year 10 will be:

$-p - (p * o_{10}/100)$.

This time you can choose p to be:

$$\frac{c_{10}}{1 + (o_{10}/100)}$$

to have the 10-year cashflow equal to c_{10}.

Repeating this process to match the residual cashflows with 9-year bonds, and then 8-year bonds, and so on, as described above, will create a bond portfolio which exactly matches all the cashflows c_1 to c_{10}.

This proves that, to be generally applicable, a hedging instrument need hedge only par bullet bonds to maturities of an exact number of years, since you can duplicate the cashflows you wish to hedge with a portfolio of such bullet bonds and thus hedge with the equivalent portfolio of hedging instruments. Such a reduced set of hedging instruments has a much better chance of achieving liquidity in the market.

6.3 CREATING A HEDGE FOR BULLET PAR BONDS

This section will demonstrate how to create a hedge contract for bullet par bonds which incorporates as many of the advantages of FRAs as possible.

The starting point is that when a par fixed bond is issued it is bought at its principal value; the present value of its future cashflows, interest plus principal, therefore equals its principal. Since there is a wide variety of par bonds available, let us pick one issued by an organisation which has the same credit standing as a prime bank, so that its short-term funding would be at Libor; for ease of explanation let us pick a definite maturity and interest frequency, say 5-year maturity with interest paid annually.

Suppose that, instead of a long-term bond, the organisation issued a 1-year bond at an interest rate of 1-year Libor; since Libor is its funding rate, the future cashflow of the bond should be valued at a zero coupon rate of 1-year Libor. Thus the cashflows at 1 year of the interest and principal can be seen to have a present value equal to the principal itself, and the bond would be issued at par.

Suppose that the organisation now arranges to issue a 1-year bond in 1 year's time, at an interest rate of the then prevailing 1-year Libor.

What will the price of the bond be at issue? The same argument as above shows that the bond will be priced at par; in fact it shows that a 1-year bond at Libor to be issued at any future date would be issued at par. This leads to:

Result 6.2 If an organisation funds at Libor, then the forward price of a bond which it will issue at the then prevailing Libor rate of a future period is par. The interest rate risk of a forward purchase of such a bond is zero.

The forward purchase is at par and the bond will be priced at par on the day when it is issued. Therefore the purchaser could remove any risk by selling the bond at par on its issue date, thus reducing his net cashflows to par in and par out, which is zero. This shows that there is no interest rate risk in such a forward purchase.

Continuing this analysis further demonstrates the truth of:

Result 6.3 An organisation which funds at Libor and wishes to raise 5-year funds should be indifferent between:

(a)   issuing at par a fixed 5-year bond with annual interest payments; and

(b)   issuing a strip of 1-year bonds paying the then prevailing 1-year Libor; the bonds are to be issued today, and at 1, 2, 3, and 4 years, and are to be sold today at a forward price of par.

The corresponding result holds for any payment frequency and any length of funding period.

Note that Result 6.2 confirms that the price for the Libor bonds in (b) will be par.

This result holds because in each case the cashflow today is the bond principal and the present value of future cashflows is also the principal. Clearly the present value of the cashflows of the 5-year fixed bond is its principal, since it is issued at par. To see that the present value of the future cashflows of the five floating bonds is the principal, start by noting that each bond has repayment at maturity equal to its principal plus the then prevailing 1-year Libor interest. Thus the value of the future cashflows of each bond at its value date will be the bond principal. Since the purchase price of each bond at its value date is the principal, the net future value of each bond except the first will be zero, and hence their net present value will be zero also. The present value of the future cashflows of the first floating bond will be the principal amount itself, since the cashflow at 1 year is not offset by any other future cashflow.

The principal repayment on each floating bond, except the last, will be met by the proceeds of the following bond; the organisation will therefore have the same use of funds over the 5-year period, regardless of which funding method it chooses. The interest rate risk will of course be different, but that is already incorporated into the pricing.

Consider now an investor who might buy the bonds; by the same argument, she too should be indifferent between the fixed bond in (a) and the floating strip in (b).

Given that both the issuer and the investor are indifferent between the two cashstreams, they should be prepared to enter into a contract where they exchange the cashstreams, *without the presence of any bonds*. Explicitly, one counterparty will pay the principal today, receive fixed interest annually for 5 years, and receive the principal back at 5 years; the other counterparty will pay the principal today, receive 1-year Libor interest annually for 5 years, and receive the principal back at 5 years. (As mentioned above, the intermediate principal flows on the strip of floating bonds net out.)

Noting that the principal flows in this contract net out both today and at 5 years, the contract can be simplified to an exchange of interest only, with one counterparty paying fixed interest annually and the other paying floating interest; the cashflows can further be reduced by having the two counterparties settle each annual payment net. Doing this creates a *single currency interest rate swap*.

The contract defined above is a *par bullet swap*; par because it is at a fair price to both counterparties, and bullet because the underlying principal does not change with time. If it can be shown that this type of swap will hedge the risk of a par bullet bond, then this will prove, by Result 6.1, that the risk of *any* fixed future cashflows can be hedged with a portfolio of such swaps.

Suppose that the organisation issuing the 5-year bond wants to hedge its resultant interest rate risk. Consider what happens if it enters into a 5-year swap where it receives fixed interest and pays floating interest. Taking the principal on the bond and swap as p, the fixed interest rate on the bond and swap as $f\%$, and the annual Libors for the 5 years as $L_0\%$, $L_1\%$, . . ., $L_4\%$, its future cashflows become:

	Bond	<- - - $\quad$ *Swap* $\quad$ - - ->
Year 1	$- (p * f/100)$	$(p * f/100) - (p * L_0/100)$
Year 2	$- (p * f/100)$	$(p * f/100) - (p * L_1/100)$
Year 3	$- (p * f/100)$	$(p * f/100) - (p * L_2/100)$
Year 4	$- (p * f/100)$	$(p * f/100) - (p * L_3/100)$
Year 5	$-p - (p * f/100)$	$(p * f/100) - (p * L_4/100)$

Netting the fixed interest flows in and out, and adding equal and opposite principal flows at each intermediate date gives:

Year 1	$-p - (p * L_0/100) + p$
Year 2	$-p - (p * L_1/100) + p$
Year 3	$-p - (p * L_2/100) + p$
Year 4	$-p - (p * L_3/100) + p$
Year 5	$-p - (p * L_4/100)$

But these are exactly the same future cashflows as if the organisation were to issue a strip of five annual bonds at 1-year Libor, and, by the above results, the present value of these cashflows will be precisely p at each annual date. It may in fact differ from p at intermediate dates, but that will involve short-term interest rate risk; there is no risk exposure to long-term rates since the present value is guaranteed to return to its original value of p every year. Figure 6.1 illustrates this hedging diagrammatically.

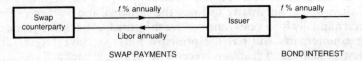

SWAP PAYMENTS   BOND INTEREST

Figure 6.1 Cashflows of swap as a hedge for a bond. There are no principal flows on the swap, and so the issuer's net principal flows are the same as for the bond. However, its receipt of fixed interest on the swap exactly offsets its payments of fixed interest on the bond, leaving it with a net Libor interest payment.

This shows that an issuer of a fixed bond can use a swap to hedge its long-term interest rate risk. Repeating the example for an investor in a fixed bond, paying fixed on a swap would reproduce the above cashflows with plus and minus interchanged, and the same result would follow, namely that the swap hedges the investor's exposure to long-term rate movements.

It is thus demonstrated that par bullet swaps can hedge the long-term interest rate risk on par bonds, and hence that they can be used to hedge the long-term risk on any fixed cashflows.

This shows that in principle a swap will trade at the same interest rate as the equivalent par bond. It should be emphasised that in practice swap rates trade independently of bonds, within limits established by market expectations and by the possibilities of arbitrage.

The above discussion is based on the credit quality of both counterparties being the same as for prime banks. This assumption will be carried through the rest of this chapter, and the pricing implications of different credit risks will be investigated in the next chapter.

6.4 INTEREST RATE SWAPS

We have seen that interest rate swaps provide a useful hedging function. This section will define swaps more rigorously, and the next section will give some information about how they are traded.

A single currency interest rate swap is a contract between two counterparties to exchange future cashstreams in the same currency; it has the effect of exchanging interest rate risk positions between the counterparties.

The most common type of swap is the fixed-to-floating bullet par swap. In this, the *fixed payer* pays a cashstream equivalent to a *fixed interest rate* applied to a *notional principal* on a series of *payment dates* from the *value date* to the *maturity date* of the swap, while the *floating payer* pays interest on the same notional principal calculated on a floating *reference rate* such as Libor. As for an FRA, a source must be specified for the reference rate.

Payment dates must also be specified for the floating interest. The payment dates on the fixed and floating side need not coincide, except for the maturity date, which must be a payment date on both sides. However, the payment dates on each side will usually be on a regular frequency, most commonly annually, semiannually, quarterly, or monthly, and will usually coincide at least annually. Where payments coincide they are settled net; where they do not coincide they are settled gross.

Interest is calculated on a series of *calculation periods*, where the first calculation period on the fixed side runs from the value date to the first fixed-side payment date, the second calculation period runs from the first to the second fixed-side payment date, and so on, with the last calculation period ending on the maturity date. The floating side calculation periods are defined similarly.

Unlike for FRAs, swap settlement is made *undiscounted* at the end of the relevant calculation period. (There are reasons for this disparity. An FRA is generally a short-term contract, and thus reducing the credit period from, say, 9 months to 3 months represents a significant reduction of risk; a swap is generally for a longer term, and reducing the credit period from, say, 5 years to $4\frac{1}{2}$ years is not a significant enough saving to justify an increase in the complexity of the settlement formula. Moreover, swaps evolved from arrangements to match cashflows rather than to reduce risk, and thus settlement was made the same as settlement in the underlying bond market.)

To make the abstract definition a bit clearer, consider a concrete example. A company issues at par a 5-year DEM100 million bond, paying interest annually at 10%. It then decides to enter into a swap with its bank to neutralise the long-term interest rate risk of the bond. The bank quotes its 5-year DEM swap rate as 9.95%/10.05%, which means that it will enter into a swap where it pays fixed at 9.95% or receives fixed at 10.05%. The company therefore enters into a swap as follows:

> The *fixed payer* is the bank, which pays at a *fixed interest rate* of 9.95% on a *notional principal* of DEM100 million on annual *payment dates* for a 5-year period. The *floating payer* is the company, which pays interest on DEM100 million on a *reference rate* of 6-month DEM Libor with semiannual payment dates.

Note that in this example the payment dates on the fixed and floating sides do not all coincide; there will therefore be some net settlements and some gross settlements.

Variations on the par bullet swap include a notional principal which varies over the life of the swap, deferred value dates, irregular payment frequencies, and *yield adjustments*, where one counterparty makes an additional payment to the other, in exchange for which the fixed or floating rate is adjusted. The pricing of these different types of swap is covered in the next two chapters.

Result 6.2 showed that a forward bond for any period at the then prevailing Libor for that period would be issued at par. Therefore, both counterparties to a swap should be indifferent as to whether the floating payer contracts to pay say, 1-year Libor annually or 3-month Libor quarterly. In fact there is a credit cost if one counterparty pays more frequently than the other, and in certain currencies there is a liquidity cost in using certain Libors; this will be discussed further in the next chapter. Usually any difference in cost will be small, giving:

Result 6.4 To a good approximation, the pricing of a swap depends only on the fixed side.

If there is a short floating period in a swap, then the Libor used to calculate the floating-side interest for that period will normally be the Libor for that period. For example, if a swap has a maturity of 5 years and 4 months, and the floating side is on a semiannual frequency with a 4-month first period, then the floating interest in the first period will be calculated on 4-month Libor. This convention ensures that Result 6.4 holds even when the floating payment dates are irregular.

6.5 TRADING SWAPS

As was done in Part II for FRAs, this section gives a brief overview of the marketplace and market terminology for single currency swaps. The part of the overview for FRAs relating to the participants in the FRA market holds for swaps also, and it is therefore not repeated here.

Bid and offer rates for single currency interest rate swaps under standard contract terms are quoted by many banks. In most currencies there is a convention for the standard frequency of the interest payments and the quotation of the interest rate on the fixed and floating sides of a swap; while swaps can be arranged on other terms, the price will be calculated with reference to the current market yield curve for a swap under the standard terms for the currency.

The liquidity in the swap market is less than for FRAs, and even banks which are nominally market makers are often reluctant to quote a two-way price. Having said that, there is certainly liquidity for swaps in the US dollar, and, to a lesser extent, in sterling, Deutschmark, yen, Swiss franc, and XEU. Swaps are available in a variety of other currencies but can be relatively illiquid. Most swaps have tenors from 1 to 10 years, with notional principals in the range US$5 million to US$100 million; outside the major currencies principals tend to be smaller and tenors tend to be shorter.

In most swaps one counterparty pays fixed interest and the other pays floating; the floating payer is said to *receive fixed*. Where a market maker quotes a two-way price, the lower rate is the bid where he will pay fixed, and the higher rate is the offer where he will receive fixed. Paying fixed is described as being *long funded*, since the fixed payer will benefit if interest rates rise; similarly, receiving fixed is described as being *short funded*.

In *basis swaps* both counterparties pay interest calculated on a floating rate; for example, one counterparty may pay interest calculated at Libor, while the other pays interest calculated at market interest rates for *commercial paper* (short-term debt securities issued by the most creditworthy companies) plus 0.07%. Basis swaps will be discussed further in Part IV.

The market standard for swaps contracts is 'ISDA Terms' produced by the International Swaps Dealers Association; a reference for this is given in the bibliography. Where a swap is to be entered into under other terms or where it is necessary to pick a specific option from the choices offered in the ISDA terms, this should be agreed at the time the deal is done; this can be important if it is necessary to make swap terms compatible with the terms of an underlying transaction. Note that ISDA terminology has certain eccentricities; for example, value date becomes 'effective date', and maturity becomes 'termination date'. You should learn these terms so as to understand ISDA swap documentation.

As with FRAs, swaps in Eurocurrencies generally have each interest rate fixing on the spot date, rather than on the first date, of each floating side calculation period; settlement will always be on the last day of the period.

Because swap contracts can be for a long tenor, credit risk is a major consideration in the swaps market; the calculation of credit risk is covered in the next chapter.

6.6 RISK PROFILE

Since a bullet swap is equivalent in terms of net cashflows to buying a bullet par fixed bond and issuing a strip of floating bonds, or vice versa, its risk profile must be equal to the sum of the risk profiles of the bonds. For example, suppose that today a company enters into a 5-year swap where it receives fixed at f % annually on a notional principal of p and pays Libor semiannually. The interest rate risk on the swap must be:

the risk on buying a 5-year par fixed annual bond; plus
the risk on issuing a strip of ten semiannual bonds at Libor.

If the company had instead paid fixed on the swap its risk would be:

the risk on issuing a 5-year par fixed annual bond; plus
the risk on buying a strip of ten semiannual bonds at Libor.

Since Result 6.2 shows that a bond to be issued with an interest rate of the appropriate Libor at some future date will always be at par, there is no interest rate risk on a floating period of a swap where the interest rate has not yet been set. Consequently, the risk on the receive fixed swap at its value date is:

the risk on buying a 5-year par fixed annual bond; plus
the risk on issuing a 6-month bond at today's 6-month Libor.

This gives

Result 6.5 The risk profile of a swap can be obtained by:

      (a)   separating the swap into its fixed and floating sides;

      (b)   equating the risk of the fixed side to the risk of the equivalent bond; and

      (c)   equating the risk of the floating side to the risk of the equivalent bond for the current calculation period where the floating rate is fixed.

In the discrete cash gaps methodology, the risk of a bond is represented by its cashflows. Thus for the 5-year swap described above, the risk of the bond equivalent to the fixed side is represented by:

Year 0	$-p$
Year 1	$(f * p/100)$
Year 2	$(f * p/100)$
Year 3	$(f * p/100)$
Year 4	$(f * p/100)$
Year 5	$p + (f * p/100)$

and the risk of the bond equivalent to the first floating period, assuming that we are at the swap's value date and have just set Libor to L_0, is represented by:

Year 0	p
Year 0.5	$-p - (L_0 * p * 0.5/100)$

Putting these together, the risk of the swap is represented by:

Year 0.5	$-p - (L_0 * p * 0.5/100)$
Year 1	$(f * p/100)$
Year 2	$(f * p/100)$
Year 3	$(f * p/100)$
Year 4	$(f * p/100)$
Year 5	$p + (f * p/100)$

The vital point to notice is that the notional principal appears twice in this cashflow representation, even though there is no exchange of principal involved in the swap. On the value date, the principals on the fixed and floating sides net to zero, but they do not net at the end of the current floating period and at the maturity date.

It can be seen from these cashflows that the interest rate sensitivity of the fixed side of the swap generally outweighs the sensitivity of the floating side. For example, if the yield curve is flat at 10%, then the change in value of the fixed side cashflows in the above swap for a 1 basis point parallel shift in the curve is 3.8 basis points of principal, while the corresponding change for the floating side is minus 0.4 basis points of principal.

6.7 HEDGING WITH SWAPS

This section gives a simple example of micro hedging interest rate risk using a single currency swap.

An investor is holding a bullet bond denominated in European Currency Units (XEU) with a face value of XEU10 million, which pays 13% annually and has maturity in 6 years. The current 6-year XEU swap rate is quoted as 10.01%/10.11%. The investor is worried that XEU rates will increase, reducing the value of his bond, and so he enters into the following swap with his bank:

> The fixed payer is the investor, who pays at a fixed interest rate of 10.11% on a notional principal of XEU10 million on annual payment dates for a 6-year period. The floating payer is the bank, which pays interest on the same notional principal on a reference rate of 6-month XEU Libor with semiannual payment dates.

The investor has removed his exposure to long-term XEU rates and ensured that every year he will receive 13% interest on the bond and pay 10.11% interest on the swap, thus guaranteeing a fixed income of 2.89% annually; he will also receive Libor semiannually on the swap and will receive the bond principal at maturity. His risk profile is changed from:

Year 1		$(13 * p/100)$
Year 2		$(13 * p/100)$
Year 3		$(13 * p/100)$
Year 4		$(13 * p/100)$
Year 5		$(13 * p/100)$
Year 6	$p +$	$(13 * p/100)$

To:

Year 0.5	$p +$	$(L_0 * p * 0.5/100)$
Year 1		$(2.89 * p/100)$
Year 2		$(2.89 * p/100)$
Year 3		$(2.89 * p/100)$
Year 4		$(2.89 * p/100)$
Year 5		$(2.89 * p/100)$
Year 6		$(2.89 * p/100)$

Where L_0 is the Libor set for the first period of the swap.

You should check that you can derive this risk profile by adding the risk profiles of the bond and of the swap, and you should experiment to see how the present values of the two risk profiles change as the zero coupon curve changes.

The same process explained in Part II for deriving the best combination of FRAs for a particular hedge can also be used for swaps. Moreover, just as FRAs can be used to take risk rather than to hedge it, so for swaps; the process of establishing the appropriate combination of instruments is again the same.

6.8 MARKING SWAPS TO MARKET

The starting point for establishing a market value for a swap is to present value its future cashflows. However, unlike an FRA, a swap is generally a medium-term contract with material future operational costs and credit risks; it is therefore appropriate to subtract a *holdback* from the present value of the cashflows to allow for these costs and risks. This section first establishes two equivalent methods for deriving the present value of the future cashflows and then discusses how to calculate an appropriate holdback.

The present value of the fixed cashflows is easy to calculate, but it is less obvious how to present value the floating cashflows. As for FRAs, there are two possible methods for establishing the present value; provided that the same midmarket rates are used as a basis, as discussed for FRAs, the two methods should give precisely the same answer.

The first method involves replacing the cashflows of the swap with the equivalent cashflows of a floating bond purchased and a fixed bond sold, or vice versa, as in Result 6.5. The present value of the swap is then the present value of the equivalent cashflows.

The second method involves comparing the swap with an equivalent swap at the current market rate. By definition, the market swap will have a present value of zero, and the only difference between the two swaps will be the difference in the fixed rate. Therefore, present valuing the difference in fixed interest at each payment date will give the value of the swap.

Note that this second method is generally applicable only for bullet swaps on their value date or on an intermediate payment date; if the swap is not bullet then there will be no easily accessible market rate for comparison (although if there is then the method will work), and if today is not a payment date then an adjustment will have to be made for the current fixed and floating periods having different lengths in the swap to be valued and in the market swap.

As an example of present valuing the cashflows of a swap, suppose that the midmarket DEM yield curves for Libor and swaps paying annually is:

	Par curve	Zero curve
Year 0.5	8.40	8.576
Year 1	8.55	8.550
Year 2	8.74	8.748
Year 3	8.84	8.855
Year 4	8.94	8.965
Year 5	9.04	9.081

Using each of the methods in turn, let us present value the cashflows of a swap with 5 years to maturity with a notional principal of DEM10 million, where you pay fixed annually at 6.70% and receive floating semiannually, and on which Libor has just been set for the current period at 8.40%.

The first method will value the swap as the present value of equivalent cashflows as follows:

	Cashflow DEM millions	Zero rate	Scaling factor	Present value DEM millions
Year 0.5	+10.42	8.576	1.04200	10.0000
Year 1	− 0.67	8.550	1.08550	−0.6172
Year 2	− 0.67	8.748	1.18261	−0.5665
Year 3	− 0.67	8.855	1.28987	−0.5194
Year 4	− 0.67	8.965	1.40977	−0.4753
Year 5	−10.67	9.081	1.54435	−6.9091

giving a net present value of DEM912,500.

The second method will value the swap as the present value of an annual payment of (9.04% - 6.70%) on DEM10 million, which equals DEM234,000, over the 5 years. This can be valued as:

	Cashflow DEM	Scaling factor	Present value DEM
Year 1	234,000	1.08550	215,569
Year 2	234,000	1.18261	197,867
Year 3	234,000	1.28987	181,414
Year 4	234,000	1.40977	165,985
Year 5	234,000	1.54435	151,520

giving a net present value of DEM912,355.

It can be seen that within rounding error the two methods agree.

The calculation of the holdback involves two components, operational costs and expected credit loss over the remaining life of the swap. Operational costs can be estimated by dividing budgeted operational expenses by the number of swaps to give an annual cost, and present valuing the cost for each future year of the swap. Expected credit losses can be estimated using the methods which will be developed in the next chapter. It is recommended there that all expected credit costs be allocated as expense to the dealer and as income to the responsibility centre which manages credit; this will have the effect of removing from the trading book all income needed to cover credit losses.

The holdback will tend to reduce over the life of a swap; at maturity future operational costs and credit losses will be zero and the holdback will become zero also.

SUMMARY

This chapter has demonstrated how the single currency interest rate swap arises as a natural contract to hedge interest rate risk in maturities beyond those available for FRAs; a swap hedges the long-term risk of a bond.

The risk profile of a swap can be represented in the cash gaps methodology as the cashflows of the equivalent fixed bond together with the cashflows of the current Libor period considered as a fixed deposit; principal flows are included in the gaps. Present valuing the cashflows in this representation gives the mark-to-market value of the swap. A swap can also be marked to market by comparing it with a market swap, but this method is hard to apply except for swaps on a Libor reset date with an exact number of periods to maturity. This chapter has concentrated on bullet swaps; the next two chapters will develop the treatment of more complex structures within a realistic framework of bid-offer spreads and other costs.

CHAPTER 7

Pricing complex interest rate swaps: theory

All interest rate risk management using swaps can be achieved using only swaps which start today and which have constant notional principal. However, organisations which have occasional complex hedging needs may find it more cost effective to enter into a single complex swap with one bank than to set up a portfolio of simple swaps with a variety of banks. Consequently, banks have to be able to calculate a fixed rate at which they will enter into such complex swaps; this is the subject of Chapters 7 and 8.

The split between the two chapters is essentially between theory and practice, or to be more precise, between theory with a little number crunching and number crunching with a little theory. This chapter derives the theory of pricing a complex swap by pricing the exact hedge position using bullet par swaps. It is shown that the market rate of a swap should be essentially independent of the payment frequency of the floating side; this allows the development of a pricing theory for the fixed side only, based on the useful concept of the *present value of 1%* interest on the terms of the swap. The chapter concludes with an analysis of how to incorporate credit risk, the opportunity cost of capital, and operational costs into the pricing model.

The next chapter will use this theory to work through various pricing examples.

It is important to realise that almost all of the complications arise because of the existence of a bid-offer spread on the yield curve. If you follow most textbooks and assume no bid-offer spread, then calculating the fixed rate on a complex swap becomes simply a matter of present valuing all cashflows and picking the fixed rate which makes the present value zero. This simplistic approach will not work in real life, since there is no direct rule which can tell you whether to use the bid or the offer side of the zero curve for a particular present valuing calculation.

7.1 PRICING THROUGH HEDGING

A bullet par swap is a swap with a constant notional principal, where the fixed side is at the market rate; the standard yield curve quoted in the interbank market is for bullet par swaps starting today or spot. To simplify terminology, such swaps will be referred to as 'simple swaps'. In this section all the simple swaps will have tenor of an exact number of years and annual fixed payments; the next section will examine how to price simple swaps with a short or long fixed calculation period.

The basic idea is that you price complex swaps by working out the effective blended fixed rate of a collection of simple swaps which would sum to the same floating payments.

The main conceptual problem is working out the rate to use in the simple swaps. The treatment here attempts to clarify this by working with reference to an organisational structure within which the complex swap rate is to be quoted. The organisation quoting the rate is a bank; it has two divisions, Trading and Marketing. It is the marketing division which quotes the price of the complex swap to the customer, but it is the trading division which quotes the price of simple swaps to Marketing. Where the bank deals a complex swap with a customer, a set of internal simple swaps is booked between Trading and Marketing, and the complex swap is booked between Marketing and the customer. The marketing division is not allowed to take on any position at a loss, nor is it allowed to take on any risk big enough to turn a profitable position into a loss; thus, from the point of view of Marketing, the cashflows on the internal simple swaps must net out with the cashflows on the external complex swap to leave zero or a net positive cashflow.

It should be clear that, although the exposition is based on this particular organisational structure, the rate which a bank quotes on a given swap should be independent of its internal organisation.

This section assumes that there are no credit risks and that the bank has no cost of capital; this means that the market-maker will be happy to quote the same swap rate to any counterparty. When the pricing of complex swaps under these idealised conditions is clarified, section 7.4 below will introduce a realistic treatment of credit and capital costs.

Since there is no difference in costs, a market maker in the trading division who is being asked to quote a rate for a particular simple swap will be indifferent as to whether the request comes from an external customer directly or through the marketing division. Thus, if a customer comes to the marketing division for a quote on a 'complex swap' which is in fact equivalent to a single simple swap where the bank pays fixed, the marketing officer will go to the market maker who will quote, say, 9.21%/9.28%, and the marketing officer will quote to the customer 9.21% or lower as she deems appropriate. For example, if she executes the deal at 9.20%, then her cashflows will be:

Internal swap	fixed in at 9.21%
	Libor out
External swap	fixed out at 9.20%
	Libor in

giving a net flow of 0.01% in. She cannot quote a rate higher than 9.21%, because then she would be taking on a position at a loss.

Grasp who pays what to whom in the above example, and you will have made your main conceptual leap towards understanding the pricing of complex swaps.

Suppose that the market maker will quote separately 9.21%/9.28% on a 5-year swap, and 9.33%/9.40% on a 10-year swap. What will he quote for the two rates simultaneously?

Assuming that the combined size of the two deals on which he is being asked to quote is no greater than the size of the individual deals on which he was happy to quote the rates above, the plausible answer is that the dealer should quote the same rates simultaneously as he quotes separately. This is because each rate he quotes should incorporate an income adequate to recompense him for the risk he is taking on; if the income incorporated in each rate separately is adequate for him to deal then it should be adequate for him to enter into the two deals together.

In fact the situation is more complex than this, since it is possible to prove:

Result 7.1 The risk on a portfolio will in general be *less* than the sum of the risks of the individual swaps in the portfolio. The risk will be the same only if the individual swaps are all to the same maturity on the same terms (including all being pay fixed or all being receive fixed) with differences only in the notional principals.

Recall that risk is defined in terms of the expected absolute change in present value over a period. For ease of explanation, consider a particular example where the market maker pays fixed on a 5-year swap and on a 10-year swap. If the yield curve has a parallel shift upwards then there will be a mark-to-market profit on both swaps, and if it has a parallel shift downwards then there will be a mark-to-market loss on both swaps; in either case, the absolute change in value of the portfolio will be the same as the sum of the absolute changes in value of the two swaps. However, if the yield curve rotates so that the 5-year swap rate goes up while the 10-year rate goes down, then there will be a profit on the 5-year swap offset by a loss on the 10-year swap; in this case the change in value of the portfolio will be less than the sum of the absolute change in value of the two swaps. Since risk is a multiple of the average, over all possible yield curve movements, of the absolute movement in present value, this example illustrates why Result 7.1 holds.

Since level shifts in the yield curve tend to be greater than rotations, the reduction in portfolio risk will be more pronounced when the portfolio includes receive fixed swaps as well as pay fixed.

Although the reduction in risk implies that a market maker should quote a lower effective bid-offer spread on a portfolio of swaps than on the same swaps individually, in practice the effect would be small, and it would be difficult to calculate in each case the reduction in risk and consequent reduction in spread. Therefore, we shall proceed using:

Assumption 7.1 A market maker will quote the same rates on swaps as a package as when he quotes on them individually.

Constructing a model to allow more aggressive quotes on a portfolio of transactions is a potentially fruitful area for obtaining a competitive advantage.

Since the marketing division cannot assume material risk, it must price its deals to its customers at, or better than, the level at which it can hedge the cashflows with the trading division; this will be the basis of the pricing theory developed below.

7.2 ELIMINATING DEPENDENCE ON THE FLOATING SIDE

The complex swaps considered in this chapter will be fixed-to-floating single currency interest rate swaps, which may differ from simple swaps by:

(a) The value date being in the future, rather than today or spot.
(b) Payment dates not being on a regular frequency.
(c) The notional principal varying over time.

The variation of the principal over the life of the swap is referred to as the *swap profile*. The swap profile must be the same on the fixed and floating sides, and, where the notional principal changes on a particular day, that day must be a payment date on both the fixed and floating sides. All floating payments will be at the Libor for the appropriate floating period.

Other types of complex swap can exist; many of them can be priced by extensions of the techniques developed here. In particular, the next chapter will consider the payment of an initial yield adjustment by one counterparty, in compensation for which the fixed or floating rate is altered.

This section will show that the fixed rate for the types of complex swap defined above is a function of the swap profile and of the fixed side payment dates only, and will be independent of the payment frequency on the floating side. The next section will look at pricing the fixed side by producing a hedge using simple swaps.

The exposition below uses the following symbols:

L_0 is the Libor set at year 0,
$L_{0.5}$ is the Libor set at year 0.5,
L_1 is the Libor set at year 1,

and so on. The currency and period of the Libor will be clear from the context.

A swap is a fair agreement because the present value of the expected floating payments equals the present value of the fixed payments; this equality is assured by the fixed and floating rates involved being market rates. (In fact, there will be a slight inequality, since the market maker will choose the fixed rate to give himself a small present value profit; this will not affect the discussion below, since in any particular case true equality could be maintained by replacing 'equal to' with, say, 'equal to £1,000 plus'.) It is useful to represent this equality on *grossed-up* swap payments, as illustrated in the following example.

Consider a swap where the notional principal is £20 million from year 0 to year 1 and £10 million from year 1 to the maturity date year 2. The floating payments are semiannual and the fixed payments are 12% annually. From the viewpoint of the fixed payer, the actual cashflows in £ millions will be:

Year 0.5 $(20 * L_0 * 0.5/100)$
Year 1 $(20 * L_{0.5} * 0.5/100)$ $- (20 * 12/100)$
Year 1.5 $(10 * L_1 * 0.5/100)$
Year 2 $(10 * L_{1.5} * 0.5/100)$ $- (10 * 12/100)$

These net payments can be restated as the sum of gross payments as follows:

	Floating payer	Fixed payer
Year 0.5	$-(20 * L_0 * 0.5/100)$	
Year 1	$-(20 * L_{0.5} * 0.5/100)$	$- (20 * 12/100)$
Year 1.5	$-(10 * L_1 * 0.5/100)$	
Year 2	$-(10 * L_{1.5} * 0.5/100)$	$- (10 * 12/100)$

Self-cancelling pairs of principal payments can be added to make the cashflows look like a series of bonds, as follows:

Year	Floating payer	Fixed payer
0	20	20
0.5	$-(20 * L_0 * 0.5/100) - 20 + 20$	
1	$-(20 * L_{0.5} * 0.5/100) - 20 + 10$	$-(20 * 12/100) - 20 + 10$
1.5	$-(10 * L_1 * 0.5/100) - 10 + 10$	
2	$-(10 * L_{1.5} * 0.5/100) - 10$	$-(10 * 12/100) - 10$

The rules for constructing the above table are:

- at Year 0 add a positive flow of the principal to each side;
- at maturity add a negative flow of the principal to each side; and

- at each intermediate payment date on either side, add a negative cashflow of the principal up to that date and a positive cashflow of the principal from that date.

These rules are guaranteed to generate self-cancelling pairs of cashflows, since each date where the principal changes must be a payment date on both sides.

It is clear that since the original swap cashflows on the fixed and floating side had equal present values, the fixed and floating side cashflows in the above table, which will be referred to as the grossed-up fixed and floating sides, must also have equal present values. Concentrate on the floating payer. His cashflows can be grouped as follows:

$$
\begin{array}{ll}
\text{Year } 0 & 20 \\
\text{Year } 0.5 & -20 - (20 * L_0 * 0.5/100) \\[4pt]
\text{Year } 0.5 & 20 \\
\text{Year } 1 & -20 - (20 * L_{0.5} * 0.5/100) \\[4pt]
\text{Year } 1 & 10 \\
\text{Year } 1.5 & -10 - (10 * L_1 * 0.5/100) \\[4pt]
\text{Year } 1.5 & 10 \\
\text{Year } 2 & -10 - (10 * L_{1.5} * 0.5/100)
\end{array}
$$

It can be seen that each of the four pairs above has the cashflows of a bond at Libor, and thus has a present value of zero. The construction above can be shown to work for any such complex swap, giving:

Result 7.2 The present value of the grossed-up floating payments of a swap is zero.

Regardless of the regularity or irregularity of the payment frequency on the floating side the present value is unchanged; since a market swap has equal present value for the fixed and floating sides, this proves:

Result 7.3 The pricing of the fixed side of a complex swap is independent of the payment dates on the floating side.

Since zero equals zero, Result 7.2 also proves:

Result 7.4 The present value of the grossed-up fixed payments of a swap is zero.

This result is needed in order to work out how to interpolate the yield curve to produce the fixed rate for, say, a $4\frac{1}{2}$-year swap.

Result 7.3, that the pricing of a swap is independent of the payment frequency on the floating side, is not strictly true for Libor periods where there is a lack of liquidity. For example, at the time of writing, there is relatively little liquidity in 3-month DEM Libor, and therefore it would be more expensive for a non-German bank to enter into a DEM swap against 3-month Libor than against 6-month Libor. Similarly, 1-month

Libor will probably be more expensive in most currencies, partly because of liquidity and partly because of increased operational costs. Such cases can be handled by a rule of thumb which states, for example, that 1-month Libor will cost 3 basis points extra. This complication is ignored in the exposition below, but you should be aware of it when you are involved in real-life transactions.

7.3 PRICING THE FIXED SIDE

Let us now look at how the marketing officer will go about constructing a hedge for the fixed side of the swap in the above example, assuming that the bank is the floating payer. Suppose that the market maker is currently quoting 1-year swaps as 12.45%/12.52% and 2-year swaps as 11.90%/11.97%. The obvious way to hedge the complex swap is with two simple swaps as follows:

> Swap A Value Year 0   Maturity Year 1
> Notional principal £10 million
> Trading pays floating semiannually
> Marketing pays fixed annually at 12.52%

> Swap B Value Year 0   Maturity Year 2
> Notional principal £10 million
> Trading pays floating semiannually
> Marketing pays fixed annually at 11.97%

The critical observation is that the sum of the swap profiles of these two swaps is equal to the swap profile on the complex swap. Since all floating payments are at Libor, the floating payment which Marketing makes to its external customer on each payment date will be the same as the total floating payment which Marketing receives from Trading on the internal swaps. If Marketing is going to eliminate its interest rate risk then it has to match its floating payments in and out in this way, since any unmatched floating payment clearly represents a risk. This gives the basic rule of constructing a hedge:

Rule 7.1 The sum of the swap profiles of the simple swaps used to construct the hedge must equal the profile of the complex swap on every date.

Where the hedge involves Marketing paying fixed on some simple swaps and receiving fixed on others, then in summing the profiles you should add the pay fixed swaps and subtract the receive fixed swaps (or vice versa), since their Libor payments will net. You will see this in action in the pricing of a deferred start swap in the next chapter.

There remains the problem that Marketing wishes to quote a single fixed rate, while the fixed cashflows on the hedge are 12.52% on the 1-year swap and 11.97% on the 2-year swap. It is necessary to work out the fixed rate which gives the same present value for the cashflows of the complex swap as for the fixed cashflows of the simple swaps. This *blended rate* will satisfy the first of the conditions derived in section 7.1, namely that Marketing cannot take on any position at a loss. After calculating the risk which Marketing is assuming through the mismatch between the hedge and the external swap, it will be possible to determine what margin it should put on its quote to compensate for risk.

In order to simplify the calculation of the blended rate, it is helpful to introduce the terminology of *the present value of 1%*, abbreviated to the *PV of 1%*:

Definition 7.1 The PV of 1% over a swap is the present value of interest payments of 1% on the swap profile on the fixed side payment dates. It will be represented by the notation PV1%(swap). Except where otherwise stated it will be calculated using the midmarket zero curve.

It will be demonstrated that the error in using the midmarket rather than the bid or offer curve is generally very small; one zero curve can thus be used consistently, helpfully reducing the complexity of calculation.

(Note that there is a sleight of hand involved here. If it is necessary to obtain present value for a *single* future cashflow beyond one year, the discount rate which it will be possible to achieve will in general be *outside* the bid-offer zero coupon spread. This is discussed in Part VI. For a portfolio of cashflows, as is the case here, the bid-offer zero coupon spread should generally encompass the true discount rate.)

Given the rates quoted above, the midmarket zero curve is:

$$\text{Year 1} \quad 12.4850\%$$
$$\text{Year 2} \quad 11.9024\%$$

Try to work out these figures for yourself, rather than assuming that there are no errors in this book. While you are at it, you can work out the bid zero rates and the offer zero rates, both of which you will be using later on.

PV1%(Swap A) is thus the present value of a cashflow of:

Year 1   1% of £10 million
which is £100,000/1.12485 = £88,900.74.

PV1%(Swap B) is the present value of two cashflows:

Year 1   1% of £10 million
Year 2   1% of £10 million
which is $(£100,000/1.12485) + (£100,000/1.119024^2) =$ £168,759.25.

PV1%(Complex swap) is again the present value of two cashflows:

Year 1   1% of £20 million
Year 2   1% of £10 million

which is ($£200,000/1.12485$) + ($£100,000/1.119024^2$) = £257,659.99.

PV1%(Complex swap) equals the sum of the PVs of 1% for the simple swaps, as it should.

In order to equate present values we need merely observe that the present value of the fixed cashflows on a swap is the fixed rate times the PV of 1%. Thus representing the blended rate as b% gives:

b * PV1%(complex swap) =
(12.52 * PV1% (swap A)) + (11.97 * PV1% (swap B)).

Substituting the values calculated above gives

b * £257,659.99 = (12.52 * £88,900.74) + (11.97 * £168,759.25),

which gives

b = (3,133,085.49/257,659.99),
which is b = 12.1598.

Therefore, a blended rate of 12.16% on the complex swap will give the marketing division a small net positive position. There is, of course, nothing to stop the marketing officer quoting a higher rate if she thinks that the customer will accept it.

If Marketing enters into the complex swap at 12.16% it will be left with cashflow mismatches and hence interest rate risk. How big will the risk be? The cashflow mismatches are:

Year 1   ((12.16 - 12.52) * £10 million/100) +
           ((12.16 - 11.97) * £10 million/100)
Year 2   (12.16 - 11.97) * £10 million/100

These work out as:

Year 1   -£17,000
Year 2   £19,000

You can check that the net present value of these flows is £59.99. If the FRA rate for the period year 1 to year 2 becomes greater than 11.765%, then the net present value of these flows will become negative.

The marketing division could hedge against this possibility by buying a 12 v 24 FRA from the trading division on a contract amount of £17,000 at the current FRA rate of around 11.32%. (This FRA rate is worked out from the midmarket zero curve; you should check that you can duplicate the calculation.) Although this micro hedging would work satisfactorily on this deal, it would become cumbersome if Marketing entered into a large number of transactions. A more practical solution might be for the market maker in the trading division to run a risk management book for

Marketing; the risk inherent in the complex deals and their internal hedges would then be incorporated into the general risk management activity of trading. Sophisticated management accounting will be needed to ensure that such a system is not abused.

It will be assumed that this problem has been resolved one way or another, and that a complex swap can be priced by taking the blended rate of the simple swaps which hedge it and rounding the rate up or down as necessary to ensure that there is enough of a positive present value in the unmatched cashflows to allow Marketing to hedge any residual risk *in principle*. Since the residual risk will generally be small, this should not prove an onerous requirement.

The above example can be reworked to show that pricing complex swaps in this way is insensitive to whether you take the midmarket, bid, or offer zero curve.

Given the above 1- and 2-year swap rates, the bid and offer zero curves are:

	Bid	Offer
Year 1	12.45	12.52
Year 2	11.867	11.937

PV1%(Swap A, bid zero curve)   = £88,928.41
PV1%(Swap B, bid zero curve)   = £168,837.47
PV1%(Complex swap, bid zero curve)   = £257,765.88
The blended rate using bid present values is 12.1597%

PV1%(Swap A, offer zero curve)   = £88,873.09
PV1%(Swap B, offer zero curve)   = £168,682.24
PV1%(Complex swap, offer zero curve)   = £257,555.33
The blended rate using offer present values is 12.1598%

Thus, in this example, using the midmarket zero curve causes at worst an error in the fourth decimal place of the blended rate; for swaps of greater maturities the error may creep into the third decimal place, but it is unlikely that it will ever be material.

7.4 CAPITAL AND CREDIT COSTS

A theory of pricing complex swaps has been developed for an idealised world where there is no credit risk and where banks incur no opportunity cost for maintaining capital; it is now necessary to try to extend the theory to the real world with its credit risks and cost of capital. Shortage of space precludes the development of a complete model for pricing credit risk or capital cost, but an extended digression will give a summary of how to go about constructing such a model. Under the assumption that you can estimate your costs for credit and capital, it will then be possible to extend the pricing theory to incorporate these costs.

This section considers the calculation of the credit and capital cost for a single swap; the next section will discuss what alterations should be made to the calculation when the new swap adds to an existing portfolio of transactions with the counterparty.

Let us start with credit, remembering that we are looking at pricing from the viewpoint of a bank. In pricing a transaction there are two ways of looking at the cost of credit; you can calculate the *expected credit loss* or you can calculate the *opportunity cost of credit*. The expected credit loss is the average amount per deal you would expect to lose if you did a great number of such deals with similar counterparties; the opportunity cost of credit is the profit which you will have to give up on other deals as a result of doing this deal, through this deal using up the available credit line for the counterparty.

Ideally, a bank should have a profit centre which effectively trades credit risk. This credit division will allocate credit lines and charge the business areas a rent for creating credit exposure. Credit's profit or loss will be the total rent it receives minus the total credit losses. On a particular deal it should demand a rent greater than the expected credit loss, otherwise its expected income will be negative. Although few banks will explicitly organise themselves in this way, most would like to think that their internal cost allocations are set up to achieve the same ends. Accordingly, it makes sense to consider a bank organised as described above in discussing the incorporation of credit risk into swap pricing.

Assume that on swaps the marketing area will pay rent to the credit area and recoup it by paying less to or receiving more from the external counterparty. (For simple swaps dealt directly between Trading and external counterparties, Trading will pay the rent to the credit area.)

The calculation of the expected credit loss on a swap is discussed below, but you should remember that the actual cost of credit charged to the marketing area will be greater than this, and will be determined by the balance of the availability of profitable deals and the size of credit lines.

The expected credit loss on any financial transaction is:

*default probability * expected positive value * default %*

where:

- default probability is the probability that a counterparty will default on a transaction;
- expected positive value is the average mark-to-market value of the transaction from your viewpoint, taking any negative value as zero; and
- default % is 100 minus the expected eventual payout from the counterparty as a percentage.

By way of explanation of the short definitions above, counterparties tend not to default on deals where you owe them money, and so the average value of a defaulted deal must be calculated by averaging over the period that the deal is worth something to you. Given the legal structure under which most swaps are executed, defaults on a swap tend to be in the framework of a bankruptcy or reorganisation, at the end of which you would expect the counterparty to pay out some percentage on its liabilities. There are of course exceptions to this, such as the UK local authority swaps of the late 1980s.

You can evaluate the default probability and default % for classes of counterparty by examining published data or your own records. You may wish to use conservative estimates for these so as not to underestimate the expected loss.

In order to evaluate the expected positive value for transactions such as swaps, you will have to construct a model of expected future interest rate movements. Below is an outline of how to construct a simplified version of such a model; brackets indicate where a more sophisticated approach could be adopted.

The starting point is an analysis of past movements in interest rates. Suppose that the standard deviation of daily rate movements has been 10 basis points over the last three years. (For simplicity the model assumes parallel yield curve shifts only; a more sophisticated model would allow for yield curve rotation.) Projecting this movement into the future allows you to build a *binomial tree* for future rates. Since there are about 250 working days in a year, the annual standard deviation of rates should be:

10 basis points * (the squareroot of 250) = 1.6%.

(This assumes that rates will be normally distributed; this cannot be exact since, for example, rates will never be negative. A more sophisticated model might use a normal distribution for the logarithm of the interest rates to get round this problem. Such models will be used in Part V on options.)

Concentrating on the 2-year swap rate, you would expect that half the time the rate will go up over the year and half the time it will go down; in either case the average movement will equal the standard deviation of 1.6%. (Accuracy could be gained by adding the cumulative movement to the implied forward swap rate at each date, rather than adding it to the current 2-year rate.) This allows the construction of a binomial tree approximating the future distribution of 2-year swap rates at yearly intervals, with the probability of each value in brackets:

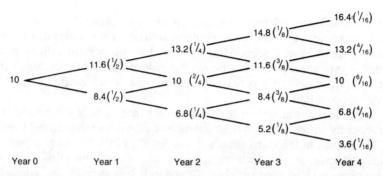

You may recognise the numerators of the probabilities as being the values found in Pascal's triangle. Although a discrete distribution has replaced a continuous one, matching standard deviations should have ensured that statistical properties are maintained to a good approximation. If more accuracy is needed for this reason you could take shorter time intervals; another possible reason for needing shorter intervals is discussed later.

What this tree is telling us is that at 3 years, for example, there is a $\frac{1}{8}$ chance that the 2-year swap rate will be 5.2%, a $\frac{3}{8}$ chance that it will be 8.4%, and so on. A 5-year swap where you are receiving fixed today at 10% on US$10 million will have a positive mark-to-market value in 3 years' time if the then prevailing *2-year* swap rate is less than 10%, since the swap will then have only 2 years left to run. Assuming that the yield curve will be flat, you can evaluate the mark-to-market value of the swap in 3 years, if the 2-year rate is then 5.2% or 8.4%, as:

Swap rate	Mark to market	Probability	Probability * value
5.2%	US$889,994	$\frac{1}{8}$	US$111,249
8.4%	US$283,765	$\frac{3}{8}$	US$106,412

The final column gives the mark to market value times the probability of that rate arising.

Since there are no other rates giving a positive mark to market, the expected positive value for this swap is the sum of the final column, which equals US$217,663. If you are told that the yield curve today is flat at 10%, then you can work out the expected positive value for a 4-year swap at 1 year, a 3-year swap at 2 years, and so on, as:

	Expected positive value US$	
Swap	*Future value*	*Present value*
5 year today	0	0
4 year in 1 year	262,628	238,753
3 year in 2 years	210,715	174,145
2 year in 3 years	217,663	163,533
1 year in 4 years	113,516	77,533
0 year in 5 years	0	0

The 0- and 5-year swaps are included to allow calculation of averages for each year below. Present valuing is done at the flat zero curve rate of 10%. (The Capital Asset Pricing Model would demand present valuing at an interest rate appropriate for the market risk of the cashflows. Since the probability of default is very small, discounting at the interbank rate is a valid approximation.)

Suppose that our historical survey shows that there is a 0.3% default probability within a year, a 0.3% chance of a default in the second year, a 0.4% chance in the third year, a 0.4% chance in the fourth year, and a 0.5% chance in the fifth year. Suppose further that this class of counterparty on average pays out 20% on its liabilities following a default. Then we can approximate the expected positive value during a year in present value terms as half the sum of the expected positive values at the start and end of the year, and the contribution to expected credit loss from a default in each year will be:

expected positive value $*$ default probability $*$ 80%.

All this is summarised in the following table:

Year	Expected positive value in present value terms	Default Probability	Contribution to credit loss
1	US$119,377	0.3%	US$287
2	US$206,450	0.3%	US$495
3	US$168,839	0.4%	US$540
4	US$120,533	0.4%	US$386
5	US$ 38,767	0.5%	US$155

The expected credit loss on the swap will be the sum of the contributions in each of the 5 years, which is US$1,863. Since PV1%(swap) equals US$379,079, it can be seen that the expected credit loss represents a cost of about 0.5 basis points per annum (bppa) on the swap rate.

Note that, particularly if the fixed and floating sides of the swap have different payment frequencies, it may be important to use intervals more frequent than annual in constructing the binomial tree, so as not to measure the risk always at the same point in an annual cycle; shorter intervals will always increase accuracy at the expense of increasing the complexity of the calculation.

It is not generally the case that a complex swap will have the same expected credit loss as the sum of the expected losses on its component simple swaps; this is because of the use of a blended rate in the complex swap and because in some part of the binomial tree one simple swap might have negative value while the complex swap has positive value. However, the difference will usually be small, and it will be practical to approximate the expected credit loss on the complex swap as the sum of the expected losses on the simple swaps. The same holds for the cost of capital discussed below.

This completes the digression relating to the calculation of the expected credit loss on a single swap. As explained above, the rent charged by Credit, which is the actual cost to Marketing, must be at least the expected credit loss. For example, for the swap above the rent might be 2 bppa.

This model assumes that credit is managed on the basis of comparing potential income with risk, but it must be noted that in practice many organisations simply refuse to deal swaps beyond a particular maturity with counterparties below a given credit standing. For example, a company might refuse to enter into a 5-year swap with any bank which was not rated at least 'double A' by one of the rating agencies. As the ratings of banks deteriorated in the late 1980s and early 1990s, this phenomenon contributed to a reduction of liquidity in the interbank swaps market, particularly at the longer maturities.

Having dealt with credit, it is time to turn to the cost of capital. Under the 'risk capital' proposals of the Bank for International Settlement (BIS), which have now been adopted by the banking regulators in the major countries of the Organisation for Economic Cooperation and Development (OECD), banks are obliged to hold capital in proportion to the *risk assets* represented by their credit risk from off-balance-sheet transactions. The formula for interest rate swaps (and also for FRAs) is:

risk assets = *weighting factor* *

(*positive mark-to-market value* + 0.5% of principal)

where

- weighting factor is   0 for counterparty OECD[1] sovereign;
  20% for counterparty OECD bank; and
  50% for other counterparties;

- positive mark-to-market value is the market-to-market value of the future cashflows of the swap if that is positive, and otherwise is 0; and

- the factor of 0.5% of principal is not included for swaps in their final year or for basis swaps.

The ratio of capital to risk assets is set by the regulators in each country, but must be a minimum of 8%.

The dependence of this formula on the mark-to-market value of the swap means that the capital required will change over the lifetime of the swap and that it will depend on prevailing interest rates. In order to predict, at the time when the swap is transacted, the expected future capital requirements, it is necessary to build a model similar to the model

---

[1]This and the following category include countries which have a special lending arrangement with the International Monetary Fund (IMF) as well as members of the OECD.

discussed for predicting expected credit losses. Since we have gone through the credit model it would involve unnecessary repetition to go through the details of a model for capital.

Assuming that capital represents a scarce resource to the bank, the bank's management will charge business units a fee for using capital. The exact fee will vary from bank to bank, but typically it will be between 10% and 20% per annum on capital employed. This will represent another cost to the trading or marketing division on each swap. There is no obvious best way of exacting this charge; here it will be assumed that at the time the deal is done a charge is agreed based on the predicted cost of capital over the life of the deal. It might be more likely in practice that the actual capital usage over the life of a deal would be the basis of the charge, or else that there would be no charge as such but each division would be evaluated on its ratio of income to capital employed.

From the formula above you can see that the cost of capital on identical deals will vary depending on the counterparty. If the counterparty is an OECD sovereign, then the cost of capital will be zero; if it is an OECD bank then the cost of capital will be only 40% of the cost of capital on an identical deal with a corporate counterparty. For example, if a swap with a corporate counterparty would have cost of capital 1.5 bppa on the swap notional principal, then the same swap with an OECD bank counterparty would have cost of capital 0.6 bppa.

All the machinery is now in place to look at the pricing of an individual swap in the presence of capital and credit costs; remember that considerations of portfolio effects on the cost of capital and credit are being left to the next section. Let us refine our bank's organisation by adding a credit division, which trades credit risk, and a management account to which all business units pay rent for their use of capital. The trading division will now quote a bid-offer swap rate appropriate for a prime bank counterparty. Such a bid-offer rate incorporates a particular cost of credit and a cost of capital. If the marketing division enters into a swap with an outside counterparty, then Trading will deal an internal swap with Marketing at a rate *inside* the original bid-offer spread by the cost of capital and credit for a bank counterparty; Marketing will pay the cost of credit for the external deal to the credit division and the cost of capital to the management account, and will ensure it is compensated for these costs by the rate it deals at externally.

This can be illustrated by returning to the example in section 7.3, where Marketing quotes on receiving fixed on a 2-year swap with profile US$20 million from value to year 1, and US$10 million from year 1 to year 2. Assume that the 1- and 2-year swap rates quoted by Trading incorporate cost of capital 0.4 bppa and credit cost 0.2 bppa, and that the external counterparty is a company, so that the cost of capital will be 1 bppa; assume further that the credit division will charge a rent of 1.5 bppa for use of the credit line. Then the original rates quoted of:

1 year 12.52%
2 years 11.97%

will be transformed into swap rates between Trading and Marketing of 12.514% and 11.964%. The blended rate calculated as before is 12.1538%. Marketing has to pay 1 bppa to the management account and 1.5 bppa to the credit division, so it will have to receive at least 12.1788% from the external counterparty to break even. Since there is a small residual risk and since swap rates are usually quoted as whole or half basis points, Marketing should quote a minimum rate of 12.18% on this swap.

7.5 PORTFOLIO EFFECTS ON CAPITAL AND CREDIT COSTS

In many jurisdictions, if a company goes into some form of receivership or liquidation the receiver or liquidator is entitled to repudiate unprofitable contracts. In the case of swaps this would mean, for example, that if a bank has two swaps with a particular counterparty, of which one has a current market value of plus £1 million and the other has a current market value of minus £1 million, then if the counterparty goes into liquidation the bank stands to lose £1 million, despite its net position being zero.

Legislative moves are under way in various countries to rectify what appears to be an inequity and to prevent such 'cherry picking' by liquidators in the case of financial contracts; the liquidator would have to decide to repudiate all of the financial contracts with a particular counterparty or none.

If such legislation is adopted, then the immediate credit risk on a portfolio of swaps with a particular counterparty will become the net total of the market values of the individual swaps. The future credit risk will in general be greater than this, and will have to be calculated by running the model of the previous section for the whole portfolio simultaneously. Being able to treat all deals with a single counterparty as a single credit exposure is referred to as *netting of credit risk*.

When you price the credit risk on a new swap with an existing counterparty, it will be necessary to calculate the credit risk on the portfolio of transactions with that counterparty with and without the new swap; the difference will be the marginal credit risk of the new swap. The complication of this process should not be underestimated, especially since other types of financial contract, including, for example, foreign exchange transactions, should be included in the netting.

Netting will be probably be relatively unimportant between banks and corporate and governmental counterparties, where swaps will tend to be either all pay fixed or all receive fixed, thus minimising the net reduction of risk. (This picture may change if contracts such as foreign exchange can be included in netting.) Since between banks there tend to be large numbers of pay and receive fixed swaps on both sides, it is in the interbank market that netting should cause the largest reduction of risk and hence of cost.

Even without legislation allowing netting, there is a portfolio effect in credit risk. To see this, remember that the model developed in the last section took a worst future case positive market value as the basis for the credit risk on a swap. If you have a portfolio of pay fixed and receive fixed swaps in the same currency, interest rates cannot simultaneously go up and down so as to make all swaps have their worst case value. It is thus possible to estimate the credit risk on a portfolio of swaps within a currency with a particular counterparty as being the greater of:

- the sum of the risks on the individual pay-fixed swaps; and
- the sum of the risks on the individual receive-fixed swaps.

(A more sophisticated analysis would note that different swaps have their projected worst cases on different future dates, and would further reduce the portfolio risk by basing it on the worst case over all future dates.)

This portfolio model can again be used to price the credit risk on new swaps as the difference in the portfolio risk with and without that swap; since only swaps are involved the potential complexity of the calculation is reduced. Again, interbank transactions would be the major beneficiary from the potential reduction in credit risk.

As far as the cost of capital is concerned, the BIS allows offsetting positive and negative mark-to-market values only for transactions 'netted through novation'. Novation under the BIS definition consists of netting all cashflows in the same currency on the same day, and thus has a very restricted application to portfolios of swaps. It is likely that in time the BIS will recognise a more general definition of netting in calculating the risk assets for swaps, and at that stage it will be necessary to extend the method of calculating the cost of capital for a proposed transaction in the same way as discussed above for the cost of credit. Again the major effect is likely to be on interbank swaps.

Netting would greatly complicate the management of a portfolio of swaps; it would necessitate central recording of all deals between all branches of an organisation and all branches of its counterparties, the maintenance of current documentation for all such deals, and the creation of the systems capacity to analyse and report credit risk and capital costs across all deals for each counterparty for every combination of jurisdiction and documentation. Further discussion of such complications is beyond the scope of this book.

7.6 OPERATIONAL COSTS

The operational cost involved in managing off-balance-sheet transactions is not insignificant. If the average cost of making payments and resetting the floating rates on a swap is, say, £100 per year, then a complex swap involving, say, five simple swaps may have a management cost of £600 per year. (This figure comes from the five internal swaps and one external swap.) A simple swap involving monthly Libor may also have operational costs of several hundred pounds per year because of the large numbers of rate resets and payments. These costs may not be immaterial in terms of basis points per annum if the notional principals involved are small.

There may be scope for increasing the automation of processing in order to reduce costs; alternatively, the amount of processing could be reduced by recording the effect of internal transactions only as additional fields on external swaps, and analysing the income transfer through management accounting reports.

To the expense of managing the swaps it may be necessary to add legal expenses for negotiating a complex agreement and the expense of additional processing controls; someone will have to pay the incremental cost. The logical area to pay is Marketing, since it can decide whether or not to enter into the external swap. Breaking out the costs which should be allocated to Marketing may be a difficult management accounting exercise, but it is important that the marketing officers should understand the cost implications of their transactions if expected profitability is actually to be delivered.

SUMMARY

The basic idea of this chapter has been that the starting point for pricing a complex swap should be the blended rate of the simple swaps which would hedge it. Care has to be taken to use the correct bid or offer rate for each simple swap. Since the fixed rate is independent of the Libor side, the blended rate is simply the single rate which gives the same present value of fixed interest as the sum of the hedging swaps. It may be necessary to allow a margin for the additional risk arising from the timing difference of the cashflows of the swap and of its hedges. The rate thus calculated then has to be adjusted for the cost of capital and credit; these can be estimated using a model which averages costs over possible future levels of interest rates. Portfolio effects should also be taken into account in calculating credit costs. In all of this, a powerful calculation tool is to work out the present value of a 1% interest flow over the swap profile.

CHAPTER 8

Pricing complex interest rate swaps: practice

As explained at the start of Chapter 7, this chapter will concentrate on working through pricing examples. Section 8.1 looks at interpolating the yield curve to price a 4½-year bullet swap. The technique developed here will allow you to calculate a rate for any simple swap with irregular fixed-side payments. The next two sections look at a deferred and an amortising swap, and sections 8.4 and 8.5 complete the examples based on the methods of Chapter 7 by looking at a swap with a *rollercoaster* profile and by showing how the pricing theory can convert swap rates between any bases and frequencies. A final section deals with swaps incorporating a yield adjustment.

8.1 SHORT PERIOD

This section uses midmarket rates and ignores the cost of capital and credit; the complications of spreads and of capital and credit costs will be introduced gradually later in the chapter.

Suppose that the yield curve for swaps paying annually, and hence also the zero curve, is flat at 11%, and you are asked to price a 4½-year swap with fixed-side payment dates at 0.5, 1.5, 2.5, 3.5, and 4.5 years. (It is the normal convention in the swap market, that if the payment frequency does not exactly divide the swap tenor, then the short calculation period should come at the beginning; of course, it is possible to have any calculation periods which both counterparties agree.)

Result 7.5 demonstrated that the present value of the grossed-up fixed-side payments of a swap was zero. Since it is clear that the rate for this swap should be independent of the notional principal, it will simplify the calculation to assume a notional principal of 100. Representing the fixed rate to be determined by f % gives the grossed-up fixed payments as:

Year 0	-100
Year 0.5	$(f * 0.5) + 100 - 100$
Year 1.5	$f + 100 - 100$
Year 2.5	$f + 100 - 100$
Year 3.5	$f + 100 - 100$
Year 4.5	$f + 100$

On the intermediate dates the plus and minus 100s cancel to give net flows:

Year 0	-100
Year 0.5	$f * 0.5$
Year 1.5	f
Year 2.5	f
Year 3.5	f
Year 4.5	$f + 100$

which has present value

$$-100 + (f * \text{PV1\%(swap)}) + (100/1.11^{4.5})$$

which must equal zero.

The last of these terms equals 62.52398, so that

$$f * \text{PV1\%(swap)} = 37.47602.$$

Since the yield curve is flat at 11%, PV1%(swap) is 3.41929. (Check this yourself to make sure that you can repeat the calculation.) Thus f must equal 37.47602 over 3.41929, which is 10.9602. The swap rate for a $4\frac{1}{2}$-year swap is thus 10.9602%, not 11%, despite the yield curve being flat.

You can obtain this result by a different route as follows: The zero curve is flat at 11% and so a 6-month swap must have a fixed rate equal to 6-month Libor, which is 10.7131%; also a 4-year swap starting in 6 months' time and having annual fixed payments must have a fixed rate of 11%. It is clear that:

PV1%(original swap) = PV1%(6-month swap) +
                      PV1%(deferred 4-year swap).

Since PV1%(6-month swap) equals $(0.5/1.11^{0.5})$, which equals 0.4746, PV1%(deferred 4-year swap) must equal

$$3.4193 - 0.4746 = 2.9447.$$

(You should check this by calculating the PV of 1% directly.)

Since you are paying 10.9602% in the first 6 months instead of 10.7131%, you are paying extra in present value terms:

$$(10.9602 - 10.7131) * \text{PV1\%(6-month swap)} = 0.1173.$$

Over the deferred 4 years you are paying 10.9602% instead of 11%, which gives a present value of

$(11 - 10.9602) * \text{PV}1\%(\text{deferred swap}) = 0.1172.$

You can see that, within a rounding error, what you lose by paying too high a rate in the first 6 months you gain back by paying too low a rate in the last 4 years. This shows that you could have derived $f\%$ from the equation:

$$(f - 10.7131) * \text{PV}1\%(\text{6-month swap}) =$$
$$(11 - f) * \text{PV}1\%(\text{deferred swap}).$$

This equation basically states that you should choose $f\%$ so that the loss in the 6 months does equal the gain in the 4 years. When the yield curve is flat, it is simple to determine the price of the deferred swap, and this is a quick way of working out f. When the yield curve is not flat, this method can still give a useful approximation.

If you practise manipulating present values of 1% in simple examples such as this, you will gain confidence in tackling more complex pricing exercises. You could try repeating this example with a bid-offer spread of, say, 10.95%/11.05% along the yield curve, and pricing the bid and offer on the $4\frac{1}{2}$-year swap. You should compare the two methods derived above to ensure that they give the same answer, remembering when using the first method to discount at the bid side of the zero curve to calculate the bid rate and at the offer side of the zero curve to calculate the offer rate.

The technique derived here will work for any simple swap with irregular payments. However, it should be recognised that the calculation assumed that all discounting could be done at the same side of the yield curve. This is a reasonable assumption in practice for swaps which have regular payments with a short first period, but if the payment days are consistently irregular, or if there is a short last period, then obtaining an accurate price would involve a more sophisticated calculation. Such swaps will not be considered further in this book.

As a final observation on the material in this section, this is the only type of rate which is derived by including the swap principal in the present value calculation; from here on results will be obtained purely by manipulating PVs of 1%.

8.2 DEFERRED SWAPS

The section incorporates a bid-offer spread on the yield curve. Credit and capital costs are initially assumed zero; later on, the effect of these being non zero is considered. Suppose that the yield curve for swaps paying annually is as follows:

| | <- - Yield curve - -> | | | Zero curve |
	Bid	Offer	Mid	Midmarket
Year 1	8.50	8.60	8.55	8.550
Year 2	8.70	8.78	8.74	8.748
Year 3	8.80	8.88	8.84	8.855
Year 4	8.90	8.98	8.94	8.965
Year 5	9.00	9.08	9.04	9.081

A customer asks the bank at what rate it will pay fixed on a 4-year swap 1 year deferred, on a notional principal of 100 with annual fixed payments.

As before, the marketing division will construct a hedge for the swap by entering into simple swaps with the trading division such that the sum of the profiles of the simple swaps equals the profile of the external swap. In this case the profile of the external swap is:

$$\begin{array}{ll} \text{Year 0-1} & 0 \\ \text{Year 1-5} & 100. \end{array}$$

This time it is not so obvious what the simple swaps should be, so it is best to try the usual trick of matching cashflows at the furthest maturity and hoping that the problem will then become simpler. Since Marketing pays fixed out to 5 years, it must receive on a 5-year simple swap with a notional principal of 100 with annual fixed payments. This simple swap matches the floating side payments in years 2, 3, 4, and 5, but creates an extra floating side payment of Libor on a principal of 100 in year 1. This means that Marketing must also pay on a simple swap with notional principal 100, annual fixed interest, and maturity 1 year. Sure enough, the sum of the profiles of these two simple swaps (remembering to *subtract* the pay fixed principal) is the profile of the external swap, and we have constructed the required hedge. It only remains to find the blended rate, which will be the maximum fixed rate which Marketing can afford to pay.

The two simple swaps are:

1 year   Marketing pays fixed annually on 100 at 8.60%; and
5 year   Marketing receives fixed annually on 100 at 9.00%.

For ease of reference, call the 1-year swap the 'short swap', the 5-year swap the 'long swap', and the external swap the 'deferred swap'. This gives:

PV1%(short swap)   is 0.9212 and
PV1%(long swap)   is 3.8990 and hence, by subtraction,
PV1%(deferred swap) is 2.9778.

Note that PV1% on the deferred swap can be calculated by subtraction because the long swap has a fixed-side payment date on the value date of the deferred swap and all its other fixed-side payments coincide with the deferred swap; the short swap must have its final payments on the value date of the deferred swap because that is also the maturity date of the 1-year swap. In the generalisation of the pricing of deferred swaps, this matching of payment dates will be a critical feature.

Assume that Marketing enters into the external swap at the breakeven blended rate b%. Between the external and internal swaps the floating cashflows vanish, and therefore the present value of the fixed cashflows must be zero, thus giving:

$$(9 * PV1\%(\text{long swap})) - (8.6 * PV1\%(\text{short swap})) = b * PV1\%(\text{deferred swap}).$$

Alternatively, recall Result 7.4 that the grossed-up fixed side payments and receipts on the external swap and the two internal swaps must have present value zero. These cashflows are:

	Short swap	Long swap	Deferred swap
Year 0	100	-100	
Year 1	-100 - 8.6	9	100
Year 2		9	-b
Year 3		9	-b
Year 4		9	-b
Year 5		100 + 9	-100 - b

The plus and minus 100s cancel out, leaving net present value:

$(-8.6 * PV1\%(\text{short swap}))$
$+(9 * PV1\%(\text{long swap}))$
$-(b * PV1\%(\text{deferred swap}));$

since these sum to zero we recover the result above.

Solving the equality gives b equals:

$$\frac{(9 * PV1\%(\text{long swap})) - (8.6 * PV1\%(\text{short swap}))}{PV1\%(\text{deferred swap})}$$

which gives

$$b = ((9 * 3.8990) - (8.6 * 0.9212))/2.9778$$

which is 9.1237.

Thus the breakeven rate on the external swap is 9.1237%. Check this by looking at Marketing's residual cashflows, which are:

	Cashflow	Present value
Year 1	0.4	0.3685
Year 2	-0.1237	-0.1046
Year 3	-0.1237	-0.0959
Year 4	-0.1237	-0.0877
Year 5	-0.1237	-0.0801
Net present value		0.0002

Within rounding error, the present values match exactly. It would be possible to go on to examine the risk in the cashflow mismatch, and to estimate what margin Marketing should charge for this risk; however, it should be clear that the residual risk should be small, and it could, in principle, be hedged if Marketing simply rounds down the rate to an exact number of basis points and pays 9.12%.

This example worked out the rate for a particular deferred swap, but if you examine what we have done you will see that the same process could be used to calculate the breakeven rate on any deferred bullet swap.

The steps from Marketing's viewpoint are:

(a)   If the deferred swap is pay fixed:

    1   Construct a simple receive fixed *long swap* to the same maturity as the deferred swap and with the same fixed side payment dates; the value date of the deferred swap should also be a fixed-side payment date of the long swap. The rate you will receive at will be the *long bid rate*, since Trading is paying fixed.

    2   Construct a simple pay fixed *short swap* to the value date of the deferred swap; the payment dates of the short swap should coincide with the payment dates of the long swap. The rate you will pay at will be the *short offer rate*, since Trading receives fixed.

    3   The blended rate $b\%$ on the deferred swap will be:

$$\frac{(\text{long bid} * \text{PV1\%(long swap)}) - (\text{short offer} * \text{PV1\%(short swap)})}{\text{PV1\%(deferred swap)}.}$$

(b)   If the deferred swap is receive fixed:

    1   Construct a simple pay fixed long swap to the same maturity as the deferred swap and with the same fixed side payment dates; the value date of the deferred swap should also be a fixed-side payment date of the long swap. The rate you will pay at will be the *long offer rate*, since Trading is receiving fixed.

    2   Construct a simple receive fixed short swap to the value date of the deferred swap; the payment dates of the short swap should coincide with the payment dates of the long swap. The rate you will receive at will be the *short bid rate*, since Trading pays fixed.

    3   The blended rate $b\%$ on the deferred swap will be:

$$\frac{(\text{long offer} * \text{PV1\%(long swap)}) - (\text{short bid} * \text{PV1\%(short swap)})}{\text{PV1\%(deferred swap)}.}$$

You can test these two formulae by checking that you derive the same pay fixed blended rate as was derived above, and by deriving the corresponding blended rate for the external swap being receive fixed. You should get a receive rate of 9.2594%. Note that this demonstrates that the bid-offer spread on the deferred swap is wider than on the long swap; this is a general phenomenon for deferred swaps and can lead to extremely wide bid-offer spreads for short swaps deferred for several years.

So far, the costs of credit and capital have been ignored. The problem in including them is that you can end up double counting the risk. Consider a deferred pay fixed swap; you will price this from a long bid rate and a short offer rate. If the bid-offer spread is widened to include the cost of credit and capital then you will be counting these costs twice for the period of the short swap.

There is no perfect answer to this problem, short of developing a model which will price the risk on the deferred swap from first principles. If you want to work from a table of costs for simple swaps along the yield curve, then you will have to make some approximation. The most sensible approach seems to be:

(a) If the deferred swap is pay fixed:
    1. Include the cost of credit and capital appropriate to the external counterparty in the long bid rate.
    2. Exclude all cost of credit and capital from the short offer rate.
(b) If the deferred swap is receive fixed:
    1. Include the cost of credit and capital appropriate to the external counterparty in the long offer rate.
    2. Exclude all cost of credit and capital from the short bid rate.

For example, if the market-maker quotes his 5-year bid at 8.50% and his 2-year offer at 9.00%, both based on a cost of capital of 1 bppa and a cost of credit of 0.5 bppa, and for the external counterparty the cost of capital is 2.5 bppa and the cost of credit is 2 bppa, then the 3-year pay fixed swap deferred 2 years will be priced off:

a long bid rate of 8.47% (incorporating external costs); and
a short offer rate of 8.985% (incorporating no costs).

This approach is conservative, in that it ignores the possibility of the deferred swap having a lower risk than the long swap; it should be clear that its risk cannot be higher.

8.3 AMORTISING SWAPS

This section uses the same yield curve as in the last section, but introduces a cost of capital and a cost of credit. Assume that the market maker has quoted his prices on the following cost of capital and credit expressed in bppa:

	Capital	Credit
Year 1	0.2	0.1
Year 2	0.3	0.1
Year 3	0.3	0.1
Year 4	0.3	0.2
Year 5	0.4	0.2

It is assumed here that the costs for pay and receive fixed swaps are the same; in practice there may be a small difference.

The marketing division is now asked to receive fixed from a corporate customer on a swap with annual payments with the following amortising swap profile:

Year 0	500
Year 1	400
Year 2	300
Year 3	200
Year 4	100
Year 5	0.

Note that the profile shows the notional principal at the start of and throughout each period. For example, the notional principal throughout the first year is 500.

You are told that the cost of credit for this customer is 0.9 bppa for swaps up to 2 years and 2.0 bppa for longer swaps; you can deduce the cost of capital for external simple swaps as being the cost of capital quoted above divided by 20 and multiplied by 50.

This lets us construct an offer side yield curve as follows:

	Market-maker quote	Bank counterparty capital and credit cost	Corporate capital and credit cost	Breakeven external quote
Year 1	8.60	0.003	0.014	8.611
Year 2	8.78	0.004	0.017	8.793
Year 3	8.88	0.004	0.028	8.904
Year 4	8.98	0.005	0.028	9.003
Year 5	9.08	0.006	0.030	9.104

We can now go on to construct the set of simple swaps which will have the same total profile as the amortising swap. As before, it is easiest to start by fitting a simple swap to the final maturity of the amortising swap.

The 5-year simple swap which is required has a principal of 100 with Marketing paying fixed at 9.08%; however, the analysis above shows that we should treat this swap as having a fixed rate of 9.104% in calculating the blended rate on the external swap, in order to take account of the capital and credit costs. (As discussed in section 7.4, there is an implicit conservative assumption that the credit and capital costs on a complex swap are the sum of the costs on the component simple swaps.)

Net of this 5-year simple swap, the amortising swap has profile:

Year 0	400
Year 1	300
Year 2	200
Year 3	100
Year 4	0
Year 5	0.

Repeating this process to fit the residual 4-year, 3-year, 2-year, and 1-year profiles, and remembering to use the midmarket zero curve to generate the PVs of 1%, gives the following simple swaps:

	Principal	Effective rate	PV1%	PV1% * rate
1 year	100	8.611	0.9212	7.9325
2 years	100	8.793	1.7668	15.5355
3 years	100	8.904	2.5421	22.6349
4 years	100	9.003	3.2514	29.2724
5 years	100	9.104	3.8990	35.4965
			12.3805	110.8718

PV1%(amortising swap) = 1% of:

$(500/1.08550^1)$ +
$(400/1.08748^2)$ +
$(300/1.08855^3)$ +
$(200/1.08965^4)$ +
$(100/1.09081^5)$

which equals 12.3805 as above.

The blended rate is thus calculated as the present value of the fixed payments on the simple swaps, which equals 110.8718, divided by PV1%(amortising swap), which is 12.3805. This give a breakeven blended rate of 8.9554%. As usual, Marketing would round this up to 8.96% or higher; as a separate exercise you can examine the risk on the residual cashflows if Marketing does receive at 8.96%.

Following through the process above will enable you to price any amortising swap. The key is to generate the simple swaps by matching the final maturity first and then working backwards.

8.4 ROLLERCOASTERS

This section uses the same yield curve and costs of credit and capital as section 8.3. Since the adjusted bid side yield curve will be needed, it is constructed below.

	Market-maker quote	Bank counterparty capital and credit cost	Corporate capital and credit cost	Breakeven external quote
Year 1	8.50	0.003	0.014	8.489
Year 2	8.70	0.004	0.017	8.687
Year 3	8.80	0.004	0.028	8.776
Year 4	8.90	0.005	0.028	8.877
Year 5	9.00	0.006	0.030	8.976

A swap profile which goes up as well as down is sometimes referred to as a rollercoaster. We shall price such a swap where the marketing division pays fixed annually on the following profile:

Year 0	100
Year 1	300
Year 2	100
Year 3	300
Year 4	200
Year 5	0.

The first step should be to construct a set of simple swaps with the same profile. However, because the profile goes up as well as down, Marketing will need to pay fixed on some simple swaps and receive fixed on others. The process can be simplified by introducing the intermediate step of finding a set of simple swaps and deferred simple swaps which will sum to the same profile as the rollercoaster. The deferred swaps can then be priced by the method derived earlier, and a blended rate for the external swap calculated by the usual route of matching present values.

(There is an equivalent method of pricing using only simple swaps; again this involves matching the furthest maturity first, and then working backwards. The advantage of the method used here is that the individual swaps used in pricing are all pay fixed or all receive fixed, so that it is easier to check the calculation for reasonableness.)

For ease of reference the term 'swapsicle' will be used to refer to a simple swap or a deferred simple swap. The first step then becomes splitting the swap profile into swapsicles. The process is to select the latest ending, earliest starting, largest swapsicle which will fit the profile, and then to subtract this swapsicle from the profile, and to select the next swapsicle, and so on, until the residual profile becomes zero.

For our swap, the first swapsicle has latest end date 5 years, earliest start date today, and largest notional principal 100. Subtracting this from the profile gives residual profile:

Year 0	0
Year 1	200
Year 2	0
Year 3	200
Year 4	100
Year 5	0.

The second swapsicle has latest end date 5 years, earliest start date 3 years, and largest principal 100, Subtracting this gives residual profile:

Year 0	0
Year 1	200
Year 2	0
Year 3	100
Year 4	0
Year 5	0.

The third swapsicle thus has maturity year 4, value year 3, and principal 100, leaving residual profile:

Year 0	0
Year 1	200
Year 2	0
Year 3	0
Year 4	0
Year 5	0.

Thus the fourth and final swapsicle has value year 1, maturity year 2, and principal 200; the residual profile is now flat at 0.

This process is represented in Figure 8.1.

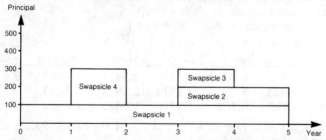

Figure 8.1 Swapsicle breakdown of rollercoaster swap profile.

We now have to find bid rates and the PV of 1% on all four swapsicles. Below is the calculation of the bid rate for the three deferred swaps using the treatment of capital and credit costs recommended at the end of section 8.2 above.

Swapsicle	Long bid	Short offer	< - - - Long	PV of 1% Short	- - -> Deferred	Deferred bid
2	8.976	8.876	3.8990	2.5421	1.3569	9.1633
3	8.877	8.876	3.2514	2.5421	0.7093	8.8806
4	8.687	8.597	3.5336	1.8425	1.6912	8.7845

To complete the picture, swapsicle 1 has bid rate 8.976% and PV of 1% of 3.8890. PV1%(external swap) is 1% of:

$(100/1.08550^1)$ +
$(300/1.08748^2)$ +
$(100/1.08855^3)$ +
$(300/1.08965^4)$ +
$(200/1.09081^5)$

which equals 7.6563.

Equating present values gives the blended rate b% from:

$$7.6563 * b = (3.8990 * 8.9760) +$$
$$(1.3569 * 9.1633) +$$
$$(0.7093 * 8.8806) +$$
$$(1.6912 * 8.7845)$$

which gives

$b = 68.4967/7.6563 = 8.9464\%.$

As usual, a careful analysis of Marketing's residual cashflows will let you determine the residual risk, and allow you to decide whether the breakeven rate is 8.945% or 8.94%.

You can test your understanding of the above process by seeing if you can calculate the corresponding blended offer rate of 9.2495% before looking at the working below. You can see how wide the bid-offer spread can become on such a swap.

The working on the blended offer rate is:

Swapsicle	Long offer	Short bid	< - - - - Long	PV of 1% Short	- - -> Deferred	Deferred offer
2	9.104	8.804	3.8990	2.5421	1.3569	9.6660
3	9.003	8.804	3.2514	2.5421	0.7093	9.7162
4	8.793	8.503	3.5336	1.8425	1.6912	9.1084

Swapsicle 1 has offer rate 9.104% and PV of 1% of 3.8890. As before, PV1%(external swap) is 7.6563.

Equating present values allows calculation of the blended rate b% from:

$$7.6563 * b = (3.8890 * 9.1040) +$$
$$(1.3569 * 9.6660) +$$
$$(0.7093 * 9.7162) +$$
$$(1.6912 * 9.1084)$$

which gives

$b = 70.8171/7.6563 = 9.2495\%.$

8.5 DIFFERENT BASES AND FREQUENCIES

You have now seen how to price the main varieties of complex swap, always working with complex swaps which pay annually. The technique developed above of matching present values of the fixed cashflows of two swaps extends in a natural way to pricing swaps paying interest on any frequency; moreover the same methods will cope with different interest bases and exact day counts.

As a simple example, if the yield curve has midmarket rates for zero coupon rates and for swaps paying annually:

	Swap	Zero
Year 0		8.400
Year 1	8.55	8.550
Year 2	8.74	8.748

then what is the midpoint rate for a 2-year swap paying semiannually?

As usual, it is easiest to work with swaps with notional principal 100. PV1%(2-year annual swap) is 1% of:

$$(100/1.08550^1) + (100/1.08748^2)$$

which equals 1.7668.

For the semiannual swap we need the zero coupon rates at 0.5 and 1.5 years; it will be assumed that the best approximation to these rates will be achieved by straight line interpolation. This gives PV1%(2-year semiannual swap) as 1% of

$$(100 * 0.5/1.08475^{0.5}) +$$
$$(100 * 0.5/1.08550^1) +$$
$$(100 * 0.5/1.08649^{1.5}) +$$
$$(100 * 0.5/1.08748^2)$$

which equals 1.8050.

Since the 2-year annual swap rate is 8.74, the semiannual fixed rate $f\%$ can be calculated by equating present values:

$$(f * 1.8050) = (8.74 * 1.7668)$$

which gives semiannual rate 8.5550%.

If the semiannual swap rate is to be $f'\%$ quoted on an actual/360 basis, then, assuming each 6-month period is an exact half year, its PV1% will be multiplied by a factor of 365/360, to give 1.8301. This gives:

$$(f' * 1.8301) = (8.74 * 1.7668)$$

which gives semiannual rate 8.4377% on an actual/360 day basis.

Suppose that the actual 6-month periods in days are 181, 184, 182, and 184, and that the annual swap is quoted on an actual/365 fixed basis. Then PV1% for the annual swap becomes 1% of:

$$(100/1.08550^{365/365}) + (100.2740/1.08748^{731/365})$$

which equals 1.7689. Ignoring the correction of the interpolated zero coupon rates for the exact number of days, PV1% for the semiannual actual/360 swap becomes 1% of:

$$(100 * 0.50278/1.08475^{181/365}) +$$
$$(100 * 0.51111/1.08550^{365/365}) +$$
$$(100 * 0.50556/1.08649^{547/365}) +$$
$$(100 * 0.51111/1.08748^{731/365}) +$$

which equals 1.8323.

Recalculating f' gives:

$$(f' * 1.8323) = (8.74 * 1.7689)$$

which equals 8.4376. This is close to the original value, but in other cases using an exact day count might lead to a more material improvement in accuracy.

The same process of equating the present values of the fixed sides of the two swaps will cope with any combination of basis and frequency. This is the general method promised in Part I for converting interest rates from one basis and frequency to another.

8.6 YIELD ADJUSTMENTS

Yield adjustments have been left to last because they turn out to be messy; they do not fit into a nice theoretical framework because they involve combining on-balance-sheet and off-balance-sheet characteristics in the one instrument.

Suppose that a bank will pay 10% annually against 6-month Libor on a 5-year swap with a particular counterparty. If the counterparty instead wishes to receive 11% as a fixed rate on the swap, one way to achieve this is for it to pay the bank a sum of money on the swap value date, in compensation for which the bank will agree to make the extra 1% payment annually on the swap notional principal. Such an arrangement is known as a yield adjustment. A yield adjustment payment is usually made on the value day of the swap but it could also, by agreement, be made on any other date. For example, certain bonds pay slightly more than their principal at maturity, and if an investor uses a swap to hedge such a bond she may wish to make a yield adjustment payment at maturity to match her receipt on the bond.

It will be assumed below that the lump sum yield adjustment payment will be paid or received by the bank at the swap value or maturity date, giving four possibilities:

(a) Bank receives at value date.
(b) Bank pays at value date.
(c) Bank receives at maturity.
(d) Bank pays at maturity.

In cases (a) and (d) the bank receives money in before it pays out; both these cases correspond to the bank taking a deposit on which it will pay a fixed rate of interest. Cases (b) and (c) involve the bank paying out before it receives in; these correspond to a fixed loan.

The pricing of a yield adjustment should be basically the same as the pricing of an amortising fixed deposit or loan. For example, if the swap notional principal in the above case is £10 million, then the required additional annual payment is £100,000. If the bank would pay out £100,000 annually for 5 years against an initial payment of £380,000, then it would seem that this should be the minimum sum which the bank should accept as a yield adjustment. Conversely, if the bank would lend this counterparty £180,000 at the value date in return for five annual repayments of £50,000, then it would seem that the bank should be prepared to make a yield adjustment payment of £180,000 on the swap value date in exchange for reducing the swap fixed rate to 9.5%.

This approach is substantially correct, but there are two complications, depending on whether the yield adjustment represents a deposit or a loan. These are dealt with in the next paragraphs, after which there is a discussion of how the deposit or loan payment should be calculated.

The first complication is that the existence of a yield adjustment where the bank receives a lump sum at value or pays at maturity reduces the credit risk on the swap, and thus should reduce the cost of credit and capital incorporated into the swap pricing. For example, if changing the fixed rate to 11% reduces the cost of credit and capital from 2 basis points per annum to 1, then the bank should calculate its effective swap rate at 10.01% and should therefore require a yield adjustment to generate a change in rate of 0.99% rather than 1%. In the case above that would mean a reduction of the required initial payment from £380,000 to £376,200.

The second complication relates to yield adjustments where the bank makes an up-front payment or receives a payment at the swap maturity date. In either case, the bank is extending credit and incurring an opportunity cost of capital. Again the bank should price the yield adjustment basically as an amortising fixed loan, which should be the mirror image of an annuity. However, the pricing of a loan should incorporate a cost of credit and a cost of capital. The cost of credit should be slightly less for a loan grafted on to a swap as a yield adjustment than for a loan on its own; this is because some of the time the swap will be at a mark-to-market loss, offsetting the credit risk on the loan. A loan has a cost of capital, since under the BIS proposals a bank has to maintain capital for its loans as well as for its off-balance-sheet exposures. Just as the possibility of offsetting losses on the swap against the yield adjustment means that the cost of credit will be lower for a swap with a yield adjustment than for a swap and a separate loan, so too the cost of capital will be less for the combined instrument than for the swap and loan separately; again the effect is likely to be small. An extension of the models derived in section 7.4 will give the appropriate costs of credit and capital, although it is questionable whether the expense of constructing a more complex model would be justified by the improved accuracy.

A more material effect comes from an asymmetry between the risk-based-capital rules for on- and off-balance-sheet instruments. In both cases there is a 0% weighting factor for OECD sovereign counterparties and a 20% weighting factor for OECD banks, but for other counterparties the weighting is 100% for on-balance-sheet-products and 50% for off-balance-sheet products. This means, for example, that if a bank would lend to an 'other' counterparty at 70 bppa above its cost of funding, where the 70 bppa represents:

  credit cost 25 bppa;

  capital cost 40 bppa; and

  profit contribution 5 bppa,

then if the loan can be classified as 'off balance sheet' by being combined with a swap, the capital cost should drop from 40 bppa to 20 bppa, so that the bank should price the yield adjustment at only 50 bppa over its funding cost. This works only for 'other' counterparties; there is no corresponding effect for OECD banks and sovereigns. Note that the regulators do not seem to mind small isolated instances of this effect, but they are unlikely to approve large loans camouflaged as yield adjustments in order to reduce their cost of capital.

The pricing of an annuity or fixed loan starts with constructing a par yield curve for bullet deposits or loans. Let us work through loan pricing, since the calculation for an annuity is merely the calculation for a loan minus considerations of credit and capital. To use a definite example, let us price a fixed loan where the bank pays a lump sum at the swap value date and is repaid £50,000 annually for 5 years in the form of a reduction of the swap fixed rate, as in the example near the start of this section. The marketing officer should know the bank's funding cost for a 1-year deposit, a 2-year deposit, and so on, up to a 5-year deposit, all paying interest annually; call these f_1% up to f_5%. There should be a model or a table to give the cost of credit and capital for loans to this counterparty to each maturity; call these c_1% up to c_5%, and assume that these are adjusted for loans related to swap yield adjustments as discussed above. On top of this there should be a requirement for a profit contribution to each maturity; call this k_1% up to k_5%. The yield curve for pricing the loan should then be f_1% + c_1% + k_1% to year 1, up to f_5% + c_5% + k_5% to year 5; call these loan rates l_1% up to l_5%.

The analysis now follows closely the demonstration in section 6.2 that par bonds paying annual interest can duplicate any cashflow on annual dates. Start with the 5-year cashflow of £50,000. In order for this to be the repayment of the interest plus principal of the 5-year loan, we must have:

$$p_5 * (1 + (l_5/100)) = £50,000, \text{ giving}$$
$$p_5 = £50,000/(1 + (l_5/100)).$$

The contribution in each year of the interest from the 5-year loan to the annual cashflow is $l_5 p_5/100$. Subtract this from £50,000 to give the contribution to the 4-year cashflow of the interest plus principal on the 4-year loan. This gives:

$$p_4 = (£50,000 - (l_5 p_5/100))/(1 + (l_4/100)).$$

Continuing the process gives:

$$p_3 = (£50,000 - (l_5 p_5/100) - (l_4 p_4/100))/(1 + (l_3/100)).$$
$$p_2 = (£50,000 - (l_5 p_5/100) - (l_4 p_4/100) - (l_3 p_3/100))/(1 + (l_2/100)).$$
$$p_1 = (£50,000 - (l_5 p_5/100) - (l_4 p_4/100) - (l_3 p_3/100)$$
$$- (l_2 p_2/100))/(1 + (l_1/100)).$$

Summing p_1 up to p_5 gives the total up front yield adjustment payment.

For example, if the values of the variables are

	f	c	k	l
Year 1	9.5%	0.6%	0.03%	10.13%
Year 2	9.6%	0.7%	0.04%	10.34%
Year 3	9.7%	0.8%	0.05%	10.55%
Year 4	9.8%	0.8%	0.05%	10.65%
Year 5	9.9%	0.8%	0.05%	10.75%

then the values of the loan principals are

p_5	£45,146.73
p_4	£40,801.38
p_3	£36,907.63
p_2	£33,449.00
p_1	£30,372.29

giving a breakeven total principal of £186,677.03. Marketing can therefore pay any sum less than this as a lump sum yield adjustment payment on the swap value day.

A variation of this method will price any of the four cases of yield adjustment payments discussed at the beginning of this section.

SUMMARY

This chapter has applied the analysis of Chapter 7 to specific types of complex swap; care has been taken not to double count credit risk when pricing deferred-start swaps. The same analysis gives a general method for comparing interest rates in different frequencies and bases; two such rates are equivalent if the present value of the interest is the same. The treatment of yield adjustments requires consideration of the portfolio effect on the cost of capital and credit from mixing on- and off-balance-sheet components in the one instrument.

Self-study questions

Unless otherwise stated, all interest is quoted on an annual basis, and each month should be considered to be an exact twelfth of a year.

3.1 You enter into a single currency interest rate swap with XYZ plc on the following terms. The swap starts on 1 July 1992 and ends on 1 July 1997. Every 6 months you pay interest at 6-month Libor on FRF200 million, and every year XYZ plc pays interest at 10% on the same amount. Where payments are concurrent they are netted.

Describe the swap using standard market terminology.

Value date:

Termination date:

Notional principal:

Fixed payer:

Fixed interest rate:

Fixed payment frequency:

Floating payer:

Reference rate:

Floating payment frequency:

3.2 Consider the swap described in question 3.1; assume that Libor is set on the spot date.

Ignoring the possibility of weekends or holidays, on what day is Libor set for the first period of the swap? If 6-month Libor is set at 9% on that day, when and how much will be the first settlement of the swap?

If Libor is set at 11% for the second floating period, when and how much will be the second settlement of the swap?

3.3   A company can borrow floating rate funds in XEU at 6-month
      Libor plus 0.70%. Instead it issues at par a 5-year bond for
      XEU50 million, paying interest at 11% annually, at a time when
      a market maker quotes 10.33%/10.43% for a 5-year XEU swap
      paying annually.

      If the company wishes to hedge the interest rate risk of the bond,
      what swap will it enter into and what will be the rate? What will
      be the company's net cashflows and what will be its residual
      risks? Assuming that XEU Libor is quoted on the same basis as
      the fixed side of the swap, how does the company's costs
      compare to the cost of raising floating debt?

      Apart from costs, why else might the company choose to raise
      funds by this method?

3.4   A company has budgeted dividend income from its American
      subsidiary in US$ millions as follows:

Year 1	1
Year 2	2
Year 3	1
Year 4	3
Year 5	2

      Assuming that the zero coupon and annual-payment swap yield
      curves are:

	Zero	Swap
Year 1	10	10
Year 2	10.210	10.2
Year 3	10.318	10.3
Year 4	10.430	10.4
Year 5	10.548	10.5

      what is the present value of the future dividends? What is the
      change in present value for a 10 basis point parallel shift in the
      zero coupon curve?

      How can the company protect itself against this risk using
      takings? How can it achieve an equivalent result using swaps?

      What swaps should the company enter into, in order to hedge its
      interest rate risk on the dividend cashstream?

3.5   A bank market maker quotes 7.21%/7.28% for a particular swap
      regardless of counterparty. A customer tells the marketing officer
      in the bank that she wants to pay fixed on the swap. If the
      marketing officer feels that he can make a spread of 1 basis point
      per annum (bppa) over the dealer's price, what rate should he
      quote to the customer?

3.6 A market maker quotes 10.31%/10.41% for a swap paying fixed annually against floating semiannually. He estimates that because 1-month Libor is relatively illiquid, he should charge a premium of 3bppa to pay or receive 1-month rather than 6-month Libor. What bid-offer spread should he quote on the same swap against 1-month Libor?

3.7 A customer requires a bank to pay fixed annually and receive floating on a swap with the following profile:

Year 0	100
Year 1	80
Year 2	60
Year 3	40
Year 4	0.

If a marketing officer is pricing this swap, what simple swaps should he use as a basis?

3.8 If 1-year Libor is 9%, and the midmarket yield curve for swaps paying fixed annually is:

2 years	8.8%
3 years	8.6%
4 years	8.5%

then, assuming that the midmarket rate for 1 year is Libor, what is the midmarket zero coupon curve?

3.9 Given the midmarket rates in question 3.8, if the 1-year swap bid rate equals Libor, and the swap bid rate is 4bppa below the midmarket rate for years 2 and 3 and 5bppa below the midmarket for year 4, how would you price the swap in question 3.7?

3.10 If the customer enters into the swap of question 3.9 at a rate of 8.56%, what is the difference in cashflows between the simple swaps entered into by the market maker and the blended swap entered into with the customer?

3.11 A dealer quotes an interbank swap bid-offer spread of 12.30%/12.37%; this incorporates a capital cost of 0.4bppa and a credit cost of 0.5bppa. What rates should a marketing officer quote to a corporate customer to earn a spread income of 1bppa, if the credit cost for the customer is 1.5bppa?

3.12 The midmarket yield curves are:

	Par rate	Zero coupon
Year 0.5	9.2	9.4116
Year 1	9.0	9.0
Year 2	8.8	8.7912
Year 3	8.6	8.5767
Year 4	8.5	8.4693

The 6-month par rate is Libor; the other par rates are given for swaps with annual fixed payments.

What would the midmarket rate be for a $3\frac{1}{2}$ year swap, with the first fixed-side period 6 months and then annual periods?

3.13 The interbank yield curve for swaps paying fixed annually is:

| | < - Yield curve - > | | | Zero curve |
	Bid	Offer	Mid	Midmarket
Year 1	8.50	8.60	8.55	8.550
Year 2	8.70	8.78	8.74	8.748
Year 3	8.80	8.88	8.84	8.855
Year 4	8.90	8.98	8.94	8.965
Year 5	9.00	9.08	9.04	9.081

The cost of capital on a 2-year interbank swap is 0.2bppa and on a 5-year interbank swap it is 0.5bppa; the cost of credit is 0.3bppa on the 2-year deal and 0.6bppa on the 5-year deal.

At what rate should a bank dealer receive fixed annually from another bank on a 3-year swap 2 years deferred?

If the corresponding credit costs for a corporate customer deal are 0.7bppa on the 2-year deal and 1.75bppa on the 5-year deal, then at what price should the bank receive fixed from the customer to have the same profitability as the interbank deal?

3.14 A swap has the following 'rollercoaster' profile:

Year 0	100
Year 1	200
Year 2	300
Year 3	150
Year 4	250
Year 5	250
Year 6	200
Year 7	150
Year 8	100
Year 9	0

How would you break the swap down into swapsicles in order to price it?

PART IV

SPREAD AND BASIS RISK

The discussion so far has focused on transactions with the banking system. It is also possible to use government bonds to manage risk, but this then introduces the *spread risk* that the riskfree and interbank yield curves will move relative to each other. The single chapter of Part IV looks at the use of government bonds in risk management and at the resultant spread risk.

A similar concept dealt with is *basis risk*, where two types of interest rates change more or less in step but can move closer or further apart; a typical example would be US dollar Libor and *commercial paper* rates. This is of particular importance to banks pricing transactions on non-Libor rates and to companies which fund through non-Libor instruments.

Since bonds are discussed extensively, an appendix at the end of Part IV deals with *duration* and *convexity*, which are risk measures commonly used in bond markets. The appendix demonstrates that duration and convexity give information about risk under parallel shifts of the zero curve only, and therefore they cannot fully substitute for the cash gaps methodology.

Bonds are described here only in as much detail as is necessary to explain spread risk. You should realise that bonds are affected by local variations, regulatory restrictions, and liquidity constraints to an even greater extent than most of the other instruments discussed in this book. You therefore must check and understand local market conditions and regulations before using bonds in risk management. In particular markets, there may be additional important issues of credit, liquidity, and pricing which are not covered in the material here.

CHAPTER 9

Spread and basis risk

Most of this chapter deals with the *spread risk* caused by the possibility of a movement of the interbank yield curve relative to the riskfree yield curve. Before discussing spread risk itself, it is necessary to show how government bonds can be used in risk management. The starting point is a brief discussion of practice in the bond markets. Following this it is possible to calculate a zero coupon curve using non-par bonds and to discuss how swap rates are quoted as a *spread* over the *yield-to-maturity* of the corresponding bond. If bonds are used in risk management they have to be funded, and section 9.4 therefore looks at *repurchase agreements*, which represent the most important funding mechanism; it turns out that a bond funded by a repurchase agreement has a similar risk to a swap. The machinery is then in place for section 9.5 to look at the risk of changes in the spread of the interbank curve over the riskfree curve. Section 9.6 completes the treatment of bonds in risk management by looking in more detail at the costs of managing risk through bonds.

Spread risk can be considered a particular type of *basis risk*, which is where the prices of two instruments which are nominally hedging each other can move independently; an example would be an FRA hedging a Eurodeposit future. The concept can be extended to a bank making markets between rates; for example, a bank may borrow US dollars at Libor and lend at a rate linked to *prime*. A final section examines the implications of basis risk.

9.1 BONDS AND ACCRUED INTEREST

This section briefly discusses bond markets and, in particular, explains the treatment of *accrued interest* in calculating the price of bonds.

The practice and theory of the world's various bond markets is a vast subject; luckily, for our purposes here, the following brief notes will suffice. Bonds are securities evidencing debt. They are issued by governments, supranational institutions, companies, and other organisations needing funding, and are bought by investors, speculators, and risk managers. They can be in any maturity up to about 40 years, with most non-government issues being 10 years or less; bonds of maturity one year or less tend to be described by some other name such as 'bills' or 'commercial paper' and to follow different pricing conventions. Because bonds carry a principal credit risk, the bond market is stratified by the credit quality of borrowers, with the weaker credits paying substantially higher rates to borrow funds. The pricing of a bond therefore depends both on the time value of money and on credit risk.

All the bonds dealt with here will be assumed to have fixed cashflows with no *embedded options*; that is, neither the issuer nor the holder will have the unilateral right to change the terms. Examples of embedded options would be where the issuer has the right at his discretion to redeem the bond before its final maturity, or where the holder of a bond has the right to convert his holding into a new bond at some future date if he then wishes to do so. Such options can have a major impact on the price of a bond. Part V will develop a theory for pricing options, although it will not look in detail at the options mentioned above.

Bonds will also be assumed to have bullet repayment of principal at maturity and to pay interest on a regular frequency; the treatment below could be extended in a natural way to cope with more complex instruments.

New bonds are issued and distributed to investors through the *primary market*; existing bonds are bought and sold in the *secondary market*. These are telephone markets in which the main participants are securities houses, banks, and investors. The quoted price of a bond is the *clean price*, which represents payment for the final principal flow and for interest accruing after the purchase date. This convention makes quoted prices more stable on a day-to-day basis and eases comparison between different bonds. When a bond is sold, the *dirty price*, which is the price actually paid, will be the clean price plus a payment for the accrued interest, calculated as explained below.

Accrued interest is the interest which would be payable on a loan or bond on a particular day if that were a payment date. For example, if a bond pays interest annually on £10 million at 10%, then the accrued interest 3 months after a payment date would be £10 million $* 10 * 0.25/100$, which equals £250,000. (In some markets a slightly different interest basis is used to calculate accrued interest compared with calculating interest on the bond itself.)

Note that the dirty price is the true market value of a bond, and it will be greater than the quoted clean price except when purchase takes place on an interest payment date. Marking a bond to market consists simply of adding the accrued interest to the published price.

Conventionally, a bond price is quoted as a price per 100 currency units of face value. For example, if a bond with a face value of FRF10 million has a clean price of FRF9.87 million, it will be quoted as 98.700. If the bond has a 9% coupon and it is 4 months since the last interest payment, then the accrued interest will be 3%, and the value of the bond will be the dirty price of 101.700.

The bid-offer spread in a government bond price is assumed below to be immaterial compared to the other costs associated with the use of bonds in risk management. In practice, you should take this spread into account when analysing the costs of using bonds.

9.2 CALCULATING THE ZERO CURVE
FROM NON-PAR BONDS

In Part I a general method was derived for calculating the zero coupon curve from the par yield curve. This was appropriate for use where the par curve was determined by Libor and swap rates, but for government bonds there may well be no bond trading at par in a particular maturity. Moreover, there may be differences in liquidity between different bonds trading to the same maturity, and, as discussed in Part I, it then becomes appropriate to use the bond with the lowest bid-offer spread to define the yield curve. It is therefore necessary to be able to calculate the riskfree zero curve from the prices of non-par bonds.

The method for calculating the zero curve in the general case turns out to resemble the original method using par bonds. The description here uses semiannual bonds, but an equivalent method would work for bonds of any frequency. Suppose there are bullet bonds paying semiannual interest for maturities 0.5, 1.0, ..., 10.0 years, with interest $m_{0.5}\%$, $m_{1.0}\%$, ..., $m_{10.0}\%$, and values $v_{0.5}$, $v_{1.0}$, ..., $v_{10.0}$. The 6-month bond is a zero coupon instrument, and its price therefore determines the 6-month zero coupon rate $Z_{0.5}$. The 1-year bond has two future cashflows; the present value of the 6-month cashflow is known since $Z_{0.5}$ is known, and thus the bond value and payment at 1 year must define the 1-year zero coupon rate $Z_{1.0}$. Similarly, $Z_{0.5}$ and $Z_{1.0}$ give the present value of the future cashflows of the 1.5 year bond except for the repayment of principal and interest at maturity; this leaves a single equation from which $Z_{1.5}$ can be determined. The process can be extended as far as required. (In some currencies, for example, the US dollar, French franc, and sterling, government bonds are traded in maturities well beyond 10 years, which is the longest common maturity for swaps.)

As an example of the calculation, suppose that the first few interest rates and present values of bonds are:

Maturity (years)	Coupon	Value
0.5	6.0	100.032
1.0	6.3	100.045
1.5	6.4	100.234
2.0	6.7	100.320

Then, using s_t to represent the scaling factor to time t, the zero rates can be calculated as follows:

For the 6-month bond,
   $100.032 = 103/s_{0.5}$, so that
   $s_{0.5} = 1.02967$, giving $Z_{0.5} = 6.022\%$.

For the 1-year bond,
   $100.045 = 3.15/s_{0.5} + 103.15/s_{1.0}$, so that
   $96.98577 = 103.15/s_{1.0}$, giving $s_{1.0}$ as 1.06356 and $Z_{1.0}$ as 6.356%.

For the 18-month bond,
   $100.234 = 3.2/s_{0.5} + 3.2/s_{1.0} + 103.2/s_{1.5}$, so that
   $94.1174413 = 103.2/s_{1.5}$, giving $s_{1.5}$ as 1.09650 and $Z_{1.5}$ as 6.334%.

For the 2-year bond,
   $100.320 = 3.35/s_{0.5} + 3.35/s_{1.0} + 3.35/s_{1.5} + 103.35/s_{2.0}$, so that
   $90.8615587 = 103.35/s_{2.0}$, giving $s_{2.0}$ as 1.13744 and $Z_{2.0}$ as 6.651%.

As in the original calculation of zero coupon rates from par rates, the computation can be simplified by accumulating a variable A_t as each new zero rate is calculated. A_t is equivalent to the present value of a 1% cashflow up to time $(t - 0.5)$, so that:

$A_{0.5} = 0$
$A_{1.0} = 0 + (0.5/s_{0.5})$,
$A_{1.5} = A_{1.0} + (0.5/s_{1.0})$, and in general
$A_{t+0.5} = A_t + (0.5/s_t)$.

This then gives

   $v_t = (A_t * m_t) + ((100 + m_t/2)/s_t)$.

If all the s_i up to $s_{t-0.5}$ are known, A_t is also known and this formula can be used to calculate s_t.
   Using A, the calculation above can be laid out as:

Year	m	v	A	s	Z
0.5	6.0	100.032	0	1.02967	6.022
1.0	6.3	100.045	0.48559	1.06356	6.355
1.5	6.4	100.234	0.95571	1.09650	6.334
2.0	6.7	100.320	1.41171	1.13744	6.651

As before, the order of calculation is A_1, s_1, Z_1, A_2, s_2, Z_2, etc.

It should be noted that there will not always be a bond exactly to each 6-month date; for example, there may not be a $2\frac{1}{2}$-year bond. It will then be necessary to use a variation of the above process to calculate the zero coupon rate to an intermediate date using a bond with that maturity. Extrapolating the zero curve will then give a value for the next exact half year.

To see this in action, suppose that the 2.4 year bond has coupon 6.6% and dirty price 100.631. Using straight line interpolation of zero coupon rates from the table above gives:

Year	Zero	Scaling factor
0.4	6.022	1.02367
0.9	6.288	1.05642
1.4	6.338	1.08984
1.9	6.588	1.12887

As 100.631 equals $3.3/s_{0.4}$ plus $3.3/s_{0.9}$ plus $3.3/s_{1.4}$ plus $3.3/s_{1.9}$ plus $103.3/s_{2.4}$, we have 88.33230 equals $103.3/s_{2.4}$, which gives $s_{2.4}$ as 1.16945 and $Z_{2.4}$ as 6.740%. Straight line extrapolation of $Z_{2.0}$ and $Z_{2.4}$ gives $Z_{2.5}$ as 6.762%.

Where the intermediate date bond is beyond the missing maturity, there will be two missing values of Z_i in the expression for the bond's present value. To solve these simultaneously, it will be necessary to use an additional equation representing the assumption that the graph of zero coupon rates against time is a straight line. The calculation will require iteration in a similar way to the calculation of yield to maturity described in the next section.

This discussion assumes that all bonds are priced consistently as the present value of their cashflows. However, other factors may affect the price, such as:

Tax   For example, a withholding tax or income tax may cause low coupon bonds to attract a premium.

Liquidity If a bond is recently issued then it may be actively traded in the secondary market; such bonds can attract a liquidity premium compared to older bonds which are seldom traded. If a particular bond issue is very small, few of the bonds may ever be traded in the secondary market, resulting in a high bid-offer spread. Other technical factors may also affect liquidity.

Options   An embedded option will change the price of a bond.

Futures   There are various exchange-traded futures contracts on government bonds; typically settlement of a contract is by delivery of one of a number of bonds, with the face value to be delivered adjusted by a formula for each different bond. As rates change, a different bond may become *cheapest to deliver* under this formula. Demand may increase for the cheapest-to-deliver bond, increasing its price.

This should give a flavour of the technical effects possible in the bond market.

Unless otherwise stated, all bonds dealt with below will be assumed to be free from such complications and to be priced at the present value of their cashflows.

9.3 YIELD TO MATURITY AND SWAP SPREADS

In comparing the riskfree and interbank yield curves, it would seem logical to look at the difference between the two sets of zero coupon rates; this will be the approach of section 9.5 below. However, the *swap spreads* quoted in the market are the differences in basis points between each swap or Libor rate and the *yield-to-maturity* of the corresponding bond; it is therefore necessary to explain this term in order to link the theory to market practice.

The yield of a bond is the *return* to an investor holding the instrument. The return on an investment is the ratio of the value of the investment instrument (plus any dividends or other payments) at the end of a period to its value at the start of the period. There are various different measures of yield, each of which focuses on a possible objective of the investor. The yield to maturity measures the total return to the investor if she holds the bond to its maturity, and it is defined by:

Definition 9.1 Yield to maturity is calculated from the flat zero coupon rate Z at which the future cashflows of a bond would have their current present value. It is the interest rate Y at the payment frequency of the bond which is equivalent to Z as an annual rate.
If the bond pays interest every t years, Y is given explicitly as $(r^t - 1) * 100/t$,
where the annualised scaling factor $r = 1 + (Z/100)$.

For a bond with an exact number of years to maturity, the formula for Y follows from the results for a flat yield curve in Part I; for other bonds the same definition is assumed to hold. There does not seem to be a market standard for converting Z to Y when the bond is not for an exact number of years; you may therefore meet yields to maturity calculated on a slightly different basis.

As an example of the calculation of Y, if a flat zero coupon rate of 10% gives the correct value of a semiannual bond, the yield to maturity will be

$$(1.1^{0.5} - 1) * 100/0.5 = 9.762\%.$$

Yield to maturity can also be defined as the flat reinvestment rate which would give a consistent yield on the bond; this is equivalent to the definition here. The internal rate of return for a cashstream was discussed in Part I; comparing definitions, you can see that yield to maturity is basically the IRR for the cashflows of the bond.

As an example of the calculation of yield to maturity, if a bond has value 100.467 and pays interest at 6% semiannually until its maturity in 3.25 years when it repays 101% of principal, then its future cashflows are:

Year	Cashflow
0.25	3
0.75	3
1.25	3
1.75	3
2.25	3
2.75	3
3.25	104

and these will have present value 100.467 if the zero coupon curve is flat at 6.745%; the yield to maturity is thus 6.635%, since a semiannual rate of 6.635% is equivalent to a flat annual rate of 6.745%.

Unfortunately, calculating yield to maturity can be done only by guessing a rate and then using the error in the resultant present value to make an improved guess, and so on. (Sophisticated mathematical methods, such as those used in bond calculators, produce consecutive estimates which quickly increase in accuracy.)

The yield to maturity attempts to summarise in one figure all the information about the attractiveness of the bond as an investment. Unfortunately, as in most attempts to summarise a complex reality, yield to maturity does not contain all the information to allow useful decision making. For example, if the zero coupon curve is as shown in Table 9.1, then two semiannual bonds, both with maturity 3.25 years but having different coupons, will have different yields to maturity, even though they are present valued using the same scaling factors.

TABLE 9.1 CALCULATION OF YIELD TO MATURITY OF TWO BONDS WITH DIFFERENT COUPONS

Year	Zero	Scaling factor	Cashflow	<- - - -6% coupon bond- - - -> PV at Zero	PV at 6.077%	Cashflow	<- - - -12% coupon bond- - - -> PV at zero	PV at 6.059%
0.25	5.0	1.012272	3	2.9636	2.9561	6	5.9273	5.9124
0.75	5.5	1.040973	3	2.8819	2.8702	6	5.7638	5.7410
1.25	5.7	1.071751	3	2.7992	2.7867	6	5.5983	5.5746
1.75	5.8	1.103697	3	2.7181	2.7057	6	5.4363	5.4131
2.25	5.9	1.137669	3	2.6370	2.6271	6	5.2739	5.2562
2.75	6.0	1.173792	3	2.5558	2.5507	6	5.1116	5.1038
3.25	6.1	1.212202	103	84.9693	85.0292	106	87.4442	87.5541
Total PV				101.525	101.526		120.555	120.555

Converting the annual zero coupon rates, the 6% bond has yield to maturity of 5.987%, while the 12% bond has yield to maturity of 5.970%, even though they are priced from the same riskfree zero curve. Although the difference is relatively small in this case, the effect can be amplified when the yield curve is steep, when the difference in coupon is larger, or when the maturity of the bonds is greater. Since swap spreads are typically in the region of 30 to 150 basis points, a difference of a few basis points caused by the choice of bond can be material. The phenomenon can be exacerbated if there is no bond with the exact maturity of the swap; for example, if there were no liquid 5-year bond then swap spreads might be quoted against the yield to maturity of a 4-year and 10-month bond. Since it is the practice of the bond market to ignore embedded options in calculating yield to maturity, the existence of such options can further distort the spread curve.

For example, if the yield to maturity of a 5-year bond is 7.00% and the 5-year swap with the same fixed payment frequency has market rate 7.60%, the 5-year spread is 60 basis points. If there is a more liquid 4-year-10-month bond with yield to maturity 7.08%, then using it as a base would give a spread of 52 basis points. If the issuer had the right to redeem the 4-year-10-month bond 2 years before its maturity, then the price of the bond might be reduced, increasing its yield to maturity to, say, 7.23%, and giving a swap spread of 37 basis points.

A final complication is that as time passes the bond used to determine, say, the 5-year spread, changes. This could change the 5-year swap spread without there being any real movement in market rates.

In the swap markets, spreads are most important for US dollar and Canadian dollar swaps, where bid and offer swap rates are commonly quoted as spreads over the yield to maturity calculated using the midmarket bond price. One advantage of quoting swap rates as spreads is that they change relatively slowly compared to the absolute swap rates, and changing spreads give an idea of the relative value of swaps and bonds.

The primary market for issuing bonds in all currencies is critically affected by swap spreads, since an issuer will typically be able to issue at a fixed spread over the government bond in a given maturity; if the issuer enters into a swap to convert his fixed funding into floating, the resultant spread over or under Libor will depend on the swap spread relative to the spread of the bond. A similar process affects bond prices in the secondary market, since investors can buy a fixed-coupon bond and simultaneously enter into a swap to convert their fixed interest income into floating interest; the spread against Libor will again depend on the difference between the swap spread and the bond spread.

Swap spreads measure the credit risk of swaps relative to government debt; since the 6-month spread is measured using a Libor placing rate, it is likely that it will be substantially higher than the 1-year spread measured using a swap rate. (The usual market quote of the 1-year spread is based on the 1-year Libor rate; the spread based on the swap rate is more useful for risk management purposes.) Thereafter you would expect spreads to widen with the increasing credit risk at greater maturities. However, as a spread is calculated against the yield to maturity of a particular bond, it is not unusual to see apparent anomalies in the swap spread curve; for example, spreads for 10-year swaps might be narrower than spreads for 7-year swaps. Only by correcting the price of bonds for the factors mentioned at the end of section 9.2 can you establish whether spreads do widen with increasing maturity.

It would be possible to reduce some of the inaccuracy in spreads by changing definition, and quoting the spread as being the parallel shift in the riskfree zero coupon curve necessary to make the present value of the grossed up fixed side of the swap, as defined in section 7.2, equal to zero. This 'zero spread' is still subject to error through anomalous pricing of particular government bonds, especially for short-dated or low-coupon swaps where the present value is most sensitive to the single zero coupon rate at maturity. Nevertheless, it gives a more accurate single figure indicator of relative value.

The measurement of 'zero spread' can be extended to non-government bonds; the spread is the parallel shift to the riskfree zero curve necessary to make the present value of the bond's future cashflows equal to its price. Unfortunately, 'zero spread' is not used in the market, and the spread of a bond over the corresponding government bond is quoted as the difference between the yields to maturity of the two instruments. Nevertheless, analysis of 'zero spread' may be a more accurate technique to identify relatively cheap or dear bonds.

9.4 REPURCHASE AGREEMENTS

It was shown in Part III that a single currency receive-fixed bullet swap was equivalent in risk to the purchase of a fixed bond and the sale of a strip of Libor bonds. Since future Libor bonds have no risk today, a bank wishing to enter into, say, a 5-year swap where it receives fixed and pays Libor semiannually on US$10 million, could therefore achieve the same result in terms of interest rate risk by buying an appropriate 5-year fixed bond paying semiannual interest and selling a 6-month bond at Libor. (It is shown below that taking funds for 6 months to fund the fixed bond has the same effect as selling a 6-month bond.)

Banks enter into swaps, rather than buying and selling bonds, because bonds have to be funded whereas swaps are off balance sheet. Moreover, bonds carry a principal credit risk and require a large holding of regulatory capital, and there is consequently a hidden cost in holding bonds. (However, as discussed in section 9.6 below, this cost is proportional to the period during which the bond is held, and thus it can be reduced if the holding is short term only.)

Government bonds are presumed to have little credit risk, especially for bonds in the domestic currency, and under the risk capital regulations of the Bank for International Settlement most such bonds carry no requirement for regulatory capital.[1] (However, some bank regulators, notably the Bank of England, go beyond the BIS requirements and do require risk capital to be held for government bonds; this creates an opportunity cost of capital for the holding of such bonds.) The two remaining problems with using government bonds to take a risk position are that government bonds are priced from the riskfree yield curve and that a purchase of bonds will have to be funded; section 9.5 below discusses the effect of the spread between the interbank and riskfree yield curves, and the rest of this section concentrates on resolving the funding issue by explaining the *repo* market.

A *repurchase agreement* or repo is an agreement whereby one counterparty borrows money from another on the security of a bond; it is assumed here that a government bond is involved. The transaction is structured as a sale and forward repurchase at a higher price, with the price difference representing the interest payment on the loan. The counterparty borrowing money in this way is said to 'repo the bond' and the effective interest rate is known as the *repo rate*. The lender of money on the repo can also be described as 'borrowing the bond' since he has the use of the bond during the repo period; this means that a dealer can sell a bond he does not own (described as a *short sale*) and deliver by borrowing the bond in the repo market.

Because the lender of money has the security of a riskfree bond, repo rates can be below rates available without collateral; this is the attraction of repos as a funding mechanism. Repos can be for any period, although the vast majority have a maturity of a few months or less, with the largest number being done for next day repurchase; a repo for next day repurchase is known as an *overnight repo*, and the phrase 'repo rate' used on its own will refer to the overnight repo rate.

The mechanics of repos are illustrated below for the US$ repo market; rates and market practice will differ in other currencies.

In the US$ market a distinction is made between 'general bonds' consisting of bonds which are seldom traded, and 'special bonds' which are actively traded, particularly where there are short sales which need to be covered by dealers borrowing the bond; in some cases repo rates on special bonds can be well below riskfree rates, since the borrower of the

---

[1] Under the BIS risk capital regulations, there is no requirement for regulatory capital for holdings of bonds issued by governments of countries which are members of the OECD or which have a special lending arrangement with the IMF; nor is capital required for holdings of domestic currency bonds issued by other governments, provided that the bank funds in the same currency. If this seems unduly generous, remember that it is the governments which agree the regulations.

bond can be made to pay a premium. It will be assumed in the example below that the collateral consists of general bonds.

Counterparties using repos to borrow are typically banks or corporations funding a bond portfolio; also holders of 'special bonds' may repo in order to borrow cheap money which they can then reinvest at market rates. Typical lenders are corporations with temporary cash surpluses and money market investment funds, together with dealers who are covering short sales. Brokers are active in the market to earn a commission by bringing borrowers and lenders together.

The transaction costs on a repo for a few days are more or less the same as for a repo with a longer period, and thus they are substantially higher as a proportion of the interest involved. Also, the credit risk on an interbank deposit for a few days is very small. For these reasons, the repo rate in very short maturities is typically only slightly below the interbank rate. For repo periods beyond a few weeks the repo rate comes well below Libor and closer to the riskfree rate.

Since the value of the bond may change during the repo period, the lender, who is lending on the security of the bond, will want to ensure that the bond is always worth more than the loan advanced on the repo plus its accrued interest. This results in the market practice that a borrower will have to put up a bond of higher value than the amount of the loan. For an overnight repo the amount of extra collateral will typically be small; for example, if you want to repo US$25 million overnight you may have to put up bonds with market value US$25.02 million. For a repo of several months, a rule of thumb is that you have to put up an extra 0.25% collateral for each month; thus if you repo a bond with market value US$25 million for 3 months you will receive cash of US$25 million over 1.0075, which equals $24.814 million. The balance of US$186,000 has to be borrowed at Libor, thus slightly increasing the net funding cost.

The borrower also has a credit risk in that he is advancing bonds worth more than the loan. Because of this, market practice is that if the market value of the bonds moves substantially from its original ratio to the loan (accrued interest on the loan is taken into account in the calculation), then the borrower or the lender can require the repo to be 'repriced'. This involves the borrower prepaying some of the loan repayment or the lender increasing the amount of the loan; alternatively, the borrower can put up more collateral or the lender can return collateral. Usually neither party would ask for a repricing if the amount involved was under, say, US$150,000. The possibility of repricing adds a slight uncertainty to the overall cost of borrowing through a repo.

As an example of a repo, suppose that you hold US Treasury bonds with face value US$24 million and market value US$26 million. The 3-month repo rate is 4.01%, compared with 3-month Libor 4.31% and 3-month government bond par rate 3.91%. (As usual, it is assumed for simplicity that interest rates are quoted on a fraction-of-a-year basis, although in practice both Libor and repo rate would be quoted on an actual/360 basis.) You have to put up 100.75% of collateral, and so you receive US$25.806 million on the repo of the bonds. If you fund the remaining US$194,000 at Libor, your average funding costs for the 3 months are

$$\frac{(25.806 * 4.01\%) + (0.194 * 4.31\%)}{26}$$

which equals 4.012%. You are thus funding the bonds at 0.102% above the riskfree rate for the 3-month period; this 10.2 bppa represents an absolute cost to you, since, if the market is efficient, funding long-term bonds exactly at short-term bond rates would be expected to give you an average zero return.

A dealer borrowing a bond through the repo market is executing a *reverse repo*; clearly, a reverse repo to one counterparty is a repo to the other counterparty, and so there is no need to repeat the description above. The only change is that the dealer will have to go to the market to do his reverse repo, and thus he will receive the repo rate minus a bid-offer spread; he will also have to lend slightly more than the value of the bond rather than slightly less.

Suppose that the bonds in the example above are 3-year notes[2] paying interest at 8% semiannually. What is the interest rate risk of a bank buying the bonds and entering into the repo? The bonds have face value US$24 million, and so their future cashflows are:

Year	US$000s
0.5	960
1.0	960
1.5	960
2.0	960
2.5	960
3.0	24,960.

The future cashflow on the repo is:

Year	US$000s
0.25	-26,065

Assuming that you fund the remaining US$194,000 of the purchase price of the bond with a 3-month taking at Libor, the future cashflow of the taking is:

Year	US$000s
0.25	-196

---

[2]US Treasury securities issued with maturities in the range 2-10 years are called *notes*; however, for all practical purposes they behave as bonds.

If the bonds' value changes and the repo is repriced then the cashflows will become more complicated. This possibility is ignored here, although you should carry out a more detailed analysis if you intend to use the repo market.

Putting together the cashflows from the bonds, repo, and balancing taking gives:

TABLE 9.2   TOTAL CASHFLOWS FROM
PURCHASE AND REPO OF BOND

Year	US$000s
0.25	-26,261
0.5	960
1.0	960
1.5	960
2.0	960
2.5	960
3.0	24,960

It is now possible to show that the risk of these cashflows is similar to that of a 3-year swap. To do this it is necessary to specify bond coupons and midmarket bond values and swap spreads; this allows zero coupon rates and spreads to be calculated as laid out in Table 9.3. The 6-month par interbank rate is a Libor rate, whereas the rates for 1 year and beyond are swap rates; as noted above, the 6-month spread is higher than the 1-year spread. Remember that the 1-year spread normally quoted in the market would be for the Libor rate over the government rate.

TABLE 9.3   CALCULATION OF RISKFREE AND INTERBANK
ZERO COUPON RATES

Year	Bond coupon	< Bond value	Riskfree Yield to maturity	Zero >	Swap spread	< Interbank Par	Zero	> Zero spread
0.25	3.91	100.000		3.968		4.310	4.380	
0.5	4.0	99.971	4.059	4.100	0.45	4.509	4.560	0.460
1.0	5.0	100.745	4.231	4.278	0.15	4.381	4.428	0.150
1.5	5.5	101.720	4.304	4.354	0.20	4.504	4.557	0.203
2.0	5.6	102.251	4.411	4.468	0.28	4.691	4.754	0.286
2.5	5.8	102.561	4.702	4.781	0.41	5.112	5.207	0.426
3.0	6.0	102.789	4.988	5.093	0.54	5.528	5.663	0.570

The zero spread is the interbank zero coupon rate minus the riskfree zero rate. The riskfree zero coupon rates are consistent with the US$26 million value of the bond in the example.

If you receive fixed on a 3-year swap on a notional principal of US$25.25 million, you will receive at about 5.528% semiannually against 3-month Libor, and the cash gaps will be:

Year	US$000s
0.25	-25,522
0.5	698
1.0	698
1.5	698
2.0	698
2.5	698
3.0	25,948.

Using the riskfree zero curve to value the bond and repo, and the interbank zero curve to value the swap and taking,[3] gives the risks of this swap and of the bond and repo cashflows of Table 9.2 as:

	Swap	Bond (plus repo and taking)
Level risk (10 bppa shift)	-US$60,861	-US$61,363
0-1 rotation (10 bppa in 0 year)	US$ 4,371	US$ 4,462
1-10 rotation (10 bppa in 10 year)	-US$14,302	-US$14,234

This shows that, provided spreads do not change, the risk of the bond plus funding is very similar to the risk of the swap.

If you sell a bond short and do a reverse repo for 3 months to cover your position, your resultant cashflows would be similar to the reverse of those in Table 9.2; the repo rate would be reduced by a spread (or by more if you have to pay a premium to borrow a particular bond) and Libor replaced by Libid, so that the cashflow at 3 months would be slightly smaller. The analysis above shows that the resultant position would have similar risk to a 3-year pay-fixed swap.

9.5 SPREAD RISK

Section 9.4 demonstrated that the risk of a bond funded through a repo is very similar to the risk of a swap. This section considers in more detail the reporting and calculation of cash gaps involving both riskfree and interbank cashflows, and then addresses the spread risk caused by the possibility of the riskfree and interbank rates moving independently.

Recalculating the example above using interbank rates throughout gives for the bond:

Level risk (10 bppa shift)	-US$60,028
0-1 rotation (10 bppa in 0 year)	US$ 4,441
1-10 rotation (10 bppa in 10 year)	-US$13,936.

Although here the difference from the original results is small, the error will tend to be larger for cashflows with longer maturities; moreover, if you are always one way round in the bond market, then the error will always be the same way. Therefore, it is worthwhile to calculate and report the risk separately on riskfree and interbank cashflows.

---

[3]There is no contradiction between this approach and the result of Part I that the measurement of risk is insensitive to the exact zero curve used, provided that the difference between the curves is constant. Part I addressed a situation where all cashflows carried the same risk, whereas here the riskfree and interbank cashflows are distinct.

The calculation of risk is straightforward; present value each cashflow using the appropriate zero curve, shift both zero curves by the same amount, present value again, and take the difference in the present values as the risk. Reporting under the discrete cash gaps methodology can be done by breaking out into separate sheets the gaps for riskfree cashflows and the gaps for interbank cashflows; a consolidation sheet can show the net gaps.

Where you hold non-government bonds, then it would be appropriate to separate the bonds into spread bands of width, say, 15 bppa, and to treat the bonds in each spread band as a separate set of cashflows for the calculation and reporting of interest rate risk. This can be done by a natural extension of the process outlined above for riskfree and interbank cashflows. Note that although it is possible to capture the interest rate risk of bonds in this way, neither this reporting nor the spread reporting described below addresses the *credit risk* of individual bonds, which may be the largest component of risk in a bond portfolio. A discussion of bond credit risk is beyond the scope of this book.

We are finally in a position to look at spread risk itself. Consider an organisation which has most of its transactions with banks, but which uses a few bond positions in hedging. It makes sense to consider a change in zero spreads as the interbank rates staying the same and the riskfree rates changing; the risk of a plus 1 basis point shift in zero spreads is thus the same as the risk of a minus 1 basis point shift in the riskfree zero coupon rates. (For an investor hedging a bond portfolio with a few swaps, it would appropriate to consider a change in spreads as affecting the interbank zero rates.)

In Table 9.3 the zero spreads are close to the swap spreads but are not identical; the discrepancy will tend to be larger for higher levels of rates and for longer maturities, where less of the value of a bond relates to its final payment of principal and interest. Since the cash gaps methodology analyses risk using zero coupon rates, it is appropriate to convert swap spreads into the equivalent zero spreads for reporting purposes. If your system cannot cope with this conversion, then the swap spreads can be used as a proxy for the zero spreads, but you should be aware of the approximations involved.

As for interest rates it makes sense to construct a model of the spread curve to allow risk management with respect to a minimal number of parameters. Given the structure of the spread curve, it probably makes sense to treat it as a hinged straight line with the hinge at 1 year, remembering that we are calculating the 1-year spread using the 1-year swap rate. (There are difficulties extending the short-term straight line segment much below 6 months, and so it may be necessary to introduce a fourth variable into the model to cover spreads under 6 months; this possibility is not considered further here.) It will be necessary to carry out an analysis of historical spreads in order to confirm that the three variable model explains a satisfyingly high percentage of the daily movements. A natural choice of descriptors might be the 1-year spread to give the level, and the difference between each of the 10-year and 6-month spreads and the 1-year spread to give the rotations. Thereafter, the analysis and reporting can follow the treatment for interest rates in Part I. This can be summarised as:

(a) For a given confidence level, identify the maximum daily movement in each descriptor.
(b) Report the cash gaps for riskfree (or, for an investor, interbank) cashflows from which spread risk will be calculated.
(c) Calculate the change in present value of the future cashflows for a 1 basis point change in each descriptor, and report.
(d) Scale up the 1 basis point change in present value for each descriptor for the maximum daily movement, and report.
(e) Check that the daily movements conform to a normal distribution so that monthly and annual movements can be predicted.

Note that any correlation between movements in absolute rates and movements in spreads would have to be taken into account in combining the two measures of risk.

Where bonds are held with spreads above interbank rates, it would be possible to report in a similar way the spread risk for each spread band; as noted above, this would not identify the risk of changes in spread due to changes in the creditworthiness of individual issuers.

9.6 THE COST OF USING BONDS IN RISK MANAGEMENT

The analysis of repos in section 9.4 above showed that funding a bond through repo would cost more than the riskfree rate for the funding period. As explained, the excess of the funding cost over the riskfree rate represents a real cost. If the bank regulators require risk capital to be held for government bonds, then this will introduce in addition an opportunity cost of holding bonds, for the same reasons as were discussed for swaps in Part III.

However, even if the carrying cost of a bond is high, it can still be relatively cheap overall if the bond is held only for a short period. For example, if interest rates are about 8% and the carrying cost of a bond is 40 bppa, then if the bond is held for 3 months to hedge a 5-year swap position the effective cost over the 5 years is only about 2.5 bppa. This can make a bond a useful interim hedge while you are waiting to put on an appropriate swap; thus a swap market maker can enter into a swap on his side of the market, and then hedge the position with a bond until he is able to enter into an offsetting swap on his side of the market again.

An alternative to buying or selling physical bonds is to buy and sell exchange-traded bond futures. The mechanics of this will be very similar to the mechanics of the Eurodeposit future discussed in Part II, except that bond futures are usually settled by delivery of the underlying bond rather than by cash settlement. Since there will be contracts only for bonds of specific maturity on specific dates, bond futures will not offer the full flexibility of buying or selling physical bonds.

Bond futures will have their own margining costs; these can often be material if the future is held for a few months. Bond futures will also have their own technical behaviour for large changes in bond value; in particular, as noted in section 9.1 above, the cheapest bond to deliver in settlement may change. The liquidity for futures on long-term bonds will be far less than the liquidity on Eurodeposit futures; this may make bid-offer spreads a material cost if you intend to adjust your position frequently, and in extreme cases it may make it impossible to take or exit positions. Because of the potential complications, it is important to investigate and understand thoroughly a particular bond futures contract before starting to use it.

9.7 BASIS RISK

Ignoring the complications of bonds, spread risk can be considered to be a particular type of *basis risk*. Basis risk exists where two positions nominally offsetting each other depend on rates which can move independently. An example of basis risk discussed in Part II was the settlement of a Chicago Eurodollar future against the corresponding FRA; because the FRA is settled against Libor determined in London time and the future is settled in Chicago time, Libor rates may change between the two determinations. Other basis risks are identified elsewhere in the book.

Another type of basis risk occurs where a bank enters into basis swaps, that is, it pays floating interest calculated on one basis and receives floating interest calculated on a second basis, plus or minus a fixed spread. For example, a bank could enter into a 4-year swap on a notional principal of US$20 million, where every 3 months it pays Libor and receives the average of the daily 3-month commercial paper (CP) rate[4] over the period plus 2 bppa. Such a swap can be marked to market against the current midmarket rate for an equivalent swap. Continuing the example above, if the midmarket rate for a 4-year

---

[4]Where a rate other than Libor is used as a reference rate it is important to agree a source. For example, a usual source for many US dollar non-Libor rates, including CP and prime, is H.15(519), which is a weekly statistical digest published by the Federal Reserve Bank.

swap became pay Libor against CP plus 5 bppa, then the value of the swap would become the value of 3 bppa on US$20 million for 4 years, less any holdback. The risk to the bank is thus that the swap rate will change, changing the present value of the future swap cashflows.

Other types of rate commonly used in basis swaps against Libor include US dollar prime, which is the average base rate quoted by major US banks, and various French franc rates based on a government index giving the average over each month of the daily domestic money market rates.

Companies which manage their interest rate risk using interbank rates, but which fund partly through commercial paper or through loans related to a bank base rate, have a basis risk which they can manage, if necessary, through entering into basis swaps with banks.

Broadly, basis risk can be calculated, reported, and managed as a simpler and less precise sort of interest rate risk; for many types of basis risk it is possible to follow the pattern described for spread risk at the end of section 9.5 above. In many cases it will be possible to use a simplified model of the risk incorporating two or one variables.

Taking the spread of 3-month US$ Libor over CP as a working example, an analysis could be made of historic spreads of Libor over CP and of basis swaps of different tenor. It would then be possible to fit a best straight line to the data for each day, and to check that this explains an adequate part of the shape of the curve of spread against maturity. Natural descriptors for the daily straight line might be the actual spread of Libor over CP and the difference between that spread and the spread on the 5-year basis swap. The data could then be analysed to give confidence levels for the daily movements in the two descriptors, and to check how the daily confidence levels can be extrapolated to longer periods.

Reporting risk can again be split into the reporting of cash gaps and the reporting of basis risk. An accurate way of incorporating CP cashflows into cash gaps is to replace each CP interest flow by Libor minus the appropriate Libor-CP spread for the tenor of the instrument. For example, if current spreads on Libor-CP swaps are:

2 year   1 basis point; and
5 year   5 basis points;

then:

(a) A 2-year loan where repayment was at CP plus 50 basis points would appear in the cash gaps in the same way as a loan at Libor plus 49 bppa.
(b) A 5-year swap of Libor against CP plus 4 bppa would appear in the cash gaps as a fixed cashflow of 1 bppa, since Libor offsets CP plus 5 bppa.

A change of 1 bppa in the Libor-CP spread in a particular maturity would cause a change in present value of each CP instrument in that maturity of 1/100 of the present value of a 1% interest flow. It is thus straightforward to calculate and report the rotation and level basis risks for 1 basis point shifts and to give confidence levels.

It is more difficult to report the basis risk in a way which allows general analysis. Cash gaps reporting will not work. Perhaps the best way is to report the net short or long principal position in CP instruments at each maturity. For example, if you pay CP interest on a Libor-CP swap on US$20 million with maturity 2 years and receive CP interest on a 5-year US$10 million loan, your net position will be:

Year	Position US$ millions
1	−10
2	−10
3	+10
4	+10
5	+10

Where there are transactions maturing within a year the average balance over the year should be taken. The logic of this report is similar to that of the funding gap methodology, which will be discussed in Part VII.

Such a report does not give enough information to calculate accurately the effect of complex changes in the spread curve, and so there will still be a need for an automated method to allow the dealer to revalue the portfolio to determine the effect of an envisaged shift in spreads. However, the report does give information to the dealer about the shape of his overall position and about the broad effects of shifts in spreads, and as such it is a useful tool.

A similar analysis and reporting framework should be established for each type of basis risk identified. As noted above, in some cases an even simpler model may turn out to be appropriate. For example, the basis risk of settlement of a future against an FRA occurs only at the settlement date of a contract, and depends only on the number of futures held times the confidence level for the difference in settlement rates.

Dealing in non-Libor instruments may involve liquidity risks as well as basis risk; a full discussion of this would raise issues of cash management beyond the scope of this book.

SUMMARY

Much of this chapter has been concerned with putting in place the basic machinery to analyse spread risk. This involved calculating the riskfree zero coupon yield curve from the prices of non-par government bonds, and defining yield to maturity and spread. It has also been necessary to look at repurchase agreements so that the package of bond plus funding can be analysed together. With all of this in place, it is possible to consider spread risk for an organisation using a few bonds to hedge a swap portfolio as the risk that the riskfree zero rates will move while the swap rates stay constant. Conversely, for an organisation using a few swaps to hedge a bond portfolio it would make more sense to consider the riskfree zero rates as constant while the interbank rates change. In either case, reporting cash gaps separately for interbank and riskfree cashflows will give immediately the risk caused by a change in spreads; an analysis of historic movements in spreads will allow quantification of the risk.

Basis risk occurs where two instruments which are nominally hedging each other have interest rates set on different bases; for example, a Libor instrument might be hedged by a commercial paper instrument. This risk can be reported as the net long or short position for each non-Libor basis in each maturity. As usual, an analysis of historic rate movements should allow a quantification of risk. In order to calculate mark-to-market values, it is necessary to replace each non-Libor floating rate by Libor plus the current market spread.

APPENDIX D

Duration and convexity

Yield to maturity attempts to express the return on a bond as a single figure. A parallel concept is *duration*, which attempts to express a bond's interest rate risk as a single figure; this can be supplemented by *convexity* as a second measure of risk. This appendix defines duration and convexity and shows that they encode the sensitivity of the value of a bond to parallel shifts in the zero curve. Since the yield curve may rotate or move in some irregular fashion, duration and convexity are therefore inadequate to give a complete description of risk.

The *Macaulay duration* of a bond is defined as the maturity of a zero coupon bond with the same present value (PV) and the same change in PV for a small parallel shift in the zero coupon curve. Duration thus gives a method of estimating the likely change in value of a bond for changes in the general level of rates.

Duration as defined above can be calculated to a very good approximation as the weighted average of the present values of each cashflow of the bond, where weighting is by maturity of each cashflow. That is:

$$d = \frac{\sum_i C_i t_i / s_i}{\sum_i C_i / s_i} \qquad \textbf{Formula D.1}$$

where

    d is the Macaulay duration
    C_i is cashflow i of the bond at time t_i
    s_i is the scaling factor to time t_i
    Σ, the upper-case Greek letter sigma, indicates that the expression to the right is to be summed. Since Σ here is indexed by the *dummy variable i*, the expression should be summed for every relevant value of i.

Since the bottom line of the expression for d is the present value of the bond, it is possible to write:

$$d = \frac{1}{PV} \sum_i \frac{C_i t_i}{s_i} \qquad \textbf{Formula D.2}$$

A zero coupon bond with the same present value and with maturity d years will have cashflow at d years of $s_d * PV$, where s_d is the scaling factor to d years. On the assumption that the yield curve is reasonably flat, simple calculus shows that, for a small parallel shift in the zero coupon curve, the change in the present value of the zero coupon bond is almost the same as the change in the present value of the original bond. Exact equality requires the zero coupon rate to d years to be a complicated average of the zero coupon rates to the cashflows of the original bond; this would be satisfied if the yield curve were flat.

As an example of the calculation of duration, consider three bonds with coupons 5%, 7%, and 10%, each with maturity 5 years and semiannual interest payments. Zero coupon rates are given in the table below, which shows the calculation of the duration of the 5% bond.

Year	Zero %	Scaling factor	Present value	PV times years
0.5	5.3	1.026158	2.43627	1.21814
1.0	6.0	1.06	2.35849	2.35849
1.5	6.2	1.094427	2.28430	3.42645
2.0	6.4	1.132096	2.20829	4.41659
2.5	6.6	1.173257	2.13082	5.32705
3.0	6.75	1.216476	2.05512	6.16535
3.5	6.9	1.263054	1.97933	6.92765
4.0	7.0	1.310796	1.90724	7.62895
4.5	7.1	1.361610	1.83606	8.26228
5.0	7.2	1.415709	72.40190	362.00948
		Totals	91.59782	407.74043

This gives duration as 407.74043/91.59782, which equals 4.45142 years.

The same calculation gives durations for the 7% bond of 4.29640 years and for the 10% bond of 4.10716 years. You can see that the duration decreases as the coupon increases; this makes sense, as it reflects the fact that more of the present value is represented by earlier cashflows.

Although Macaulay duration has been defined for an individual bond, it can also be calculated for a portfolio of bonds using the same formula. Alternatively, if you know the duration for each bond, you can work out the duration of the portfolio as the weighted average duration of the individual bonds, where the weighting is by the present value of each bond. (This is logical, since a bond with a bigger present value should have a bigger impact on the final result.) It can be shown straightforwardly that the average duration calculated in this way is the same as the duration which would be calculated by substituting all the cashflows of all the bonds in the above formula.

It should be emphasised that the above procedure can be used only for a portfolio of assets or for a portfolio of liabilities; if you mix cashflows in and out then the calculation becomes meaningless. Where you have both assets (such as bonds owned) and liabilities (such as fixed debt) you have to work out a duration for your assets separately and a duration for your liabilities separately. This lets you compare the sensitivities of the value of your assets and of your liabilities to parallel shifts in the yield curve, and to hedge or take positions as required.

Duration as defined above lets you calculate the sensitivity of your bond to parallel yield curve shifts; by slightly redefining duration it becomes even more straightforward to calculate this sensitivity.

Consider the zero coupon bond with the same risk as your original bond; as noted above, it has maturity d years and present value PV, and hence its cashflow at maturity must be $PV * s_d$, where s_d is the scaling factor to d years. This cashflow is a constant which we can call K, and the present value of the zero coupon bond can therefore be written K/s_d. If Z_d is the zero coupon rate to d years, then s_d equals $(1 + (Z_d/100))^d$. Simple calculus then gives the change in the value of the zero coupon bond for a small shift delta in Z_d as

$$\frac{-PV * d * \text{delta}}{(1 + (Z_d/100))}$$

Therefore, if we use a different definition of duration of $d/(1 + (Z_d/100))$ we can simplify the formula for the sensitivity of the zero coupon bond, which, remember, equals the sensitivity of the original bond. This leads to the definition of *modified duration* d_m (also known as Hicks duration) which equals:

$$\frac{\text{Macaulay duration}}{(1 + (Z_d/100))}$$ **Definition D.1**

where Z_d is the zero coupon rate to d years.

The change in present value for a small parallel shift of delta in the yield curve can then be written as $-PV * d_m * \text{delta}$.

An exact formula for modified duration is derived below, but for most purposes substituting the approximation to Macaulay duration in Formula D.1 or D.2 into Definition D.1 will give adequate accuracy.

For example, take the 5% coupon bond for which we worked out a Macaulay duration of 4.45142 years above. The zero coupon rate to 4.45142 years is 7.09028%, taking a straight line interpolation between the 4 and $4\frac{1}{2}$ years. This gives d_m equals 4.45142 over 1.0709028, which equals 4.15670 years. By the derivation above, the change in present value of the bond for a 0.01% parallel increase in the zero coupon curve should be $-PV$ times 4.15670 times 0.01%, which equals -0.03807, giving a new present value of 91.55975. We can work out the present value under the new yield curve as:

Year	Zero %	Scaling factor	Present value
0.5	5.31	1.026207	2.43616
1.0	6.01	1.0601	2.35827
1.5	6.21	1.094582	2.28398
2.0	6.41	1.132309	2.20788
2.5	6.61	1.173532	2.13032
3.0	6.76	1.216818	2.05454
3.5	6.91	1.263468	1.97868
4.0	7.01	1.311286	1.90653
4.5	7.11	1.362182	1.83529
5.0	7.21	1.416369	72.36814
		Total	91.55977

The theory thus gives a very good fit here and justifies modified duration as a useful tool. The accuracy would be lower if the yield curve were not so close to a straight line around d and d_m; the exact definition below will resolve this.

As will be explained below, modified duration is usually defined in terms of the derivative of the present value with respect to parallel shifts in the yield curve; this will lead to a value close to that given by the formula above. Instead of defining modified duration in terms of shifts in the zero curve it is sometimes defined in terms of shifts in the par curve; this creates complexities which are not covered here, and which can in any case be finessed by dealing with shifts in the zero curve and then translating the answer into an effect on the par curve.

The excellent agreement between the present value of 91.55975 predicted by the modified duration and the present value of 91.55977 actually calculated, starts to break down when delta becomes larger. This is shown in Figure D.1.

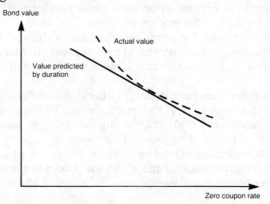

Figure D.1   Bond value as a function of the level of interest rates. The curvature of the actual value line is exaggerated.

The difference between the straight line relationship between price and interest rates predicted by the modified duration formula and the curved relationship actually observed is described by the *convexity* of the bond. Convexity is a measure of 'how convex' the dotted curved line is; an explicit definition in terms of derivatives of *PV* is given below.

Unlike duration, convexity can be usefully defined for a portfolio of assets and liabilities. It can become particularly important where the sensitivity of the portfolio present value to parallel shifts in the zero curve is hedged to zero; this will occur when the duration and present values of the assets equal the duration and present values of the liabilities. The change in portfolio value for yield curve parallel shifts then becomes totally dependent on convexity, as shown in Figure D.2.

Other things being equal, positive convexity is obviously the thing to aim for. As explained below, convexity is proportional to the second derivative of the present value of a bond with respect to parallel shifts in the yield curve, and so positive convexity corresponds to a positive second derivative.

The definition of convexity depends on calculus. The present value of a bond (or portfolio) can be expressed as a polynomial in the level of the zero curve Z; as usual, we assume that any shift in the zero curve will be parallel, so that the zero curve can then be described by a single

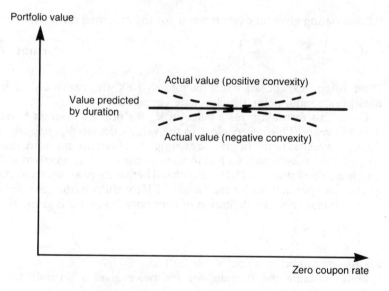

Figure D.2   Portfolio value as a function of the level of interest rates. The curvature of the actual value line is exaggerated.

variable. Then from elementary calculus we have the Taylor expansion:

$$PV = K_0 + (K_1 * \text{delta}) + (0.5 * K_2 * \text{delta}^2)$$
$$+ \text{ terms in delta}^3 \text{ and higher powers}$$

Equation D.1

where K_0 = Value of PV at original position of zero curve

$$K_1 \quad = \frac{dPV}{dZ}$$

$$K_2 \quad = \frac{d^2PV}{dZ^2}$$

delta = parallel shift in zero curve

For very small values of delta, the value of PV will be very close to K_0 plus the term ($K_1 *$ delta). But we already have from the definition of modified duration that the change in the value of the bond for a small shift of delta in the yield curve is $-PV * d_m * \text{delta}$.

Equating the two formulae gives $d_m * PV = \frac{-dPV}{dZ}$

Since PV is given by the formula $\sum_i \frac{C_i}{s_i}$ where $s_i = (1 + (Z_i/100))^{t_i}$,

differentiating gives an exact formula for the modified duration of:

$$d_m = \frac{1}{PV} \sum_i \frac{t_i * C_i}{(1 + (Z_i/100))^{t_i + 1}}$$

Formula D.3

(You might expect an extra factor of 100; this vanishes as it is incorporated into delta, which is a percentage.)

Using this formula gives a value of d_m for our 5% coupon bond of 4.15460 years. This is very close to the value calculated previously; the difference relates to the imprecise assumption about the appropriate zero coupon rate to use which we had to make to convert duration to modified duration. The value of 4.15460 calculated here is more accurate, in that it gives better predictions for the value of PV for shifts in the zero curve.

In a similar vein, the definition of convexity c is that it is given by:

$$c * PV = \frac{d^2PV}{dZ^2}$$

c is also measured in years.

Differentiating the formula for PV twice gives a formula for the convexity of

$$c \quad = \frac{1}{PV} \sum_i \frac{t_i * (t_i + 1) * C_i}{(1 + (Z_i/100))^{t_i + 2}}$$

Formula D.4

Using this formula to calculate the convexity of our 5% coupon bond gives a value of 22.419 years.

It is possible to use the duration and convexity to predict the effect of a parallel shift in the zero curve on the value of the bond. Equation D.1 predicts that, if the zero curve has a parallel shift of +0.1%, then the new value of PV will be:

$$91.59782 + (K_1 * 0.1\%) + (0.5 * K_2 * 0.1\%^2).$$

But from the discussion following Equation D.1 we have:

$$K_1 = -d_m * PV \qquad \text{and}$$
$$K_2 = c * PV$$

so that the new present value equals:

$$91.59782 - (4.15460 * 91.59782 * 0.1\%)$$
$$+(0.5 * 22.419 * 91.59782 * 0.1\%^2)$$

which is 91.21829, thus giving an exact fit to the actual value, which can be calculated directly.

By adjusting the value of duration and convexity of your portfolio you can hedge or take trading positions. However, you will still be exposed to non-parallel movements of the yield curve, and therefore you are far safer using the cash gaps methodology, which is also more straightforward and understandable, to manage your positions.

The discrete cash gaps methodology as developed in Part I implicitly gives the value of convexity; Part VII shows how a measure of convexity can be incorporated explicitly into cash gaps reporting.

Self-study questions

Unless otherwise stated, all interest is quoted on an annual basis, and each month should be considered to be an exact twelfth of a year.

4.1 A bond pays interest semiannually at 8%. It is quoted at a price of 98.765 for delivery 2 months after an interest payment. What is the clean price to buy DEM20 million of the bond, and what is the dirty price? What is the value of the bond?

4.2 Government bonds pay interest semiannually. Representative dirty prices for bonds of different maturities are:

Maturity (years)	Coupon	Value
0.5	8.30	100.123
1.0	8.24	100.028
1.5	8.06	99.986
2.0	8.01	99.954

Calculate the riskfree zero coupon yield curve to 2 years.

4.3 A government bond with an annual coupon of 8% matures in 2 years and 6 months and has a clean price of 99.023. What is its dirty price? What flat zero coupon rate would make the dirty price the present value of the future cashflows of the bond? What is the yield to maturity?

If the 2-year swap spread is 52, what is the market fixed rate on a 2-year swap paying semiannual interest?

4.4 You buy at par a 5-year US$10 million government bond, which pays interest semiannually; you finance the purchase by borrowing funds at Libor for 6 months. You then enter into a 5-year swap where you pay fixed and receive Libor semiannually on US$10 million.

Would you expect to make or lose money if swap spreads widened? What risks do you have other than spread risk?

4.5   If the riskfree and interbank zero curves are:

Year	Riskfree	Interbank
0.5	3.836	4.040
1.0	4.100	4.500
2.0	4.564	5.082
3.0	4.991	5.621
4.0	5.544	6.178
5.0	6.059	6.759

and the 5-year bond rate is 5.85% and the 5-year swap rate is
6.5%, then what is the risk to the net position in question 4.4:

(a) If riskfree rates stay the same and zero spreads increase by
    1 bppa in every maturity.

(b) If zero spreads stay the same and riskfree and interbank zero
    rates increase by 1 bppa in every maturity.

4.6   A bond with $3\frac{1}{2}$ years to maturity pays an annual coupon of
      7.5%. What are its modified duration and convexity, if the zero
      coupon curve is:

Year	Zero
0.5	7.1
1.5	7.3
2.5	7.5
3.5	7.7?

If there is a parallel shift of 10 bppa in the zero curve, what new
value of the bond is predicted using duration and convexity as
risk measures? What is the actual new value of the bond? What
drawbacks do duration and convexity have as measures of risk?

PART V

INTEREST RATE OPTIONS

Part V deals with *options*, that is, contracts where one counterparty has the right, but not the obligation, to enter into an *underlying contract* with another counterparty at some future date. Typical underlying contracts of interest rate options are economically equivalent to an FRA or a swap; the party with the right to choose will enter into the underlying contract only if the fixed rate is better for her than the then prevailing market rate.

Options allow hedging, investment, and risk-taking strategies which cannot be achieved through passive holdings of a portfolio of non-option instruments. (To some extent, the effect of an option can be duplicated by dynamically adjusting a portfolio of non-option instruments, but this may involve extensive transaction costs and will introduce additional risks.)

Since risk is defined in terms of variability of present value, the ultimate goal is to determine an exact pricing formula for interest rate options and to analyse the sensitivity of the price to changes in the determining variables. The focus is on the most common and most tractable types of options; many more exotic options can be priced only by numeric methods.

It turns out that the theory of option pricing can produce only an approximate price for interest rate options; to see why this is so, it is necessary to develop the theory of pricing options where the underlying contract is the purchase or sale at a fixed price of an asset with certain well-defined properties, and then to try to apply the resultant pricing model to interest rate options.

The first two chapters of Part V, Chapters 10 and 11, therefore deal with the pricing of such options on general assets; the final product of these chapters is the *Black Scholes* pricing formula. Chapter 12 then looks at interest rate options, concentrating on their mechanics, economics, and market. Chapter 13 uses a derivative of the Black Scholes formula to price the various types of interest rate options; emphasis is placed on identifying potential inaccuracies of the pricing formulae. Finally, Chapter 14 uses the pricing formulae for the various interest rate options to derive formulae for the sensitivity of the price to changes in the determining variables; this allows a discussion of the reporting and management of an option portfolio.

A standard textbook on options is *Options Markets* by John Cox and Mark Rubinstein, published by Prentice Hall. This concentrates on options on shares, and therefore much of the material is peripheral to the subject of interest rate options; however, as far as possible the terminology and notation used here is consistent with *Options Markets* and you are referred to it as a useful source for further information on the general theory of option pricing. Much of the development of the theory in Chapters 10 and 11 closely parallels the treatment of *Options Markets*.

A more brutally mathematical treatment of option pricing is to be found in *Options, Futures, and Other Derivative Securities*, by John Hull, also published by Prentice Hall; this has the advantage of including material explicitly on interest rate options. The review of numerical methods for pricing options at the end of Chapter 13 follows this book. If you intend to use options which cannot be priced using Black Scholes, then *Options, Futures, and Other Derivative Securities* is a good starting point for learning the full mathematical pricing theory.

Not every reader will need the full detail of Part V. If you are already comfortable with options on general assets then you can skip Chapters 10 and 11 altogether; if you are already using interest rate options and need the exact pricing and sensitivity formulae for reference, then you will find these in Chapters 13 and 14. For the reader who wishes a general overview of the subject without too much detail, the chapter description at the head of each chapter attempts to signpost the material which you have to understand in order to follow the outline of the main argument.

Inevitably, there is a great number of reasonably complex mathematical formulae involved in the exposition of the subject. The mathematically unsophisticated should still be able to derive a useful understanding of the material if they are prepared to take the details of the mathematics on trust.

CHAPTER 10

Options

The interest rate risk arising from any set of future fixed and Libor cashflows can be hedged by a static portfolio of swaps and FRAs. However, there are interest rate risks which cannot be hedged by any such portfolio. For example, consider a 5-year bond which pays interest semiannually at the lower of 6-month Libor and 9%, referred to as a 'capped floating rate note'. It turns out that neither the issuer of nor the investor in such a bond can hedge the resulting interest rate risk with a static portfolio of swaps and FRAs. (It is possible to construct a hedge by dynamically adjusting a portfolio of swaps and FRAs as interest rates change, but such a dynamic hedge may have high transaction costs and cannot, in fact, eliminate all risk.) There is, therefore, a requirement for a new class of hedging instruments: interest rate options.

As explained in the introduction to Part V, this and the next chapter look at options on general assets; after mastering this material, you will be able to look at interest rate options in the subsequent chapters.

This chapter defines an option contract and looks at what can be said about option pricing without extended calculation. After a series of definitions, the first key result is *put-call parity* for *European* options; this allows the derivation of *put* prices from *call* prices, and thus simplifies the search for an exact pricing formula. The next section identifies five variables which affect the price of an option, these are the *strike price*, the current price of the underlying asset, the time to the *exercise date*, the interest rate, and the *volatility*. The last section is aimed at developing your intuition for the behaviour of the price of the option as the determining variables change; it does this by using simple arguments to prove various constraints on the option price. If you are aiming simply for an overview then you can skip this section.

10.1 DEFINITIONS

An option contract, normally referred to simply as an 'option', is a contract between two counterparties, a *writer* (or *seller*), and a *buyer* (or *holder*). The buyer pays the writer a *premium*, and in return the buyer has the right, but not the obligation, to enter into an *underlying contract* with the writer during some specified *exercise period*. The *option period* is from the contract date to the end of the exercise period; it ends on the *maturity* date.

An example of an option contract would be: you pay me £50 today to have the right to buy my car in a year's time for £2,000. You are the buyer, I am the writer; the premium is £50, the underlying contract is your purchase of my car for £2,000, and the exercise period is the one day a year from now. The option period is from today for one year. Presumably you will choose to *exercise the option*, that is to take up your right under the option to buy my car, if and only if the market value of the car in one year's time turns out to be at least £2,000.

Another example would be a film producer paying a writer US$50,000 to have the right to buy the screen rights for his new banking textbook for US$500,000 at any time during the next 2 years. The buyer would be the producer, the writer (appropriately) would be the writer; the underlying contract would be the purchase of the film rights for US$500,000, and the exercise and option periods would both be the next 2 years. Presumably the producer would exercise the option only if he thought that the film rights were worth more than US$500,000 at the time.

An option in which the exercise can take place only on a particular day is called a *European option*; an option with an extended exercise period is an *American option*. (These names are historical rather than geographical; they relate to which types of options used to be traded where.) The first of the examples above is a European option, and the second is an American option. By necessity, the exercise date on a European option is also the option maturity.

The theory to be developed below will be for European options only; this is because the vast majority of interest rate options are of this type or can be approximated closely by a similar European option, and because excluding American options allows a much cleaner theoretical structure. Chapter 13 will say a little about how the theory could be extended to include American options.

The definition of an option above is extremely general; let us focus on options where the underlying contract is the purchase or sale at a specified price of an asset with certain properties. These properties are:

(a) The asset must be one of a large class of similar assets.
(b) At all times the asset must have a publicly known price.
(c) The asset must remain intact over the option period.

Point (c) means that if, for example, I write an option for you to buy my car and I sell the stereo before the exercise date, then the sale proceeds would be included with the car if you exercise the option to buy.

A typical example of such an asset would be a fixed number of quoted shares in which there is expected to be no dividend during the option period; for ease of reference these two chapters on general options will assume that all the underlying assets are such quoted shares. Chapter 12 will identify corresponding assets for interest rate options.

An option in which the underlying contract is for the buyer to buy the asset from the writer is a *call option*; an option for the buyer to sell the asset to the writer is a *put option*. The specified price at which the underlying purchase or sale will take place if the option is exercised is the *strike price*. (In *Options Markets* the term used is 'striking price'; 'strike price' is more current in interest rate markets, and so it is used here.)

Both the original examples were call options. An example of a put option would be where I pay you £10 to have the right to sell you my two shares in Graham & Trotman for £500 each in three months. Note that this is a European put option on quoted shares, which fits in with the restricted universe of options with which we are working. It is assumed without further mention that there will be no dividends within the option period in this example or in any of the examples below.

Such put and call options allow hedgers and investors to follow strategies which would not be practical were they restricted to forward contracts to buy and sell assets; this is discussed further for interest rate options in Chapter 12.

We are interested in risk management, where risk is defined in terms of variability of present value. In order to understand the risk characteristics of options it is therefore necessary to be able to calculate their market price under any circumstances. To allow the development of such a pricing theory it will be assumed that:

(d) The market bid-offer spread on the asset is zero.
(e) Transaction costs are zero (so that any arbitrage will be exercised)
(f) Bid-offer spreads on interest rates are zero.
(g) Tax effects can be ignored.

Although these assumptions are obviously not wholly accurate, economies of scale mean that major participants in wholesale markets can come close to zero spreads and transaction costs. Also, as financial institutions converge on recognising all trading income on a mark-to-market basis, there become fewer cases of differences in tax treatment for income from different products; any remaining difference which allows a profitable arbitrage will tend to be removed by legislation. Consequently, you would expect option prices to be close to the prices predicted by a theory based on the above assumptions; this can be checked by a statistical analysis of actual option prices.

To remove fussy detail it is also assumed that:

(h) The option premium is paid on the contract date. (We could alternatively work with the present value of the premium.)

(i) You can sell shares you do not have today and deliver them by buying them in on the option exercise day. (Otherwise we would have to discuss a mechanism of borrowing shares. Since there will be no dividend until after the exercise date, the purchaser does not lose out by your late delivery.)

(j) Options are transferrable from one holder or writer to another at any time, on payment of their current value. (Otherwise we would have to speak continually of one counterparty entering into a back-to-back option with another market participant to realise an arbitrage; this would have the same economic effect as transferring an option for its current value.)

(k) There is effectively a single market price for the asset in the underlying contract on the exercise day, or, equivalently, exercise must be at a particular time on the exercise day. (This ensures that the decision to exercise will be a simple yes or no, and will not involve a succession of decisions through the day. It is a good approximation for most interest rate options.)

The following terminology is often used to describe options:

Definition 10.1 A call option on which the strike price is below the current share price is *in the money*; if the strike is above the share price it is *out of the money*. A put is in the money if the strike is above the share price and out of the money if the strike is below the current share price. A call or put is *at the money* if the strike equals the share price.

An option will be exercised only if it is in the money at maturity; otherwise it will be allowed to lapse.

The following notation will be used:

S Current price for one share
S^* Price for one share at exercise date
C Current value of a call option
P Current value of a put option
K Strike price for one share
t Years from contract date to exercise date
$Z\%$ Zero coupon rate to exercise date at contract date
r The annualised scaling factor $1 + (Z/100)$

Sometimes it will be necessary to look at a day intermediate between the contract date and the exercise date; t will then be the time in years from the intermediate day to the exercise date, and $Z\%$ will be the zero coupon rate to the exercise date prevailing on the intermediate day.

The theory is developed using the riskfree yield curve, that is, the yield curve defined by government bonds. However, Chapter 13 explains that the interest rate options market uses the interbank yield curve in pricing; the justification for this will be discussed in that chapter.

The development of the theory starts by establishing the variables which will affect the price of an option and by establishing qualitatively how the option price depends on each variable; in some cases it will be possible to establish a quantitative relationship. You should be able to develop some feel for option pricing by working through this material.

10.2 PUT-CALL PARITY

In general it is far from clear how to price options. However, on the option maturity date the pricing becomes more accessible, and so this section will concentrate on the price of puts and calls immediately before they are exercised or lapse. This will allow the demonstration of a relationship between put and call options on the same asset at the same strike price on the same date; this relationship is know as *put-call parity*.

The exposition will rely heavily on payoff diagrams; you met these in Part II as a useful way of displaying price relationships by graphing the value of an asset or liability in particular circumstances against the possible values of a single variable. Payoff diagrams are sometimes called *price diagrams* because they show the price of a portfolio in different circumstances; the two terms will be used interchangeably.

Figure 10.1 shows payoff diagrams for the holders of a put and a call option on a single share at maturity. The variable along the x axis is

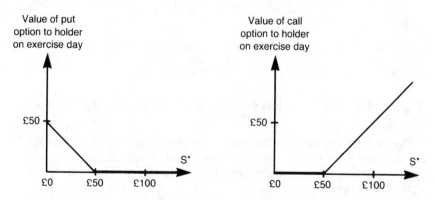

Figure 10.1   Payoff to the holders of a put and call option on a single share at maturity.

$S\star$, the share price on the exercise date, and the y axis shows the value of the option. For both the put and call the strike price K is £50.

In each case the holder will exercise the option only if it is in the money; consequently, the option cannot be worth less than zero. If the option is exercised, then it will be worth the difference between the strike price K and the share price $S\star$, since the holder can sell (buy) a share at K and buy (sell) it back in the market at $S\star$. This can be expressed as:

Result 10.1 The value of a call at its maturity is max(0, $S\star$ - K), where the symbol max(A, B, ..., Z) equals the largest of A, B, ..., Z. The value of a put at its maturity is max(0, K - $S\star$).

It can be seen that the holder of a call option has unlimited potential for gain, while the holder of a put option cannot gain more than the strike price. In both cases the holder cannot lose anything since he is under no obligation to exercise. (The original payment of premium represents a sunk cost, which is not relevant in considering the economics of the option at maturity.)

Since the writer and the holder of an option must have equal and opposite gains and losses, the payoff diagrams for the writers of the same options as above must be as in Figure 10.2:

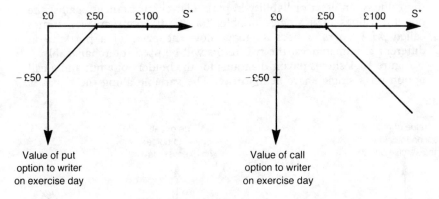

Figure 10.2 shows payoff to writers of a put and call option on a single share at maturity.

Figure 10.2 Payoff to writers of a put and call option on a single share at maturity.

Figure 10.3 shows payoff diagrams for the buyer of a share and for an investor in a riskfree zero coupon bond which matures on the option exercise day and which pays £50 on maturity. The snapshot is again at the option exercise day.

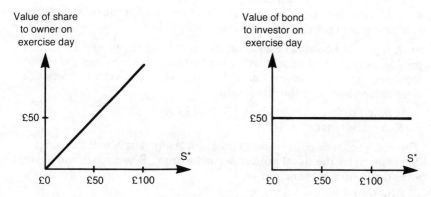

Figure 10.3 Payoff to buyer of share and investor in riskfree zero coupon bond.

Benefitting from other people's research, we can now draw payoff diagrams for two separate portfolios:

- portfolio A consists of buy call, sell put; and
- portfolio B consists of buy share, sell bond paying strike price at maturity.

The payoff diagrams are shown in Figure 10.4.

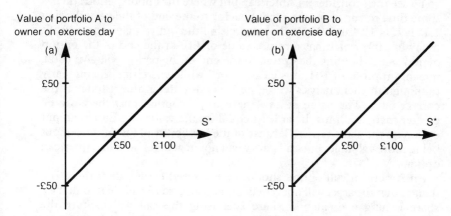

Figure 10.4 Payoff to owners of option and non-option portfolios on option exercise date.

The payoff of portfolio A equals the payoff of portfolio B; the two portfolios must therefore have the same value at all times, since if one is more expensive at any time before the exercise date, then there will be a riskless arbitrage as follows:

- immediately buy the cheaper portfolio and sell the more expensive, giving a positive net cashflow; and
- at the exercise date sell the bought portfolio and buy the sold portfolio, giving a zero net cashflow.

Such a pair is known as *equivalent portfolios*, and the route to an exact pricing formula will rely heavily on constructing equivalent portfolios involving options, assets, and bonds. The equivalent portfolios constructed here give the relationship:

At time t before exercise date, $C - P = S - Kr^{-t}$.
(Remember that $r^{-t} = 1/r^t$.)

The result holds since the value of the bond at any time before the exercise day is given by the usual present value formula. Rearranging the terms gives the equivalent relation:

Result 10.2 $P = C - S + Kr^{-t}$.

This relation is known as put-call parity, since it expresses the price of a put in terms of the price of a call and of known variables. Because of this relationship, the search for an option pricing formula can concentrate on calls only; a formula for call prices will allow the pricing of puts through put-call parity.

Note that put-call parity does not hold in general for American options; this is because it is sometimes worthwhile to exercise an American put option before the end of the option period, and hence the price of an American put may be different from the price of a European put.

To see this, consider an American put where the option period still has some time to run, with the scaling factor to the end of the period being 1.1. If K is 101 and S is 1, then exercising the put will give you a profit today of 100, which has a future value of 110 at the end of the option period. Since holding the option to the end of the period will give you a maximum profit of 101, it is clearly worthwhile exercising the put early (although further analysis would be needed to determine if today is the correct day). The value of an American put option may therefore be greater than, and must be at least equal to, the value of a European put option on the same terms. Because of the possibility of the American put being more valuable, put-call parity will not in general hold for American options.

An American call option should be exercised early only if there is a danger that the asset will not remain intact; an example of this would be a share issuing a dividend, where exercising the call will capture the dividend as well as the share. If the asset does remain intact, then you are better off holding the option to maturity, since the exercise price will have a lower present value then and since you retain the choice of not exercising if the asset price drops. Under assumption (c) above, the asset will remain intact to maturity, and thus the European call options discussed here will have the same value as American call options on the same terms; however, in the more general case the value of an American call may be greater than the value of an equivalent European call.

We have now seen:

(a) the price of a call at maturity is max$(0, S^\star - K)$;
(b) the price of a put at maturity is max$(0, K - S^\star)$; and
(c) at all times, $P = C - S + Kr^{-t}$.

As a simple exercise, you can prove that put-call parity holds at the exercise date, by considering the three cases where $S^\star$ is greater than, equal to, and less than K.

10.3 VARIABLES DETERMINING OPTION PRICING

This section identifies the different variables which will determine the price of a call option before maturity; as demonstrated above, the price of put options will follow by put-call parity.

We already know that the call price is dependent on the stock price S and on the strike rate K, since these appear in the formula for the price of a call at maturity. The formula for put-call parity involves two further variables, r a function of the zero coupon rate, and t the time to maturity; it is shown below that these two variables do indeed affect the price of a call option. In addition to these you will discover *volatility*, for which the lowercase Greek letter sigma, written σ, will be used; σ measures the likely size of future changes in the asset's value and is similar to the standard deviation of the expected distribution of future prices, which we met in Part I.

It will turn out that, given the assumptions above, S, K, r, t, and σ are the only variables which affect the price of an option.

The next section is devoted to deriving various constraints imposed on the option price by the values of these variables, but the first of these constraints is derived here since it is needed to demonstrate that t and r do affect the option price.

Consider C plus the present value of K; this cannot be less than S, since, if it is, you could enter into the following arbitrage:

Buy a call, deposit the present value of the strike price for time t, and sell the share. If the share value at the option maturity date is above the exercise price, then exercise the option to buy the share; otherwise, buy in the share at the market price $S^\star$, and deliver the share.

Your cashflows are:

Time 0	$+S$	(sell share)
	$-C$	(buy call)
	$-Kr^{-t}$	(deposit)
Time t	$+K$	(maturing deposit)
	$-\min(K, S^\star)$	(exercise or buy share)

The symbol min $(A, B, ..., Z)$ equals the smallest of $A, B, ..., Z$.
Since the cashflow at time 0 is positive and the cashflow at time t is positive or zero, you have successfully executed a profitable arbitrage.

Therefore the original situation cannot arise, and we have the result:

Result 10.3 $C + Kr^{-t}$ is greater than or equal to S.

If t is greater than 0, then usually we would expect the strict inequality to hold. Since we are generally interested in the call price, we can rearrange the terms as:

Constraint 10.1 C is greater than or equal to $S - Kr^{-t}$.

This constraint can be used to show that the call price is dependent on r and t. Consider a call on a share with current price S; the strike price is K, the time to maturity is t and the interest variable is r. Suppose that the variables are:

S	£100
C	£40
K	£77
t	1
r	1.1

You can check that $C + Kr^{-t}$ equals £110, which is greater than S.

Suppose that all the variables stay the same except that r becomes 1.3. If C remains unchanged then $C + Kr^{-t}$ equals £99.23, which is less than S, contradicting Constraint 10.1. Therefore C must change, and so C is dependent on r. A similar argument shows that C is dependent on t. It will be shown below that C is dependent on the two variables separately, and not just on the expression r^t.

To show that the call price depends on σ demands a rigorous definition of volatility. Consider a time sequence of the price of a particular share at close of business each day for, say, a year. The ratio of each pair of successive prices would have some statistical distribution. You might expect that the distribution would be normal, but this would mean that there was a finite probability that the ratio could be negative, leading to a negative share price. A more self-consistent assumption is based on the idea that investors will expect that the growth in the share price will be a constant proportion of the share price itself, thus giving them on average a constant yield on their investment. This leads to the assumption that the *logarithms* of the ratios of successive prices are normally distributed, and it is this assumption which is borne out by studies which have been done on share prices. A variable whose logarithm is normally distributed is said to be *lognormally distributed*; in order to develop an exact option pricing theory it will be assumed that the ratio of successive prices of the underlying asset is lognormally distributed. (This is, in fact, equivalent to the price itself being lognormally distributed.)

Note that all logarithms referred to are *natural logarithms*, that is logarithms to the base e, which equals $2.718281828459...$

Although there is evidence that quoted share prices are reasonably close to lognormally distributed, it is not necessarily the case for other assets; if necessary, the theory could be amended to cope with other distributions, although you would not expect to obtain a closed-form pricing formula for a general distribution.

The mean of the distribution of the logarithms of the ratios measures the average daily change in the price, and the standard deviation measures the dispersion of daily changes around the mean. The actual standard deviation of the logarithms as measured from a time sequence is known as *historic volatility*. The volatility used in pricing options is the market expectation of the standard deviation of the logarithm of future ratios of successive prices of the asset; this is known as *market volatility*. Volatility is quoted on an annualised basis, that is, it is adjusted to the value which it would have if the underlying period measured were one year.

If you are trying to build your intuition, you can start by considering the volatility to be the standard deviation of the price ratios themselves; you will need to remember the logarithm only when it comes to looking at exact pricing formulae.

Suppose that for a particular share the volatility is zero. This means that the future share price is completely predictable; in particular the price $S^\star$ on a call expiry date can be predicted. Therefore, at the time that the call is entered into, the buyer's cashflows can be predicted exactly as:

Time 0	$-C$
Time t	$\max(S^\star - K, 0)$.

If $S^\star$ is not greater than K then the option is worthless, otherwise it is worth the present value of $(S^\star - K)$. But the present value of K is Kr^{-t}, and the present value of $S^\star$ must be the current share price S, since otherwise there would be an opportunity for riskless arbitrage; this gives

$$C = S - Kr^{-t}.$$

To demonstrate the dependence on volatility, choose K to be Sr^t so that C becomes zero.

Now suppose that all the variables except for volatility stay unchanged, but volatility becomes positive for the period to time t. This means that the market expectations of S at option maturity are distributed around the original $S^\star$, with a positive probability that the stock price will be greater than the original $S^\star$. If this does happen, then the option will have a positive value at time t. The present value of the option, C, is the present value of each possible state of the option at time t times the probability of that state occurring. Since the option will have positive future value in some states and zero future value the rest of the time, the contribution to the present value must be positive from some states and zero from the others. C must therefore be greater than zero.

This shows that changing the volatility can change the price of a call, and that the call price is therefore dependent on the volatility.

Note that the above working did not specify the discount rate to use to value the possible future profit; this is because the discount rate depends on the risk of the future cashflows, and we have not yet developed a theory to enable us to determine this risk for an option. Historically the problem of determining the discount rate was a major obstacle to developing a consistent theory of option pricing; Chapter 11 will show this problem can be sidestepped in deriving an exact pricing formula.

You have now seen that the five variables, S, K, t, r, and σ are needed to price an option. How do you know that there are no other variables needed? The answer is that you will not know until you have seen an explicit pricing formula, and you are therefore asked meanwhile to take the list of five on trust.

However, you might worry that market expectation of the asset price at maturity should affect the option price, and therefore it is worth a brief digression to give a plausible reason why it cannot do so. Suppose the market expectation of $S^{\star}$ increases while S, K, t, r and σ stay the same; you might suspect that a call would become more expensive and a put would become cheaper. But from put-call parity

$$P = C - S + Kr^{-t}.$$

Therefore, either C and P both increase, or they both decrease, or they both stay the same. It seems easier to believe that they both stay the same than that a put becomes more expensive or a call becomes cheaper. A proof will have to await the pricing formula.

10.4 CONSTRAINTS ON OPTION PRICES

This section shows how the call price is constrained by the values of the five determining variables. In *Options Markets* the term used for this is 'general arbitrage relationships' which seems unhelpful; this book refers to 'constraints'.

We already have our first constraint; for ease of reference it is repeated here:

Constraint 10.1 C is greater than or equal to $S - Kr^{-t}$.

We already know that C is never negative. It is also clear that if C is greater than S, buying the asset and writing the call would be a riskless arbitrage. This gives immediately:

Constraint 10.2 C is greater than or equal to zero.

and

Constraint 10.3 C is less than or equal to S.

This lets us draw Figure 10.5.

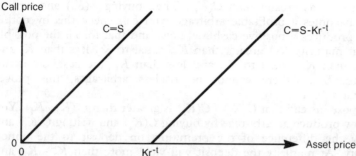

Figure 10.5   Price diagram of call option value against asset price. C must be on or between the two 45 degree lines.

We can now turn to C as a function of the strike price K. Three constraints are stated and then proved. All three use the symbol $C(K_i)$ to mean the value of C for strike price K_i.

Constraint 10.4   If K_2 is greater than K_1 then $C(K_1)$ is greater than or equal to $C(K_2)$.

Constraint 10.5   If K_2 is greater than K_1 then $r^{-t}(K_2 - K_1)$ is greater than or equal to $C(K_1) - C(K_2)$.

(You can read this as stating that an increase in the present value of the strike price cannot cause a greater decrease in the call price; for an American call, only the weaker condition of $K_2 - K_1$ being greater than or equal to $C(K_1) - C(K_2)$ can be proved.)

Constraint 10.6   The price diagram of C against K is *convex up*; this means that if you join any two points on the line $C(K)$ by a straight line, the straight line must lie on or above $C(K)$. This mathematical usage should become clear if you examine Figure 10.6 which incorporates all three constraints on C as a function of K; you should see that 'convex' has its normal meaning.

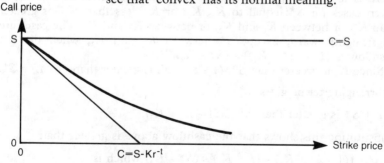

Figure 10.6   Price diagram of call option value against strike price. Constraints on C as a function of K. The line must have the shape shown and must be above the sloping line and below the horizontal line.

The proof of the first two constraints is straightforward. Suppose that $C(K_2)$ was greater than $C(K_1)$. Then buying $C(K_1)$ and writing $C(K_2)$ becomes a profitable arbitrage; you can check this by noting that it produces a positive cashflow now, and that for all the possible cases at maturity ($S^\star$ greater than K_2, equal to K_2, less than K_2 and greater than K_1, equal to K_1, and less than K_1) the cashflow is not negative. Since there cannot be riskless arbitrages, this proves Constraint 10.4.

Suppose instead that $C(K_1)$ - $C(K_2)$ is greater than $r^{-t}(K_2 - K_1)$. You can now produce an arbitrage by buying $C(K_2)$ and writing $C(K_1)$ and putting the difference of the premiums on deposit to the option maturity. At maturity the deposit will yield more than $K_2 - K_1$, and you can check all the possible cases for $S^\star$ to establish that your net outflow on the two options cannot be greater than $K_1 - K_2$. This shows that if Constraint 10.5 is breached then there will be a riskless arbitrage, and thus Constraint 10.5 must hold. (For an American call exercise might be immediate, and therefore to ensure that the strategy above gives deposit proceeds of $K_2 - K_1$ it is necessary to have the difference in the call prices greater than the difference in the strike prices themselves; this explains the weaker constraint for American calls.)

Proving the third constraint involves slightly more work. Start by noting that if K_2 is between K_1 and K_3, then there is an L between 0 and 1 such that:

$$K_2 = (L * K_1) + ((1 - L) * K_3).$$

If Constraint 10.6 does not hold, then there exist K_1 and K_3 with a K_2 between them such that $C(K_2)$ is above the straight line joining $C(K_1)$ and $C(K_3)$, and thus:

$$C(K_2) \text{ is greater than } (L * C(K_1)) + ((1 - L) * C(K_2)).$$

The arbitrage this time is writing $C(K_2)$ and buying L of $C(K_1)$ and $(1 - L)$ of $C(K_3)$. This gives a positive cashflow today. To show that there is a zero or positive cashflow at maturity involves looking at seven cases for $S^\star$: equal to K_1, K_2, or K_3, less than K_1, or greater than K_3, or between K_1 and K_2, or between K_2 and K_3. The cases are all straightforward, except $S^\star$ between K_2 and K_3, when the net cashflow is $(L * (S^\star - K_1)) - (S^\star - K_2)$.

Since K_3 is greater than $S^\star$, $(1 - L) * K_3$ is greater than $(1 - L) * S^\star$.

Rearranging terms gives

$$L * S^\star \text{ is greater than } S^\star - ((1 - L) * K_3).$$

Substituting this shows that the cashflow above is greater than

$$S^\star - ((1 - L) * K_3) - (L * K_1) - (S^\star - K_2) \text{ which is}$$

$$K_2 - ((L * K_1) + ((1 - L) * K_3)) \text{ which is 0.}$$

Thus for this case the cashflow at maturity is positive; the other six cases follow easily, thus proving that if the constraint does not hold then there will be a riskless arbitrage. Constraint 10.6 is thus proved.

Consider now the dependence of C on t. The symbol $C(t_i)$ will represent the value of C for time t_i. It is easy to show:

Constraint 10.7   If t_2 is greater than t_1 then $C(t_2)$ is greater than or equal to $C(t_1)$.

If this constraint does not hold then you can construct an arbitrage by buying $C(t_2)$ and writing $C(t_1)$. Your cashflow today is positive. At t_1, there are two cases; if the option is not exercised then you have definitely made a profit, so consider the case where the option is exercised. You will receive K, which you put on deposit to t_2; you have to deliver the asset, but do not buy it in until t_2. If $S^\star$ at t_2 is greater than K then exercise the option, paying out K from the maturing deposit (and keeping the interest) and delivering the asset against $C(t_1)$; if $S^\star$ is less than K then simply buy in $S^\star$ and you do even better. This proves that Constraint 10.7 must hold.

It seems likely that if volatility increases the price of a call will increase, but this cannot be demonstrated by a simple arbitrage relation. Similarly, if interest rates increase then the price of a call seems likely to increase, following the example in section 10.3. Proofs of both of these results will have to await the exact option pricing formulae in the next chapter.

SUMMARY

This chapter has been concerned with setting up a framework for discussing options on general assets; the next chapter will develop a pricing formula for such general options, while interest rate options will not be considered until chapter 12. In order to develop a pricing theory it is necessary to specify a set of assumptions and limitations on the options to be considered. These allow a proof of the key result of put-call parity for European options, which means that the search for a pricing formula need consider only call options. At least five variables affect the price of an option: strike rate, current asset price, time to exercise, zero coupon interest rate to the exercise date, and volatility. It will be shown in the next chapter that, within the theoretical framework, these five suffice. Even without a pricing formula, arguments based on the possibility of arbitrage can demonstrate a series of constraints on the price of an option; consideration of these constraints can help build your intuition about options.

CHAPTER 11

Option pricing formula

This chapter demonstrates how an exact option pricing formula can be derived. The treatment parallels Chapter 5 of *Options Markets*, and you are recommended to that work for full rigorous proofs; in working through the proofs there you should remember that they are derived for *American* options.

The alternative to deriving a formula is simply to state it. The advantage of working through the derivations is that it should give you more understanding and confidence; critically, it should also help you to recognise the limitations of the theory.

Here a full mathematical treatment is given for the single period binomial model. It is then shown how the single period model can be extended into a multiple period binomial model, and the pricing formula for this is derived. This allows the introduction of *delta hedging*, which is central to the management of option positions. A limiting process is then applied to the multiple period model to produce the Black Scholes pricing formula, which is the standard formula used (with adjustments in certain circumstances) by participants in options markets. Finally the implications of the Black Scholes formula are discussed, with the intention of developing your intuition in the use of options.

Even if you are aiming simply for an overview then it should still be worthwhile for you to look at the detail of the single period binomial model, since this contains the basic trick whereby an exact pricing formula for options can be obtained. However, you can safely skim the detailed mathematics of the derivation of the multiple period binomial model pricing formula and of the Black Scholes formula, provided that you take the trouble to see how the general shape of the formulae emerges.

You should bear in mind that we are still working with general assets under the various assumptions listed in Chapter 10; interest rate options are not considered until the next chapter.

11.1 SINGLE PERIOD BINOMIAL MODE

This section finally succeeds in pricing a call option before its maturity. It achieves this by working with what appear to be very artificial assumptions; in subsequent sections you will see that these assumptions are not in fact so artificial, and that the single period model can be extended into a general pricing tool.

The options considered in this section are European call options with an underlying asset which has a price S today at the start of a period and which will definitely have one of two prices at the end of the period:

uS with probability q; or
dS with probability $(1-q)$.

(The constants u and d stand for up and down, with u greater than d; u must be greater than 1, although d does not have to be less than 1.)

A unit of currency deposited in riskfree bonds at the start of the period will grow to $\breve{r}$ units at the end of the period; $\breve{r}$ is thus the scaling factor for the period. ($\breve{r}$ is used here in place of s to avoid confusion with the asset price S; the symbol used in *Options Markets* is r without the breve accent, but that is being used here for the annualised scaling factor.) In order to prevent the possibility of a riskless arbitrage, $\breve{r}$ must be greater than 1 and must be between d and u.

At the start of the period, what is the value C of a call option with a strike price of K?

We shall use the trick of creating an equivalent portfolio. Portfolio X will contain our call option, and portfolio Y will contain Δ units of S and value B of riskfree bonds. (Δ is the uppercase Greek letter delta.)

We know that the value of portfolio X at the end of the period will be:

if the price goes to uS, $C_u = \max(0 , uS - K)$; and
if the price goes to dS, $C_d = \max(0 , dS - K)$.

Portfolio Y will have value at the end of the period of:

if the price goes to uS, $\Delta uS + \breve{r}B$; and
if the price goes to dS, $\Delta dS + \breve{r}B$.

If we choose:

$$\Delta = \frac{C_u - C_d}{(u - d) * S} \text{ and}$$ **Equation 11.1**

$$B = \frac{uC_d - dC_u}{(u - d) * \breve{r}}$$

then portfolio Y will have the same value as portfolio X at the end of the period whether the price is uS or dS. (You should take the trouble to check this for yourself.) Portfolios X and Y are therefore equivalent portfolios, and, because of our assumption of zero transaction cost, they must have the same value at the start of the period or else there would be a riskless arbitrage. Therefore the value of the call option at the start of the period must be the value of portfolio Y, which is $\Delta S + B$.

Expanding the expressions for Δ and B gives:

$$C = \frac{1}{\check{r}}\left[\left(\frac{\check{r} - d}{u - d}\right)C_u + \left(\frac{u - \check{r}}{u - d}\right)C_d\right] \qquad \textbf{Equation 11.2}$$

We have thus priced a one period call option.

The expression for C can be simplified by defining the variable p as:

$$p = \frac{(\check{r} - d)}{(u - d)}$$

giving

$$C = \frac{1}{\check{r}}(pC_u + (1 - p)C_d) \qquad \textbf{Equation 11.3}$$

The variable p in Equation 11.3 will always be between zero and one; it can be seen to be the probability of an up movement on the assumption that investors are *risk neutral*, that is they do not demand a premium for investing in a risky asset, and that the expected return on S is therefore the riskfree scaling factor $\check{r}$. (You can check that $puS + (1 - p)dS = \check{r}S$.) Equation 11.3 can thus be interpreted as stating that the value of the call at the start of the period is the present value, discounting at the riskfree rate of return, of the expected value of the call at the end of the period on the assumption that investors are risk neutral. It turns out that this concept of *risk-neutral valuation* can be extended to the pricing of general options because of a mathematical property of the differential equation governing the price of options. Risk-neutral valuation is not needed further here in the derivation of the Black Scholes formula, but it is an important pricing tool in its own right; it will be mentioned again in the review of numerical methods for pricing options at the end of Chapter 13.

The expression for C derived above contains S, K, $\check{r}$, u, and d. (Note that q is represented indirectly through its effect on the value of S, but it does not appear explicitly here or in any of the other pricing formulae derived below.) Of the five variables derived in Chapter 10, two, namely S and K, are in the above list. In fact, $\check{r}$ used here represents r^t in the original notation; consequently both r and t are present as variables.

What of the volatility σ? Volatility was defined as the standard deviation of the logarithm of the ratio of successive prices of an asset. The standard deviation of a variable is the squareroot of the variance, where the variance is the average of the square of the difference between the variable and its expected value.

In the case of the single period binomial model, the possible values of the price at the end of the period are uS with probability q and dS with probability $1 - q$, and hence the expected value of the logarithm of the ratio of the prices at the end and at the beginning of the period is $q\log(u) + (1 - q)\log(d)$; call this E.

The variance of the logarithm of the ratio is

$$q(\log(u) - E)^2 + (1 - q)(\log(d) - E)^2.$$

It can thus be seen that the volatility is a function of q, u, and d. Since we have two equations linking q, u, and d to the expected value of the price and to its volatility, both of which are assumed to be known from the market, it is possible to eliminate the dependence on q and to treat the volatility as being a function of u and d.

The discrepancy of having six variables rather than five contributing to the option price will be resolved when the Black Scholes formula is derived as a limiting case of a multiple period binomial model; u and d will be subject to an additional constraint and will become effectively one variable, which will be directly related to σ.

Before going on to the multiple period model in the next section, let us work out an option price using the single period formula. Suppose that a house is worth £200,000 today. We may be on the edge of a recession, in which case the house will be worth only £190,000 in a year; alternatively, there may be a boom, in which case it will be worth £240,000. The riskfree interest rate for the year is 10%. On the rather unrealistic assumption that all the conditions of Chapter 10 are satisfied in this case, what should you pay for a call option to buy the house at £220,000 in a year's time?

We have:

$S = $ £200,000
$K = $ £220,000
$\check{r} = 1.1$
$u = 1.2$
$d = 0.95$

The value of the option in a year will be either

$C_u = $ £20,000 or $C_d = 0$.

To construct the equivalent portfolio (using a cheaper house, perhaps) we would have:

$$\Delta = \frac{(20,000 - 0)}{(1.2 - 0.95) * 200,000}$$

$$= 0.4$$

$$B = \frac{((1.2 * £0) - (0.95 * £20,000))}{(0.25 * 1.1)}$$

$$= -£69,091$$

This gives:

$$C = (0.4 * £200,000) - £69,091$$

$$= £10,909.$$

The equivalent portfolio has a short position in bonds; it can be shown that this is always the case for call options. You should check that the equivalent portfolio has the same value as the call today and also at maturity, whether prices go up or down.

11.2 MULTIPLE PERIOD BINOMIAL MODEL

We have priced a call option with the unrealistic assumption that the asset price can change only once before the option maturity. The assumption can be made slightly less unrealistic by allowing the asset price to change twice, as shown in Figure 11.1.

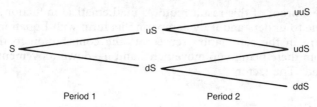

Figure 11.1 Two period binomial model of share price.

We now have a two period model, and the assumption is that in each period *independently* the asset price can change by a multiple of u with probability q, or by a multiple of d with probability $(1-q)$; we also require that the riskfree scaling factor in each period is $\check{r}$. (It is possible to have different interest rates in each period in the binomial model, but in order to derive the Black Scholes formula later on we work with the special case where $\check{r}$ is constant.)

The basic trick is to value a portfolio containing one call option by calculating from right to left in the diagram above. Writing in the values of the call at the various nodes of the diagram as C_{uu} etc. gives Figure 11.2.

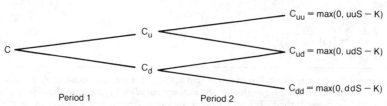

Figure 11.2 Two period binomial model showing call prices at each node.

Using Equation 11.3 we can immediately price:

$C_u = (1/\check{r}) * (pC_{uu} + (1-p)C_{ud})$ and
$C_d = (1/\check{r}) * (pC_{ud} + (1-p)C_{dd})$

where p is $\dfrac{(\check{r} - d)}{(u - d)}$ as before.

We can now use the same process of forming an equivalent portfolio of assets and bonds to price C in terms of C_u and C_d. The form of Equation 11.3 will remain the same, giving:

$$C = \frac{1}{\check{r}}(pC_u + (1-p)C_d) \quad \text{so that}$$

$$C = \frac{1}{\check{r}^2}[p^2 C_{uu} + 2p(1-p)C_{ud} + (1-p)^2 C_{dd}]$$

The same procedure can be extended to n periods, giving: [1,2]

$$C = \frac{1}{\check{r}^n}\sum_{j=0}^{n}\left(\frac{n!}{j!\,(n-j)!}\right)p^j(1-p)^{n-j}\max(0,\ u^j d^{n-j}S - K)$$

A rigorous proof of this result requires mathematical induction, but it is possible to understand it by comparing its form with Equation 11.3. Each term in the summation represents the contribution to the call value from there being j up movements and $n-j$ down movements over the period. The factor

$$\frac{n!}{j!\,(n-j)!}$$

is the number of different ways of having precisely j ups out of n choices. Each factor of p comes from an up movement, and each factor of $(1-p)$ comes from a down movement. The max( ) expression is the value of a call option at the end of the period if there are precisely j up movements.

The formula for C can be simplified by including only these terms which are greater than zero, that is, by ensuring that there are enough up movements j so that $u^j d^{n-j}S$ is greater than K. Let a be the smallest whole number such that $u^a d^{n-a}S$ is greater than K. Taking logarithms of both sides gives a as the smallest whole number greater than $\log(K/Sd^n)$ over $\log(u/d)$. When j is less than a, the max( ) term will be zero, and so we need only sum over j greater than or equal to a, giving:

$$C = \frac{1}{\check{r}^n}\sum_{j=a}^{n}\left(\frac{n!}{j!\,(n-j)!}\right)p^j(1-p)^{n-j}(u^j d^{n-j}S - K)$$

---

[1] The symbol Σ, the uppercase Greek letter sigma, indicates that the expression to the right is to be summed for every value of the *dummy variable*. In this case the dummy variable, written beneath the Σ, is j, and it takes the values from 0 to n inclusive in steps of $+1$. This is a variant of the $\sum_i$ notation used in Appendix D:

As a straightforward example,

$$\sum_{k=1}^{5} k^2$$

is $1^2 + 2^2 + 3^2 + 4^2 + 5^2$ which is 55.

[2] The symbol $n!$ (read 'n factorial') means, for any whole number, $n*(n-1)*(n-2)*\ldots*3*2*1$. Thus 4! is $4*3*2*1$, which is 24. By convention, 0! equals 1; 1! also equals 1.

We can further simplify the expression for C by splitting it into two terms as

$$C = S \sum_{j=a}^{n} \left(\frac{n!}{j! \, (n-j)!}\right) p^j \, (1-p)^{n-j} \, u^j \, d^{n-j} \, \check{r}^{-n}$$

$$-K\check{r}^{-n} \sum_{j=a}^{n} \left(\frac{n!}{j! \, (n-j)!}\right) p^j \, (1-p)^{n-j}$$

These two terms can each be simplified by recognising that they are multiples of the *complementary binomial distribution* function $\Phi(a; n, q)$. (Φ is the uppercase Greek letter phi.) This function gives the probability that a random sequence of n ups and downs, in which each up is chosen independently with a probability of q, and hence in which each down is chosen with a probability of $1-q$, contains at least a ups, and it is given explicitly by:

$$\Phi(a; n, q) = \sum_{j=a}^{n} \left(\frac{n!}{j! \, (n-j)!}\right) q^j \, (1-q)^{n-j}$$

By its definition, $\Phi(a; n, q)$ is always between 0 and 1; as a increases the value of $\Phi(a; n, q)$ must decrease. Values of the complementary binomial distribution are available from tables.

Using Φ in the above expression for C gives the final form for the binomial pricing formula for a call option:

$$C = S\Phi(a; n, p') - K\check{r}^{-n}\Phi(a; n, p) \qquad \textbf{Equation 11.4}$$

where

$$p \quad = \quad \frac{(\check{r} - d)}{(u - d)}$$

$$p' \quad = \quad \frac{u}{\check{r}} p$$

$$a \quad = \quad \text{smallest whole number} > \frac{\log(K/Sd^n)}{\log(u/d)}$$

If a is greater than n the call is worthless.

The binomial pricing formula is the sum of two terms, one a multiple of S, and one a multiple of K. These can be interpreted as:

(the present value of the asset $*$ the probability of exercise) −
(the present value of the strike price $*$ the probability of exercise).

The complication is that discounting has to be done at a different rate for S and K, reflected in the use of a different probability parameter in Φ in the two terms. The Black Scholes pricing formula will turn out to have the same two-term structure.

If we create an equivalent portfolio at the start date of the option, then we will have to adjust it after each period's up or down movement in order to maintain the equivalence. Following through this process for every period will get us to the option maturity with the same value for our portfolio as for the option, provided that u and d remain constant. This process is known as *delta hedging*.

To see this in practice, let us recalculate our option on a house using a two period model. The house is worth £200,000 today and can go up by a factor of 1.0954 or down by a factor of 0.9747 in a 6-month period. (These values are chosen to recover the original up and down movements as extreme possibilities over 1 year.) The riskfree interest rate for 6 months is 4.8809%, which compounds to an annual rate of 10% as before. What is the price of a call option at 1 year with a strike price of £220,000?

We have:

$$
\begin{aligned}
S &= £200,000 \\
K &= £220,000 \\
\check{r} &= 1.0488 \\
u &= 1.0954 \\
d &= 0.9747 \\
n &= 2.
\end{aligned}
$$

Since there are only two periods involved we can work out the relevant values of Φ by hand. First we calculate a:

$\log(K/Sd^2)$ over $\log(u/d)$ is $\log(1.15785)$ over $\log(1.12383)$ which equals 0.14656 over 0.11674, which is 1.25544.

Consequently a is the smallest whole number greater than 1.25544, giving a equals 2.

Now let us calculate p and p'. p is $(\check{r} - d)$ over $(u - d)$, which is $(1.0488 - 0.9747)/(1.0954 - 0.9747) = 0.6139$. p' is $p * (u/r)$, which is $0.6139 * (1.0954/1.0488) = 0.6412$.

In order to work out $\Phi(2; 2, p)$, consider the binomial tree:

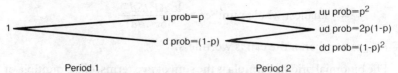

Period 1   Period 2

It can readily be seen that $\Phi(2; 2, p)$, which is the probability of there being at least two up movements in two periods, is p^2.

This lets us write the price of the call option as

$S\Phi(2; 2, p') - K\check{r}^{-2}\Phi(2; 2, p)$ which equals
$(£200,000 * 0.6412^2) - (£220,000 * 1.0488^{-2} * 0.6139^2) = £6,852$.

This is less than the value of £10,909 given by the one period model; this is reasonable, since the assumptions about price movements in the one period model were more extreme.

Let us now see how to construct an equivalent portfolio of assets and bonds and how to manage it over the two periods in order to duplicate the option.

We start off with a portfolio of ΔS plus B. Unfortunately, we have a formula to calculate the delta Δ only for a one period option, and so to calculate the delta at the start of our multiple period option we first have to calculate the option values at the end of the first period. Using these values, we can then work out the equivalent portfolio at the start of the first period.

For simplicity we work out the option values at each node of the tree below by calculating one period options from right to left; for a many-period option it would be easier to calculate the values at the end of the first period directly, using Equation 11.4.

Note the rounding difference of £1 in the value of C.

Substituting C_u and C_d from the above table in the formula for Δ in Equation 11.1 gives:

$$\Delta = (£11{,}707 - £0)/((1.0954 - 0.9747) * £200{,}000)$$
$$= 0.48496$$
$$B = (u * £0) - (d * £11{,}707))/((u - d) * \check{r})$$
$$= -(0.9747 * £11{,}707)/((1.0954 - 0.9747) * 1.0488)$$
$$= -£90{,}140$$

The equivalent portfolio is thus to buy a similar house at £96,992 and sell £90,140 of bonds, for a net outlay of £6,852.

At the end of the first period, the house price will have gone up or down; let us assume first that it goes down. The value of the call option is now zero, since the house price after two periods can now be a maximum of ud times £200,000, which equals £213,573 and is thus less than the strike price K. The value of our equivalent portfolio is now:

$(£96{,}992 * d) - (\check{r} * £90{,}140)$, which is £1.

Therefore, if we sell our portfolio we will match, to within a rounding error, the option value of £0 for the rest of its life.

What happens if the house goes up in price in the first period? The value of the portfolio is now:

$(£96{,}992 * u) - (\check{r} * £90{,}140)$, which is £11,706,

which matches the value of the option. Now, if we want to create an equivalent portfolio for the second period we shall have to adjust our portfolio. In fact, again using Equation 11.4, we shall have to hold £165,700 of the asset and sell £153,993 of the bond. This new portfolio has value £11,707, and so we can exchange our old portfolio for it at no cost, again to within a rounding error. If the house price goes down in the second period, our equivalent portfolio will end up with value £0, which is the same as the option. If the house price goes up, then our portfolio will be worth:

$$(£165,700 * u) - (\check{r} * £153,993),$$

which is £20,000, matching the option value exactly.

Thus you can see that the multiple period binomial model has given the correct option price, since we have succeeded in duplicating the effect of the option by dynamically adjusting an equivalent portfolio. Throughout the above example we assumed that the values of u and d were constant, which corresponds to an assumption of constant volatility. If u and d were allowed to vary, then the delta hedging strategy would result in a residual profit or loss compared to holding the option itself. This point is revisited later in this chapter.

11.3 BLACK SCHOLES

The Black Scholes pricing formula for options was derived in a paper entitled 'The pricing of options and corporate liabilities' by Fischer Black and Myron Scholes in *Journal of Political Economy*, May–June 1973 issue, pp. 637-59. That paper used complex mathematics to obtain the result; the treatment we shall follow here, while still involving extended calculation, uses a limiting process based on the binomial method which should be easier for the non-mathematician to understand. This treatment was derived originally by William Sharpe, and was published in a paper entitled 'Option pricing: a simplified approach' by John Cox, Stephen Ross, and Mark Rubinstein in *Journal of Financial Economics*, Vol. 7, September 1979, pp. 229-63.

The basic idea is to let the number of periods n in the multiple period binomial model become very large, while choosing u, d, q, and $\check{r}$ as functions of n so that the model continues to generate consistent asset prices and uses consistent interest rates. In the limit as n goes to infinity, the Φ function in Equation 11.4 is replaced by the normal distribution function and we obtain the Black Scholes formula.

Before showing how to choose u, d, q, and $\check{r}$ as a function of n, let us briefly review the properties of the normal distribution, which we met in Part I. The standard normal distribution is defined by the familiar bell-shaped curve shown below in Figure 11.3.

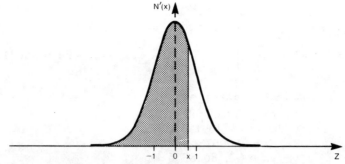

Figure 11.3 Standard normal density function.

The standard normal distribution $N(x)$ has a mean of zero and a standard deviation of 1; it is given by the area under the curve shown above of the standard normal density function:

$$N'(z) = \frac{1}{\sqrt{2\pi}}\, e^{-\frac{z^2}{2}}$$

This equals as an integral $\displaystyle\int_{-\infty}^{x} \frac{1}{\sqrt{2\pi}}\, e^{-\frac{z^2}{2}}\, dz$

Here π, the lower-case Greek letter pi, has its usual mathematical meaning of the ratio of a circle's circumference to its diameter, and equals 3.1415926535898...

$N(x)$ is the shaded area in the diagram; it gives the probability that a normally distributed random variable with mean zero and standard deviation one will have a value less than or equal to x.

$N(x)$ is always between 0 and 1, and it tends to 0 as x tends to minus infinity and to 1 as x tends to infinity. By symmetry, $N(-x) = 1 - N(x)$. Figure 11.4 shows $N(x)$:

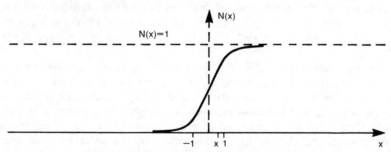

Figure 11.4 Standard normal distribution.

Values of $N(x)$ can be obtained from tables, but it also possible to approximate it by functions which can be calculated directly. One such approximation is based on a function given in *Numerical Recipes in C: The Art of Scientific Computing*, referred to in the bibliography.

This gives for x greater than or equal to zero:

$$N(x) = 1 - 0.5 \; erfc \left(\frac{x}{\sqrt{2}} \right) \qquad\qquad \textbf{Formula 11.1}$$

where

$$
\begin{aligned}
erfc(z) = t * \exp(-z^2 &- 1.26551223 + \\
(t * (1.00002368 + \\
(t * (0.37409196 + \\
(t * (0.09678418 + \\
(t * (-0.18628806 + \\
(t * (0.27886807 + \\
(t * (-1.13520398 + \\
(t * (1.48851587 + \\
(t * (-0.82215223 + \\
(t * 0.17087277)))))))))))))))))))
\end{aligned}
$$

where $t = 1/(1 + (0.5 * z))$
and $\exp(y) = e^y$, where e, as before, is the basis of natural logarithms
2.718281828459...

If x is less than 0, then $N(x) = 1 - N(-x)$, where $N(-x)$ is calculated from the formula above. The error in $N(x)$ from this formula will be less than 0.0000001.

Clearly, Formula 11.1 is most usefully applied as part of a spreadsheet or of a computer program. As a check of your programming, to seven decimal places $N(0)$ should be 0.5, $N(5.4)$ should be 1, and $N(0.242)$ should be 0.5956099.

Now let us return to the problem of choosing consistent values for u, d, q, and $ř$ as functions of n; we shall identify these as $u(n)$, $d(n)$, $q(n)$, and $ř(n)$. (This differs from the notation of *Options Markets*.) It is easy to choose a value for $ř(n)$, since we are working with a flat yield curve and we want to maintain the same total scaling factor across the option period. We retain our original use of r as the scaling factor for 1 year, so that the scaling factor for the option period of t years is r^t. To maintain consistency within the binomial model with n periods we must use $ř(n) = r^{t/n}$.

We shall derive $u(n)$, $d(n)$, and $q(n)$ assuming that price changes are continuous, that is, that there are no jumps in price; basically this means that as n tends to infinity u and d tend to 1. In each period of the binomial model the asset price changes either by a factor of u with probability q, or by a factor of d with probability $1 - q$. If we work instead with the change in the logarithm of the asset price in one period, it will be $\log(u)$ with probability q or $\log(d)$ with probability $1 - q$.

If we look at the change in the logarithm of S over the whole option period it will be $\log(S^\star) - \log(S)$, which equals $\log(S^\star/S)$.

Since $S^\star$ is formed from S plus a series of j ups plus $(n - j)$ downs, $\log(S^\star/S)$ equals $j \log (u) + ((n - j) \log (d)) = j \log(u/d) + n\log(d)$.

Therefore the expected value of $\log(S^{\star}/S)$ is
$E(j)\log(u/d) + n\log(d)$
where $E(x)$ is the expected value of the variable x.

Similarly the variance of $\log(S^{\star}/S)$ is
$\text{Var}(j)(\log(u/d))^2$
where $\text{Var}(x)$ is the variance of the variable x.

Each of the n possible upwards moves has probability q, and thus $E(j) = nq$. Also, in each period the possible values for j are 1 with probability q and 0 with probability $(1 - q)$, with $E(j)$ being q. This gives the variance of j for a single period as $q(1 - q)^2 + (1 - q)(0 - q)^2$, which equals $q(1 - q)$, and so for n periods $\text{Var}(j) = nq(1 - q)$. Putting all this together gives:

$E(\log(S^{\star}/S)) = (q\log(u/d) + \log(d))n$ and
$\text{Var}(\log(S^{\star}/S)) = q(1 - q)(\log(u/d))^2 n.$

Since we are trying to make the binomial model consistent with the known behaviour of the asset price, we must choose $u(n)$ and $d(n)$ so that the above formulae give the expected value and the expected variance for $\log(S^{\star}/S)$. Suppose that the expected value of $\log(S^{\star}/S)$ for 1 year is μ, where μ is the lower-case Greek letter mu; then it can easily be shown that the expected value for $\log(S^{\star}/S)$ for t years is μt. (The argument is the same as that used in Part I to show that the scaling factor for t years is r^t). The definition of the volatility σ as the standard deviation of $\log(S^{\star}/S)$ for 1 year gives immediately that the variance of $\log(S^{\star}/S)$ for 1 year is σ^2, and again this can be extended to show that the variance of $\log(S^{\star}/S)$ for t years is $\sigma^2 t$.

This gives:

$(q\log(u/d) + \log(d))n$ tends to μt; and
$q(1 - q)(\log(u/d))^2 n$ tends to $\sigma^2 t$
in the limit as n tends to infinity.

Our condition that price movements are continuous gives:

$\log(u)$ tends to 0; and
$\log(d)$ tends to 0
in the limit as n tends to infinity.

We can achieve all this most simply by choosing:

$$u(n) = e^{\sigma\sqrt{t/n}} \qquad d(n) = e^{-\sigma\sqrt{t/n}} \qquad q(n) = \frac{1}{2} + \frac{1}{2}\left(\frac{\mu}{\sigma}\right)\sqrt{\frac{t}{n}}$$

You can check with a little algebraic manipulation that these values do satisfy the four limit conditions above. Note that $u(n) = 1/d(n)$; this effectively makes u and d into one linked variable, as promised above.

Moreover, it can be shown that in the limit as n tends to infinity, with $u(n)$, $d(n)$, and $q(n)$ defined as above, $\log(S^*/S)$ tends to a normal distribution; the limiting case of the multiple period binomial model thus recovers the correct distribution for $\log(S^*/S)$, and hence should give the correct value for the option price.

In order to establish the limit form of Equation 11.4 as the number of periods tends to infinity, it is necessary to find the limit of $\Phi(a; n, p)$ and $\Phi(a; n, p')$. This involves more sophistication than we are using here, and so we simply state the result that

$$\text{if } x = \frac{\log (S/Kr^{-t})}{\sigma\sqrt{t}} + \frac{1}{2}\sigma\sqrt{t}$$

then $\Phi(a; n, p')$ tends to $N(x)$ and $\Phi(a; n, p)$ tends to $N(x - \sigma\sqrt{t})$ as n tends to infinity.

Substituting this result in Equation 11.4 immediately gives the Black Scholes formula for the price of a call option on a continuously traded asset whose price is lognormally distributed:

$$C = SN(x) - Kr^{-t}N(x - \sigma\sqrt{t}) \qquad \textbf{Equation 11.5}$$

$$\text{where } x = \frac{\log (S/Kr^{-t})}{\sigma\sqrt{t}} + \frac{1}{2}\sigma\sqrt{t}$$

and σ =
the standard deviation of the logarithm of the asset price over 1 year.

The Black Scholes formula will be the basis of all our subsequent analysis of options. The next section will begin the analysis of its implications, but it is worth noting here that the only variables which appear in the formula are S, K, r, t, and σ. The list of five determining variables in section 10.3 has thus turned out to be exhaustive, as promised. In particular, μ, the variable related to the expected value of S^*, does not appear in the formula.

Since the price formula for a European call option can be derived using Black Scholes plus put-call parity, put options for general assets are not considered separately; when it comes to interest rate options, explicit formulae will be derived for puts as well as calls.

This section closes with a numerical example, again using the option to buy a house. What would the price of the call be if the volatility of the house price were expected to be 11.6%? (Note that the normal market convention is to quote volatilities as a percentage.)

We have

$$S = £200,000$$
$$K = £220,000$$
$$t = 1$$
$$r = 1.1$$
$$\sigma = 0.116$$

giving $C = (£200,000 * N(x)) - (£220,000 * r^{-t}N(x - \sigma\sqrt{t}))$

where $x = \dfrac{\log(200,000/(220,000 * 1.1^{-1}))}{0.116 * \sqrt{1}} + \dfrac{1}{2} * 0.116 * \sqrt{1}$

$= \dfrac{\log(1)}{0.116} + 0.058$

$= 0.058$

and $x - \sigma\sqrt{t} = -0.058$

giving $C = (£200,000 * N(0.058)) - (£200,000 * N(-0.058))$

Using Formula 11.1 to calculate $N(z)$ gives $N(0.058) = 0.5231257$,
and $N(-0.058) = 0.4768743$

Substituting these gives $C = £9,250$.

11.4 SENSITIVITIES OF BLACK SCHOLES TO ITS VARIABLES

In order to manage an option position it is necessary to know how option prices will change with changes in the underlying variables.

This can be expressed for the Black Scholes formula for a call option price by taking the partial derivative[3] of the option price C with respect to each of the five variables. Remembering that

$$N'(x) = \frac{1}{\sqrt{2\pi}} e^{-\frac{x^2}{2}}$$ allows us to prove:

---

[3] A partial derivative of a function of many variables is the analogue of the ordinary derivative of a function of a single variable of elementary calculus. It is defined as the ratio of the change in the value of the function to the change in the value of a single determining variable, in the limit as the change becomes small, *while all the other determining variables remain constant.*

Thus, for example, if f is a function of x, y, and z, then $\dfrac{\partial f}{\partial x}\Big|_{y,z}$ is the limit, as Δx tends to zero, of

$$\frac{f(x + \Delta x, y, z) - f(x, y, z)}{\Delta x}$$

Usually it is clear which variables are held constant, and the partial derivative is written simply $\dfrac{\partial f}{\partial x}$.

$$SN'(x) = r^{-t}KN'(x - \sigma\sqrt{t}) \qquad\qquad \textbf{Identity 11.1}$$

This identity together with substantial algebraic manipulation gives:

Delta $\quad \dfrac{\partial C}{\partial S} = N(x)$ $\hspace{4cm}$ always > 0

$\quad\quad\;\; \dfrac{\partial C}{\partial K} = -r^{-t}N(x - \sigma\sqrt{t})$ $\hspace{3cm}$ always < 0

-Theta $\quad \dfrac{\partial C}{\partial t} = \dfrac{S\sigma}{2\sqrt{t}}\, N'(x) + Kr^{-t}\log(r)N(x - \sigma\sqrt{t})$ $\hspace{1cm}$ always > 0

Vega $\quad \dfrac{\partial C}{\partial \sigma} = S\sqrt{t}N'(x)$ $\hspace{3.6cm}$ always > 0

$\quad\quad\;\; \dfrac{\partial C}{\partial r} = tKr^{-(t+1)}N(x - \sigma\sqrt{t})$ $\hspace{2.5cm}$ always > 0

Note that three of the partial derivatives are important enough to have their own names; remember that theta is *minus* the partial derivative with respect to time. The results for volatility and interest rates constitute the proofs promised at the end of section 10.4.

The second order partial derivative of C with respect to S is also important enough to merit a name of its own:

Gamma $\quad \dfrac{\partial^2 C}{\partial S^2} = \dfrac{\partial(\text{delta})}{\partial S} = \dfrac{1}{S\sigma\sqrt{t}}\, N'(x)$ $\hspace{2cm}$ always > 0

The importance of gamma is explained in the next section.

The best way to visualise the effect of changing variables on the call option price and on delta, theta, vega, and gamma, is to draw your own price diagrams. Figure 11.5 gives *representative* curves for various relationships; you should exercise caution in assuming that the pricing formula will always behave as shown.

11.5 DELTA AND GAMMA HEDGING

As for the binomial pricing model, the Black Scholes formula has two terms, one in S and one in K. These can again be interpreted as the present value of the asset price minus the strike price times the probability of the option being exercised. However, this time the pricing formula gives a direct way of constructing an equivalent portfolio; the term in S tells you how much of the asset to buy, and the term in K tells you how much of the riskfree bond to sell. This follows directly from the partial derivatives of C with respect to S and K. (The multiple period binomial pricing formula does not have this property, which is why we had to work out an equivalent portfolio by a recalculation in section 11.2 above.)

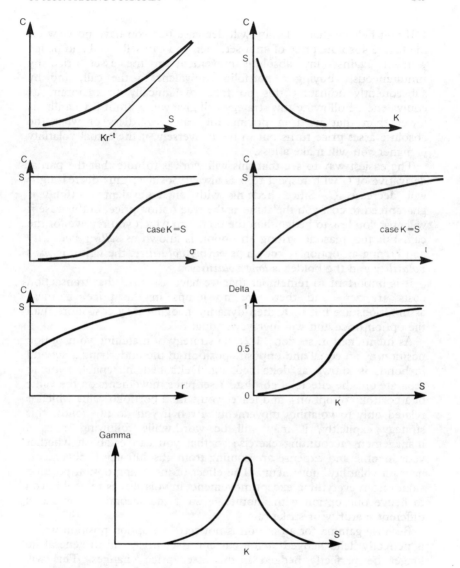

Figure 11.5 Representative pricing relationships for call options.

The derivation of the Black Scholes formula assumed that volatility was a constant. In fact, implied volatility can be observed only by calculating backwards from quoted option prices, and in general neither implied nor historic volatility remain constant over extended periods.

If you believe that volatility will decrease but you have no view on the future absolute price of an asset, then you can sell a call and hedge yourself against any absolute movement in the asset price by simultaneously buying a portfolio equivalent to the call, and by subsequently adjusting this portfolio dynamically to maintain its equivalence. Following this strategy will give you a profit if volatility is lower than that used in pricing the call, regardless of what the absolute asset price turns out to be; conversely, if the actual volatility is higher you will make a loss.

The easiest way to see that this will work is to note that the partial derivative of C with respect to σ is always positive; thus decreasing σ will decrease C. Since hedging with an equivalent portfolio is guaranteed to cost you the same as the true option price, in this case it will cost you less to hedge than the premium which you receive for the call. For this reason, writing an option is known as *selling volatility* and buying an option is known as *buying volatility*; the writer is *short volatility* and the holder is *long volatility*.

It is important to remember that we have assumed that transaction costs are zero and there are no jumps in the price; if these assumptions are not met, then dynamic hedging may cost more than the option price and will involve residual risk.

As mentioned in section 11.2, the strategy of matching your option position by an equal and opposite position in the underlying asset and in bonds is known as delta hedging. Delta hedging enables you to separate out the effects of absolute asset price movements on the value of a portfolio of options, and leaves you with a portfolio value which is related only to volatility movements. Even if you do not follow this strategy explicitly, it may still be worthwhile following it as a management accounting exercise so that you can establish whether your income and expense are coming from absolute level movements or from volatility movements. The effect of insulating option position values from everything except movements in volatility is to enable you to hedge one option with another, even if the second option has a different maturity or strike rate.

Because gamma for an option is not zero, an option position which is perfectly delta hedged at the current asset price will in general no longer be perfectly hedged if the asset price changes. This will necessitate increasing or decreasing the hedge, with consequent administrative and transaction costs. In order to reduce the necessity to change the delta hedge, a strategy is often followed of *gamma hedging*. This involves hedging a bought option with a sold option which has opposite gamma. The residual delta of the position can then be hedged with a forward, which will have effectively zero gamma. However the asset price changes (within reasonable limits), the change in delta of the two options will cancel, leaving the position delta hedged. By following this strategy, the transaction costs of delta hedging a portfolio can be minimised.

It can be seen from the diagrams of gamma and delta against asset price at the end of section 11.4 above, that delta changes most rapidly when the asset price moves close to the strike price, and thus gamma hedging is most appropriate for such positions. In the extreme case when the option is at the money and the time to expiry is very short, the gamma of a single option will tend to infinity, and thus gamma hedging will become vital.

SUMMARY

This chapter has developed exact pricing formulae for options on general assets. Given the restrictive assumption that the asset price can change only once between today and the exercise date it is possible to develop the single period binomial pricing model for call options. Allowing the asset price to change a fixed number of times gives the multiple period binomial model. Finally, allowing the number of periods in the binomial model to tend to infinity gives the Black Scholes pricing formula for call options as a limiting case. Satisfyingly, the Black Scholes formula involves precisely the five variables identified as necessary in the last chapter, namely strike rate, current asset price, time to exercise, interest rate to the exercise date, and volatility. Put-call parity can be used to price European puts.

Since risk is measured as the change of present value for a change in each risk factor, the risk of an option value can be expressed in terms of the first derivative of the pricing formula with respect to each of its defining variables. The derivative with respect to the asset price is called delta, and a delta hedging strategy for an option portfolio based on selling delta of the underlying asset will protect the value of the portfolio for small changes in the asset value. The hedge will have to be adjusted as the asset value, and hence delta itself, changes. The net profit or loss of this strategy will depend on the relationship between actual volatility over the period and the volatility priced into the options. Gamma hedging is a refinement of delta hedging which involves in addition matching the second derivative of the option value with respect to the asset price; this reduces the transaction cost of repeatedly adjusting the delta hedge. Gamma hedging requires the use of options in the hedge portfolio.

CHAPTER 12

Interest rate options

You now have enough background information to consider interest rate options. As noted in the introduction to this part it will take three chapters to cover the material. This chapter looks at the economic rationale for interest rate options, reviews the major option instruments, and applies the results of sections 10.2 and 10.4 to derive pricing relationships. The next chapter looks at exact pricing formulae, and the concluding chapter discusses risk management of portfolios of interest rate options.

12.1 WHY INTEREST RATE OPTIONS ARE NECESSARY

The theory developed in Chapters 10 and 11 demonstrates that under a restrictive set of assumptions an option position can be replicated by dynamic hedging using bonds and the underlying asset of the option. Under these assumptions there is no need for options contracts at all! However, in real life, several of the assumptions break down, making it impossible in practice to replicate the effect of an option. This section briefly reviews some of the ways in which the assumptions of these chapters break down, with particular reference to the management of interest rate risk.

Since we have not yet defined an interest rate option, it is assumed in this and the next section that we are talking about an option on an underlying asset whose price is sensitive to movements in a particular interest rate; we shall not need to be too specific about which asset and which interest rate. Section 12.3 below will define specific interest rate option contracts.

For convenience, the eleven assumptions of section 10.1 are repeated here:

(a) Asset one of large class.
(b) Publicly known price.

(c) Asset remains intact.
(d) Zero bid-offer spreads on asset.
(e) Zero transaction costs.
(f) Zero bid-offer spreads on interest rates.
(g) Tax effects immaterial.
(h) Option premium paid on contract date.
(i) Short positions in asset allowed without penalty.
(j) Options can be assigned.
(k) Single market price for asset on a particular day.

To these must be added the following assumptions used to derive the Black Scholes pricing formula in Chapter 11:

(l) Asset price lognormally distributed.
(m) Asset price changes infinitesimal.
(n) Yield curve flat.
(o) Zero coupon rate to the option maturity does not change.
(p) Volatility remains unchanged over the option life.

The first batch of these assumptions were needed to obtain the option pricing relationships and dependencies of Chapter 10, and the second batch were needed to obtain the Black Scholes pricing formula.

Of the assumptions in the first batch, (a), (b), (c), (g), and (i) are reasonable for a wide class of interest-sensitive assets, (h) is a technicality which we can assume will be satisfied, and (j) is economically equivalent to the reasonable assumption that an option position can be closed out by an equal and opposite transaction in the marketplace. Assumption (k) will be satisfied if we choose an asset with a price based on a rate which is set daily, such as a particular Libor; alternatively, we can require exercise at a particular time on the exercise day, so that (k) also becomes a technicality. Of the first batch of assumptions above, this leaves (d), (e), and (f) as contentious.

For a bank or other financial institution active in the market for interest rate risk management products, transaction costs and effective bid-offer spreads will be relatively low; for a corporate or other *end user* (that is, an organisation using risk management products only to hedge risk) utilising these products occasionally, transaction costs and bid-offer spreads will be relatively high. As mentioned at the end of Chapter 11, these costs and spreads will be particularly important when the option gamma is high. Assumptions (d), (e), and (f) will thus be better satisfied for major financial institutions, which will have a price advantage relative to corporate users in replicating or managing option positions. It may therefore be possible for financial institutions to assume the option risk of corporates and to manage it more cheaply than the corporates could themselves.

Assumption (m) is not necessarily true for interest rates; occasionally there are sudden large rate movements. Dynamic management of an equivalent portfolio will not cope with such movements.

Assumption (p) is obviously not satisfied in practice, since the volatility used to price an option is merely the market's current estimate of future price movements; like other market estimates it changes with sentiment and as new information becomes available. Because future volatility is basically unknowable, a risk-averse hedger should use an option rather than an equivalent portfolio.

To summarise the above briefly: end users have more reason to use options than do banks, since their cost of dynamically managing an equivalent portfolio will be higher. In addition, options cope with two types of risk which a replicating portfolio does not: jumps in interest rates and changes in volatility. For these reasons alone, options are a useful additional hedging tool.

The other three assumptions in the second batch, (m), (n), and (o), are emphatically not met for interest rate options. Empirical studies show that interest rates are not lognormally distributed, yield curves in general are not flat, and it is inconsistent to assume that one zero coupon rate remains unchanged while the interest rate on which the asset price is based changes. The failure of these assumptions impacts the accuracy of a pricing formula for interest rate options; this in turn makes it more difficult to calculate an exact equivalent portfolio. These problems are discussed in more detail in Chapter 13.

12.2 ECONOMIC RATIONALE FOR
INTEREST RATE OPTIONS

The previous section demonstrated that options could not satisfactorily be replicated by equivalent portfolios, especially for corporate or other end users. This section reviews types of exposure which oblige these organisations to transfer risk to banks or other financial institutions using interest rate option instruments. In addition, it discusses how options allow investors or other risk takers with a particular market view to take positions which would otherwise not be possible.

Forward contracts such as FRAs or swaps are used to manage the interest rate risk arising from assets and liabilities; option contracts are used to manage the risk arising from contingent assets and liabilities. Such contingencies may be explicit in debt agreements or may be implicit in economic risk. An equivalent viewpoint is that forward contracts have values which vary with the value of the underlying asset, while the value of option contracts is dependent on the volatility of the asset value also. Exposures requiring management through options are thus those depending on volatility.

Below are some examples of exposures to interest rate volatility; the list is meant to be illustrative rather than exhaustive, with the aim of introducing you to some of the sources of supply and demand in the options markets.

Where a heavily leveraged company borrows at a floating rate, there is a danger that rates will rise above the point where the debt can be serviced. Banks lending in such circumstances often insist on the borrower insuring against such an eventuality by buying an interest rate option to limit its maximum interest expense; we shall see in the next section that a *cap* would be such an option. Other companies financed through floating debt may choose to limit their maximum interest expense in this way without the lender's insistence.

Many corporate bonds are issued with call options; that is to say, at certain times the issuer can announce early redemption, usually at the face value of the bonds or at a slightly higher price. Such a call option may be included for reasons which have nothing to do with interest rate risk management. For example, the bonds may be issued under a restrictive covenant which prevents the issuer taking over another company; if the issuer does wish to mount a takeover, then it will be easier to do so by calling the bonds, even at a loss, than by negotiating a change of covenant with the bondholders. An investor in such bonds faces the risk that if interest rates drop so that the value of the bond goes above par then the issuer may exercise its right to call the bond at a price below its current market value. This risk is equivalent to the investor writing a call option on the bond to the issuer, which is similar to writing an option on a single currency interest rate swap.

Investors differ in their market views and risk preferences, and there are times when some investors wish to assume an interest rate option position. This can provide an arbitrage opportunity for the issue of corporate bonds with embedded options or for the issue of *warrants*, which are securities with a pure option payoff. An example of a warrant would be a security entitling its holder to buy a share at a particular strike price at a given future date; the warrant in this case would be equivalent to a call option on the share, but warrants can incorporate any type of option, including interest rate options. The issuers of such bonds or warrants assume the risk of the option position, which they then need to hedge. These instruments can have extremely complex structures; for example, the holder of one bond could be given the right to exchange his holding for a bond with a different maturity. Evaluating an option such as this, which is driven by the difference between the interest rates to two maturities, is beyond the scope of this book. Private placements in particular often involve a complex option structure, since they can be tailored exactly to the needs of the investor.

Another type of debt issued by corporations and institutions is *floating rate notes*, which are bonds in which the interest payments are linked to a floating rate such as Libor. These are sometimes 'capped', that is, they will never pay above a certain level, regardless of movements in Libor. The issuers of these notes include the cap to prevent their interest expense exceeding a certain level. The investors are assuming an option risk equivalent to their writing a cap to the issuer, and again they can hedge the risk by buying a cap from a bank. A variant of this is where the notes have a 'floor', that is, they will never pay below a certain level. Such notes can be an attractive way for investors to buy an option; alternatively, some investors may choose to 'strip the floor', by writing an equivalent *floor* contract to a bank and receiving an up-front payment.

All of the above examples involve debt. Another source of volatility risk is contract tenders or takeover bids, where a corporation bids to make a long term investment involving significant interest rate risk. Since the investment is contingent on events outside the corporation's control, the appropriate management of the risk may involve an option contract rather than a forward.

A similar source of option risk occurs in retail financial services when fixed price investment or debt instruments are offered to the public during a fixed sales period. If interest rates move against the financial institution then the public is more likely to buy the instrument; the institution may therefore find that it has written a free interest rate option.

Lastly, volatility risk can arise through economic exposure. A well-known example is the housebuilding trade, where interest rate rises above a certain level will severely impact the demand for new houses. Because there is no symmetrical increase in demand when rates fall, the risk has the properties of an option. Suppliers of consumer durables may also find themselves affected in this way.

There are many such examples of corporates and institutions which lose when interest rates are volatile; such organisations are described as naturally short of interest rate volatility. It is harder to identify organisations which are naturally long of volatility; perhaps banks benefit from increased volatility since their customers then need more risk management products! If you can identify an organisation which is long in interest rate volatility, then you may be able to engage in profitable business supplying volatility to the market.

In addition to these requirements driven primarily by hedging, investors or risk takers may wish to use interest rate options to take risk positions which could not be achieved through the use of forwards alone. For example, suppose a closely run election is coming up, and you believe that if one party wins interest rates will move sharply up while if the other party wins they will move sharply down; you cannot take advantage of this view using forwards, but you can by using options. You need to buy one option which will give you a payoff if interest rates go up, and a second option which will give you a payoff if interest rates go down; you will see in section 12.3 below that an appropriate strategy might be to buy a *cap* and a *floor*. This is an example of buying options in the belief that volatility will increase. Other strategies could be used if you believe that volatility will decrease or if you have some more specific view about the future movement of volatility.

This concludes the review of the sources of interest rate option positions in the marketplace. We now turn to the instruments which are used to transfer and to assume interest rate option risk.

12.3 TYPES OF INTEREST RATE OPTION

What candidates are there for the underlying asset of an interest rate option? The four commonest interest rate hedging instrument are FRAs, Eurodeposit futures, interest rate swaps, and government bonds, and there are option instruments based on each of these. In the subsections below, each is examined in turn.

12.3.1 Caps and floors

Let us consider a particular option on an FRA. The FRA has value 30 June, maturity 30 September, contract amount US$100,000, and contract rate 8%; we buy, for a premium of US$250, the European option exercisable on 30 June to pay fixed on the FRA and receive Libor. Suppose that at 30 June, Libor is 10%; we shall exercise the option, and receive a net 2% on US$100,000 for 3 months, discounted back to 30 June at Libor.

One curious feature of this option is that the asset we receive on exercise is cash and the exercise price seems to be zero. In order to put this contract within the theoretical framework developed in Chapters 10 and 11, it is necessary to look at it in a slightly different way, and to identify the asset as the receipt of Libor on US$100,000 for 3 months, and the strike price as the payment of 8% on US$100,000 for 3 months. The netting of these two amounts in the FRA settlement has no economic significance in the pricing of the option. Since the strike price is a multiple of the FRA contract rate of 8%, the 8% contract rate is referred to as the *strike rate*.

The advantage of this description is that the 3-month Libor expected to prevail on 30 June does have many of the characteristics of an asset which were needed as assumptions in Chapters 10 and 11, and therefore it is possible to use the theory developed there to price options on FRAs. In particular, 3-month Libor on 30 June is traded in the market as an FRA rate, with a potentially large number of transactions and, through brokers, a publicly known price; also an FRA does not 'pay dividends', that is, there is only one cashflow on an FRA and it is determined solely by the Libor at its value date. The bid-offer spreads and transaction costs on an FRA are not zero, but they are small enough to allow the analysis leading to the pricing model to be considered reasonably accurate. The main difference from our assumptions is that FRA rates do not seem in practice to be lognormally distributed; this is discussed further in Chapter 13.

Treating the Libor interest as the underlying asset of the option and the contract rate interest as the strike price lets us speak of options on FRAs using the same terminology as for options on other assets; we shall need this when we come to look at pricing models. However, options on FRAs have a terminology of their own, as explained below.

Suppose that we had an outstanding Libor loan for US$100,000 repricing on 30 June. If we consider together the loan and the call option on Libor in our example, then there are two possibilities for Libor on 30 June:

- Libor is less than or equal to 8%
  We do not exercise the option and our interest expense is Libor.
- Libor is greater than 8%
  We exercise the option receiving (Libor - 8%) and pay Libor on the loan. Our net interest expense is therefore 8%.

By using the option we have ensured that our interest expense will never exceed 8% plus the cost of the call. This is described as 'capping' our interest expense, and therefore the option is known as an interest rate *cap*.

Our cap is for a single period; such a cap is sometimes referred to as an *interest rate guarantee* (IRG). It is more common to see caps involving a succession of periods in the same way as a swap; the constituent IRGs of a multiple period cap can be referred to as 'caplets'. If we exercise our cap it settles discounted at the beginning of the period; the market practice is that caps settle undiscounted at the end of the period, and we shall assume below that this is the settlement used. With the assumption that the credit risk of the delayed settlement is negligible, the two settlement methods are economically equivalent.

The standard terminology for a cap is that on the transaction date the *buyer* of the cap pays a *premium* to the *seller* or *writer*. On the cap *value date* and thereafter on a series of *payment dates* until the last payment date before the cap *maturity date*, the *strike rate* is compared to a floating *reference rate* such as Libor. If the reference rate is greater than the strike rate, then the writer of the cap pays interest calculated on the *notional principal* of the cap, at an interest rate of the difference between the reference rate and the strike rate, over the period until the next payment date; the interest is paid at the next payment date. If the reference rate is below the strike rate then there is no payment.

In the example above, we are the buyer and the premium is US$250. The value date is 30 June and the first payment date and cap maturity is 30 September. The strike rate is 8% and the reference rate is 3-month dollar Libor, with the notional principal being US$100,000. Assuming that our cap settles at the end of the period, then the settlement amount will be 2% on US$100,000 for 92 days, which equals US$511, since dollar Libor is expressed using a year of 360 days.

The spot date convention is used for most caps, so that in the above example the reference rate would be the Libor prevailing on 28 June; settlement would still be on 30 September.

Buying a cap is equivalent to buying a call option to receive floating on an FRA; a put option to pay floating on an FRA is an interest rate *floor*. Just as a cap lets a borrower limit her maximum interest expense, a floor lets an investor guarantee a minimum interest income. To see this working, suppose that an investor buys a floor on sterling at 10%. If sterling Libor is greater than 10% then the investor will receive Libor on his portfolio minus the cost of the floor. If Libor is less than 10% then the investor will receive Libor on his portfolio and (10% - Libor) on the floor, giving a net 10% minus the cost of the floor. The terminology used for floors is the same as for caps and it is therefore not repeated; however, it is worth noting that the term 'interest rate guarantee' may refer to a single period floor as well as to a cap.

If a borrower caps her interest expense by buying a cap, she may want to subsidise the expense of the cap by selling a floor and giving up possible gains should interest rates drop below the floor strike rate. This arrangement of buying a cap and writing a corresponding floor is know as buying a *collar*; if the premium on the cap equals the premium on the floor so that the net premium is zero, then the overall deal is a 'zero-cost collar'.

The payoff diagrams for a one period cap or floor have the characteristic 'hockey stick' appearance seen in Figure 12.1.

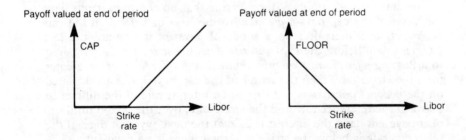

Figure 12.1 Payoff at end of period to buyer of a single period cap or floor.

Adding the inverse of the floor to the cap gives the payoff diagram for a collar shown in Figure 12.2.

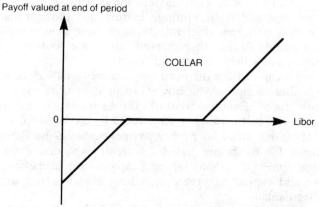

Payoff valued at end of period

COLLAR

0   Libor

Figure 12.2 Payoff at end of period to buyer of a single period collar.

Many collars are bought by floating-rate borrowers; combining a one-period floating loan with a collar gives the net interest expense shown in Figure 12.3.

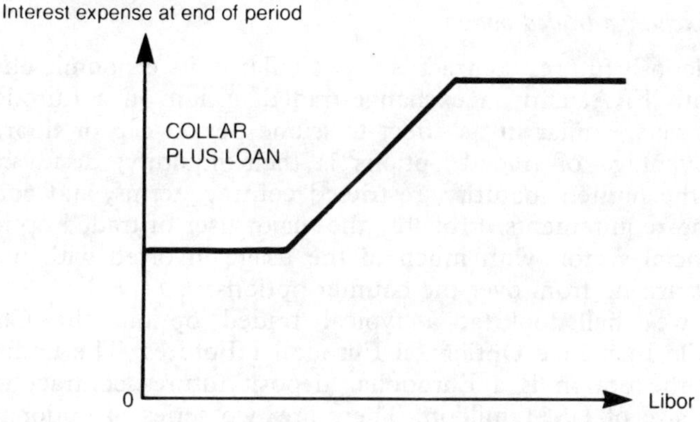

Interest expense at end of period

COLLAR
PLUS LOAN

0   Libor

Figure 12.3 Net interest expense at end of period for loan plus collar.

Combining options and debt in this way can produce a variety of geometries of payoff diagrams, with names such as strangles, bear spreads, butterfly spreads, and a whole menagerie of others. If you ignore the name and concentrate on the shape of the payoff line, you can work out which shape of payoff, and hence which combination of options, best suits your needs. This subject is not pursued further here, since the logic of this book is to teach you to understand thoroughly the mechanics, pricing, and risk of each instrument; when you have learned this you will be able to use the instruments in any combination.

Two-way prices in caps and floors are quoted primarily by large banks, for the same currencies and maturities as FRAs and interest rate swaps. Banks aim to earn income through the bid-offer spread available on caps and floors, through trading, and through managing residual option positions efficiently through equivalent portfolios of FRAs and swaps. As in other markets, there are brokers trying to match buyers and sellers in caps and floors.

If you sell a cap or floor then you have no credit risk, since you can have no further receipt; if you buy a cap or floor then you have the same credit risk as if you entered into the corresponding swap, since your receipts will be the same as they would be on the swap, although you will of course make no further payments. Since the BIS capital requirements for banks are based on credit exposure, there is no capital requirement for a bank selling a cap or floor. In the absence of credit risk and capital requirements, selling caps is a very attractive business for banks.

It should be noted that options, such as caps and floors, which are dealt directly between two counterparties, are described as *over-the-counter* (OTC) options, in contrast to options traded on an exchange; 'over-the-telephone' might be a more appropriate terminology today.

12.3.2 Exchange-traded options

A Eurodeposit futures contract is very similar in its economic effect to a 3-month FRA, and an exchange-traded option on a Eurodeposit future is very similar in its effect to a one period cap or floor. The main advantage of traded options is their liquidity; disadvantages include the limited maturity, restricted contract terms, and complex margining requirements. Probably the major user of traded options is the financial sector, with much of the usage involved with hedging positions arising from over-the-counter options.

Here we shall look at a typical traded option, the Chicago Mercantile Exchange Option on Eurodollar Futures. The underlying asset of the option is a Eurodollar deposit futures contract with a contract size of US$1 million. There are two series of options, puts and calls, corresponding in effect to caps and floors. A major difference is that the traded option is an American option, which can in theory be exercised at any time. In fact, it is never worthwhile to exercise a put option of this nature early, but it may under certain conditions be worthwhile to exercise a call option early; this complicates obtaining an exact pricing formula.

This seems to be the reverse of the normal situation for American puts and calls; the reason is that futures prices are quoted 'upside down', so that what looks like a call is really a put! To see this, consider that the underlying futures contract has a maximum price of 100 and no minimum price, so that the call offers limited gains to the holder, while the put, in principle, offers unlimited gains.

There can be an option on any of the four futures contracts in a year, at any strike rate which is a multiple of 0.25 above 91.00, 91.00 itself or a multiple of 0.50 below 91.00. As for Eurodollar futures, the quoted traded option price represents 'US$25 for an 01'; for example, a price quote of 0.50 represents US$1,250 for a contract.

Since buying a futures contract is equivalent to receiving fixed on an FRA, we have the following equivalences:

- Cap   – traded put option; and
- Floor – traded call option.

Consider the following example. Suppose that the price of a June call option on the Eurodollar future at a strike rate of 92.00 is 0.43. This means that we can buy for US$1,075 the right to buy one June future at a price of 92.00; the mechanics of exercise are discussed below. As noted above we are in effect buying a floor at a strike rate of 8%. When we buy a call our contract is with the exchange. Unlike the process of buying a future, we have to pay immediately the price of US$1,075; we do not have to pay any margin at any stage, since our liability is limited to the initial price.

The writer of the option also has a contract with the exchange, but he will not receive the full US$1,075 price, since he has to put up some initial margin. Thereafter, at the end of each trading day, the option contract is marked to market at its closing price and the writer pays or receives a variation margin according to whether the price has gone up or down. The calculation of the margin is not simple, since the exchange will require the total margin to meet its immediate risk plus an extra amount to cover future market movements. Suppose that in our case the price of a June future is 92.10. If we exercise the option today we will realise a profit of US$250, and so the exchange must ensure that it has at least US$250 net margin from the option writer. The calculation is further complicated by the fact that the exchange will assess the amount needed to cover future market movements on the whole portfolio of options and futures held by the writer, so that if there are offsetting risks the margin will be reduced. This results in extremely complex rules for margining, which it is not appropriate to discuss further here; for further information, you should contact a futures and options broker or the exchange itself.

To return to our example, we may decide to close out our option when the price goes to 0.63. We do this by writing an identical option; the exchange will pay us the full price of US$1,575 which it receives from the buyer of the option. We have no margining requirement because our position nets to zero. The exchange still has its margin from the writer of the original option which we bought, and in effect the buyer of the option from us has stepped into our shoes.

A second way in which we can close out the option is to exercise it and buy a future. Suppose we do this when the future price is 92.50; we have to pay the initial margin on the future, but we shall receive a variation margin from the exchange of US$1,250, being the difference between the market price and our exercise price. The exchange will have the funds for this variation margin from the net margin paid by the writer of the option. Since each option counterparty deals only with the exchange, the exchange will select at random a writer of a call option at a strike of 92.00 on the June future, and will advise her that her option has been exercised and that she is now short a futures contract; her net margin above the US$1,250 will be returned to her, and she will have no further exposure on the original option which she wrote.

The third way to close out an option is to hold it to maturity, when we shall receive cash settlement from the exchange. If the future price at maturity is at or below 92.00 then we receive nothing, and the writer of the option receives back his net margin; if the future price is, say, 92.20, then the exchange assumes that the option is exercised and we receive US$500 and the writer receives his net margin less US$500.

It is worth noting that at the London International Financial Futures Exchange the margining process for traded options is different from that described above, with both writer and buyer putting up margin payments; this is described as a 'futures style' traded option.

The risk characteristics of a Eurodeposit future are similar to an FRA with a contract amount higher than the contract size of the future by a ratio equal to the scaling factor from today to the end of the future's underlying deposit period. A traded put option should be exercised only at maturity, which will be at the value date of the underlying period; this reduces the uncertainty of the equivalent underlying FRA contract amount. A traded call will be exercised early only if the future's price is high, that is, if interest rates, and thus the scaling factor, are low; again this reduces the uncertainty of the contract amount. It is therefore not too much of an approximation to treat a traded option as being equivalent to a single period cap or floor, with strike rate equal to 100 minus the strike rate of the traded option, calculation period equal to the underlying deposit period of the future, and notional principal equal to the future's contract size times

$$(1 + ((100 - \text{future price}) * 0.25/100)),$$

the factor in brackets being the scaling factor for 3 months at a zero coupon rate corresponding to the current future price. (An adjustment should be made for the exact number of days in the calculation period and for the day convention used in quoting Libor in the currency.)

Such a treatment will not be exact, since there will still be uncertainty as to the exact discount factor at maturity, and there will still be the possibility of early exercise; moreover, for the writer of a traded option there will be uncertainty as to the size and timing of variation margin payments. However, given the approximations which we shall meet in Chapter 13 when we come to price interest rate options, it may not be worth worrying about these relatively minor uncertainties, and we shall assume that the price and risk characteristics of a traded option in normal circumstances will be a fixed multiple of those of the corresponding cap or floor. It is worth summarising and highlighting this analysis as:

Result 12.1 A traded option on a Eurodeposit future behaves like a single period cap or floor, with notional principal equal to the underlying principal of the future times the scaling factor for the underlying period of the future based on the current future price.

Because of this, the pricing and risk management of traded options are not covered explicitly in this book; it is assumed that the price and risk measures follow to a reasonable approximation from those to be derived for caps and floors.

12.3.3 Swaptions

An option on an interest rate swap is known as a swaption. Most of this subsection deals with the most common type of swaption, which is a European option on a bullet swap; at the end there are a few words about more complex swaptions.

If you buy an option on which the underlying asset is a swap on which you will receive fixed, then you are said to *buy the right to receive,* or to buy a *receiver's swaption*; if you would pay fixed on the swap then you are said to *buy the right to pay* or to buy a *payer's swaption*.

Let us look at a particular swaption. The swap will have value 31 August and maturity 5 years later; the notional principal will be £10 million, and we would be the fixed payers at 12% semiannually, with floating interest also semiannual. We buy the option, paying a premium of £50,000. In accordance with market practice, the exercise must be before 11am London time on 31 August; if the swap had floating rate calculated on a spot rather than on a same day basis, then the normal market practice would be for exercise to be by 11am two working days before 31 August.

We have bought 'the right to pay on a 5-year £10 million swap out of 31 August'. The period from today to 31 August is the option period. On 31 August we will exercise the swaption if, and only if, the 5-year swap rate is above 12%.

As for an option on an FRA, we have to separate the fixed and floating sides of the swap in order to produce a floating asset and a fixed liability. Here the asset will be the receipt of 6-month Libor on £10 million semiannually for 5 years, and the liability, whose present value at 31 August will be the strike price, will be the payment of 12% on £10 million semiannually for 5 years. We have bought a call option on the floating asset.

For an option on an FRA, the payment of the strike price and the payment of the floating amount are made on the same day, and there is thus no difficulty about incorporating them in a pricing model; for a swaption the strike price is paid as a succession of payments over time, as are the floating payments, and, therefore, we must future value each set of payments to the same day in order to incorporate them into a model.

When we have chosen our underlying asset and our strike price as above and made the necessary approximations, we shall be able to fit swaptions into the general theory of options developed in Chapters 10 and 11.

Section 12.2 above gives several applications for swaptions; the common thread is that they involve buying the right to lock in a fixed investment or borrowing rate for a many-period instrument. The payoff diagram for a swaption will be similar to the payoff diagram for a cap or floor, except that the payoff has to be present valued and thus will be proportionally less for higher interest rates. Figure 12.4 is the payoff diagram for the swaption in our example, assuming that the present values of the fixed and floating payments depend only on the 5-year swap rate at 31 August.

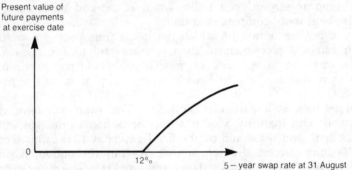

Figure 12.4 Payoff at exercise date to holder of payer's swaption. The curvature of the payoff line is exaggerated for clarity.

You should recognise the similarity of this diagram to the payoff diagram for a cap; a receiver's swaption would give a payoff similar to a floor, but again with a curved line. Payer's and receiver's swaptions can be combined to produce the swaption equivalent of a collar, and more exotic payoff diagrams can be obtained through a suitable portfolio of instruments.

Prices in swaptions are made by the same banks which are involved in swaps and caps. Option periods are from around one month to several years, with shorter option periods being the most common; the underlying swaps will have similar final maturities and notional principals to swaps traded in the market. Again the banks will aim to earn spread income by providing this service, and they will also look to use swaptions in managing their own positions and in proprietary trading. Brokers are also active in the swaption market.

It should be recognised that the swaption market can be very illiquid; this provides opportunities for spread income, but it also creates risks in using these instruments.

Whether you sell or buy a swaption you have a potential credit risk, since if the swaption is exercised the resultant swap will give a credit exposure to both parties. Since there is a credit risk, banks will have to hold capital under the BIS risk capital regulations whether they buy or sell a swaption; the capital required is calculated using the same formula as for a single currency swap, and the capital and credit costs can be predicted using a model similar to that discussed for swaps in Part III. To reduce credit exposure, some swaptions settle on a cash basis; that is, if the swaption is exercised the seller pays the mark-to-market value of the future swap payments to the buyer and there is no ongoing swap contract. Under this arrangement, known as a 'cash settlement swaption', there is no credit risk or capital requirement for the seller, although there is for the buyer up to the exercise date. Unfortunately, there does not seem to be an agreed market practice for valuing cash settlement swaptions on exercise, so you are advised to include a detailed formula for this in your contract.

It is possible to have swaptions in which the underlying swap has a complex structure; for example, you could have a swaption in which the underlying contract is an amortising swap. Having an underlying complex swap rather than a simple swap does not change the logic of the analysis above, but it adds yet another complication to pricing and position management. Such swaptions therefore should carry an increased spread to compensate for the increased risk.

It is also possible to have American swaptions. These come in two basic varieties, which can be characterised as *trombone* and *wasting*. ('Trombone' is not a standard market term, but is has the advantage of being descriptive.) A trombone option is an option on a swap with a constant tenor – like the slide of a trombone. For example, a trombone option on a 5-year swap might have exercise period 31 July to 30 September; if the option is exercised on 31 August then the swap will run for 5 years starting on 31 August, and if it is exercised on 15 September then the swap will run for 5 years from 15 September. In contrast, a wasting swaption has an underlying swap with a fixed maturity. For example, a wasting swaption might have exercise period 31 January to 31 December and underlying swap with maturity 31 December 5 years later. Whenever the swaption is exercised, the swap will run from that date to 31 December 5 years later. A trombone swaption would be appropriate where the position to be hedged is a loan to be fixed for a period of years; a wasting swaption might relate to the hedging of an existing bond with a fixed maturity. A variation of American swaptions is where exercise can be on one of a discrete set of days, rather than over a continuous period; for example, you might sell the right to enter into a 5-year swap at a fixed rate on any 1 June or 1 December for the next 3 years.

The pricing and management of American swaptions is beyond the scope of this book; this should not be taken as implying that there is a satisfactory theory in existence anywhere else. The main problem is that there is more than one possible underlying contract for an American swaption, and the theory developed above handles only options on a single asset price. At the end of Chapter 13 there is a brief review of numerical methods for pricing options; this will be relevant to the pricing of American swaptions.

12.3.4 Options on government bonds

A European option on a particular government bond has the characteristics of a cap, floor, or swaption. For example, an option to buy a 3-month US Treasury bill with a face value of US$10,000,000 in 6 months' time at a price of US$9,880,000, is equivalent to a floor on the 3-month riskfree interest rate in 6 months' time. To see this, consider that the scaling factor locked into the underlying contract is 1.012146 for a 3-month period, corresponding to a deposit rate of 4.858% on the assumption that the period is an exact quarter of a year. If the price of the bill in 6 months is above US$9,880,000, corresponding to a lower deposit rate, then the option will be exercised; the holder of the option thus has a lower limit on his return over the 3-month period, and hence the option is equivalent to a one period floor. By a similar analysis, an option to sell a particular government bond at a fixed price on a particular future date can be seen to be equivalent to a European payer's swaption, where the fixed swap rate is replaced by the yield to maturity of the government bond.

An American option on a particular government bond is complicated by the fact that the underlying asset price is demonstrably not lognormally distributed; in particular, as the maturity date of the bond approaches the price will become very close to the face value of the bond. This is similar to the situation for a wasting swaption. As noted above for American swaptions, the pricing of such instruments involves numerical methods which are beyond the scope of this book; there is a brief review at the end of Chapter 13.

There are also traded options on government bonds; the most popular of these have the appropriate government bond future as their underlying contract. As noted in Part IV, government bond futures generally have the additional complication that exercise can be into one of a number of bonds, at the choice of the seller; as the structure of the yield curve changes, a different bond may become cheapest to deliver. Traded options on government bonds thus have all the complications of American bond options, together with the additional complication of different bonds being delivered. Accurate pricing of these instruments should therefore again involve numerical methods.

An advantage of traded options on government bonds compared to over-the-counter options is their greater liquidity; it can be expensive (or, in some markets, due to regulations or lack of liquidity, impossible) for banks to delta hedge options on physical bonds, and this feeds through into a large bid-offer spread for such over-the-counter options.

As a summary of this section, there are options on government bonds corresponding to caps, floors, swaptions, and traded options. Except for the traded options on bond futures, which can be delta hedged through the futures contract, these instruments tend to be relatively illiquid. Sophisticated numerical pricing methods are appropriate for all but the simplest options on government bonds.

12.4 CONSTRAINTS ON INTEREST RATE OPTION PRICES

This section briefly applies the analysis of sections 10.2 and 10.4 to identify pricing constraints on interest rate options. As mentioned above, it does not deal with traded options, since these are being regarded as effectively the same as caps and floors; nor does it deal with options on government bonds which are assumed either to be the same as caps, floors, or swaptions, or to require numerical pricing methods.

12.4.1 Put-call parity

You will recall from section 10.2 the put-call parity relationship that

$$P = C - S + Kr^{-t}$$

where
  P is the price of a European put;
  C is the price of a call on the same terms;
  S is the price of the asset;
  K is the strike price;
  r is the riskfree scaling factor for 1 year; and
  t is the number of years to maturity.

The relationship is exact only if there are no bid-offer spreads; if spreads are included, then the equality becomes only a close approximation.

For an FRA with maturity at time t, this relationship becomes:

Result 12.2 The price of a floor at strike rate K% equals
  (the price of a cap at strike rate K%)
  − (the present value of Libor interest on the FRA terms)
  + (the present value of a fixed payment of K% on the FRA terms).

Note that present valuing the strike payment should be done at the riskfree rate. What rate should be used to discount the future floating payment? The only way to sell the present value of the Libor interest is to enter into the FRA, receiving fixed and paying floating, and then selling forward the fixed payment. The appropriate discount rate for borrowing from a bank is Libor; the risk on the FRA payment can be made smaller by netting it against the strike payment, and so the appropriate discount rate must be between Libor and the riskfree rate. It is reasonable to assume that this rate is close enough to the riskfree rate to make the error in discounting using the riskfree rate immaterial, especially if the time t is short.

If the strike rate equals the FRA contract rate, that is, if the cap and floor are at the money, then this gives:

Result 12.3 For one period caps and floors at the money, the floor price equals the cap price.

This result also follows from the fact that buying the cap and selling the floor is equivalent to entering into a market FRA.

For many period caps and floors, the put-call parity relationship is the sum of the put-call parity relationships for the individual periods.

For a swaption, put-call parity is:

Result 12.4 The price of a receiver's swaption at strike rate $K\%$ =
   (the price of a payer's swaption at strike rate $K\%$)
   − (the present value of Libor interest on the swap terms)
   + (the present value of a fixed payment of $K\%$ on the swap terms).

Again there is a complication with regard to the discount rate to use to present value the floating payments, and again the equality will be only approximate when bid-offer spreads are taken into account.

If the strike rate equals the forward swap rate then the relationship becomes:

Result 12.5 At the money, the price of a receiver's swaption equals the price of a payer's swaption.

This also follows from the fact that buying a payer's swaption and selling a receiver's swaption gives the same future cashflows as entering into a market swap.

12.4.2 Constraints on interest rate option prices

This subsection goes through the constraints derived in section 10.4, using the same numbering as was used there; the results are stated for a one period cap only, since the results for many-period caps and for floors and swaptions are similar in form. It is assumed that it is a good approximation to do all present valuing at the riskfree rate. Because of this, and because of the existence of bid-offer spreads, all the equalities below should be taken as only approximate.

Constraint 10.1 C is greater than or equal to $S - Kr^{-t}$

The cap price is greater than or equal to the present value of (the market FRA contract rate – the strike rate over the FRA terms)

Constraint 10.2 C is greater than or equal to zero

The cap price is never negative; this result does not depend on approximations!

Constraint 10.3 C is less than or equal to S

The cap price is never greater than the present value of the market FRA rate over the FRA terms; again, this does not involve approximation.

Constraint 10.4 If K_2 is greater than K_1, then
$C(K_1)$ is greater than or equal to $C(K_2)$

If strike rate K_2 is greater than K_1, then a cap at K_2 is not more expensive than a cap at K_1.

Constraint 10.5 For European calls, if K_2 is greater than K_1 then $(K_2 - K_1)r^{-t}$ is greater than or equal to $C(K_1) - C(K_2)$

If the strike rate increases, the cap price cannot decrease by an amount greater than the present value of the difference in the strike rates over the FRA terms.

Constraint 10.6 The price diagram of C against K is convex up.

The cap price must have the relationship to the strike rate shown in Figure 12.5. S is the present value of the market FRA contract rate over the FRA contract terms.

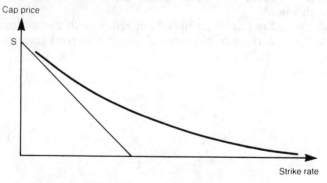

Figure 12.5 Relationship of cap price to strike rate.

Constraint 10.7 If t_2 is greater than t_1 then
$C(t_2)$ is greater than or equal to $C(t_1)$

For a flat yield curve, the price of a cap cannot decrease as the time to the underlying period increases. If the yield curve does not remain flat, then there is no exact relationship for caps based on this constraint.

We have now done as much as we can on interest rate options without having an exact pricing formula; the next chapter produces a 'best-efforts' pricing formula to enable us to continue our analysis of pricing and risk.

SUMMARY

This chapter has introduced interest rate options and placed them within the framework of the theory of options on general assets developed in chapters 10 and 11. Interest rate options do not satisfy all of the assumptions needed to derive a pricing theory for general options; this impacts the accuracy of the pricing formulae for interest rate options which will be developed in the next chapter.

The instruments covered in this chapter were caps and floors, traded options on Eurodeposit futures, swaptions, and options on government bonds; these correspond to options on FRAs, Eurodeposit futures, swaps, and bonds. The key step in the analysis is to identify the underlying asset and the strike price. For a single period cap, the asset is the floating interest of the FRA, and the strike price is the fixed interest; if the option is exercised these are settled net. A cap is a strip of European call options on FRAs; a floor is a strip of European puts. Similarly, a payer's swaption corresponds to a call option on a swap, while a receiver's swaption corresponds to a put option on a swap; in each case the asset is the present value at exercise of the floating interest. Traded options on Eurodeposit futures behave very much like caps or floors, while options on specific government bonds behave very much like swaptions. American swaptions and the more complex options on bonds cannot be priced by the methods derived in this book.

Put-call parity for European options together with the constraints on option prices derived in chapter 10 hold for interest rate options also.

CHAPTER 13

Exact pricing for
interest rate options

Chapter 11 derived the Black Scholes pricing formula, and Chapter 12 demonstrated that certain central assumptions of that derivation were not satisfied for interest rate options. This chapter derives a pricing formula for interest rate options based on Black Scholes; because of the additional complexity inherent in interest rates this pricing formula will be to some extent an approximation. The route to this formula involves pricing an option on the forward price of an asset, and then looking more closely at volatility. This allows the derivation of the pricing formula, which is considered separately for caps, floors, and swaptions. The chapter ends with a discussion of numerical methods for pricing options.

A pricing formula gives in principle all that is needed to manage an option portfolio, since the effect of changing variables on the value of the portfolio can be determined by revaluing each contract. However, it is more efficient to generate explicit formulae for the sensitivity of option prices to changes in the underlying variables, and this will be done in the next chapter.

13.1 OPTIONS ON FORWARD CONTRACTS

FRA and swap rates equate to future valued cashflows, and thus any option pricing formula for options on FRAs or swaps must involve the forward price of the underlying asset rather than today's price.

Consider an asset to be held as an investment which has a market price S for immediate delivery and a market price S' for delivery at time t. Assuming that the asset will remain intact to time t, what is the relationship between S' and S?

We initially assume zero spreads and zero transaction costs, so that all arbitrages will be exercised. Consider two portfolios:

- portfolio X contains – the asset; and
- portfolio Y contains – a forward contract to buy the asset; and
  - value S of a riskfree zero coupon bond.

Both portfolios cost S today and will contain the asset at time t. If the annualised riskfree scaling factor is r, then the value of the bond at time t will be Sr^t. If this is more or less than S', then there will be an arbitrage, since one of the portfolios will be a cheaper way of acquiring the asset, and it will be possible to buy one portfolio and sell the other to generate a riskfree profit. Therefore the two portfolios must have the same value, proving:

Result 13.1 S', the forward price of an investment asset at time t, is Sr^t.

In the real world, spreads and transaction costs will allow the spot and forward prices to diverge from this relationship by a small amount.

We have made the implicit assumption that the forward contract has no credit risk; it will generally be possible to find a counterparty with low credit risk, but you will always have some risk, and therefore the arbitrage cannot be totally riskfree. However, in general you can make the risk minimal, and so the assumption should be met closely enough to maintain the precision of Result 13.1 to within a small spread in real-world conditions.

This lets us replace S in the Black Scholes formula of Equation 11.5 by $S'r^{-t}$, to produce a call option pricing formula in terms of the forward price S'.

$$C = S'r^{-t}N(x) - Kr^{-t}N(x - \sigma\sqrt{t})$$

and equivalently

$$C = r^{-t}(S'N(x) - KN(x - \sigma\sqrt{t}))$$ **Equation 13.1**

$$\text{where } x = \frac{\log(S'/K)}{\sigma\sqrt{t}} + \frac{1}{2}\sigma\sqrt{t}$$

Although S' is a forward price, C is the cost of the option today. The formula is exact to within the limits discussed above for assets meeting the various assumptions of Chapters 10 and 11.

Equation 13.1 is known as the Black formula, after Fischer Black, who derived it in a paper entitled 'The pricing of commodity contracts' in *Journal of Financial Economics*, Vol. 3, January to March 1976, pp. 167-79.

When we come to consider appropriate assets for interest rate options we run into a problem. The floating side of an FRA, for example, is traded only as *part of* a forward contract, as discussed in Chapter 12; in order to buy the right to receive the floating payment you must buy an FRA, and thus you must take the credit of the banking system. If you lend to a bank then the appropriate discount rate to use to value future payments is Libor; however, the appropriate discount rate to use to present value the floating side of an FRA will be between Libor and the riskfree rate, since the netting of the floating payment with the fixed payment on the FRA greatly reduces the risk, but does not eliminate it.

Therefore for the floating side of an FRA, the relationship $S' = Sr^t$ does not hold exactly when r is the riskfree scaling factor. However, generally the discount rate should be close enough to the riskfree rate for r to be a good approximation to the appropriate discount rate.

Even with this approximation, it is not clear that we can use the Black formula to value options on FRAs or other interest rate options, since we still have problems with the assumptions of a flat yield curve, unchanging interest rates, and lognormal distribution of asset prices. The next section shows how the market copes with these problems by loading them on to the value of volatility.

13.2 THE ROLE OF VOLATILITY

The derivation of the Black Scholes formula assumed that the volatility of the underlying asset was known and constant; in practice, future volatility is unknown and variable. Since volatility is the only variable in the formula which is not directly observable, the market estimate of volatility has to be back calculated from the market price of options; this value is referred to as *implied volatility*, and the bid-offer spread on the option price gives a bid-offer spread on the implied volatility. When the assumptions which go into the Black Scholes and Black formulae are not well met, then the formulae become less accurate, and market makers will protect themselves by making *ad hoc* adjustments to their prices and by widening their spreads; because the volatility is calculated from the market price using Black Scholes in reverse, this will shift the value of volatility calculated and widen its spread.

Since all that you can observe in the market are the prices quoted for options, it is possible to look at the pricing process in a different way. The Black Scholes model is very successful in giving the correct relative value of two options. Even if an asset does not exactly meet the assumptions necessary for Black Scholes, it may be easier for a market maker to assume that Black Scholes will give the correct *relative* values for different options on the asset, and to use the volatility implied by other option prices on that asset, on the assumption that they *were* calculated using Black Scholes. Provided he is not asked to quote on an option with extreme parameters, this strategy might well provide the best way of interpolating consistent prices.

In interest rate options there are various competing models, but the Black formula seems to be the market standard, with market makers making their own *ad hoc* adjustments to their estimates of volatilities to compensate for the failure of interest rate options to satisfy certain critical assumptions. It is thus possible to price interest rate options using the Black formula incorporating the market estimate of volatility implied by market option prices, even though you know that the resultant price is at best an approximation; at least it is an approximation incorporating full information about the market.

If you are unhappy about this, consider that there is a thriving market in company shares, even though there is no practical way to find the 'true value' of a company at any time; market participants take the market value as the true value. From time to time, such as in October 1987, there is a large readjustment of *all* share prices, but *differentials* between share prices tend to change relatively slowly. Market makers in shares can thus concentrate on the value of one share relative to another, although anyone holding a large net position is at risk to any readjustment of share prices as a whole.

The same holds for interest rate options; it is possible that the market may suddenly adjust the price of *all* options, but the relative values of different options should change only slowly. Thus, provided that your net option position is small, you are not greatly at risk in using an inexact pricing formula. If, however, you are running a large option position and using results calculated from the pricing formula to delta hedge your position, then you are at risk from a wholesale adjustment of option prices, since the value of the hedge will not move in parallel with the change in value of the options. *It is not clear that this market risk is generally understood.*

For assets for which the assumptions of the Black Scholes or Black formulae are closely met, implied volatility should bear some resemblance to historic volatility; indeed, in the absence of changes in the structure of the economy or of the market, you would expect the two volatilities to be equal. Also, over a long period, implied volatility should average out close to average historic volatility. For interest rate options this need not be the case, since implied volatility contains a conscious or unconscious adjustment to historic volatility to fit the imperfections of the pricing formula; thus you would not expect historic volatility to be a good predictor of implied volatility for interest rates. However, in the absence of radical changes in the market you would expect the difference between implied volatility and historic volatility to be relatively constant; implied volatility should thus be affected by the same factors as historic volatility, such as changes in the balance of supply and demand for options, and economic uncertainty. This means that it may be reasonable to trade an option position and to manage its risk on the assumption that implied volatility changes will follow the pattern of changes in historic volatility. Careful analysis of historic data needs to be done to justify this assumption.

You should now understand why the Black formula is used to price interest rate options and the risks involved; the next section looks at the application of the formula.

13.3 USE OF THE BLACK FORMULA TO PRICE CAPS

You have now seen how the Black formula can be used to value interest rate options. Standard practice in the market seems to be to use an adjusted Black formula with interbank interest rates, that is, the zero curve derived from the Libor and swaps yield curve, instead of the riskfree interest rates which are incorporated in the original formula. It is unclear what theoretical justification there is for this, although there is a discussion below as to whether the use of interbank rates compensates for the *mean reversion* inherent in interest rate movements. The argument in section 13.2 above shows that the market should adjust its estimate of volatility so that options are correctly priced relative to each other using the adjusted formula. Since the market uses the adjusted formula it is used here, but you should be aware of the possibility that more accurate results could be obtained by using riskfree interest rates in deriving prices.

The adjusted formula is:

$$C = r^{-t}(S'N(x) - KN(x - \sigma\sqrt{t}))$$ **Equation 13.2**

where C is the price of a European call option

$$x = \frac{\log(S'/K)}{\sigma\sqrt{t}} + \frac{1}{2}\sigma\sqrt{t}$$

S' = forward price of asset at time t
K = strike price
t = time to expiry in years
Z = zero coupon rate to time t based on interbank yields
r = $1 + (Z/100)$
σ = volatility of S' as a fraction

For a one period cap, the assumption is that the floating interest of the corresponding FRA is an asset with lognormal distribution. Since the effective value date of the floating interest is the maturity of the cap, and the end date for volatility to have effect is the value date, it is necessary to incorporate the two different dates into the pricing formula as shown below.

$$C = r_m^{-t_m}(S'N(x) - KN(x - \sigma\sqrt{t_v}))$$ **Equation 13.3**

where C is the present value of the cap price

$$x = \frac{\log(S'/K)}{\sigma\sqrt{t_v}} + \frac{1}{2}\sigma\sqrt{t_v}$$

$S' = M * f$

K = strike rate $* f$

M = Market FRA rate

f = cap notional principal $*$ period in years/100

Z_m = zero coupon rate to time t_m based on interbank yields

$r_m = 1 + (Z_m/100)$

t_v = time in years to the value date of the cap

t_m = time in years to maturity of cap

σ = volatility of value of floating interest of FRA as a fraction

In making the substitutions above the assumption was that the floating interest of an FRA is an asset whose value at the FRA maturity has a lognormal distribution. Empirical studies show that this assumption is not wholly accurate, and that the value shows a tendency to return to its mean rather than to drift off to zero or infinity; this property is referred to as *mean reversion*.

Mean reversion will reduce the value of an option, since the chances of extremely profitable exercise are reduced; the effect will be most pronounced for long-dated options. There is no adjustment in Equation 13.3 to recognise this. However, the use of interbank interest rates rather than riskfree interest rates in Equation 13.3 will decrease the option prices given by the formula, and again the effect will be greater for longer maturities; it may thus be that the use of interbank rates introduces a compensating error which corrects the pricing formula for mean reversion. More analysis needs to be done to determine if this is in fact the case.

To avoid the inclusion of superfluous factors in the formulae, it is assumed that interest rates are quoted on a full year basis and that all relevant periods are a given fraction of a year; in practice you will have to adjust the formulae here for actual/360 and actual/365 day basis quotes and for the exact number of days in periods. In the case of single period caps, this involves redefining f as:

the notional principal $*$ days in the period/(100 $*$ day basis).

The above symbols will keep their meaning through the next two chapters. For completeness it is worthwhile adding:

Z_v = zero coupon rate to cap value date, and

$r_v = 1 + (Z_v/100)$

which will be needed later.

Let us price a one period cap using Equation 13.3. Our cap will have value at 9 months and maturity at 1 year, with a notional principal of £10 million. Midmarket zero rates are 10% to value date and 10.13% to maturity, with volatility 15%. What is the price at which a market maker will sell a 10% cap?

You will notice that we do not have what seems like a crucial piece of information, namely the market FRA rate. This is because the midmarket FRA rate can be deduced from the zero coupon rates using Result 4.3 from Part II:

If the scaling factor to t_1 years is s_1, and to t_2 years is s_2, then m, the implied Libor rate for the period t_1 to t_2, and hence the market FRA rate, is:

$$\frac{((s_2/s_1) - 1) * 100}{t_2 - t_1}$$

Using this result gives $m = 10.13$.

Is the midmarket FRA rate the correct rate for a market maker to use? The answer must surely be no, since a market maker in FRAs would not receive fixed on an FRA at midmarket, and a cap is effectively an option to the buyer to pay fixed on an FRA to the market maker. The appropriate rate to give the market maker a viable bid-offer spread will therefore be the FRA offer rate, which will be assumed to be 10.16%. This should remind us that the volatility being used should be the (higher) offer-side volatility; let us assume that the 15% volatility we have been given is the offer side. We can now price the cap as follows:

t_v	=	0.75
t_m	=	1
Z_v	=	10
Z_m	=	10.13
$K\%$	=	10
σ	=	0.15
f	=	25,000
r_v	=	1.1
r_m	=	1.1013
$r_m^{-t_m}$	=	0.9080178
m	=	10.16
S'	=	£254,000
K	=	£250,000
$\log(S'/K)$	=	0.0158733
$\sigma\sqrt{t_v}$	=	0.1299038
x	=	0.1871446
$x - \sigma\sqrt{t_v}$	=	0.0572408
$N(x)$	=	0.5742264
$N(x - \sigma\sqrt{t_v})$	=	0.5228234

giving the price of the cap C as £13,754.

It should be well worth your while to build a simple spreadsheet to take the inputs as shown and produce the cap price.

The volatility of 15% used in the above example is the volatility for a particular asset price, the floating side of an FRA with value

9 months from today and maturity 3 months later. (Note that the dates of the FRA remain constant, so that the 9 v 12 FRA we are considering today would have been a 12 v 15 FRA 3 months ago; this complicates computing historic volatilities.) The volatility for a different sterling FRA will in general be different; for example, the 9 v 15 FRA may have volatility 14% or the 6 v 9 FRA may have volatility 16%.

Using the available market cap prices it is possible to calculate an implied *volatility curve*. As indicated above, there will be a separate volatility curve for different Libors; usually the shorter the contract period of the underlying FRA the higher the volatility. Volatility tends to decrease with increasing maturity of the FRA, since mean reversion in interest rate movements comes into force. Thus the usual shape of the volatility curves will be as shown in Figure 13.1.

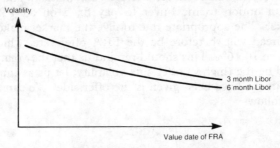

Figure 13.1   Representative curves of FRA rate volatility against time.

Because of the imperfections of the cap pricing formula, it is sometimes possible to observe different volatilities being used in the market to price caps on the same Libor and maturity but different strike rates. When this happens, it is generally the case that the implied volatility is lowest for caps in or at the money and highest for caps far out of the money; this is known as 'the volatility smile'. The market logic seems to be that transaction costs make the small premium on an out-of-the-money cap an inadequate recompense for the risks involved. However, the difference in pricing due to the use of a higher volatility tends to be small.

Most caps are for multiple periods; the market convention is that if the cap starts today or spot the first period will not be included. Thus a 5-year cap with spot value date on 6-month XEU Libor at a strike rate of 10% will have no settlement in 6 months' time, even if XEU Libor today is 9%; the last period of the cap will still run from $4\frac{1}{2}$ years to 5 years.

The price of a multiple period cap is simply the sum of the prices of the individual caplets. The implied volatility for each caplet will in general be different, as will the FRA rate.

There is a problem in choosing the FRA rate to use where the maturity of a caplet is beyond the maturity for which there is a liquid market for FRAs. The theoretically correct way to calculate the market price of, say, a 5- v 5½-year pay-fixed FRA, is to work out at what price you could hedge such an FRA by receiving fixed on a 5½-year swap and paying fixed on a 5-year swap. Such an approach gives a very wide bid-offer spread for such long-dated FRAs, and this would tend to raise considerably the price of long-dated caps.

Luckily, there is an argument for using a rate finer than the achievable market rate. Provided that the caplet is part of a strip starting today, delta hedging of the cap will be done primarily using swaps starting today. Thus, since we are accepting in our pricing formula the assumption that we can delta hedge at close to zero transaction cost, we can afford to price our caplet at the yield curve implied by pay-fixed swaps starting today. If s_v and s_m are the scaling factors to the FRA value and maturity implied by the bid side swap yield curve, the implied FRA bid rate is again given by the formula of Result 4.3:

$$\frac{((s_m/s_v) - 1) * 100}{t_m - t_v}$$

For example, if the Libor curve is flat at 12% and for swaps paying annually the yield curve is flat at 12% bid and 12.05% offer, then the FRA rate for a 5- v 5½-year FRA calculated from the bid side of the zero curve is 11.66%; the corresponding offer rate would be 11.71%. The corresponding rates achievable through hedging by paying fixed at the market offer on one swap and receiving fixed at the market bid on a second swap are 11.19% and 12.18%. Obviously, a caplet priced off an FRA rate of 12.18% will be much more expensive than one priced off a rate of 11.71%. The usual assumption in the market is, therefore, that each FRA rate used in pricing a cap or floor should be the rate implied by the bid or offer side of the swap yield curve; implied volatilities should be consistent if they are calculated on that basis.

This analysis assumes that the delta of each constituent caplet of the cap will be the same. In practice, the delta will be different for caplets of different maturities, and hence delta hedging using swaps will allow only an approximate match in individual maturities; the situation will be exacerbated if the cap is far out of the money, since the delta on the short maturity caplets will be very small while the delta on the longer maturities may be quite large. The uneven delta across the caplets will either reduce the accuracy of the hedge or will increase the hedge cost; in either case the assumption of zero transaction cost for delta hedging becomes inappropriate. This should be recognised by using a more conservative estimate of the FRA price than that implied by the swap bid rates, especially in the further maturities. Alternatively, a higher estimate of volatility should be used to increase the price of caps sold and a lower estimate should be used to decrease the price of caps bought.

In practice, to minimise the cost of adjusting a delta hedge, a market maker running an interest rate option portfolio will often try to maintain a gamma hedge through selling and buying options to obtain a zero gamma position. Usually the best that can be achieved is an approximate hedge where a long gamma position in one maturity is matched by a short position in another.

Let us look at a simple example of a market maker buying a multiple period cap. The cap will have value today and maturity in 2 years, and will be on 6-month Libor on a notional principal of £10,000,000, with a strike rate of 10.00%. The sterling bid-offer yield curve is:

6 months	11.5%/11.625%	(Libor)
1 year	11%/11.125%	(Libor)
18 months	10.5%/10.57%	(swap)
2 years	10%/10.07%	(swap)

Sterling swaps are quoted on the basis of semiannual interest. The bid-offer volatility curve for 6-month Libor is:

6 months	18%/20%
18 months	16%/18%.

The corresponding zero coupon yield curve is:

	bid	mid
6 months	11.831%	11.897%
1 year	11%	11.062%
18 months	10.749%	10.784%
2 years	10.190%	10.226%

Since the market maker is buying the cap he will use the bid FRA rates and the bid volatility rates. In practice there would be market rates for FRAs in these maturities, but it is assumed here that we have to calculate the FRA rates from the zero bid curve. Using Result 4.3 gives FRA rates:

6 v 12	9.929%
12 v 18	9.999%
18 v 24	8.355%.

Remember that there will be no settlement on the 0 v 6 caplet. This leaves three caplets to price with the following parameters:

	6 v 12	12 v 18	18 v 24
FRA rate	9.929%	9.999%	8.355%
$K\%$	10%	10%	10%
f	50,000	50,000	50,000
S'	496,450	499,950	417,750
K	500,000	500,000	500,000
Z_m	11.062%	10.784%	10.226%
t_v	0.5	1.0	1.5
t_m	1.0	1.5	2.0
σ	18	17	16

Inserting these values into Equation 13.3 gives caplet prices:

6 v 12	12 v 18	18 v 24
£21,201	£29,023	£7,152

giving a total cap price of £57,376.

The discussion above looked at pricing new transactions. In marking a portfolio of caps to market it will generally be appropriate to base the valuation on midmarket interest and volatility rates; this is because there will be a large number of offsetting bought and sold caps, leaving a relatively small net position. However, as for swaps, it will be necessary to subtract from this valuation for each deal an allocation of income to the credit area, an allocation to the management account for the cost of capital, and a holdback calculated on the basis of future operational costs. It may be appropriate to increase the holdback to allow for the inaccuracy inherent in the hedging of option positions. As noted in Chapter 12 there will be no credit or capital cost for caps sold; however there will still be a need for a holdback.

This analysis will carry through for the valuation of floors and swaptions; it will therefore not be repeated for these instruments in the sections below.

13.4 PRICING FLOORS

Floors can be priced using put-call parity. Result 10.2 demonstrated that, under the assumption of no bid-offer spreads, the price of a put option was:

$$P = C - S + Kr^{-t}.$$

Since we are now working with S' instead of S, this relationship becomes:

$$P = C - (S' - K)r^{-t}.$$

In the original derivation, r was the riskfree zero coupon rate; in the practice of the interest rate option market, r is the interbank zero coupon rate. In principle this should sometimes give opportunities for riskfree arbitrage, but in practice the nominal mispricing will be less than the relevant bid-offer spread.

How should the bid-offer spread be included in the put-call parity relationship? The relationship above is true at maturity, but if we attempt to create the right-hand-side portfolio today by buying a call and a bond and selling the asset, we shall have to buy the call and bond at the market maker's offer price and sell the asset at the bid, while constructing the left-hand-side portfolio involves buying the put at the offer price. Assuming that the bid-offer spread on the bond can be ignored (since in practice we shall absorb the bond into our net funding position), the equivalence of these two portfolios shows that:

P_{offer} is not greater than $C_{\text{offer}} - (S'_{\text{bid}} - K)r^{-t}$

since otherwise we would buy the right hand side portfolio instead of buying the put.

Similar arguments show that:

P_{bid} is not less than $C_{\text{bid}} - (S'_{\text{offer}} - K)r^{-t}$
C_{offer} is not greater than $P_{\text{offer}} + (S'_{\text{offer}} - K)r^{-t}$
C_{bid} is not less than $P_{\text{bid}} + (S'_{\text{bid}} - K)r^{-t}$

Putting these relationships together shows that
P_{offer} is in the range:

$$C_{\text{offer}} - (S'_{\text{offer}} - K)r^{-t} \text{ to } C_{\text{offer}} - (S'_{\text{bid}} - K)r^{-t}$$

and P_{bid} is in the range:

$$C_{\text{bid}} - (S'_{\text{offer}} - K)r^{-t} \text{ to } C_{\text{bid}} - (S'_{\text{bid}} - K)r^{-t}$$

This gives:

Result 13.2 The maximum possible bid-offer spread for a put option is:

$$P_{\text{offer}} = C_{\text{offer}} - (S'_{\text{bid}} - K)r^{-t}$$
$$P_{\text{bid}} = C_{\text{bid}} - (S'_{\text{offer}} - K)r^{-t}$$

It will be assumed that put-call parity holds for floors and caps in the form of Result 13.2, but you should remember that floor bid-offer spreads may be within the spread defined there.

It is sometimes possible to observe different implied volatilities being used for caps and floors; this may be due to an imbalance in supply and demand or to a market belief in the direction of rate movements. So long as the cap and floor prices sit within the bid-offer spreads in the equations above, there will be no opportunity for arbitrage.

We are now in a position to price a floor using put-call parity. Suppose that a market maker wishes to buy a one-period floor on 3-month Libor on a principal of DEM20,000,000, at a strike rate of 7.5%, where the value date of the floor is at 1 year, the zero coupon rate to 15 months is 8.2%, the 12 v 15 FRA rate is 8.00%/8.07%, and the bid side volatility is 14%. Assuming that the period of the floor is 91 days, what should the market maker's bid price be?

The market maker will first establish the bid price of the cap, which he needs for use in Result 13.2. Which FRA rate should he use in calculating the cap price? He should choose the FRA rate which gives the lower price for buying a cap, and so the appropriate rate is the FRA bid rate, which in this case is 8%.

As an aside, we can now summarise the appropriate FRA rates for a market maker to use in the Black formula in pricing caps and floors:

Buy cap or floor   FRA bid rate;
Sell cap or floor   FRA offer rate.

To return to our calculation, we now have all the variables we need to price the floor. We have to remember that the convention for quoting Deutschmark Libor rates is to use a basis of a year of 360 days, and therefore to use Equation 13.3 to price the corresponding cap we must remember to set f equal to:

$$\frac{DEM20{,}000{,}000 * 91}{360 * 100}$$

This gives

t_v	$= 1$
t_m	$= 1.25$
Z_m	$= 8.2$
$K\%$	$= 7.5\%$
σ	$= 0.14$
f	$= 50{,}555.56$
r_m	$= 1.082$
S'	$= DEM404{,}444$
K	$= DEM379{,}167$
$\sigma\sqrt{t_v}$	$= 0.14$
$\log(S'/K)$	$= 0.0645385$
x	$= 0.5309893$
$x - \sigma\sqrt{t_v}$	$= 0.3909893$
$N(x)$	$= 0.7022869$
$N(x - \sigma\sqrt{t_v})$	$= 0.6520974$

giving the price of the cap as DEM33,331. Using Result 13.2, the price of the floor is:

$$P_{bid} = C_{bid} - (S'_{offer} - K)r^{-t}$$

where

C_{bid}	$=$	DEM33,331
S'_{offer}	$=$	$f * 8.07$
	$=$	DEM407,983
K	$=$	DEM379,167
r^{-t}	$=$	$1.082^{-1.25}$
	$=$	0.9061830

This gives the price of the floor as:

DEM33,331 - (DEM28,816 * 0.9061830)
which equals DEM7,218.

If the offer side volatility is 16%, then the cap offer price is DEM38,134, S'_{bid} is DEM404,444, and the floor offer price is DEM15,228.

The cap bid-offer spread is DEM4,803 and the floor bid offer spread is DEM8,010. This wider spread might be appropriate, or a market maker might choose to narrow the spread on the floor compared to Result 13.2 to bring it more in line with the spread on the cap.

The pricing of multiple period floors follows exactly the pricing of multiple period caps.

13.5 PRICING SWAPTIONS

This section first prices European options to pay fixed on bullet swaps, and then uses put-call parity to price European options to receive fixed.

An example of an option to pay fixed would be the right to enter into a 3-year swap where you receive at 6-month Libor and pay semiannually at 10% on £10,000,000, where the exercise date and swap value date are both in 1 year's time. What is the underlying asset of this option, and what is the strike price? As discussed in the previous section, the underlying asset is taken as the floating receipts on the swap and the strike price is taken as the fixed payments. In order to use the Black formula to value the asset we have to make the assumption that its value will be lognormally distributed; again this assumption is not met accurately in practice, causing inaccuracy in the derived option price.

As for caps and floors, this inaccuracy will feed through into adjustments in the volatility used in the market. Note that the volatility of a swaption will be a function both of the tenor of the underlying swap and of the option period; it will thus be described by a set of curves, one for each swap tenor. In general, volatility tends to decrease with an increasing option period and with increasing tenor of the underlying swap; this continues the trend we saw for caplets of different maturities for different Libors. As for caps and floors, the market volatility used for receivers' and payers' swaptions or for swaptions with differing strike rates may be slightly different.

To fit the asset and strike price into Equation 13.2 we have to future value each as of the value date of the underlying swap. Since the fixed and floating sides of a swap at the market fixed rate have equal value, we can value our floating asset by equating it to the value of the fixed payments on a market swap over the same period and notional principal. We saw in Part III how to determine the fixed rate for a deferred swap; once we have the fixed rate we simply apply it to the notional principal and discount each payment to the exercise date using the interbank zero coupon curve. Since the strike price is also a fixed payment over the swap life, we could follow the same process of applying the strike rate to the notional principal and discounting it back to the exercise date. However, by choosing the payment dates of the market swap to coincide with the payment dates of the fixed side of the underlying swap of the swaption, we can simplify the computation, as shown in the example below.

Let us work out the price at which a market maker would write a payer's swaption, where the option period is 1 year and the underlying 2-year swap has notional principal of £20,000,000, with the market maker receiving fixed annually at 11% and paying Libor semiannually. Volatility for a 2-year swap starting in 1 year's time is 12% bid, 14% offer.

The sterling yield curve is:

	Bid	Offer
6 month	11.375%	11.50% (Libor)
1 year	11.375%	11.50% (Libor)
2 year	11.00%	11.06% (Swap)
3 year	10.90%	10.96% (Swap)

Sterling swaps are quoted on the basis of semiannual payments.

The market maker estimates her cost of funds as being Libor out to 1 year; this gives midmarket rates:

	Semiannual par curve	Zero coupon	Annual par curve
1 year	11.196	11.500	11.500
2 year	11.03	11.319	11.329
3 year	10.93	11.206	11.224

The market swap rate for a 2-year swap 1-year deferred is calculated by the method of Chapter 8 as follows. The long swap is from today for 3 years, and the short swap is from today for 1 year. Working on a principal of 100:

PV1%(short swap)   = 0.89686
PV1%(long swap)   = 2.43098
PV1%(deferred swap) = 1.53412

long bid   = 11.194%
long offer = 11.254%
short bid   = 11.430%
short offer = 11.500%

(These are rates for annual fixed payments. The bid-offer spread has been kept as 6bppa for the 3-year rate but has been reduced on the 1-year rate to estimate the reduced spread on off-balance-sheet instruments.)

The market maker's bid rate on the deferred swap is then:

$$\frac{(\text{long bid} * \text{PV1\%(long swap)}) - (\text{short offer} * \text{PV1\%(short swap)})}{\text{PV1\%(deferred swap)}}$$

which equals

$$\frac{(11.194 * 2.43098) - (11.5 * 0.89686)}{1.53412}$$

which equals 11.015%.

Similarly the offer rate on the deferred swap is:

$$\frac{\text{(long offer} * \text{PV1\%(long swap))} - \text{(short bid} * \text{PV1\%(short swap))}}{\text{PV1\%(deferred swap)}}$$

which equals

$$\frac{(11.254 * 2.43098) - (11.43 * 0.89686)}{1.53412}$$

which equals 11.151%.

The market maker is writing an option where she will receive fixed; should she price it using the bid or the offer swap rate? If she were going to enter into the swap directly she would use the offer swap rate, and therefore she should use the offer swap rate in pricing the option; the offer rate here is 11.151%.

S' is thus the value at 1 year of 11.151% at year 2 and 11.151% at year 3; on the notional principal of £20,000,000 this equals £2,230,200 on each date. The scaling factor to 1 year is 1.11500, to 2 years it is 1.23919, and to 3 years it is 1.37526. This gives the present value of the cashflows as £1,799,724 and £1,621,657, totalling £3,421,381; future valuing this to 1 year gives S' equals £3,814,840.

We could value K by the same method, but by observing that the strike price is the value at 1 year of an 11% annual cashflow over the swap we can immediately write:

$K = S' * (11\%/11.151\%)$, which gives K as £3,763,182.

We now have all the variables for the Black formula.

S' = £3,814,840
K = £3,763,182
t = 1
Z = 11.5%
r = 1.115
σ = 0.14

These give

r^{-t} = 0.896861
$\log(S'/K)$ = 0.0136339
$\sigma\sqrt{t}$ = 0.14
x = 0.1673850
$x - \sigma\sqrt{t}$ = 0.0273850
$N(x)$ = 0.5664664
$N(x - \sigma\sqrt{t})$ = 0.5109237

so that the offer price of the swaption is

$C = 0.896861 * ((£3,814,840 * 0.5664664)$
$\quad - (£3,763,182 * 0.5109237))$

which equals £213,704.

To find the price at which the market maker should bid for the swaption, the above calculation should be repeated using the bid swap rate of 11.015% and the bid volatility of 12%. This gives S' as £3,768,313, and the swaption price is then £163,899.

Pricing a receiver's swaption can be done using put-call parity in the same way as for pricing a floor; the receiver's swaption price is:

$$P = C - (S' - K)r^{-t}$$

where C is the price of the payer's swaption.

Using Result 13.2, the bid side of S' can be used to price the offer side of P and the offer side of S' can be used to price the bid of P; this gives the maximum spread without the possibility of an arbitrage, and in practice the market spread might be less.

For example, to price the market maker's offer on a receiver's swaption on the same terms as the swaption in the example above, we start with the offer price for C of £213,704. The bid side of S' is based on the bid rate for the deferred swap of 11.015%, giving:

$$S' = £3,768,313$$
$$K = £3,762,984$$
$$r = 1.115$$
$$t = 1.$$

This gives the offer rate for the receiver's swaption as

$$P_{offer} = £213,704 - ((£3,768,313 - £3,762,984) * 0.8968610)$$
$$= £208,925.$$

The equivalent calculation shows that the bid rate should be

$$P_{bid} = £163,899 - ((£3,814,840 - £3,762,984) * 0.8968610)$$
$$= £117,391$$

The wide bid-offer spread on the receiver's swaption gives the market maker the opportunity to improve one or both sides, if she so wishes.

If the underlying swap is not bullet but has some complex profile, then it is still possible to price the swaption using the method developed above. The values of S' and K can be calculated in the same way, and an appropriate volatility rate can be chosen to represent the average volatility of the component swapsicles of the swap. It is probably wise to widen the bid-offer spread on the volatility to take account of the increased illiquidity of such a swaption and of the additional approximations that go into the pricing.

Before leaving swaptions it is worthwhile observing that the price of a payer's swaption will always be less than the price of the corresponding cap, since the cap gives you the right to receive Libor minus the strike or to pay nothing, while if you exercise the swaption you may still end up paying in some periods of the swap. For the same reason, a receiver's swaption will always be cheaper than the corresponding floor.

13.6 NUMERICAL METHODS FOR PRICING OPTIONS

This section makes no attempt to explain numerical pricing methods in detail; it aims merely to give a brief overview. Three numerical methods are dealt with below: *Monte Carlo* simulation, *lattices*, and *finite diference* methods. A good source for further information on all of these is *Options, Futures, and Other Derivative Securities*.

In the absence of an analytic formula, the obvious way to estimate the price of a European option is to simulate repeatedly the random movement of the asset price over the option period. Each such simulation can be described as a *simulation run*, and the terminal value of the option can be calculated for each simulation run based on the asset price at the exercise date; the present value of the option can then be calculated by present valuing the terminal value. By averaging over a large number of such simulation runs, a good estimate of the option value should be obtained. This method is known as a Monte Carlo simulation, by analogy with the process at work in a casino.

The problem is knowing which scaling factor to use in the present valuing, since the scaling factor depends on the systematic risk of the underlying cashflows. This issue can be avoided by using risk-neutral valuation, which was mentioned in Chapter 11 as a general property of many types of option. This involves two steps. First, for each simulation run adjust the random movement of the asset price so that it conforms to the movement which would exist were investors indifferent to risk; this means that the expected terminal asset price must be the asset price today future valued at the riskfree scaling factor. Secondly, for each simulation run, discount the terminal value of the option using the riskfree scaling factor. If you revisit the derivation of the binomial pricing models in Chapter 11 you can see how risk-neutral valuation is used in practice.

The Monte-Carlo method can be extended to options dependent on more than one asset price; in each simulation run each asset price is generated based on its own risk-neutral random movements and the terminal option price is again discounted at the riskfree rate. The Monte Carlo method has the advantage that it is relatively efficient for options involving several assets, since the time to compute each simulation run is, more or less, simply multiplied by the number of assets.

In order to run a Monte Carlo simulation you need to be able to understand the random process followed by asset prices. This requires an understanding of the mathematics of *stochastic processes*; again *Options, Futures, and Other Derivative Securities* is a good source text. A particular problem with interest rate options is that the random process governing the evolution of interest rates over time is not well understood; this means that any pricing technique for interest rate options can be only approximate.

The Monte Carlo method works only for European options, since it cannot directly determine when it is best to exercise an American option before the end of its exercise period.

The binomial pricing model for European call options which was developed in Chapter 11 is an example of the lattice approach to pricing options. A binomial (or indeed polynomial) tree is built representing the full distribution of possible movements of the asset price over the period, and the value of the option is then calculated at each node working from the end of the period backwards. Again it is necessary to understand the random process followed by the asset price. Risk-neutral valuation can also be used in this method to simplify the calculation of the value at each node.

An advantage of this method compared to a Monte Carlo simulation is that it can be used to price American options, provided that these depend only on the current state of the asset and not on its history. This is because each evaluation of a node incorporates full information about the future but none about the past. A disadvantage is that for options involving more than one asset the size of the tree can rapidly grow to become unmanageable.

The original paper by Black and Scholes derived their celebrated pricing formula by demonstrating that the call option price f satisfied the equation:

$$\frac{\partial f}{\partial t} + \log(r)S\,\frac{\partial f}{\partial S} + \frac{1}{2}\,\sigma^2 S^2 \frac{\partial^2 f}{\partial S^2} = \log(r)f \qquad \textbf{Equation 13.4}$$

They then produced an analytic solution for this equation which satisfied the known boundary condition of the option price at the maturity date.

In fact, Equation 13.4 can be shown to be true for the price of any option which is dependent only on the value of an asset whose price is lognormally distributed. It can thus be used to price European put options directly, and in principle it can be used to price other sorts of options such as American puts.

However, there is no known exact analytic solution to equation 13.4 for American put options, and therefore it is necessary to solve numerically. The finite difference method is a numerical procedure for solving such differential equations. It involves constructing a grid of equally-spaced asset prices and equally-spaced time intervals across the option period. The option will have a value at each grid point, which can be represented by a matrix of values f_{ij}. The procedure is to create a version of Equation 13.4 at each grid point by approximating the partial derivatives of f_{ij} in terms of the differences between f_{ij} and its neighbours, and then to solve simultaneously for all the f_{ij}. The known boundary condition of the value of the option at its maturity date uniquely determines all the f_{ij}.

Where the asset price is distributed other than lognormally, the option price should still satisfy some differential equation, which can then be solved by the finite difference method. The method can also be used for options involving more than one asset price, although again the complexity of the calculation increases rapidly with the number of assets involved.

A drawback of all these methods is the computational complexity involved; they all can take an appreciable amount of computer power to calculate a price. Since there is a need to manage option positions as well as to price options, it will be necessary to determine regularly the sensitivity of options to changes in the underlying variables; this involves recalculating the option price for each sensitivity to be measured. For a sizeable portfolio this can rapidly become a large use of computing time.

An alternative approach is to develop an analytic formula which approximates the correct solution; this has been done with varying success for certain types of options.

As we have seen, interest rate options have prices sensitive to movements in interest rates up to the maturity of the underlying asset. Consequently, any numerical method which seeks to improve on the Black formula for European interest rate options must incorporate a coherent model of possible future yield curve movements. There does not currently seem to be any promising candidate for such a model.

However, numerical methods are still essential for American swaptions, options on bonds, and other complex types of interest rate option, where there is as yet no analytic pricing formula.

It should be noted that where there is no agreed analytic formula for valuing an option, there may well be difficulties agreeing the valuation for financial accounting purposes.

SUMMARY

This chapter has derived an exact pricing formula for caps and floors and for European swaptions. The Black Scholes formula leads to the Black formula for the value of a European call option using the forward price of an asset as a variable. Assuming that the market will adjust its estimate of volatility for interest rate options to take account of their failure to meet some of the key assumptions made in chapters 10 and 11, it is possible to use the Black formula to price such options. The circular nature of this reasoning exposes the interest rate option market to the risk of a systematic readjustment of all market volatilities; this can be compared to the systematic risk of the equities market.

The Black formula gives directly a pricing formula for single period caps and European payer's swaptions. Put-call parity then gives a formula for floors and European receiver's swaptions. Numerical methods can approximate the value of more complex interest rate options.

CHAPTER 14

Risk management
of interest rate options

This chapter discusses the management of the risk inherent in interest rate options, where, as usual, risk is defined in terms of the variability of the present value of a portfolio of instruments.

In order to manage risk, it is necessary to measure how the value of the portfolio changes with changes in the variables which determine the individual option values, to quantify the likely movements in these variables in order to quantify the likely total movement in value, and to understand how to hedge the risks thus calculated.

Again caps, floors, and swaptions are considered separately, sensitivities being determined for each instrument. There is then a brief discussion on how to quantify risk through analysing historic data and how to report risk; this will be further developed in Part VII. A concluding paragraph looks at hedging and risk taking using options.

The development of the results is, of necessity, highly mathematical. This is the price of the analytic approach, but the alternative, of calculating risks by repricing options for different values of the variables, involves more work and gives no easily applicable general results. It is possible to follow the development of the argument while taking the detail of the mathematics on trust. Alternatively, you may wish to ignore the development altogether, and simply refer to the results for the sensitivities of each instrument which you will find in the appropriate section.

14.1 SENSITIVITIES OF CAP PRICES

This section develops the risk measurements for caps; this will involve resolving most of the chapter's conceptual issues and hard mathematics, so that the next two sections, on floors and swaptions, should prove easier reading.

The most important risks to be managed are interest rate and volatility risk, but other possible risks also have to be considered. The starting point will be the sensitivity of the cap price to changes in the underlying variables in the pricing formula of Equation 13.3, namely S', K, r_m, t_m, t_v, and σ; when these are determined it will be possible to look in more detail at the nature of the interest rate risk.

Since the underlying FRA has constant period, any change in t_v must be matched by a corresponding change in t_m; it therefore makes sense to consider sensitivity to a single time variable, which can be written as t. The constants t_v and t_m will represent the original times to the FRA value and maturity dates, and t will represent a variable time to the value date, so that the corresponding variable time to the maturity date equals $t + (t_m - t_v)$. An exception to this will be where t_m is used in the expression for *future valued theta*; there t_m will be considered a variable.

This gives five sensitivities to calculate. Each sensitivity is defined in terms of the ratio of the change in C to the change in the value of a particular variable while the other four variables are held constant. For example, the sensitivity with respect to σ is the limit, as the small amount $\Delta\sigma$ tends to 0, of

$$\frac{C(S', K, r_m, t, \sigma + \Delta\sigma) - C(S', K, r_m, t, \sigma)}{\Delta\sigma}$$

This can be recognised as the partial derivative:

$$\frac{\partial C}{\partial \sigma}\bigg|_{S', K, r_m, t}$$

where the symbols to the right of the vertical line indicate the variables being held constant; in general it will be obvious which variables should be constant, and partial derivatives will be written using the simpler notation:

$$\frac{\partial C}{\partial \sigma}$$

The basic property of partial derivatives needed here is that, for a function such as $C(S', K, r_m, t, \sigma)$, for a small change in one variable, say a change of $\Delta\sigma$ in σ,

$$C(S', K, r_m, t, \sigma + \Delta\sigma) \approx C(S', K, r_m, t, \sigma) + \Delta\sigma \frac{\partial C}{\partial \sigma}$$

where the symbol $\approx$ should be read as 'is approximately equal to'.

The approximation will improve as $\Delta\sigma$ tends to zero. The error in the value predicted by this formula is a function of the second derivative of C with respect to the same variable; the larger the second derivative the lower the accuracy.

This property allows you to investigate the behaviour of a function for small changes in its determining variables by simply looking at the partial derivatives of the function with respect to each variable. A practical application of this at the end of this section shows how to predict changes in the value of a cap as the determining variables change.

The five sensitivities can now be calculated by taking partial derivatives of Equation 13.3 for the value of a single period cap; for convenience the equation is repeated here:

$$C = r_m^{-t_m}(S'N(x) - KN(x - \sigma\sqrt{t_v}))$$

where

C is the present value of the cap

$x \quad = \dfrac{\log(S'/K)}{\sigma\sqrt{t_v}} + \dfrac{1}{2}\sigma\sqrt{t_v}$

$S' \; = m * f$

$K \; = $ strike rate $* f$

$m \; = $ Market FRA rate

$f \; = $ cap notional principal $*$ period in years/100

$Z_m \; = $ zero coupon rate to time t_m based on interbank yields

$r_m \; = 1 + (Z_m/100)$

$t_v \; = $ time in years to the value date of the cap

$t_m \; = $ time in years to maturity of cap

$\sigma \; = $ volatility of value of floating interest of FRA as a fraction

Also needed below are:

$Z_v \; = $ zero coupon rate to cap value date

$r_v \; = 1 + (Z_v/100)$

$F \; = $ Cap notional principal

In order to simplify the calculation of the partial derivatives of C with respect to its determining variables you should remember that:

$$N'(x) = \frac{1}{\sqrt{2\pi}}e^{-\frac{x^2}{2}}$$

This lets us prove the equivalent of Identity 11.1:

$$S'N'(x) = KN'(x - \sigma\sqrt{t_v}) \qquad\qquad \textbf{Identity 14.1}$$

Using Identity 14.1 it becomes straightforward to prove:

Delta $\quad \dfrac{\partial C}{\partial S'} = r_m^{-t_m}N(x)$ $\qquad\qquad\qquad$ always > 0

$\dfrac{\partial C}{\partial K} = -r_m^{-t_m}N(x - \sigma\sqrt{t_v})$ $\qquad\qquad$ always < 0

-Theta $\quad \dfrac{\partial C}{\partial t} = \dfrac{r_m^{-t_m}\sigma S'N'(x)}{2\sqrt{t_v}} - C\log(r_m)$ $\qquad > = $ or < 0

Vega $\quad \dfrac{\partial C}{\partial \sigma} = r_m^{-t_m}S'N'(x)\sqrt{t_v}$ $\qquad\qquad\qquad$ always > 0

$\dfrac{\partial C}{\partial r_m} = -\dfrac{t_m}{r_m}C$ $\qquad\qquad\qquad\qquad$ always < 0

It is worthwhile comparing the results above with the corresponding partial derivatives for Black Scholes derived in section 11.4. The derivatives with respect to S', K, and σ above are equivalent to their forms for Black Scholes, and the sign of each of these is also the same. The formula for theta has changed, and theta can now be negative, zero, or positive instead of always negative.

$\frac{\partial C}{\partial r}$ has also changed its form, and it is now always negative, whereas under Black Scholes it was always positive.

The change in sign of theta and of $\frac{\partial C}{\partial r}$ deserves further discussion.

Under Black Scholes the partial derivatives other than delta involve holding S constant, while under Black they involve holding S' constant. Since

$$C = r_m^{-t_m} (S'N(x) - KN(x - \sigma\sqrt{t_v})),$$

decreasing t while holding the other variables constant has two effects: it increases the factor outside the brackets since

$$\frac{\partial}{\partial t} r_m^{-t_m} = -\log(r_m)r_m^{-t_m},$$

and it decreases the factor inside the brackets since

$$\frac{\partial}{\partial t} (S'N(x) - KN(x - \sigma\sqrt{t_v})) = \frac{S'N'(x)\sigma}{2\sqrt{t_v}}$$

If the option is substantially in the money then the first of these factors will dominate and C will increase, and if the option is substantially out of the money then the second factor will dominate causing C to decrease; somewhere between the two extreme cases the behaviour will switch over. This contrasts with the simpler form of theta for Black Scholes which has two terms which are both always negative, encapsulating the idea that the 'time value' of the option decreases as time to maturity decreases. In fact, we can recover a decreasing time value for the Black formula for caps if we look at the sensitivity to movements in t of the future value of C at time t_m. This gives:

Future valued theta $-\dfrac{\partial (Cr_m^{-t_m})}{\partial t} = -\dfrac{S'N'(x)\sigma}{2\sqrt{t_v}}$ $\qquad$ always < 0

Under Black Scholes $\frac{\partial C}{\partial r}$ is always positive, whereas under Black it is always negative. The explanation is in the relation $S' = r_m^{t_m}S$. If S' is held constant while r_m increases then S must decrease, and if S is held constant while r_m increases then S' must increase; this accounts for the apparent discrepancy.

The sensitivities derived above provide sufficient information to manage volatility and certain other risks for caps; section 14.5 below discusses further the reporting and management of such risk. However, in order to manage interest rate risk within the theoretical framework of Part I, it is necessary to know the sensitivity of the option price to changes in zero coupon interest rates; this will be the major topic of the rest of this section.

C is sensitive to changes in zero coupon rates in two ways, through consequential changes in S' and consequential changes in r_m; the other price-determining variables K, t, and σ, have no sensitivity to changes in interest rates. S' is dependent upon the zero coupon rates to t_v and t_m, Z_v and Z_m, while r_m is dependent only on Z_m. From a basic property of partial derivatives:

$$\frac{\partial C}{\partial Z_m}\bigg|_{Z_v,K,t,\sigma} = \frac{\partial C}{\partial S'}\frac{\partial S'}{\partial Z_m}\bigg|_{Z_v} + \frac{\partial C}{\partial r_m}\frac{\partial r_m}{\partial Z_m}\bigg|_{Z_v} \qquad \text{and similarly}$$

$$\frac{\partial C}{\partial Z_v}\bigg|_{Z_m,K,t,\sigma} = \frac{\partial C}{\partial S'}\frac{\partial S'}{\partial Z_v}\bigg|_{Z_m} + \frac{\partial C}{\partial r_m}\frac{\partial r_m}{\partial Z_v}\bigg|_{Z_m}$$

Therefore, in order to calculate the sensitivity of C to changes in interest rates, it is necessary to calculate the partial derivatives of S' and r_m with respect to Z_v and Z_m. Using Result 4.3, S' can be expressed in terms of Z_v and Z_m as:

$$F\left(\frac{(1 + (Z_m/100))^{t_m}}{(1 + (Z_v/100))^{t_v}} - 1\right)$$

Remembering that r_v is $1 + (Z_v/000)$ and r_m is $1 + (Z_m/100)$, it is easy to calculate:

$$\frac{\partial S'}{\partial Z_m} = \frac{Ft_m}{100} r_m^{t_m-1} r_v^{-t_v}$$

$$\frac{\partial S'}{\partial Z_v} = -\frac{Ft_v}{100} r_m^{t_m} r_v^{-t_v-1}$$

Also $\dfrac{\partial r_m}{\partial Z_m} = 1/100$ and $\dfrac{\partial r_m}{\partial Z_v} = 0$

This gives

$$\frac{\partial C}{\partial Z_m}\bigg|_{Z_v} = \frac{Ft_m N(x)}{100 r_m r_v^{t_v}} - \frac{t_m C}{100 r_m} \qquad \text{almost always} > 0$$

$$\frac{\partial C}{\partial Z_v}\bigg|_{Z_m} = -\frac{Ft_v N(x)}{100 r_v^{t_v+1}} \qquad \text{always} < 0$$

For Black Scholes, we created a portfolio which was equivalent to the option in its price sensitivity to small changes in the value of S by buying delta of S and selling zero coupon bonds to make the total portfolio value C. The corresponding portfolio for the cap involves buying the future-valued delta of the underlying asset, where the future valued delta is the scaling factor $r_m^{t_m}$ times the delta calculated above. Since the asset is the floating interest of an FRA, we have to buy the FRA and invest enough money today to pay the fixed side of the FRA at t_m. As an FRA has no cost, for the equivalent portfolio to have value C we must:

Buy (pay fixed) future-valued delta of the FRA and buy C of the bond.

(As usual it is assumed that we can buy a zero coupon bond giving an interbank yield rather than a riskfree yield; this approximation is needed to derive the result for an equivalent portfolio below.)

It is easy to see that the above portfolio must have the same sensitivity to changes in the FRA rate as does C; however, it turns out that it also has the same sensitivities as C to *independent* changes in Z_v and in Z_m.

To prove this, write out the equivalent portfolio explicitly as $N(x)$ of the FRA plus C of the bond; call its present value

$$PV(\text{portfolio}) = PV(\text{FRA}) + PV(\text{bond}).$$

Let us start by considering partial derivatives with respect to Z_m. We shall consider S' to be a function of Z_m, with the original value of Z_m written as $\underline{Z}_m$. Then the future value of the FRA is $N(x) * (S'(Z_m) - S'(\underline{Z}_m))$; the present value of the FRA, $PV(\text{FRA})$, is therefore $N(x)r_m^{-t_m}(S'(Z_m) - S'(\underline{Z}_m))$. Also, the future value of the bond is $Cr_m^{t_m}$, where r_m is $1 + (\underline{Z}_m/100)$ so that its present value, $PV(\text{bond})$, is $C\underline{r}_m^{t_m}r^{-t_m}$.

Since $N(x)$, C, and $\underline{Z}_m$ are fixed, we have

$$\frac{\partial PV(\text{FRA})}{\partial Z_m} = N(x)r_m^{-t_m}\frac{\partial S'}{\partial Z_m} - \frac{N(x)t_m}{100}r_m^{-t_m-1}\,(S'(Z_m) - S'(\underline{Z}_m))$$

But at $Z_m = \underline{Z}_m$, $S'(Z_m) - S'(\underline{Z}_m) = 0$, so that the factor in $(S'(Z_m) - S'(\underline{Z}_m))$ vanishes, giving

$$\frac{\partial PV(\text{FRA})}{\partial Z_m} = \frac{N(x)Ft_m}{100r_m r_v^{t_v}}$$

We have also

$$\frac{\partial PV(\text{bond})}{\partial Z_m} = C\underline{r}_m^{t_m}\frac{-t_m}{100}r_m^{-t_m-1}$$

$$= -\frac{t_m C}{100r_m}$$

which gives

$$\frac{\partial PV(\text{portfolio})}{\partial Z_m} = \frac{N(x)Ft_m}{100r_m r_v^{t_v}} - \frac{t_m C}{100r_m}$$

which is the same as $\frac{\partial C}{\partial Z_m}$ calculated above. A similar calculation shows that

$$\frac{\partial PV(\text{portfolio})}{\partial Z_v} = \frac{\partial C}{\partial Z_v}.$$

This proves:

Result 14.1 A portfolio consisting of $N(x)$ of the FRA and C of a zero coupon bond has the same instantaneous sensitivity to interest rate movements as the cap.

The next two sections will prove the corresponding result for floors and swaptions.

Using Result 14.1, it is possible to report and manage the interest rate risk of a cap as if it consisted of an FRA and bond position; this allows the incorporation of caps in the cash gap methodology developed in Part I.

The sensitivities of the cap value to Z_v and Z_m give the basic information for managing the interest rate risk of a cap; these sensitivities can be explored further to produce the cap equivalent of gamma. Under Black Scholes, gamma was the second derivative of the option value with respect to the asset price, and it gave information on how rapidly a delta hedge would have to be adjusted as the price of the asset changed. In addition, gamma measured how the sensitivity of the option price to the asset price would change as the asset price itself changed; this was particularly important where delta hedging had reduced the portfolio sensitivity to the asset price to zero. For a cap, it is more useful to know how the hedge will have to be adjusted for a change in Z_v or Z_m, and so, since the delta hedge position is $N(x)$ of the FRA and C of the bond, the equivalents of gamma are:

$$\frac{\partial N(x)}{\partial Z_m} = \frac{N'(x)Ft_m}{100S'\sigma\sqrt{t_v}} r_m^{t_m-1} r_v^{-t_v}$$

$$\frac{\partial N(x)}{\partial Z_v} = -\frac{N'(x)F\sqrt{t_v}}{100S'\sigma} r_m^{t_m} r_v^{-t_v-1}$$

and $\dfrac{\partial C}{\partial Z_m}$ and $\dfrac{\partial C}{\partial Z_v}$, which are calculated above.

These show the sensitivity of the hedge position to changes in the zero coupon rates; in order to know how the sensitivity of C to the zero coupon rates changes as the zero rates themselves change it would be necessary to calculate $\dfrac{\partial^2 C}{\partial Z_m^2}$, $\dfrac{\partial^2 C}{\partial Z_v^2}$, and $\dfrac{\partial^2 C}{\partial Z_m \partial Z_v}$; this may be important in particular circumstances, but the expressions are not derived here.

The two partial derivatives of $N(x)$ above relate to the value of an FRA hedge at the cap value date. It may be more useful to report gamma in consistent present value terms for options with different expiry dates; this is considered further in section 14.5 below.

You can examine any other sensitivity similarly by calculating the appropriate partial derivative. For example, you might be interested in the effect of a change in the market volatility σ on the hedge ratio $N(x)$; you would investigate this by calculating $\frac{\partial N(x)}{\partial \sigma}$.

This section concludes with a numerical example to consolidate the material.

Section 13.3 priced a sample cap with:

$$
\begin{aligned}
t_v &= 9 \text{ months} \\
t_m &= 1 \text{ year} \\
Z_v &= 10\% \\
Z_m &= 10.13\% \\
F &= £10,000,000 \\
\sigma &= 0.15 \\
K\% &= 10\% \\
m &= 10.16\%
\end{aligned}
$$

to give a value of £13,754. The original pricing used the correct side of the interest and volatility bid and offer rates; however, as noted in Chapter 13, in marking a portfolio to market, and consequently in analysing risk, it makes more sense to use midmarket rates throughout. In order to use the same figures as this example, it will therefore be assumed that the offer-side volatility of 15% corresponds to midmarket volatility of 14%, and that the midmarket FRA rate is 10.1296%, which to within rounding is the rate implied by the zero coupon rates. It is also assumed here that we have bought the cap.

Using the midmarket FRA rate and volatility gives a cap price of £12,577.54. Below, each sensitivity of this price is calculated and its meaning is demonstrated for a typical small change in the determining variable. Remember that the sensitivities will change as the values of the determining variables change, and therefore the partial derivatives will predict accurately the change in C or $N(x)$ only for small changes in the underlying variables.

Delta $\frac{\partial C}{\partial S'} = 0.5141624$

If S' changes by £1 then C will change by £0.5141624. Thus, if S' changes from £253,240 by £250 to £253,490 (corresponding to a change in the market FRA rate from 10.1296 to 10.1396), C should change by approximately £128.54 to £12,706.08. In fact the new value of C is £12,706.44.

$\frac{\partial C}{\partial K} = -0.4705158$

If K changes by £1 then C will change by about -£0.4705158. Thus if $K\%$ increases from 10% to 10.01% so that K increases from £250,000 to £250,250, C should change by -0.4705158 times £250, which is

Theta - $\dfrac{\partial C}{\partial t}$ = -6,099

Vega $\dfrac{\partial C}{\partial \sigma}$ = 78,347

$\dfrac{\partial C}{\partial r_m}$ = -11,421

Future valued theta

- $\dfrac{\partial (Cr_m^{t_m})}{\partial t}$ = -8,053

$\dfrac{\partial N(x)}{\partial Z_m}$ = 1.1929743

-£117.63, to become £12,459.91. The actual new value of C is £12,460.28.

If t_v and t_m both decrease by 0.01 year while S' remains constant, then C will decrease by £60.99. (It would be no use giving the definition in terms of a change in time of 1 year, since the behaviour of C is clearly not linear over such a long period.) Thus if t_v becomes 0.74 and t_m becomes 0.99, while S' remains constant, we would expect C to be about £12,516.55. In fact C is £12,516.24.

If σ increases by 1% then C will increase by £783.47. (Remember that σ is expressed as a fraction, so that an increase of 1 in σ represents an increase of 100%.) Thus if σ increases from 14% to 15%, C should increase from £12,577.54 to about £13,361.01; in fact, it increases to £13,361.20.

If r_m increases by 0.01, corresponding to an increase of 1% in Z_m, then C decreases by £114.21. Thus if Z_m increases from 10.13% to 11.13% while S' remains constant, r_m will increase from 1.1013 to 1.1113, and you would expect C to decrease from £12,577.54 to about £12,463.33. In fact, C decreases to £12,464.36.

If t_v and t_m both decrease by 0.01 year while S' remains constant, then the future value of C at time t_m will decrease by £80.53. Thus if t_v becomes 0.74 and t_m becomes 0.99, you would expect the future value of C to decrease from £13,851.64 to £13,771.11. The future value actually becomes £13,770.84.

If Z_m increases by 0.01% with a consequential change in S', then N(x) will increase by about 0.0119297. (As N(x) cannot be greater than 1, this relation obviously holds only for small shifts in Z_m.) Thus, if Z_m increases from 10.13 to 10.14, so that m becomes 10.1668% and S' becomes £254,171, you would expect N(x) to increase from 0.5662470 to 0.5781767; in fact $N(x)$ becomes 0.5781237. This represents a change in the FRA hedge from £5,662,470 to £5,781,237, a change of £118,767 for a 0.01% change in Z_m.

$$\frac{\partial N(x)}{\partial Z_v} = -0.8957877$$

If Z_v increases by 0.01% with consequential changes in m and in S', then you would expect a decrease in $N(x)$ of about 0.0089579. Thus if Z_v increases from 10% to 10.01%, so that m decreases to 10.1016% and S decreases to £252,541, you would expect $N(x)$ to go down from 0.5662470 to 0.5572891; in fact $N(x)$ becomes 0.5572619.

$$\frac{\partial C}{\partial Z_m} = 47,755$$

If Z_m decreases by 0.01% with consequential changes in m and S', then C will go down by about £477.55. Thus if Z_m decreases from 10.13% to 10.12%, C should decrease from £12,577.54 to about £12,099.99; in fact C becomes £12,105.04.

$$\frac{\partial C}{\partial Z_v} = -35,944$$

If Z_v decreases by 0.01% with consequential changes in m and S', then C will increase by about £359.44. Thus if Z_v goes from 10% to 9.99%, C should go from £12,577.54 to about £12,936.98; in fact C becomes £12,939.87.

You can see how close the values of C and $N(x)$ predicted by the partial derivatives are to the values actually calculated.

In this example, the sensitivity of the FRA hedge ratio is of the order of £100,000 for a 1 basis point shift in Z_m or Z_v, while the corresponding sensitivity of the bond hedge is of the order of only £400. A dealer delta hedging the interest rate risk of this cap without the benefit of sophisticated reporting would therefore concentrate on adjusting the FRA hedge. Section 14.5 below resolves this potential inaccuracy by recommending integration of the reporting of the FRA and bond sensitivities. Because of transaction costs a dealer will not adjust a delta hedge for every small rate movement; instead she will adjust the hedge periodically, hoping not to be caught out by large shifts in rates. The sensitivities calculated above show the risks in this approach.

For a multiple period cap or for a portfolio of caps, the sensitivities are simply the sum of the sensitivities of the individual caplets; where some caps are sold rather than bought, their sensitivities should be subtracted rather than added to reach the total.

14.2 SENSITIVITIES OF FLOOR PRICES

In investigating the sensitivities of cap values it made sense to use midmarket interest rates and volatilities and midmarket prices. Similarly, using the midmarket version of put-call parity greatly simplifies the analysis of the sensitivities of floor values.

From put-call parity, the price of a single period floor is

$$P = C - r_m^{-t_m}(S' - K)$$

where C is the price of the corresponding cap.

So for any variable, say v:

$$\frac{\partial P}{\partial v} = \frac{\partial C}{\partial v} - \frac{\partial}{\partial v}(r_m^{-t_m}(S' - K)) \qquad \textbf{Equation 14.1}$$

Before applying this formula to calculate the sensitivity of the floor price to its determining variables, it is worth observing that, from the symmetry of the normal distribution:

$$1 - N(x) = N(-x) \qquad \textbf{Identity 14.2}$$

This identity allows a useful simplification of the formulae for the various sensitivities.

Using Equation 14.1 together with Identity 14.2 gives for a single period floor:

Delta $\qquad \dfrac{\partial P}{\partial S'} = -r_m^{-t_m}N(-x) \qquad\qquad$ always < 0

$$\frac{\partial P}{\partial K} = r_m^{-t_m}N(-x + \sigma\sqrt{t_v}) \qquad\qquad \text{always} > 0$$

-Theta $\qquad \dfrac{\partial P}{\partial t} = \dfrac{r_m^{-t_m}\sigma S' N'(x)}{2\sqrt{t_v}} + \log(r_m)r_m^{-t_m}(S'N(-x) - KN(-x + \sigma\sqrt{t_v}))$

$$ > = \text{ or } < 0$$

Vega $\qquad \dfrac{\partial P}{\partial \sigma} = r_m^{-t_m}S'N'(x)\sqrt{t_v} \qquad\qquad \text{always} > 0$

$$\frac{\partial P}{\partial r_m} = t_m r_m^{-t_m-1}(S'N(-x) - KN(-x + \sigma\sqrt{t})) \qquad > = \text{ or } < 0$$

Future valued theta

$$-\frac{\partial(Pr_m^{t_m})}{\partial t} = -\frac{S'N'(x)\sigma}{2\sqrt{t_v}} \qquad\qquad \text{always} < 0$$

$$\frac{\partial P}{\partial Z_m} = -\frac{Ft_m N(-x)}{100r_m r_v^{t_v}} + \frac{t_m(S'N(-x) - KN(-x + \sigma\sqrt{t_v}))}{100r_m^{t_m+1}} \qquad \text{always} < 0$$

$$\frac{\partial P}{\partial Z_v} = \frac{Ft_v N(-x)}{100r_v^{t_v+1}} \qquad\qquad \text{always} > 0$$

It is worthwhile comparing each formula with the corresponding formula for a cap, and examining the similarities and differences. In particular, you should observe that the formulae for vega and for future valued theta are the same for caps and floors.

The future value of delta at t_m is $N(-x)$. The portfolio consisting of FRAs and zero coupon bonds which has the same instantaneous interest rate risk as the floor is:

Sell (received fixed) future delta of the FRA and buy P of the bond.

This can be proved in the same way as in the corresponding proof for caps, by showing that:

$$\frac{\partial PV(\text{portfolio})}{\partial Z_m} = \frac{\partial PV(\text{FRA})}{\partial Z_m} + \frac{\partial PV(\text{bond})}{\partial Z_m} = \frac{\partial P}{\partial Z_m} \qquad \text{and}$$

$$\frac{\partial PV(\text{portfolio})}{\partial Z_v} = \frac{\partial PV(\text{FRA})}{\partial Z_v} + \frac{\partial PV(\text{bond})}{\partial Z_v} = \frac{\partial P}{\partial Z_v}$$

The details of the proof follow from the expressions for the partial derivatives. This result can be stated as:

Result 14.2 A portfolio consisting of $-N(-x)$ of the FRA and P of a zero coupon bond has the same instantaneous sensitivity to interest movements as the floor.

Since any derivative of $N(-x)$ is simply minus the equivalent partial derivative of $N(x)$, any sensitivity of the FRA hedging ratio for a floor will be the same as the equivalent sensitivity for the corresponding cap.

This section on floors ends with a worked example. This time we shall consider a one period floor with:

t_v	=	2 years
t_m	=	2.5 years
Z_v	=	11%
Z_m	=	10.96%
F	=	£20,000,000
σ	=	0.13
$K\%$	=	10%

Z_v and Z_m give

$$m = 10.5232948\%$$

The floor price generated by these values is £39,985.49. As in the cap example, each sensitivity is calculated below.

Delta $\frac{\partial P}{\partial S'} = -0.2744401$ If S' increases by £1 then P should decrease by about £0.2744401. Thus, if S' changes from £1,052,329 to £1,053,329, corresponding to an increase of m to

10.5332948%, then P should change by -0.2744401 times £1,000 to £39,711.05; in fact P changes to £39,711.79.

$\frac{\partial P}{\partial K} = 0.3287868$

If K increases by £1 then P should increase by about £0.3287868. Thus, if the strike rate increases to 10.01% so that K increases from £1,000,000 to £1,001,000, P should increase to about £40,314.28; in fact P increases to £40,315.10.

Theta - $\frac{\partial P}{\partial t} = -9,738$

If t_v and t_m decrease in step by 0.01 years while m and hence S' remain the same, P should decrease by about £97.38 to £39,888.11; the actual value of P is £39,887.82.

Vega $\frac{\partial P}{\partial \sigma} = 427,598$

If σ increases by 1%, then P should increase by about £4,275.98 to £44,261.47; in fact P increases to £44,271.81.

$\frac{\partial P}{\partial r_m} = -90,090$

If r_m increases by 0.01, then P should decrease by £900.90. Thus if Z_m increases by 1% with S' constant, and in consequence r_m increases from 1.1096 to 1.1196, then P should decrease to £39,084.45. In fact P becomes £39,098.74.

Future valued theta

$-\frac{\partial (Pr_m^{t_m})}{\partial t} = -18,023$

If t_v and t_m decrease in step by 0.01 years while m and S' remain the same, then the future value of P should decrease by £180.23 from £51,858.33 to £51,678.10; the actual value is £51,677.79.

$\frac{\partial N(x)}{\partial Z_m} = 0.9135846$

If Z_m increases by 1% with consequential changes in m and S', then $N(x)$ should increase by about 0.9135846. (Obviously linearity must break down long before $N(x)$ exceeds 1.) Thus if Z_m increases to 10.97%, $N(x)$ should increase from 0.6440708 to about 0.6532066; in fact $N(x)$ becomes 0.6531448. Since the delta hedge FRA amount is £20,000,000 times $N(-x)$, the hedge changes by £181,480.

$\frac{\partial N(x)}{\partial Z_v} = -0.7306043$

If Z_v increases by 1% with consequential changes in m and S', then $N(x)$ should decrease by about 0.7306043. (This time linearity must break down before $N(x)$ reaches 0.) Thus if Z_v increases to 11.01%, $N(x)$ should decrease to about 0.6367648; in fact $N(x)$ becomes 0.6367264. The hedge FRA therefore changes by £146,888.

$$\frac{\partial P}{\partial Z_m} = -131{,}074$$

If Z_m increases by 1% with a consequential change in S', then P should decrease by about £131,074. (Obviously this must break down well before a 1% change, since P cannot become negative.) Thus if Z_m increases from 10.96% to 10.961%, P should decrease to £39,854.42; the actual value is £39,854.59.

$$\frac{\partial P}{\partial Z_v} = 104{,}101$$

If Z_v increases by 1% with a consequential change in S', then P should increase by about £104,101. Thus if Z_v goes up from 11% to 11.001%, P should increase to about £40,089.59; in fact P becomes £40,089.70.

Again in this example, the sensitivities of the delta hedge FRA to changes in Z_v and Z_m are far greater than the corresponding sensitivities of the hedging bond, and therefore, to a good approximation, the dealer would be justified in ignoring the bond in the hedging process. However, if there is a systematic bias in the portfolio then the total sensitivity of the delta-hedge bonds may become large, and it is therefore important to monitor this sensitivity at least periodically. Even better would be to incorporate the sensitivities of the FRA and bond in a single report, as discussed in section 14.5 below.

For a multiple period floor or for a portfolio of floors, the total sensitivity is simply the sum of the sensitivities of the individual one period floors, where the sensitivities of floors bought are added and the sensitivities of floors sold are subtracted. Where caps and floors are in the same portfolio, their sensitivities may be added to give the total sensitivity for the portfolio.

14.3 SENSITIVITIES OF SWAPTION PRICES

We have an analytic formula for the price of European swaptions only, and this section will therefore deal only with sensitivities for European swaptions. If you need to work out sensitivities for other types of swaptions then you will have to use numerical methods, such as those discussed in section 13.6, or else develop an analytic approximation to the price.

As before, in looking at sensitivities rather than absolute prices, it is possible to make the simplification of working with midmarket rates only. This allows the valuation of S' directly from the midmarket zero coupon curve, as follows:

For each payment period of the underlying swap, the zero coupon yield curve defines an FRA rate and a scaling factor from today to the maturity of the period. The contribution of each payment period to S' is the FRA rate times the swap notional principal over that period, discounted to today at the scaling factor for the end of the period, and then forward valued to the value date of the swap using the appropriate scaling factor for that date. Summing over all the payment periods gives S'. This represents a significant reduction in computation compared to the method of section 13.5, especially for non-bullet swaps.

K can be valued in the same way, by valuing the fixed interest rate over each payment period, present valuing it to today, and then future valuing it to the swap value date.

Since the swaption pricing involves valuing S' at the value date of the underlying swap, which is effectively the expiry date of the option, there is only one time factor t_v which comes into the pricing formula. You will recall that a payer's swaption, where the option holder has the right to pay fixed and receive floating on the underlying swap, is a call option on the floating asset. For convenience Equation 13.2 is repeated here as the pricing formula for a payer's swaption:

$$C = r_v^{-t_v}(S'N(x) - KN(x - \sigma\sqrt{t_v}))$$

where

C is the price of a European payer's swaption

$$x = \frac{\log(S'/K)}{\sigma\sqrt{t_v}} + \frac{1}{2}\sigma\sqrt{t_v}$$

S' = forward price of asset as defined above at time t_v
K = strike price as defined above
t_v = time to expiry in years
r_v = $1 + (Z_v/100)$
Z_v = zero coupon rate to time t_v based on interbank yields
σ = volatility of S' as a fraction

Given this pricing formula, the sensitivities of the swaption price give essentially the same formulae as the sensitivities for a one period cap, with both t_m and t_v replaced by t_v. Z_v is now the zero coupon rate to the value date of the underlying swap, and Z_m is the zero rate to the maturity date of the swap.

Delta $\quad \dfrac{\partial C}{\partial S'} = r_v^{-t_v} N(x)$ $\hspace{4cm}$ always > 0

$\qquad\quad \dfrac{\partial C}{\partial K} = - r_v^{-t_v} N(x - \sigma\sqrt{t_v})$ $\hspace{2.5cm}$ always < 0

-Theta $\quad \dfrac{\partial C}{\partial t} = \dfrac{r_v^{-t_v} \sigma S' N'(x)}{2\sqrt{t_v}} - C\log(r_v)$ $\hspace{1.5cm}$ $> = $ or < 0

Vega $\quad \dfrac{\partial C}{\partial \sigma} = r_v^{-t_v} S' N'(x) \sqrt{t_v}$ $\hspace{3cm}$ always > 0

$\qquad\quad \dfrac{\partial C}{\partial r_v} = - \dfrac{t_v}{r_v} C$ $\hspace{4.5cm}$ always < 0

Future valued theta

$$- \dfrac{\partial (C r_v^{t_v})}{\partial t} = - \dfrac{S' N'(x) \sigma}{2\sqrt{t_v}} \hspace{3cm} \text{always} < 0$$

Where the underlying swap is bullet, the calculation of S' can be further simplified as follows. S' for the underlying FRA of a cap was valued as:

$$F\left(\dfrac{r_m^{t_m}}{r_v^{t_v}} - 1\right).$$

For a cap S' is valued as at t_m, but for a swaption S' is valued as at t_v. You can see that the FRA formula must hold for the value of S' at t_m for the underlying bullet swap of the swaption, since the value of the floating side payments is unchanged, regardless of the choice of floating side payment dates. Taking the extreme case in which there is only one floating payment at the swap maturity recovers the effective cashflows of an FRA, and so the value of S' at t_m must be given by the FRA formula.

Since we want to value S' for the swaption at t_v, we simply divide the FRA formula by the scaling factor to t_m and multiply it by the scaling factor to t_v to give:

$$S' = F\left(1 - \dfrac{r_v^{t_v}}{r_m^{t_m}}\right).$$

The only interest rates involved in this formula are Z_v and Z_m and so it seems that, as for caps and floors, the only interest rate sensitivities for a swaption are with respect to Z_v and Z_m. However, unlike the situation for caps, there is also a sensitivity of K to changes in zero coupon rates. (This is not the case for a cap because there K is both paid and valued at the FRA maturity date.) Since K is the sum of the values at t_v of cashflows at each fixed payment date of the swap, K will have a sensitivity to the zero coupon rate to each payment date. Let us call these payment dates t_1, t_2, ..., t_n, where t_n equals t_m; below, these dates will be referred to generically as t_i, with the zero coupon rate to each t_i being Z_i and the annualised scaling factor to each date being r_i.

Since there are now three determining variables of C which have interest rate sensitivity, the derivatives of C with respect to Z_v and Z_m become:

$$\frac{\partial C}{\partial Z_v} = \frac{\partial C}{\partial S'}\frac{\partial S'}{\partial Z_v} + \frac{\partial C}{\partial r_v}\frac{\partial r_v}{\partial Z_v} + \frac{\partial C}{\partial K}\frac{\partial K}{\partial Z_v}\Big|_{Z_i} \quad \text{and}$$

$$\frac{\partial C}{\partial Z_m} = \frac{\partial C}{\partial S'}\frac{\partial S'}{\partial Z_m} + \frac{\partial C}{\partial r_v}\frac{\partial r_v}{\partial Z_m} + \frac{\partial C}{\partial K}\frac{\partial K}{\partial Z_m}\Big|_{Z_v, Z_1, ..., Z_{n-1}}$$

Moreover, we now have:

$$\frac{\partial C}{\partial Z_i} = \frac{\partial C}{\partial K}\frac{\partial K}{\partial Z_i}\Big|_{Z_v, Z_1, ..., Z_{i-1}, Z_{i+1}, ..., Z_m}$$

Similarly, the derivatives of $N(x)$ become:

$$\frac{\partial N(x)}{\partial Z_v} = \frac{\partial N(x)}{\partial S'}\frac{\partial S'}{\partial Z_v} + \frac{\partial N(x)}{\partial K}\frac{\partial K}{\partial Z_v}\Big|_{Z_i}$$

$$\frac{\partial N(x)}{\partial Z_m} = \frac{\partial N(x)}{\partial S'}\frac{\partial S'}{\partial Z_m} + \frac{\partial N(x)}{\partial K}\frac{\partial K}{\partial Z_m}\Big|_{Z_v, Z_1, ..., Z_{n-1}} \quad \text{and}$$

$$\frac{\partial N(x)}{\partial Z_i} = \frac{\partial N(x)}{\partial K}\frac{\partial K}{\partial Z_i}\Big|_{Z_v, Z_1, ..., Z_{i-1}, Z_{i+1}, ..., Z_m}$$

If K_i is the fixed side cashflow at t_i, then:

$$K = r_v^{t_v}\sum_{i=1}^{n}\frac{K_i}{r_i^{t_i}} \quad \text{so that}$$

$$\frac{\partial K}{\partial Z_v} = \frac{t_v}{100 r_v}K \quad \text{and}$$

For $i = 1, 2, ..., n$ $\quad \dfrac{\partial K}{\partial Z_i} = -r_v^{t_v}\dfrac{t_i K_i}{100 r_i^{t_i+1}}$

This gives:

$$\frac{\partial S'}{\partial Z_v} = -\frac{t_v F r_v^{t_v-1}}{100 r_m^{t_m}}$$

$$\frac{\partial S'}{\partial Z_m} = \frac{t_m F r_v^{t_v}}{100 r_m^{t_m+1}}$$

$$\frac{\partial C}{\partial Z_v} = \frac{-N(x)t_v F}{100 r_m^{t_m} r_v} - \frac{t_v C}{100 r_v} - \frac{t_v K N(x - \sigma\sqrt{t})}{100 r_v^{t_v+1}}$$

$$\frac{\partial C}{\partial Z_m} = \frac{N(x)t_m F}{100 r_m^{t_m+1}} + \frac{t_m K_n N(x - \sigma\sqrt{t_v})}{100 r_m^{t_m+1}}$$

$$\frac{\partial C}{\partial Z_i} = \frac{t_i K_i N(x - \sigma\sqrt{t_v})}{100 r_i^{t_i+1}}$$

$$\frac{\partial N(x)}{\partial Z_v} = -\frac{N'(x)F\sqrt{t_v}\,r_v^{t_v-1}}{100 S' \sigma r_m^{t_m}} - \frac{N'(x)\sqrt{t_v}}{100 \sigma r_v}$$

$$\frac{\partial N(x)}{\partial Z_m} = \frac{t_m N'(x)F r_v^{t_v}}{100 S' \sigma \sqrt{t_v} r_m^{t_m+1}} + \frac{t_m N'(x)K_n r_v^{t_v}}{100 K \sigma \sqrt{t_v} r_m^{t_m+1}}$$

$$\frac{\partial N(x)}{\partial Z_i} = \frac{t_i N'(x)K_i r_v^{t_v}}{100 K \sigma \sqrt{t_v} r_i^{t_i+1}}$$

Using the partial derivatives derived above, the following result can be proved to be true for a swaption on a bullet swap:

Result 14.3 A portfolio consisting of $N(x)$ of the underlying swap and C of a zero coupon bond to the option expiry date has *approximately* the same instantaneous sensitivity to interest rate movements as a payer's swaption.

Again the proof would consist of showing that the sensitivities of the portfolio to changes in Z_v and Z_i equal the sensitivities of the swaption price. The result is an approximation since there are some terms in $N(x)$ and some in $N(x - \sigma\sqrt{t_v})$; the former terms come from the derivatives of S', and the latter come from the derivatives of K. This differs from the corresponding result for a cap, which did not rely on an approximation, since for a cap K has no sensitivity to the interest rates. Because of the approximation involved in Result 14.3, accurate management of the interest rate risk of a swaption portfolio requires sophisticated reporting; there is no short cut as there was for caps and floors.

If the underlying swap is not bullet, then there is no simple formula for S', and the present value of S' will have sensitivity to the zero coupon rate to every date when the swap amortises or accretes. Breaking down the swap into its component swapsicles allows S' to be expressed as the sum of S' for a series of bullet swaps; this allows a tractable analytic solution for the sensitivities. Alternatively, S' can be expressed as the sum of the value of the floating interest in each floating period of the underlying swap; this again gives a method for computing the sensitivities through an analytic formula. Where the underlying swap is not bullet then Result 14.3 will still hold in general, but the approximation involved is likely to be greater.

A European receiver's swaption can be priced through put-call parity in the same way as a floor, to give a value $P = C - r_v^{-t_v}(S' - K)$. Using this relation together with Identity 14.2 that $1 - N(x)$ equals $N(-x)$ allows the calculation of the sensitivities for a European receiver's swaption on a bullet swap as:

Delta $\quad \dfrac{\partial P}{\partial S'} = -r_v^{-t_v}N(-x)$ $\hfill$ always < 0

$\dfrac{\partial P}{\partial K} = r_v^{-t_v}N(-x + \sigma\sqrt{t_v})$ $\hfill$ always > 0

-Theta $\quad \dfrac{\partial P}{\partial t} = \dfrac{r_v^{-t_v}\sigma S'N'(x)}{2\sqrt{t_v}} + \log(r_v)r_v^{-t_v}(S'N(-x) - KN(-x + \sigma\sqrt{t_v}))$
$\hfill >$ =or < 0

Vega $\quad \dfrac{\partial P}{\partial \sigma} = r_v^{-t_v}S'N'(x)\sqrt{t_v}$ $\hfill$ always > 0

$\dfrac{\partial P}{\partial r_v} = t_v r_v^{-t_v-1}(S'N(-x) - KN(-x +\sigma\sqrt{t_v}))$ $\hfill > $ = or < 0

Future valued theta

$-\dfrac{\partial(Pr_v^{t_v})}{\partial t} = -\dfrac{S'N'(x)\sigma}{2\sqrt{t_v}}$ $\hfill$ always < 0

$\dfrac{\partial P}{\partial Z_m} = -\dfrac{N(-x)t_m F}{100r_m^{t_m+1}} - \dfrac{t_m K_n N(-x + \sigma\sqrt{t_v})}{100r_m^{t_m+1}}$ $\hfill$ always < 0

$\dfrac{\partial P}{\partial Z_v} = \dfrac{N(-x)t_v F}{100r_m^{t_m}r_v} + \dfrac{t_v S'N(-x)}{100r_v^{t_v+1}}$ $\hfill$ always > 0

$\dfrac{\partial P}{\partial Z_i} = -\dfrac{t_i K_i N(-x + \sigma\sqrt{t_v})}{100r_i^{t_i+1}}$ $\hfill$ always < 0

As before, the following result could be proved:

Result 14.4 A portfolio consisting of receiving fixed on $N(-x)$ of the underlying swap and P of a zero coupon bond to the option expiry date has approximately the same instantaneous sensitivity to interest movements as a receiver's swaption.

The sensitivity of a portfolio of swaptions is the sum of the sensitivities of the individual swaptions bought minus the sum of the sensitivities of the individual swaptions sold. For a portfolio of caps and floors and swaptions the total sensitivity is the sum of the sensitivities for the individual instruments.

This section ends with another worked example; since the ground has already been covered for caps and floors, only a few of the sensitivities are calculated for the sample swaptions.

The swaptions to be considered have underlying swap with value date 0.25 years and maturity 1.25 years; both fixed and floating payments are semiannual.

$$
\begin{aligned}
t_v &= 0.25 \text{ years} \\
t_m &= 1.25 \text{ years} \\
Z_v &= 10\% \\
Z_{0.75} &= 10.1\% \\
Z_m &= 10.2\% \\
F &= \pounds 10,000,000 \\
\sigma &= 0.16 \\
K\% &= 10\%
\end{aligned}
$$

The value of the payer's swaption C is $\pounds 28,866.06$, while the value of the receiver's swaption P is $\pounds 29,072.22$.

Representative sensitivities are:

Theta - $\dfrac{\partial C}{\partial t} = -55,156$ — If t_v and t_m reduce in step by 0.01 year with S' and K constant, C should decrease by $\pounds 551.56$. In fact C reduces by $\pounds 558.02$ to $\pounds 28,308.04$.

Theta - $\dfrac{\partial P}{\partial t} = -55,135$ — If t_v and t_m reduce in step by 0.01 year with S' and K constant, P should decrease by $\pounds 551.35$. In fact P reduces by $\pounds 557.82$ to $\pounds 28,514.40$.

Vega $\dfrac{\partial C}{\partial \sigma} = 180,959$ — If σ increases by 0.001 to 0.161, then C (and P) should increase by $\pounds 180.96$. In this case agreement is exact, with C increasing by $\pounds 180.96$ to $\pounds 29,047.02$ and P increasing by $\pounds 180.96$ to $\pounds 29,253.18$.

$\dfrac{\partial C}{\partial Z_v} = -11,425$ — If Z_v increases by 0.01 to 10.01%, then C should decrease by $\pounds 114.25$. In fact, C decreases by $\pounds 114.11$ to $\pounds 28,751.95$.

$\dfrac{\partial C}{\partial Z_{0.75}} = 1,530$ — If $Z_{0.75}$ decreases by 0.01 to 10.09%, then C should decrease by $\pounds 15.30$. In this case agreement is again exact, with C decreasing by $\pounds 15.30$ to $\pounds 28,850.76$.

$\dfrac{\partial C}{\partial Z_m} = 54,146$ — If Z_m increases by 0.01 to 10.21%, then C should increase by $\pounds 541.46$. In fact, C increases by $\pounds 544.45$ to $\pounds 29,410.51$.

$\dfrac{\partial P}{\partial Z_v} = 10,767$ — If Z_v increases by 0.01 to 10.01%, then P should increase by $\pounds 107.67$. In fact, P increases by $\pounds 107.80$ to $\pounds 29,180.02$.

$\dfrac{\partial P}{\partial Z_{0.75}} = -1,639$ — If $Z_{0.75}$ increases by 0.01 to 10.11%, then P should decrease by $\pounds 16.39$. In fact P decreases by $\pounds 16.38$ to $\pounds 29,055.84$.

$\dfrac{\partial P}{\partial Z_m} = -51,339$ — If Z_m decreases by 0.01 to 10.19%, then P should increase by $\pounds 513.39$. In fact, P increases by $\pounds 516.49$ to $\pounds 29,588.71$.

$$\frac{\partial N(x)}{\partial Z_v} = -0.1218204$$

If Z_v increases by 0.01 to 10.01%, then $N(x)$ should decrease by 0.0012182. In fact $N(x)$ decreases by 0.0012183, from 0.5148220 to 0.5136037. This corresponds to a change in the hedge notional principal of £12,183.

$$\frac{\partial N(x)}{\partial Z_{0.75}} = 0.0173910$$

If $Z_{0.75}$ increases by 0.01 to 10.11%, then $N(x)$ should increase by 0.0001739. In this case the agreement is exact, with $N(x)$ increasing by 0.0001739 to 0.5149959; this corresponds to a change in the hedge notional principal of £1,739.

$$\frac{\partial N(x)}{\partial Z_m} = 0.5790378$$

If Z_m increases by 0.01 to 10.21%, then $N(x)$ should increase by 0.0057904. In fact, $N(x)$ increases by 0.0057850 to 0.5206070, corresponding to a change in the delta hedge principal of £57,850.

The other sensitivities of the swaption values could be calculated and analysed similarly.

14.4 QUANTIFYING EXPECTED CHANGES IN VOLATILITY

The methodology developed above expresses the sensitivity of the value of an option portfolio to changes in its price-determining variables. The actual change in portfolio value over a period will be the sensitivity times the change in the determining variables, and therefore, in order to quantify the risk, it is necessary to estimate the likely magnitude of changes in the values of the variables.

Of the variables, only interest rates and volatility are market-determined rates; the magnitude of future interest rate movements was discussed in Part I, and so this section concentrates on quantifying the likely movements in volatility.

The passage of time will also affect the value of the portfolio, but this is easy to quantify since we know that time passes at a fixed rate; the sensitivity of portfolio value to the passage of time is discussed in the next section. The other variable K is fixed after an option position is taken; the sensitivity of the option price to K is relevant when pricing options but it does not affect the subsequent risk.

In order to quantify likely future movements in a market rate, it is necessary to begin with the reasonable assumption that the future will be not too unlike the past. It is then possible to examine a time series for the rate in question and to work out the average and standard deviation of the daily or weekly changes over a period. If the distribution of daily changes appears to be stable over, say, the previous year, then it is then not unreasonable to predict that the average daily change over the next year will be the same as it was over the previous year.

There are problems with this approach for both interest rates and volatilities. For interest rates the problem was, if anything, an overabundance of data, since the yield curve up to 10 years could contain 15 or more points representing separately traded instruments. The treatment recommended in Part I for predicting the magnitude of interest rate movements therefore involved using a simple model to represent the yield curve using two or three variables.

For volatility the problem is the opposite, the difficulty of obtaining historic data. Except for short-dated traded options, the interest rate option market is highly illiquid, especially for swaptions, and therefore it is hard to establish a time sequence representing true market volatilities. From the available data it seems that market volatilities do not conform to a normal or lognormal distribution but that they exhibit periodic jumps; it is difficult to quantify the likely size of such jumps with the same sort of confidence levels that are possible with lognormally distributed variables, and also with such a distribution there is no simple relationship between the expected movement over one day and the expected movement over a longer period.

Perhaps the solution is to use changes in historic volatility as a proxy for changes in implied volatility, as discussed in section 13.2; more analysis needs to be done to establish if this is a viable route. If there is no source for implied volatilities and historic volatilities are not the answer, then, in order to quantify the risk you are running against changes in volatility, you are left with making a subjective analysis of the likely changes in implied volatility in the future. Despite the guesswork involved it is important to make and document such an analysis, in order that dealers and management will understand the framework within which risk is being managed.

14.5 REPORTING, MANAGING, HEDGING, AND TAKING OPTION RISK

This section looks at the reporting and management of an option portfolio. It considers in turn the sensitivity of option values to interest rate and volatility changes, the sensitivity of hedge ratios to changing interest rates, and the sensitivity of value to the passage of time. A concluding paragraph discusses hedging and risk taking using options.

For first order interest rate risk the goal is to report options in the discrete cash gaps methodology developed in Part I. This is simple for caps and floors, since Results 14.1 and 14.2 demonstrated an equivalent portfolio of FRAs and zero coupon bonds which had the same instantaneous interest rate risk as the cap or floor; thus reporting the cash gaps of the equivalent portfolio will correctly report the interest rate risk of the cap or floor.

For swaptions there is no equivalent direct method, since the equivalent portfolio is not exact. However, using the formulae derived above, it is straightforward to calculate all the interest rate sensitivities of the swaption value C or P,

$$\frac{\partial}{\partial Z_v}, \frac{\partial}{\partial Z_i} \text{ for } i = 1, ..., n - 1, \text{ and } \frac{\partial}{\partial Z_m},$$

and to translate these into the corresponding cash gap in each maturity. This can be done most simply by observing that a cash gap of G_i at time t_i has a sensitivity to Z_i of

$$-\frac{t_i G_i}{100 r_i^{t_i + 1}}.$$

Thus, if the sensitivity of the option value to Z_i is S_i, then the equivalent cash gap is

$$-\frac{100 r_i^{t_i + 1} S_i}{t_i}.$$

This relation allows the generation of the equivalent cash gap at t_v and at each fixed payment date of the swaption.

For more complex instruments which are priced by numeric methods, the same procedure will allow the representation of interest rate sensitivities in equivalent cash gaps. The cash gaps thus reported can be used to calculate the required delta hedge for the portfolio.

The reporting of interest rate risk can thus be done in a consistent way for all options, and the interest rate risk added to the risk from non-option instruments.

If we could rely on the accuracy of the option pricing formulae then this would be sufficient. However, given the approximations involved in option pricing and hence in the sensitivities calculated for options, it seems advisable in addition to report separately on the interest rate risk of the option position, so that senior management can be aware of the possible risk being run.

In Part VII other methods of reporting interest rate risk will be derived; since these will use discrete cash gaps as a common starting point, the representation of interest rate risk on options as cash gaps described above will enable the inclusion of options in all of the other methodologies.

The reporting of volatility risk can most easily be done in terms of sensitivity of portfolio present value to, say, a +1% change in volatility to each maturity; this would mean for example, consolidating into a 3-6 month 'bucket' the total sensitivity to all options expiring within 3-6 months. The full time span of option maturities could be covered by, say, quarterly buckets for the first 2 years and annual buckets thereafter. This would give a report as illustrated below:

Exhibit 14.1 Representation of report of volatility risk.

Period	1Q93	2Q93	3Q93	4Q93	94	95	96	97	98	total
Sensitivity	-100	80	40	-75	100	120	50	20	-10	225

All sensitivities are currency unit 000 change in present value for +1% change in volatility to the midpoint of the period.

The implicit assumption in this reporting methodology is that there is a strong positive correlation between volatilities for different instruments to the same option expiry date. If this assumption does not provide enough accuracy for managing positions then the report should be broken out by tenor of underlying; for example, all the positions against 3-month Libor could be on one page while all the positions for swaptions with underlying tenor 5-7 years could be on another page. The report would still foot to the totals above.

Such a reporting methodology would identify the risk and direction of large volatility positions, and would thus enable the management of such positions. When it is required to close a volatility gap identified by this methodology, the contribution to volatility sensitivity of a proposed new option position should be added to the existing report to determine whether the new position will have the desired effect.

The reporting of the gamma risk of the sensitivity of the delta hedge ratios to changes in zero coupon rates can also be done using a gap methodology, where the gap in each maturity bucket in this case would be the change in the delta hedge for, say, a +0.1% change in the zero coupon rate to that maturity. For example, if the option portfolio had an equivalent cash gap in year 1994 of 1,200, and a change in zero coupon rate to each date in 1994 of +0.1% would change the cash gap to 1,275, then the gamma risk for 1994 maturity would be +75.

Note that gamma as defined here is calculated from all cash gaps equivalent to the option positions; it thus includes terms in

$$\frac{\partial N(x)}{\partial Z} \text{ as well as in } \frac{\partial C}{\partial Z} \text{ and } \frac{\partial P}{\partial Z}.$$

If the gamma is positive as in the example above, then hedging in the event of an increase in the zero coupon rate Z would involve creating an equal and opposite negative cashflow; here the cashflow to be created for a 0.1% movement in Z would be -75. If we assume that the scaling factor to 1994 is 1.25, then the required hedge would be equivalent to selling a zero coupon bond with principal today of 60. If we sell this bond at 60 and Z comes back down by 0.1%, then delta will decrease by 75 and we shall have to buy back the bond. However we shall be buying it back at a price higher than 60, since the scaling factor to the final payment of 75 will have decreased. We would lose similarly if Z went down and then up. It can thus be seen that positive gamma as defined here corresponds to being short volatility.

A large gamma gap would indicate that a delta would need to be repeatedly adjusted for relatively small rate movements. To close such a gap you should add the gamma of a proposed position to the existing gaps to see if it will have the effect of reducing the unacceptable gap.

A gap of the same nominal amount is more important for a longer than for a shorter maturity, since, as noted above, the sensitivity of the present value of a cash gap of G at time t to a change in the zero coupon rate Z is $-\dfrac{tG}{100r^{t+1}}$, where r is the annualised scaling factor. It is possible to correct for this by reporting each gap as the equivalent gap at 1 year which has the same sensitivity to a parallel shift in the zero curve; this is known as the *1-year equivalent* gap, and it is given by $\dfrac{s_1^2 tG}{r^{t+1}}$, where s_1 is the scaling factor for 1 year. For accuracy of calculation, the 1-year equivalent should be calculated separately for each component of the gap within the maturity bucket.

Gaps reported in this way should provide more useful information to the dealer, since they will let him compare like with like. This would give a report as illustrated below:

Exhibit 14.2 Representation of report of gamma.

Period	1Q93	2Q93	3Q93	4Q93	94	95	96	97	98	total
Sensitivity	100	-70	60	-20	20	30	100	-20	40	240

All sensitivities are currency unit 000 one year equivalent gaps for a change of +0.1% in the zero coupon rate to the midpoint of the period.

The alternative is to report 'raw' gamma without conversion to 1-year equivalents; the total gap should then not be included as it becomes a misleading figure.

Assuming that the option portfolio is delta hedged, gamma also shows the earnings impact of changes in the zero coupon curve.

The last reporting to be considered is theta. This tells the dealer two things. First, in the absence of any rate changes, theta will be the daily change in the value of his portfolio and thus will be his profit or loss. Secondly, theta measures the runoff of the time value of the options in the portfolio, and thus if the dealer thinks that rates are entering a period of little change he will be pleased to have high positive theta so that he can take a high daily time value into profit. Conversely, if he thinks that in the short term rates will be volatile, he may wish to have negative theta to take advantage of movements in his own favour.

The simplest way to report theta is to give a single figure for the whole portfolio; typically this would be the one day change in portfolio value. Since a dealer may have different perceptions about rate movements in different maturities, it is worthwhile to report theta by maturity bucket. This could involve, for example, reporting the total theta for all options maturing in each quarterly bucket to 2 years and each annual bucket thereafter.

Such a methodology would enable the dealer to take advantage of different expectations of volatilities in different maturities.

The reporting methodology suggested above is not necessarily the best that could be devised, nor is it exhaustive, but it should demonstrate the sort of reporting possible and necessary to manage interest rate option risk.

When a reporting methodology has been set up it is possible to impose position limits; typically these would be imposed in terms of maximum interest rate risk and maximum volatility risk in each currency. Other more detailed limits might be appropriate in particular situations. There will be further discussion of reporting and of dealing limits in Part VII.

With adequate reporting, hedging or position taking becomes straightforward. Determine what position you would like to have; if this is materially different to the position which you do have, then consider what instruments you might buy or sell to obtain the desired position. Add the sensitivities of each proposed transaction to your existing positions to determine the resultant position, and enter into the transaction which gets you closest to your desired position for the cheapest cost. As discussed in the previous section, you should use your expectations of average future rate movements to determine what size of position is material; this is important in eliminating the transaction cost of repeated small hedging transactions.

SUMMARY

This chapter has derived the sensitivities of cap, floor, and European swaption values to changes in the underlying variables; the sensitivities are the partial derivatives of the value with respect to each of the variables. Manipulating the derivatives of the value with respect to changes in the zero coupon rate to each maturity allows the calculation of a set of future cashflows with the same instantaneous interest rate risk as the option; this enables the representation of interest rate options within the cash gaps methodology. An alternative route to representing an option as cash gaps is to identify an equivalent portfolio of non-option instruments.

In addition to interest rate risk, option values are sensitive to changes in market volatility; managing an option portfolio thus requires the reporting of volatility risk. Gamma for interest rate options is the sensitivity of the hedge ratios to changes in the zero coupon rates; the higher the gamma the more likely it is that a delta hedge will have to be adjusted repeatedly. Management of an option portfolio therefore also requires reporting of gamma. Reporting theta gives useful information on profit runoff and on the effect of short-term volatility on portfolio value.

PART V

Self-study questions

Unless otherwise stated, all interest is quoted on an annual basis, and each month should be considered to be an exact twelfth of a year. Values of the normal distribution function needed in the questions are given in the table below.

x	$N(x)$ to 4-figure accuracy
0.001	0.5004
0.002	0.5008
0.005	0.5020
0.006	0.5024
0.058	0.5231
0.059	0.5235
0.063	0.5251
0.064	0.5255
0.071	0.5283
0.072	0.5287
0.104	0.5414
0.105	0.5418
0.154	0.5612
0.155	0.5616
0.220	0.5871
0.221	0.5875
0.527	0.7009
0.528	0.7013
0.717	0.7633
0.718	0.7636

Values of $N(x)$ for intermediate values of x can be estimated using linear interpolation, that is:

$$N(x_3) = \frac{(N(x_2) * (x_3 - x_1)) + (N(x_1) * (x_2 - x_3))}{x_2 - x_1}$$

where $x_1 < x_3 < x_2$.

5.1   You enter into a contract with your bank whereby you pay the bank US$1,000 today, and in 6 months you have the right, but not the obligation, to buy 200 ounces of gold from the bank at US$370 per ounce. Describe this contract using the standard option terminology below.

Buyer:

Writer:

Premium:

Exercise period:

Option period:

Maturity date:

Underlying contract:

Is the option European or American? Is it a put or a call option? What is the strike price?

5.2   Suppose that US$1,000 is a fair midmarket price for the option in question 5.1. If dollar 6-month Libor is 7%, and gold is trading today at US$350 per ounce, what is the midmarket price for an option to sell 200 ounces of gold in 6 months' time at US$370 per ounce?

5.3   The price of gold today is US$365 per ounce, and 6-month dollar Libor is 7%. If your bank offers you an option at a premium of US$1,000 to buy 200 ounces of gold in 6 months at US$370 per ounce, how can you make money without risk? Make clear what assumptions you use.

5.4   If the price of a call option is greater than the price of the asset, how can you make money without risk? What basic assumption are you making?

5.5   Assuming zero transaction costs and zero credit risk, which of the following combinations of European call option prices allow riskfree arbitrage?

Strike price	10	12	14
(A)	6	5	
(B)	6	7	
(C)	6	3	
(D)	8	7	
(E)		7	5.5
(F)	8	7	5.5
(G)	8	7	6.5

For each combination allowing riskfree arbitrage, which options should you buy and sell to lock in a profit?

5.6   A 3-month European call option on a share costs £50, and a 6-month option at the same strike price costs £40. How can you lock in a profit? What key assumptions do you have to make in doing this?

5.7   A racehorse is worth £4 million today. If it wins the Derby next year it will be worth £10 million; otherwise it will be worth only £2 million. If £1 invested in Treasury bills today would be worth £1.12 on Derby Day, what is a fair value today for a call option to buy the horse at £5 million immediately after the race?

Assuming that you can buy a share in the horse today and that you can assume a short position in Treasury bills, show how you can construct a portfolio which will have the same price as the option regardless of who wins the Derby.

What is the delta of the option today?

5.8   A share is priced today at £100. Each quarter the price will either go up by 10% or down by 10%; there will be no dividend over the next year. The annual riskfree interest rate is 12.551%. What is the cost of a European call option with a strike price of £100 and an option period of 1 year?

What is the value of the option at the end of the year if the share enjoys four up movements? What will the value be if it has three up movements followed by a down movement? What will the value be in 9 months if there have been three up movements to that date?

5.9   A share price is £100 today and has a volatility of 19%; there will be no dividends over the next year. The riskfree annual interest rate is 12.55%. What is the cost of a European call option with a strike price of £100 and an option period of 1 year?

5.10 Which of the following debt instruments contain embedded interest rate options? Which contain other sorts of options?

(A) A floating rate note paying Libor plus 1% quarterly.

(B) A floating rate note paying Libor plus 1% quarterly where the issuer has the right to call the note at par on any payment date.

(C) A floating rate note paying Libor plus 1% quarterly where the issuer has the right to call the note at par plus accrued interest on any date. Accrued interest is calculated as:

$$\frac{\text{original interest rate times days in period to repayment}}{100 \text{ times day basis}}$$

(D) A bond paying 10% fixed annually.

(E) A bond paying 10% fixed annually which the issuer must offer to repurchase at par on any payment date when it fails to meet certain covenant conditions.

(F) A bond paying 10% fixed annually which the issuer can redeem at 101% of face value on any payment date.

(G) A domestic mortgage at 13% fixed for 6 years which the borrower can repay at any time for a payment of 105% of the principal outstanding.

(H) A loan at a fixed rate of 8% which the borrower can extend if required for an extra year at the same rate.

(I) A floating rate note paying the higher of quarterly Libor and 6%

5.11 You pay £90,000 to enter into a contract with a bank whereby every 6 months for 5 years, starting in 6 months' time, if sterling 6-month Libor is greater than 12% then the bank will pay you £50,000 ∗ (Libor - 12) 6 months later. Express this contract in the standard terminology of interest rate options.

To help pay for this contract, you enter into a second contract whereby the bank pays you £45,000 and you contract to pay, over the same dates, if 6-month Libor is less than 7%, £50,000 ∗ (7 - Libor). Express this second contract in the standard option terminology.

What is the combination of the two contracts called?

5.12 Draw a diagram of cashflow at the 1-year date against Libor at the 6-month date under the combined contracts of question 5.11; positive cashflow means that you receive payment.

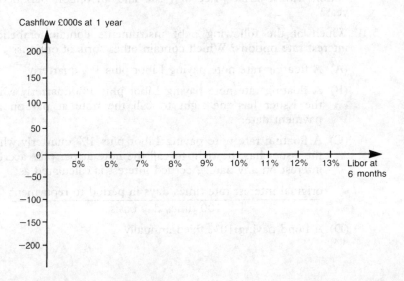

5.13 You buy a traded call option on the June Eurodollar deposit futures contract at the Chicago Mercantile Exchange; the strike rate is 94.00 and the price is 0.34. The value of an 01 on the future or option is US$25.

How much do you pay to the exchange?

If you hold the traded option to maturity when the futures price is 94.20, what is the final settlement? What would the final settlement be if the price were 93.50?

To what over-the-counter option transaction does your purchase approximate?

5.14 You sell a receiver's swaption; do you have a credit risk? Would you have a credit risk if the swaption was for cash settlement? In interest rate risk terms, which of the following most resembles selling a receiver's swaption:

selling a cap;
selling a floor;
buying a cap; or
buying a floor?

5.15 Assuming that all bid-offer spreads are zero and that the zero coupon curve is flat at 10%, what is the 6 v 12 FRA rate? If the price of a single period cap at 11% on 6-month Libor with value date 6 months is 0.05% of principal, what is the price of an equivalent 11% floor?

If the price of an 11% cap on 6-month Libor with value date 1 year is 0.13% of principal, what is the price of an equivalent 11% floor?

5.16 If a share costs £100 today and the sterling riskfree zero coupon yield curve is flat at 10.25%, what will be the price of a forward contract to buy the share in 6 months? Assume zero spreads, no dividends in the period, and the ability to borrow shares.

If the forward contract has a higher or lower price than you predict, demonstrate how you can make a riskfree profit.

5.17 A market maker is asked to quote a bid-offer price on a 1-period cap with the following parameters:

Value	12 months
Maturity	15 months
Principal	£200,000,000
Strike rate	11%

The zero coupon rate to 1 year is 10.97% based on a cost of funds of Libor, and the 12 v 15 FRA is quoted as 10.94%/11.01%. The market 12-month volatility on 3-month Libor is 11%/13%. On the above information, what prices should the market maker quote? Why might she quote different prices?

5.18 Using the same rates and volatilities as question 5.17, what should be the maximum bid-offer spread for an 11% floor?

5.19 What are the variables affecting the value of a single period cap? Which of these variables can change after the cap is agreed? Of the remaining variables, how many are independent?

The set of variables you have produced could be replaced by various other sets of the same number of independent variables. Can you select a set which would be most suitable for reporting and management?

5.20 A one-period cap has the following parameters:

Value   15 months
Maturity   18 months
Principal   £100,000,000
Strike rate   11%

The zero coupon rate to 15 months is 10.9%, and the zero coupon rate to 18 months is 10.95%. Cap volatility to 15 months is 14%.

What is the FRA rate implied by the zero coupon rates?

What is the value of the cap?

If the 15-month zero rate stays the same, while the 18-month zero rate increases by 0.02%, what is the new FRA rate? What is the new value of the cap? What is the change in value?

What is the partial derivative $\frac{\partial C}{\partial Z_m}\big|_{Z_v}$ at the original zero rate to maturity of 10.95%? What is the product of the partial derivative and the change of 0.02% in Z_m? How does this compare to the change in value of the cap calculated above?

5.21 You are given the following information about interest rates in the Ruritanian Rouble over the past 3 years.

The daily rates were analysed by taking each day a best straight line fit to fourteen points of the 0-10 year zero coupon yield curve; the resultant straight line predictor of the yield curve had an r^2 of 0.90 over the period.

The straight line each day was specified by two variables: the level, defined as the overnight rate, and the slope, defined as the 10 year rate minus the overnight rate. The standard deviation of the daily change in level was 0.07%, and the standard deviation of the daily change in slope was 0.03%.

The volatility used in pricing single period caps on 3-month Libor with value date 3 years was recorded weekly. The standard deviation of weekly changes in this volatility was 0.25%.

The distributions of daily changes in level and slope and weekly changes in volatility were all reasonably close to a normal distribution.

The economy of Ruritania has not changed structurally over the past 3 years, nor is much change expected while the current Grand Duke (a healthy 60 year old) remains the head of state.

You are responsible for running an interest rate option portfolio in Ruritanian Roubles. If the sensitivity of your portfolio present value is RUR1,000 for every 1bppa change in the level of the yield curve, about how large a change in the value of your portfolio would you expect to see overnight?

How large a change would you expect to see over 1 year of 256 trading days?

If the sensitivity of your portfolio value to changes in slope is RUR5,000 for every basis point change in slope, how large a consequent change in value would you expect to see overnight and over 1 year?

If the Vega of your portfolio is RUR200,000 for every 1% change in volatility, assuming that the 3 v 3.25 year cap volatility is representative, what is the expected weekly change in portfolio value due to volatility changes, and what is the expected annual change assuming a year of 49 weeks?

A movement in a normally distributed variable greater than two standard deviations in a particular direction ('one tailed') would be expected only about 2.3% of the time. What loss on the portfolio due to changes in volatility would you expect not to be exceeded on a weekly basis more than 2.3% of the time?

The risk of the portfolio has been described in three numbers, the sensitivities to shifts in yield curve level, yield curve slope, and volatility. What are the limitations of this method of reporting risk?

5.22 Today's date is 22 March, so that the June Eurodollar deposit future has the underlying period of a 3 v 6 FRA, the September future has the underlying period of a 6 v 9 FRA, and the

December future has the underlying period of a 9 v 12 FRA; the FRA rates are in the range 6.12% - 6.52%. As usual, the future price is quoted as 100 minus the implied interest rate with an 01 worth US$25. Deltas are quoted as a percentage. Vega is quoted as US$ per percent change in volatility.

Assume that the bid-offer spread on futures and on options is one 01 and that margining costs are small.

The December put option at a strike of 93.50 is priced at 0.29, corresponding to a volatility of 16%; the delta is 53%. If you are convinced that the volatility is too high, what position in futures and options can you take in order to benefit if volatility decreases? If vega is US$44 per %, what profit would you expect to make if volatility decreased to 14%? What happens if volatility stays static or increases? What other concerns will you have in managing this position?

Restate your futures and options position in terms of FRAs and caps or floors.

PART VI

CROSS CURRENCY INTEREST RATE RISK MANAGEMENT

Up to now there has been an explicit or implicit assumption that interest rate risk is being considered for one currency at a time; in practice, however, organisations have to cope with interest rate risk across many currencies simultaneously. This adds two dimensions to the risk management process. First, the interest rates in different currencies are locked together by the possibility of arbitrage through the *forward foreign exchange* market; this gives opportunities for managing interest rate positions through forward foreign exchange, and it makes the capital markets in one currency accessible to a borrower or lender in another currency. Secondly, because of the possibility of offsetting rate movements in different currencies, the risk of a multicurrency portfolio of transactions may be less than the sum of the risks of the transactions in each currency.

Coverage of these matters will take three chapters. Chapter 15 demonstrates the *interest rate parity* relationship between interest rates and foreign exchange rates, and shows how to use this relationship to hedge interest rate risk through the forward foreign exchange market. Chapter 16 looks at *cross currency interest rate swaps*, and Chapter 17 looks at *medium term foreign exchange* transactions, which turn out to involve primarily interest rate risk. This last chapter also considers the marking to market and risk management of cross currency positions.

Although much of the discussion revolves around the use of foreign exchange transactions, the management of foreign exchange risk, that is, the risk that the present value of a firm or portfolio will change if *spot foreign exchange rates* change, is not addressed, since this is a large subject deserving a book to itself. Consequently, care has to be taken to ensure that all the instruments created through foreign exchange transactions do not themselves involve foreign exchange risk. It is not immediately obvious that this can be done, but please keep an open mind until you have read the chapters that follow.

CHAPTER 15

Foreign exchange swaps

This chapter briefly reviews the *foreign exchange* market and demonstrates the *interest rate parity* relationship; this leads to a description of *foreign exchange swaps*. Applications for foreign exchange swaps are then discussed, including synthetic FRAs and synthetic interest rate swaps.

15.1 FOREIGN EXCHANGE MARKET

A foreign exchange deal is a contract between two counterparties, each of which agrees to deliver to the other on a particular day a specified amount in a different currency. For example, counterparty A could contract to deliver FRF57,890,000 in two days' time to counterparty B, while in return B contracted to deliver on the same date US$10,000,000. The ratio of the two currency amounts, 5.789 in this example, is the *exchange rate* applicable to the deal. While occasional foreign exchange deals are agreed for *split delivery*, where the two counterparties deliver their currency amounts on different days, the vast majority of deals transacted have delivery of both amounts on the same day, and it is assumed below that all deals do have exchange on the same day. In the example above, counterparty A can be said to be 'selling French francs and buying dollars', while counterparty B can be said to be 'selling dollars and buying francs'; each foreign exchange deal is thus simultaneously a sale and a purchase for each counterparty.

Most foreign exchange deals have a bank as at least one counterparty; banks make markets in foreign exchange to earn spread and trading income, to manage their own risk, and to provide a service to their customers. Banks can achieve such a stranglehold on the foreign exchange market because they perform the useful economic function of providing liquidity with minimum credit risk.

The foreign exchange market is vast; the Bank for International Settlement recorded in 1989 that the daily volume of foreign exchange deals transacted by banks worldwide was about US$640,000,000,000, which was over US$100 for every person on the planet. Given the large volume it is not surprising that the market is liquid, with typical interbank bid-offer spreads on *spot* deals between major currencies of three parts in ten thousand, representing US$300 on a principal of US$1 million. Such small spreads apply to normal size interbank deals; these would typically be for an amount equivalent to between US$5 million and US$20 million. For smaller or larger deals wider spreads would be quoted.

The description of market practice which follows applies to major currencies, which in this context can be taken to include any currency in which there is a reasonably liquid money market.

The market convention is that deals for immediate delivery are settled on the *spot date*, which is two business days from the transaction date; there is a standard method for adjusting the spot date to cope with holidays. The rate which is commonly quoted as 'the foreign exchange rate' is the *spot rate* for spot delivery. It is possible to deal for delivery on the deal day or the next day instead, but, as you will see, this will involve an adjustment to the spot rate.

Any deal for settlement after the spot date is known as a *forward deal*. Typically, two counterparties will agree to exchange currency amounts a fixed number of months forward; the months are counted from the spot date, with an adjustment if the forward date is a weekend or holiday. Exchange can also be agreed on an intermediate date. The market exchange rate for delivery on a particular forward date is known as the *forward exchange rate*. The forward market is very liquid out to 6 months, less liquid out to a year, and relatively illiquid beyond a year; this impacts the arbitrage which is possible between foreign exchange rates and interest rates.

A large percentage of foreign exchange deals involve the US dollar as one of the currencies; moreover many *cross deals* which do not involve the dollar are actually managed by the bank dealer selling the first currency against the dollar in one transaction and buying the second against the dollar in another. However, there is a growing number of banks running *cross books* in which the dealer will manage a position of, say, yen against Deutschemark, without exchanging either currency into the dollar.

A foreign exchange rate can be quoted between any pair of currencies, but the most usual quote is of a currency against the US dollar. There are two ways of quoting the rate against the dollar:

In the most common, *direct* method

US$1 = $x *$ currency unit

where x will be used consistently here and below as the exchange rate.

For example, if the Deutschmark/dollar exchange rate is quoted as 1.7305, then this means that US$1 will be exchanged for DEM1.7305.

In the less common, *inverted* method

currency unit = US$*x*.

For example, if the European Currency Unit/dollar exchange rate is quoted as 1.2120, this means that XEU1 will be exchanged for US$1.2120.

The only major currencies which are normally quoted against the dollar by the inverted method are sterling, European Currency Unit, Irish punt, Australian dollar, and New Zealand dollar.

A bank quoting a two-way price will use a shorthand description such as 1.7305/10. If this is a direct quote, such as for the Deutschmark against the dollar, then it would mean that the bank would buy US$1 and sell DEM1.7305, or would sell US$1 and buy DEM1.7310. If it is an inverted quote, such as for sterling against the dollar, then the bank would buy £1 for US$1.7305 or sell £1 for US$1.7310. In either case the bank is buying one currency and selling another, but in the first quote the left-hand side is a bid rate to buy the dollar and simultaneously an offer rate to buy the Deutschmark, and in the second it is an offer rate to sell the dollar and a bid rate to buy sterling. You can appreciate from this that it is best to avoid the terminology 'bid' and 'offer' in foreign exchange unless you are being very specific as to which currency you regard as being bid or offered. It is possible to avoid confusion by remembering the basic principle that a dealer will buy cheap and sell dear; working this through will show which side of the quote is which.

There will be a normal convention for quoting the exchange rate between any frequently traded pair of currencies; this will specify whether the quote is direct or inverted and will give the number of decimal places to be included. For example, the XEU against the US$ is quoted using the inverted method with four decimal places, so that a rate of 1.3105 means that XEU1 is exchanged for US$1.3105, while sterling/yen is quoted using the direct method with respect to sterling, with two decimal places, so that a rate of 210.72 means that £1 is exchanged for JPY210.72.

The smallest normally-quoted movement in a foreign exchange rate is referred to as a *pip*, or as a foreign exchange point or *FX point*. In the examples above, an FX point for US$ against XEU would be US$0.0001, and for sterling against yen an FX point would be JPY0.01. You need to understand the definition of FX points when you look at the quotation of forward exchange rates below.

Spot foreign exchange rates change rapidly in response to economic or political news or to changes in the balance of supply and demand for a particular currency. Typically, the rate between a pair of currencies will change every couple of minutes during the trading day; however, since most movements will be only a few FX points and there will be a large number of mutually offsetting ups and downs, the net daily change will be relatively small. Forward rates will also move up and down during the day, but, for reasons to be explained in the next section, the *difference* between the spot and a particular forward rate will generally be relatively stable. The convention in the market, therefore, is to quote forward foreign exchange rates in terms of the differential with the corresponding spot rate; the differential measured in FX points is known as the *forward points* and will be far less volatile than the spot rate.

For example, if the spot dollar-sterling exchange rate is 1.7010 and the three month forward rate is 1.6930, then the forward points are minus 80. The dollar being worth relatively more in 3 months' time than today is referred to as the dollar being at a premium forward and sterling being at a discount; because there will always be one currency at a premium while the other is at a discount this terminology can become confusing, and so it will not be used further here.

Foreign exchange dealers are addicted to shorthand ways of expressing rates. A spot rate of 1.7210/1.7220 will be universally expressed as 1.7210/20, and between dealers it would be customary to ignore the 'big figure' and to quote this rate as simply 10/20. The quotation of forward points is similarly laconic. If the 3-month forward rate were 1.7280/95, then the forward points would be quoted as 70/75. If instead the forward rates were 1.7130/1.7145, then the forward points would be -80/-75; however, they would be universally quoted as 80/75. There would seem to be an ambiguity of sign, but this can be resolved by the principle that the forward market will never be more liquid than the spot market. If the forward points were +80/+75 then the forward rate bid-offer spread would be 5 points, as against a spread of 10 on the spot rate; consequently, it can be deduced that the sign must be minus. If the forward points were, say, -100/-80 then this would again be quoted as 100/80. This time the ambiguity can be resolved by the principle, already noted, that a dealer will buy cheap and sell dear; if the points are added rather than subtracted, then the forward rate will be 1.7310/1.7300, which would quickly put the dealer out of business. Consequently it can again be deduced that the forward points must be subtracted.

Where the quotation of the forward points as positive would be genuinely ambiguous, then minus signs are used. For example, if the forward points were -80/-80 then they will be quoted with the signs included, since otherwise you could not deduce that the sign should be negative. Similarly, forward points of -1/+2 will always be quoted with the signs included.

It will be shown below how the basic instruments of spot and forward foreign exchange deals can be combined to produce instruments with suitable characteristics for managing interest rate risk.

15.2 INTEREST RATE PARITY

The previous section mentioned that the differential between a forward foreign exchange rate and the corresponding spot rate tended to be relatively stable. To demonstrate why this should be so involves showing the existence of a potential arbitrage between the spot and foreign exchange markets and the money markets; this will lead to the interest rate parity relationship, which forms the basis for the use of foreign exchange to manage interest rate risk.

Suppose we start off with no money at all. Let us borrow dollars for 3 months from spot. We shall sell the dollars we borrow for sterling at today's spot rate and deposit the sterling for 3 months; at the same time, we shall enter into a 3-month forward foreign exchange deal to sell the sterling proceeds of our deposit back to dollars. We shall use the dollar proceeds of the forward foreign exchange deal to repay our dollar loan.

The cashflows are:

	Sterling		Dollar	
Spot	Buy £	+	Sell US$	−
	Deposit £	−	Borrow US$	+
3 months	Sell £	−	Buy US$	+
	Repay deposit	+	Repay loan	−

Suppose that the rates are:

Spot	1.7000
US$ loan	6% (on 12-month basis)
£ deposit	12% (on 12-month basis)
Forward	1.6830

Then, if we borrow US$100, the cashflows will be:

	Sterling		Dollar	
Spot	Buy £	+58.82	Sell US$	−100.00
	Deposit £	−58.82	Borrow US$	+100.00
3 months	Sell £	−60.58	Buy US$	+101.96
	Repay deposit	+60.58	Repay loan	−101.50

and we shall be left with a zero sterling net cashflow and a positive US$ net cashflow at 3 months of US$0.46.

Clearly such a situation allows us to generate riskfree income by entering into the above transactions on a scale of millions rather than hundreds of dollars, and so this combination of foreign exchange and interest rates cannot persist for long.

The possibility of arbitrage thus constrains the possible combinations of foreign exchange and interest rates; to proceed further, it is necessary to examine the relationship in more detail.

If there are zero transaction costs, the arbitrage in the above example will vanish if the dollar loan rate increases so that the repayment on the loan becomes US$101.96; this will happen at a loan rate of 7.84%. Recreating the cashflows for the above transactions with this new dollar loan rate, and separating out the money market and foreign exchange cashflows gives:

| | Money market | | Foreign exchange | |
	Sterling	Dollar	Sterling	Dollar
Spot	−58.82	+100.00	+58.82	−100.00
Forward	+60.58	−101.96	−60.58	+101.96

Assuming for the moment that there are zero bid-offer spreads in foreign exchange, we could enter instead into equal and opposite foreign exchange deals to obtain cashflows:

	Sterling	Dollar
Spot	−58.82	+100.00
Forward	+60.58	−101.96

But these cashflows are identical to the cashflows from the money market transactions above. Thus the same cashflows can be constructed from either:

(a) spot and forward foreign exchange deals; or
(b) a sterling deposit and a dollar loan.

It is thus clear that if the foreign exchange rates get out of line with money market rates then an arbitrage will be possible; as usual, such an arbitrage would act to move rates back in line so that the possibility of arbitrage vanishes.

Let us now calculate a formula for this arbitrage relation. This will be done twice, once in a world of zero transaction costs and zero bid-offer spreads, and once in the real world. A general transaction will be used, where we borrow currency A and deposit currency B, and sell currency A spot and buy currency A forward, each time against currency B.

The following symbols will be used consistently below:

x spot foreign exchange rate, direct with respect to A
f forward exchange rate, also direct with respect to A
t years from spot to forward date
e_A spot exchange amount in currency A
e_B spot exchange amount in currency B
i_A deposit interest rate in currency A as percentage
i_B deposit interest rate in currency B as percentage
s_A scaling factor for currency A over period spot to forward date
s_B scaling factor for currency B over period spot to forward date

Then we have

$$e_B = xe_A$$
$$s_A = (1 + (i_A * t/100)) \text{ and}$$
$$s_B = (1 + (i_B * t/100)).$$

The spot foreign exchange has cashflows:

Currency A $-e_A$
Currency B $+e_B$

The deposit in currency B has cashflows

Spot $-e_B$
Forward $+s_B e_B$

The loan in currency A has cashflows

Spot $+e_A$
Forward $-s_A e_A$

The forward foreign exchange has cashflows

Currency A $+s_A e_A$
Currency B $-f s_A e_A$

The net spot cashflow in each currency is zero, as is the forward cashflow in currency A. The only cashflow which does not necessarily equal zero is the forward cashflow in currency B, $s_B e_B - f s_A e_A$, which equals $x s_B e_A - f s_A e_A$. If this is greater than zero then there is a riskfree arbitrage, so this expression must be less than or equal to zero. However, repeating the analysis for the equal and opposite set of transactions, where we borrow currency B and deposit currency A, gives residual cashflow $-(x s_B e_A - f s_A e_A)$, which again must be less than or equal to zero to avoid the possibility of arbitrage. This shows that the expression $x s_B e_A - f s_A e_A$ must equal zero, giving:

Result 15.1 If there are no spreads or transaction costs then f is $x * s_B/s_A$.

This is the basic interest rate parity relationship, showing how the forward foreign exchange rate is dependent on the spot rate and on interest rates.

Since x is the number of units of B for one unit of A for spot exchange while f is the number of units of B for one unit of A for forward exchange, the interest rate parity relationship shows that the currency with the higher interest rate will be worth relatively less forward than spot. The longer the time period and the greater the interest rate differential, the greater the effect will be.

The same analysis holds if the 'forward' date is in fact today or the next day instead of the spot date. The 'scaling factors' will then be less than one; for example, s_A will be $\dfrac{1}{1 + (i_A * t/100)}$, where t is the time in years from the exchange date to the spot date. In this case the currency with the higher interest rate will be worth relatively more than at spot, although the effect will be small since t will be small.

In the real world, the above ideal relationship will not hold exactly, because of the existence of bid-offer spreads and transaction costs. However, by following through the above calculation carefully, incorporating bid and offer rates as appropriate, it is possible to identify boundaries beyond which the forward rate cannot move without potentially allowing arbitrage.

Using the terms 'bid' and 'offer' with foreign exchange rates to identify the bid and offer rates for *currency A*, and then reworking the above example with currency A again being borrowed, gives residual forward cashflow in currency B of $x(\text{bid})s_B(\text{bid})e_A - f(\text{offer})s_A(\text{offer})e_A$, which must be less than or equal to zero. This gives:

Result 15.2 $f(\text{offer})$ is not less than $x(\text{bid}) * s_B(\text{bid})/s_A(\text{offer})$

A similar analysis of the equal and opposite transactions involving depositing currency A and borrowing currency B gives:

Result 15.3 $f(\text{bid})$ is not greater than $x(\text{offer}) * s_B(\text{offer})/s_A(\text{bid})$

Results 15.2 and 15.3 together constitute the interest rate parity relationship for the real world with its bid-offer spreads. The existence of transaction costs should widen these arbitrage limits, but, since transaction costs for interbank short-term foreign exchange and money market transactions are very small as a fraction of the principals involved, it can be assumed for most practical purposes that the arbitrage limits are as shown in these results.

The arbitrage limits can be illustrated with an example incorporating realistic bid-offer spreads. Suppose that the spot dollar/sterling exchange rate is 1.7110/20 and the 3-month interest rates on a 12-month basis are

    sterling 12.00%/12.125%   and
    dollar   6.00%/6.125%.

It is most convenient to take sterling as currency A, since the exchange rate is quoted directly with respect to sterling; this makes the spot bid 1.7110 and the spot offer 1.7120.

Then the 3-month forward exchange rate must satisfy the following:

offer not less than $1.7110 * (s_B(\text{bid})/s_A(\text{offer}))$
$= 1.7110 * (1.015/1.0303)$
$= 1.6856$; and

bid not greater than $1.7120 * (s_B(\text{offer})/s_A(\text{bid}))$
$= 1.7120 * (1.0153/1.03)$
$= 1.6876$.

Also, of course, the bid must be less than the offer.

If we assume that the forward rate will have a bid-offer spread of 15 points, then the constraints above allow a movement of the forward bid rate between 1.6841 and 1.6876, and a movement of the offer rate between 1.6856 and 1.6891. This represents a movement of the forward points between 269/264 and 234/229, and compares with a midmarket forward rate of 1.6866 implied by the zero spread version of interest rate parity acting on the midmarket spot and interest rates.

This section began by stating that interest rate parity constrained the differential between spot and forward rates to be relatively stable. This example shows that there will still be some room for a fluctuation in the forward points before arbitrage becomes possible. However, even before rates move to the possible extreme, it will become cheaper for dealers to close out particular positions through the money market and forward exchange market rather than through the spot exchange market; this will tend to push forward rates towards the theoretical midmarket.

Since interest rates tend to be less volatile than spot foreign exchange rates, and since for a particular forward rate the range allowable for the forward relative to the spot is small, the forward points will tend to be relatively slow changing.

15.3 FOREIGN EXCHANGE SWAPS

The last section showed that a spot and forward foreign exchange deal which reversed each other were together equivalent to an interest rate risk in each currency. Such a pair of offsetting foreign exchange deals is known as a *foreign exchange swap*. A swap may have its initial exchange spot and its reexchange forward, or it may have both legs forward to different dates. Swaps may be used in cash management or in risk management. For example, a UK bank which takes a deposit in French francs may enter into a foreign exchange swap to sell the francs spot for sterling and to buy back the franc principal plus interest at the maturity of the deposit; this allows the bank to meet its franc cashflows and avoid franc interest rate risk, while contributing sterling to its own funding position. Other applications for foreign exchange swaps will be introduced throughout the rest of Part VI.

In the examples above, the spot and forward exchanges had principals with equal present value. As has been shown, such a swap is a pure interest rate instrument, involving no foreign exchange risk. Swaps are also traded with the spot and forward principal in one currency being identical; such a swap will involve a foreign exchange risk on the difference in present values of the spot and forward exchanges, and this will impact its pricing. All the swaps discussed below will be of the first type, so that they will not involve foreign exchange risk.

The period of a swap may be described in a similar way to an FRA, so that, for example, a swap with initial exchange in 3 months and final exchange in 6 months will be described as a '3 v 6' or a '3 against 6' swap, and will be said to have value in 3 months and maturity in 6 months. However, it is not common to use the shorthand FRA description for a swap starting in an inexact number of months; for example, you are unlikely to hear a request for a swap as a '3 v 6 over the 22nd'.

Interest rates tend to be less volatile than spot foreign exchange rates. Also, a foreign exchange swap is equivalent to being long interest rates in one currency and short in another, and since there tends to be positive correlation between the movements in Libor for the same period in different currencies, the net interest rate risk of a swap is further reduced. Consequently, the risk of entering into a swap is far less than that of entering into an *outright* foreign exchange deal.

As for outright forward foreign exchange deals, the market in foreign exchange swaps is most active out to 6 months and is not very liquid beyond a year. Since the risk of a swap is lower than the risk of an outright forward deal, it is not surprising that market makers quote very fine rates on swaps. The rates are based on the forward points, as explained below.

Suppose that the spot dollar/Deutschmark rate is 1.7310/20 and the 6-month forward points are 150/155, so that the outright 6-month forward rate is 1.7460/75. Then a market maker will sell Deutschmarks spot at 1.7310, and will buy Deutschmarks forward outright at 1.7475; however, if she enters into a swap where she sells the Deutschmark spot and buys them back forward, which would be described as her *selling and buying the Deutschmark*, then she will sell at 1.7310 and buy at 1.7465. In other words, she will sell at the spot offer for Deutschmarks and will buy back at the spot offer plus the bid forward points, thus improving the forward price for a swap by the full spot bid-offer spread. The effective bid-offer spread on the swap is thus the spread on the forward points, which in this case is 5 points; here this is less than the bid-offer spread on the spot rate.

Conversely, if the market maker *buys and sells the Deutschmark*, that is, she buys the Deutschmark spot and sells it forward, then the rates will be 1.7320 spot and 1.7470 forward. Again the spot rate is the same as for an outright deal, while the forward rate is the 'wrong' side of the spot plus the correct forward points. As before, the effective bid-offer spread on the swap is 5 points.

The interest rate parity relationships demonstrated in the previous subsection will also act as a constraint on forward swap rates. Revisiting the example from the end of the previous section gives the result for the forward swap rates that:

the offer rate is not less than 1.6856; and
the bid rate is not greater than 1.6876.

Making the assumption that the bid-offer on the forward points is 5 FX points gives a tighter constraint for the forward swap rates than for the outright forwards. The swap bid must be in the range 1.6851 to 1.6876, and the offer must be in the range 1.6856 to 1.6881. The range allowable for the forward points is unchanged.

As we have seen, a foreign exchange swap has no foreign exchange risk, and it has the same interest rate risk as a placing in one currency and a taking in another. The credit risk of a swap is far less than the credit risk of a taking and placing, since throughout the life of the transaction the swap asset and liability can be netted, although there will be some credit risk if exchange rates change so as to make the asset worth more than the liability. On the initial and final days of a swap its credit risk becomes equivalent to that on a placing, since the counterparty may not deliver his currency amount to you even though you deliver your currency amount to him; however, this *delivery risk* is shortlived and thus is small compared to the principal risk throughout the life of a placing. (There is an equivalent delivery risk on any foreign exchange transaction.) Because of the reduced credit risk, the risk-based capital requirements for foreign exchange swaps will also be far less than for placings. Since the bid-offer spreads in swaps tend to be smaller in present value terms than the bid-offer spreads on placings and takings, swaps are generally the cheapest way of creating a short-term interest rate instrument with a short position in one currency and an equivalent long position in another.

One application for such an instrument was described at the start of this section, the use of a swap to turn a taking in francs into a sterling position; a similar technique can be used to reduce interest rate risk cheaply whenever a long position in one currency is offset by a short position in another. The rest of this chapter looks at using this capability to produce synthetic FRAs and synthetic interest rate swaps.

15.4 SYNTHETIC FRAs

A *synthetic financial instrument* is a set of transactions which collectively have the same cashflows, and hence the same market risk, as the desired instrument. Ideally, the net credit risk should also be similar. For example, it may be possible to create a desired interest rate position in a particular currency more cheaply by using a foreign exchange swap together with an interest rate instrument in a second currency. When the position so created is equivalent to an FRA, the set of transactions is referred to as a *synthetic FRA*.

In principle any currency can be used to create a synthetic FRA position in a second currency, but in practice it is usually only the US dollar which ever gives the required better rate; this is because of the very high liquidity in both the market for foreign exchange swaps between the US dollar and other currencies and the market for US dollar interest rate instruments. The US dollar is therefore used in the description of a synthetic FRA here, and will also be used in the description of synthetic interest rate swaps in the next section.

Suppose that the 3 v 6 FRA rate in dollars is 6.12%/6.17%, and the corresponding rate in Deutschmarks is 8.43%/8.50%. It will be assumed for simplicity that all rates are quoted on the basis of a 12-month year, so that each 3-month period is an exact quarter of a year; in practice the calculation would have to be adjusted for rates quoted on a 360-day basis and for the exact number of days in each period. Suppose further that the relevant foreign exchange rates and forward points are:

spot dollar/Deutschmark   1.7425/35
3-month forward points   95/97
6-month forward points   190/193.

Then if you wish to enter directly into a 3 v 6 Deutschmark FRA where you pay fixed, you would pay 8.50%, since you will have to pay at a market maker's offer rate. Consider instead the effect of entering into the following set of transactions:

- Pay fixed on a 3 v 6 dollar FRA with a contract amount of, say, US$1 million at a rate of 6.17;
- Enter into a 3 v 6 foreign exchange swap where you sell and buy the dollar; the principal on the 3-month leg will be US$1 million at a rate of 1.7520, and on the 6-month leg it will be US$1,015,425 at a rate of 1.7618.

First it is shown how the dollar principals on the swap are calculated, and then it is demonstrated that the risk of the combined transactions is *almost* the same as that of a Deutschmark FRA.

We are trying to create a synthetic pay-fixed Deutschmark FRA. An FRA has one payment, which is the net of a fixed and a floating interest amount paid discounted at the start of the calculation period; an economically identical instrument can be constructed by combining a fixed and a floating interest amount paid undiscounted and gross at the end of the period. Principal payment and receipts can then be added at the beginning and end of the period, again without changing the interest rate risk characteristics of the instrument. If we now group:

(a) the start principal payment with the floating interest rate receipt and with the end principal receipt; and
(b) the start principal receipt with the fixed interest payment and the end principal payment;

then we have successfully produced a floating placing and a fixed taking which combined have the risk characteristics of the FRA.

This follows the treatment of FRAs in Part II, where it was demonstrated that the 'grossed up' floating payments can be ignored in calculating risk; this was encapsulated in Result 6.2 that the risk of purchasing at par a future bond to be issued at the then prevailing Libor was zero.

This lets us ignore the floating side in analysing risk. Concentrating on the fixed side, since a foreign exchange swap is equivalent to a fixed taking in one currency and a fixed placing in a second currency, the Deutschmark fixed taking can be created through a 3 v 6 swap.

This will leave us with a 3 v 6 fixed placing in dollars, which we can neutralise by paying fixed on a dollar FRA to leave us with a position equivalent to a floating dollar placing; this floating placing will have no risk. Starting with a US$1 million FRA, it is clear that the 3-month swap principal must be US$1 million. The 6-month principal on the swap should be the same as the FRA contract amount plus interest; this equals US$1,015,425. The 3-month swap rate is the market maker's outright 3-months bid rate for dollars; this is the spot bid of 1.7425 plus the corresponding forward points of 95, which gives 1.7520, for a Deutschmark principal of DEM1,752,000. The 6-month swap rate is the 'wrong' side of the spot plus the correct side of the forward points, that is the spot bid of 1.7425 plus forward points of 193, to give a forward rate of 1.7618, for a Deutschmark principal of DEM1,788,976.

Since the fixed side of the dollar FRA matches the swap, we have neutralised the fixed dollar position of the FRA and left ourselves with a fixed Deutschmark position. The Deutschmark cashflows are equivalent to a taking with principal DEM1,752,000 and interest DEM36,976, which is equivalent to an interest rate of 8.44%. This compares favourably with paying fixed on the Deutschmark FRA at 8.50%.

The risk of the above set of transactions is equivalent to the combined risk of the fixed side of the Deutschmark FRA and the floating side of the dollar FRA. Since the risk of the floating side in each currency has been shown to be zero, we have thus succeeded in constructing a synthetic FRA through using a foreign exchange swap.

The assumption that Libor represents the cost of funding begs the question of bid-offer spreads; if in 3 months' time we attempt to close out the synthetic FRA with a dollar taking and a Deutschmark placing, then we may receive only Libid on the placing. If this is an issue, as it may be for a bank not making a market in Deutschmark money market instruments, then it will be possible to close out the synthetic FRA position by doing an equal and opposite 0 v 3 swap in 3 months; this will create a position equivalent to a dollar taking and a Deutschmark placing. There is a basis risk here, since the interest rates achieved through the 0 v 3 swap may be worse than Libor; this risk can be estimated by analysing historic values for the equivalent interest rates achievable through 0 v 3 dollar/Deutschmark swaps, and assuming a reasonable value for the cost of closing out a Libor-Libor position through such a swap.

The synthetic FRA which we have created has a rate 6 basis points better than the market FRA rate. If the historic interest equivalent rates of a 0 v 3 swap have consistently been closer than 6 basis points to Libor, then the synthetic FRA offers the better value, whereas if the historic rates have been more than 6 points from Libor then the market FRA seems cheaper.

Synthetic FRAs are a useful tool, especially for organisations active in the forward foreign exchange market as well as being involved in interest rate risk management, since the interest rate dealer may be able to obtain an advantageous rate from the in-house foreign exchange dealer for a swap which will involve no credit risk and reduced transaction costs. It is important to ensure that the management accounting satisfactorily reports positions and profitability on such internal swaps.

15.5 SYNTHETIC INTEREST RATE SWAPS

Just as a synthetic FRA can be created using an FRA in one currency together with a foreign exchange swap, a synthetic interest rate swap can be created using an interest rate swap in one currency and a series of foreign exchange swaps. Because of the complexity of calculating the necessary transactions and entering into them simultaneously, and because of the reduced liquidity in longer-dated foreign exchange swaps, it is less likely that a cheaper interest rate swap rate can be achieved through the synthetic deal. Moreover, where such a synthetic swap is feasible it is likely to have a fairly short tenor. Despite the infrequency of application, you should be aware of how to go about constructing a synthetic swap, since market circumstances may sometimes make the synthetic cheaper. In particular, if there is a forward foreign exchange market in a particular currency but no interest rate swap market, then the only way to obtain the effect of a swap may be through the synthetic transaction.

The construction of a synthetic FRA worked because an FRA is equivalent in market risk to a fixed taking and a floating placing, where the floating placing carries no interest rate risk; similarly, a synthetic interest rate swap can be constructed as a strip of fixed takings together with a strip of floating placings. (Or alternatively, of course, floating takings and fixed placings.) Again the floating placings can be ignored in terms of risk, and the foreign exchange swap market used to reproduce the cashflows of the fixed takings.

For ease of exposition, it is again assumed that we are trying to create a synthetic instrument where we pay fixed interest in Deutschmarks. The required bullet interest rate swap will have value date in 3 months and maturity in 15 months, with fixed and floating interest paid each 6 months. Suppose that the offer rate for an equivalent dollar interest rate swap is 6.44%. Then we can attempt to construct our synthetic fixed cashflows by:

- paying fixed on an equivalent dollar swap with value 3 months and maturity 15 months;
- entering into a dollar/Deutschmark 3 v 9 foreign exchange swap to neutralise the fixed dollar taking for the period 3 months to 9 months; and
- entering into a 9 v 15 foreign exchange swap to neutralise the fixed dollar taking for the period 9 months to 15 months.

Since this procedure duplicates the process through which we successfully created a synthetic FRA, it will create two consecutive FRAs which will have a very similar risk profile to the required swap. Unfortunately, in general, the risk profile will not be identical because the contract rates on the two FRAs will be different, owing to the shape of the yield curve reflected in the forward points. In order to make the two synthetic FRAs have the same rate it is therefore necessary to add additional transactions which move a part of the fixed interest payment from, say, the second period to the first. The easiest way to do this is to use placings and takings in Deutschemarks, choosing these to make the effective interest rate the same in both periods. However, if there is greater liquidity in the dollar, then it should be possible to achieve a slightly better rate by making placings and takings in dollars, before calculating the foreign exchange swaps in such a way that the resultant synthetic FRAs all have the same rate; the calculations for this are complex and will not be discussed further.

Since the object of the exercise is to create an instrument with desired risk characteristics, it may not be necessary to make the synthetic swap have precisely the cashflows of an interest rate swap; this may remove the necessity for takings and placings discussed above. The only limitation on using such 'imperfect' synthetic instruments will be the capacity of the management accounting to produce correct position reporting and income allocation; this is discussed further in Chapter 17.

The discussion above considers a bullet swap, but the same process can in principle create a synthetic instrument equivalent to any complex swap; since complex swaps may be considerably less liquid, it may be more likely that there will an opportunity to find cheaper pricing through the synthetic instrument. Note that this method can synthesise a swap only when all its payments are concurrent; if you wish to synthesise a swap which, for example, pays annually and receives semiannually, then you will have to use money market transactions to create the semiannual payments.

The implicit assumption throughout the above discussion was that the construction of synthetic instruments involves being a price taker for every transaction entered into. A market maker who can incorporate a customer transaction at his own side of the bid-offer spread into a synthetic instrument may be able to obtain a substantially better rate; an investment in systems and in creative thought will be necessary to achieve the maximum potential from such opportunities.

SUMMARY

This chapter has extended the discussion to consider interest rate risk in different currencies simultaneously. The key result is interest rate parity, which establishes a relationship between the spot and forward foreign exchange rates for a pair of currencies and the interest rates within each currency. This allows the use of foreign exchange swaps to transfer short-term interest rate risk between currencies without creating foreign exchange risk. Foreign exchange swaps have applications in the management of cash and in the creation of synthetic FRAs and swaps; other applications will be shown in the next two chapters.

CHAPTER 16

Cross currency swaps

Cross currency interest rate swaps offer a mechanism for converting a cashflow in one currency into a cashflow with equivalent present value in a second currency; this allows an organisation to borrow funds in one currency and utilise them in a second currency without market risk, and thus allows access to the capital markets in any currency if borrowing rates in that currency become advantageous. Cross currency swaps also have applications as a risk management tool, although banks managing extensive interest rate and foreign exchange positions will generally be able to find a cheaper combination of instruments to manage their risk.

This chapter starts by describing the economic rationale for cross currency swaps; it then describes the mechanics of the instrument and its pricing. Pricing involves a discussion of credit and capital costs, and of the process of hedging the cross currency risk inherent in a swap. The chapter concludes with a brief review of applications for cross currency swaps. A discussion of how to report and manage the additional risks inherent in dealing in cross currency swaps is held over until Chapter 17.

16.1 ECONOMIC RATIONALE FOR CROSS CURRENCY SWAPS

No financial instrument will become widespread unless there is an economic rationale for its use. In the case of cross currency swaps, an original economic rationale based on regulatory restrictions on foreign exchange transactions has been replaced by a new rationale based on access to cheaper capital markets in foreign currencies.

When exchange controls were in force, in the United Kingdom and elsewhere, in the 1970s, banks invented back-to-back loans to circumvent the restrictions on the purchase of foreign currency. The basic idea was that, for example, a British company wanting US dollars would arrange for its US subsidiary to borrow dollars from a bank while at the same time the company itself deposited sterling with the bank. The initial value of the deposit would equal the initial value of the loan, and the bank would have a legal right of offset between the two; consequently the bank's credit exposure was low, and thus it could charge a relatively small spread, making the transaction cheaper for the company than buying dollars at an artificially high rate.

By the early 1980s, banks realised that this type of transaction was an efficient method of converting funds in one currency into funds in another, even when no exchange controls were involved. Thus, for example, if a Swiss company could borrow Swiss francs from retail investors at a relatively cheaper rate than it could borrow US dollars, then it could borrow francs and lend them to a bank which would simultaneously lend it dollars cheaper than it could have borrowed them directly. In time, the cashflows of two independent loans became the cashflows of a single off-balance-sheet instrument which became known as a cross currency interest rate swap. (The single currency interest rate swap developed from its cross currency cousin.)

The market in cross currency swaps has now matured, so that there is a broad range of transactions possible, with a consistent terminology and a standard basis for documentation. All the variants of swap are similar economically to a loan in one currency back to back with a deposit in another currency; variations include irregular cashflows, increasing or amortising principals, and matching reductions of interest rates in the two currencies.

The essence of the prototype cross currency swaps was the reduction of credit risk by the matching of asset and liability principals, and the management of the risk by the bank counterparty as a loan in one currency and a deposit in another. Banks quickly realised that they could hedge the cashflows and the risk of cross currency swaps more cheaply through the forward foreign exchange market, as will be explained in section 16.3 below. This allowed banks to reduce their bid-offer spreads on cross currency swaps while maintaining profit margins, and thus contributed to the growth in the market for the instrument. This growth coincided with, and contributed to, the explosive growth in the Eurobond debt market in the 1980s.

With the introduction of risk-based capital requirements for banks at the end of the 1980s, a cost of capital was introduced into the banks' pricing; at the same time, banks became more keenly aware of the credit risk involved in cross currency swaps. The cost of capital and credit can be substantial for a cross currency swap, as we shall see in section 16.4 below, and so liquidity in the instrument has probably dropped since the late 1980s.

In addition to its use in accessing the capital markets, a cross currency swap can also be used to hedge interest rate risk. The relatively wide spread on cross currency swaps acts to make them an unattractive hedging instrument for professional market participants such as the larger banks, but the specificity of risk profile achievable through a swap can make it a useful hedging tool for end users.

16.2 MECHANICS OF CROSS CURRENCY SWAPS

A cross currency interest rate swap is an agreement between two counterparties to exchange future cashstreams in two currencies. The *currency A payer* will pay a cashflow denominated in currency A, and the *currency B payer* will pay a cashflow denominated in currency B. The swap runs from its *effective date*, usually referred to as the *value date*, to its *termination date*, usually referred to as the *maturity date*.

Often, but not always, there will be an *initial exchange* of currency amounts on the value day, in which each counterparty receives the currency which it will subsequently pay; thereafter each counterparty will pay its own currency only. This corresponds to the initial drawdown of a loan in which the borrower receives the currency amount he will subsequently repay. There will always be a *final exchange* of currency amounts on the maturity day.

Usually the cashflows after the value date are equivalent to the principal and interest on a loan and deposit; all the swaps dealt with here are assumed to be of this type. Interest is calculated in each currency over successive *calculation periods* from the value date to the maturity date, and is paid on a series of *payment dates*; the payment dates may differ between the two currencies, but the maturity date will always be a payment date in both currencies. As for loans, periodic swap payments are normally on a regular frequency, such as quarterly, semiannually, or annually; the frequencies may be different in the two currencies.

Figure 16.1 on the next page shows the cashflows of a typical cross currency swap with initial exchange.

Following the convention of the Euromarkets, floating interest rates in cross currency swaps are set on the spot date, that is two London business days before the start of the relevant calculation period. If the swap is being used to hedge an interest rate position where Libor is set on the first day of each calculation period, then consideration should be given to agreeing same-day setting for the swap also; this is most common in sterling.

When the cashflows are calculated as interest and principal, then the initial exchange, if any, and the final exchange will be for the principal amounts; on the maturity date there will also be an exchange of interest payments. If the underlying principal changes, then generally it will accrete or amortise by the same proportion on the same dates in both currencies, so as to maintain a constant exchange rate. As in the final exchange, each amortisation will involve an exchange of the amortising principal amounts; as in the initial

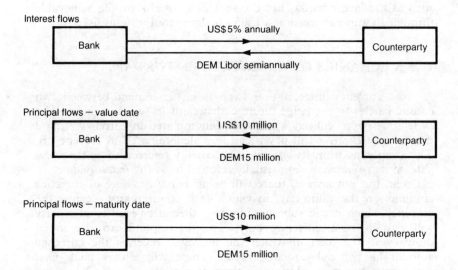

Figure 16.1 Cashflows of a typical cross currency swap. The bank pays fixed at 5% annually on a principal of US$10 million, and receives fixed at 6-month Libor semiannually on a principal of DEM15 million. There is an initial exchange of principals.

exchange, each accretion may or may not involve an exchange of the principal accretions.

In order to minimise the credit risk for both counterparties, the principals in the two currencies are usually equal at the foreign exchange rate to the value date prevailing when the swap is agreed. As will be shown in section 16.3 below, if the swap does have an initial exchange of principals then its pricing will not be sensitive to the exact exchange rate chosen, unless there are material compensating off-market interest rates in each currency. If there is no initial exchange, then the swap creates a foreign exchange position and its price will be sensitive to the exchange rate used; in this case, agreeing the exchange rate will be an important part of the execution of the transaction.

Other variations possible include the payment of a yield adjustment by one counterparty, in exchange for which the other counterparty pays more or receives less interest in the relevant currency.

Given the variety of exchange rates, principal and payment schedules, and compensating off-market rates possible, you will appreciate that a wide variety of transactions can come under the umbrella of cross currency swaps; this is considerably different from the situation for, say, FRAs or forward foreign exchange deals, where only a few parameters are needed to define a transaction. A market standard for documentation has been developed to cope with the definition of swap transactions; this is the same ISDA terms and conditions produced by the International Swap Dealers Association which was mentioned in Part III as the standard documentation for single currency swaps. ISDA terms will not be discussed further here, but it is again important for market participants to examine and understand the standard conditions so that they know when they have to negotiate changes for particular transactions.

When pricing is examined in the next section, you will see that, in principle, any bank which deals in forward foreign exchange in a currency can manage a cross currency swap which has a floating interest rate in that currency, and a bank dealing in addition in single currency interest rate swaps in the currency can manage a cross currency swap which has a fixed interest rate in the currency. Banks will enter into cross currency swaps with their customers at a rate which allows them to hedge the transaction at a profit. Consequently, cross currency swaps are available in major currencies with interest calculated on either a fixed or floating basis. Typical principal amounts would be the equivalent of US$5 million to US$100 million, with typical maturities between 1 and 10 years. Because of the cost of credit and capital, effective bid-offer spreads will widen with increasing maturity of the swap; however, since banks do not in general quote a two-way swap price to end users, the size of the spread is camouflaged.

16.3 HEDGING AND PRICING

Banks will price a cross currency swap at a rate which allows them to hedge the risk of the transaction and to cover their associated costs at a profit. This section looks at hedging a cross currency swap and develops a quantitative understanding of the cost of hedging; the strategy is to look at micro hedging a single swap, and then to consider how the cost for this can be translated into costs for macro hedging a portfolio of swaps. The next section goes on to look at the cost of capital and credit.

The starting point is to consider a *Libor-Libor* cross currency swap, where we shall pay floating interest at Libor on a dollar principal and receive floating interest at Libor plus 10 basis points on a Swiss franc principal. The swap will have value date spot and maturity 2 years later, with interest paid semiannually in both currencies; there will be an initial exchange of principals at the current spot rate, and the principals will be unchanged during the life of the swap, so that there will be a full exchange of principals at the maturity date. The principals are assumed to be US$1 million and CHF1.3 million at the current spot rate of 1.3000. How should we go about hedging this transaction?

The first point to note is that this swap does not involve us in any material foreign exchange risk, since the net present value of the cashflows in each currency is close to zero. To see this, consider first the cashflows in dollars. We receive the initial exchange amount of

US$1 million, and thereafter we pay interest at Libor semiannually; on the maturity date we also repay the principal amount of US$1 million. We can create an economically equivalent set of cashflows by adding a principal payment and a principal receipt at each intermediate 6 month date. This lets us group the cashflows as follows:

Year 0   US$1,000,000
Year 0.5   - US$1,000,000 - interest at Libor

Year 0.5   US$1,000,000
Year 1.0   - US$1,000,000 - interest at Libor

Year 1.0   US$1,000,000
Year 1.5   - US$1,000,000 - interest at Libor

Year 1.5   US$1,000,000
Year 2.0   - US$1,000,000 - interest at Libor

Each of the four sets of cashflows is equivalent to the cashflows of a taking at Libor, and, as shown previously, the present value of a future taking at the then prevailing Libor is zero.

In francs, the cashflows are similarly equal to a series of four placings at Libor plus 10 basis points; the present value of each placing is slightly greater than zero because of the 10 basis point spread, but the effect of this on the risk of the instrument will be very small. (A 5% change in the spot rate will cause less than a US$25 change in the present value of one of the placings.)

This demonstrates that, to a good approximation, there is no foreign exchange risk in entering into this swap.

Nor do we have any material interest rate risk beyond the current 6-month period, since there is no variability of present value for a future taking or placing at Libor. Consequently, the only risk needing hedging is the interest rate risk of the first 6-month period, where it can be assumed that the Libors have been set at today's rates since the swap is starting at spot. Since it has been shown that the risk is the same as the risk of a 6-month dollar taking and a corresponding 6-month franc placing, we know that we can hedge the risk by doing an equal and opposite 6-month foreign exchange swap between dollars and francs, where we sell and buy the dollar.

Because of interest rate parity, we would expect that the effective interest rate attainable in the foreign exchange swap would be close to Libor in each currency. We can adjust the amount of the forward reexchange so that the dollar amount we receive is precisely US$1 million plus 6 months' interest at dollar Libor, and we would then expect the franc amount to be close to CHF1.3 million plus 6 months' interest at franc Libor.

Suppose that in fact it equals CHF1.3 million plus 6 months' interest at Libor plus 4 basis points per annum (bppa). This then means that in the first 6 months our net cashflows, based on the grouping into a series of placings and takings, are:

	Dollar		Franc	
	Swap	Hedge	Swap	Hedge
Year 0	+1 million	−1 million	−1.3 million	+1.3 million
Year 0.5	−1 million	+1 million	+1.3 million	−1.3 million
	−Libor	+Libor	+Libor	−Libor
			+10 bppa	−4 bppa

This gives a net residual cashflow of +6 bppa in Swiss francs at 6 months, with all other cashflows hedged. If it is assumed that the achievable effective interest rates on foreign exchange swaps have been stable for many years at receiving dollar Libor and paying franc Libor plus 4 bppa, then it is not unreasonable to project these rates as the likely rates on future foreign exchange swaps.

If, as is unlikely, the spot exchange rate turns out to be exactly 1.3000 at each 6-month date, then if we 'roll the hedge' by entering into a new 0 v 6 swap every 6 months, our cashflows will be:

	Dollar		Franc	
	Swap	Hedge	Swap	Hedge
Year 0	+1 million	−1 million	−1.3 million	+1.3 million
Year 0.5	−1 million	+1 million	+1.3 million	−1.3 million
	−Libor	+Libor	+Libor	−Libor
			+10 bppa	−4 bppa
Year 0.5	+1 million	−1 million	−1.3 million	+1.3 million
Year 1.0	−1 million	+1 million	+1.3 million	−1.3 million
	−Libor	+Libor	+Libor	−Libor
			+10 bppa	−4 bppa
Year 1.0	+1 million	−1 million	−1.3 million	+1.3 million
Year 1.5	−1 million	+1 million	+1.3 million	−1.3 million
	−Libor	+Libor	+Libor	−Libor
			+10 bppa	−4 bppa
Year 1.5	+1 million	−1 million	−1.3 million	+1.3 million
Year 2.0	−1 million	+1 million	+1.3 million	−1.3 million
	−Libor	+Libor	+Libor	−Libor
			+10 bppa	−4 bppa

There is thus a residual cashflow of +6 bppa every 6 months on the Swiss franc principal, with all other cashflows matched; this demonstrates the basic principle of *Libor-Libor hedging* a cross currency swap, as illustrated in Figure 16.2 on the next page.

However, the assumption that the exchange rate will return to its current value every 6 months is clearly unreasonable. Consider what happens if the spot exchange rate in 6 months is, say, 1.2000. At the

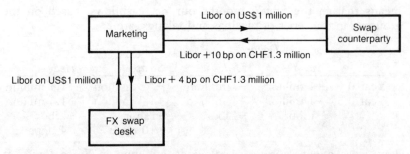

Figure 16.2 Interest cashflows of cross currency swap plus hedge, where the
spot rate equals the ratio of the swap principals.

6-month date we can still put on a 0 v 6 swap to get the following
cashflows:

	Dollar		Franc	
	Swap	*Hedge*	*Swap*	*Hedge*
Year 0	+1 million	−1 million	−1.3 million	+1.3 million
Year 0.5	−1 million	+1 million	+1.3 million	−1.3 million
	−Libor	+Libor	+Libor	−Libor
			+10 bppa	−4 bppa
Year 0.5	+1 million	−1 million	−1.3 million	+1.2 million
Year 1.0	−1 million	+1 million	+1.3 million	−1.2 million
	−Libor	+Libor	+Libor	−Libor
			+10 bppa	−4 bppa

This time the hedge has not been so successful, and there are residual
net franc cashflows:

Year 0.5   +6 bppa interest on CHF1.3 million
           −CHF0.1 million

Year 1.0   +6 bppa interest on CHF1.2 million
           +10 bppa interest on CHF0.1 million
           +CHF0.1 million
           +Libor on CHF0.1 million

However, it is possible to match the CHF0.1 million principal and
interest payments with a CHF0.1 million taking from year 0.5 to year
1.0 at Libor, as illustrated in Figure 16.3 on the next page, giving net
cashflows:

Year 0.5   +6 bppa interest on CHF1.3 million

Year 1.0   +6 bppa interest on CHF1.2 million
           +10 bppa interest on CHF0.1 million

If at year 1.0 the spot exchange rate becomes 1.5000, then the net
Swiss franc cashflows of the cross currency swap and the hedge will
be:

Year 1.0   +6 bppa interest on CHF1.3 million
           +10 bppa interest on CHF0.1 million
           +CHF0.2 million

Year 1.5   +6 bppa interest on CHF1.3 million
           −4 bppa interest on CHF0.2 million
           −CHF0.2 million
           −Libor on CHF0.2 million

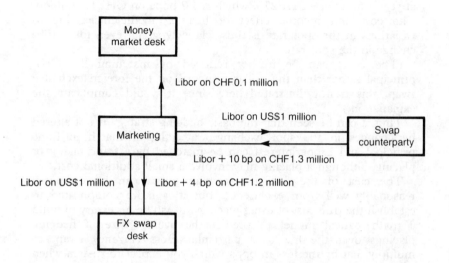

Figure 16.3 Interest cashflows of swap plus hedges where the spot rate is 1.2 and the ratio of principals is 1.3. At the start of the hedge period the CHF principal cashflows will be: maturing foreign exchange (FX) swap −1.3 million, new FX swap +1.2 million, money market taking +0.1 million, giving a net zero principal cashflow. The net CHF principal flow at the end of the period will also be zero, since a money market transaction will be added to the initial exchange of the FX swap in the following period to make it up to CHF 1.3 million.

This time there is a surplus of CHF0.2 million for 6 months which we could hedge by placing the funds in the market at Libid, which equals Libor minus 12.5 bppa. In fact, following on from the discussion of foreign exchange swaps in the previous chapter, we could probably swap the franc surplus into our home currency and use it to fund our own operations, rather than placing the funds with the market. Let us assume that we do this, realising an effective CHF interest rate of Libor minus, say, 8 basis points per annum. This will give residual cashflows of:

Year 1.0   +6 bppa interest on CHF1.3 million
           +10 bppa interest on CHF0.1 million

Year 1.5   +6 bppa interest on CHF1.3 million
            −4 bppa interest on CHF0.2 million
            −8 bppa on CHF0.2 million

The two residual cashflows at year 1.0 net at CHF440, which is
6.8 bppa on CHF1.3 million; similarly the three residual cashflows
at year 1.5 net at +CHF270, which is 4.2 bppa on CHF1.3 million.
The cost and income effect of hedging inefficiencies due to
variations in the spot rate is thus relatively small, even for a 15%
change in the spot rate.

(The costs can be further reduced by matching the CHF
principal rather than the dollar principal on the foreign exchange
swap; this is not illustrated here since it would complicate the
explanation.)

Thus it can be seen that the basic hedging strategy is not altered
by changes in the spot exchange rate; the mismatch in franc
principal and Libor interest can be matched by a franc taking or
placing, although a placing may involve a small additional cost.

The cost of the foreign exchange swaps can be estimated
reasonably well from experience, but it is more complicated to
establish the true cost of using placings. It will be necessary to build
a mathematical model to predict the average size of hedging
placings over the life of a particular cross currency swap, to
multiply that by the loss in bppa which you expect to sustain when
entering into such a placing, to present value the losses so
calculated, and then to express the present value in terms of bppa
on the swap principal over the swap life.

The details of such a mathematical model are discussed in the
next section; here it will be noted simply that the expected cost of
hedging with placings on a swap will generally be small. A bank
which is active in the forward foreign exchange market or which
manages a large number of cross currency swaps may be able to
offset some of its foreign exchange swap hedging internally, thus
reducing its costs both for direct Libor-Libor hedging and for the
hedging of residual placings.

Suppose that the mathematical model shows that for the swap in
the example above the expected cost to us of hedging with placings
will be 2 bppa. Since the expected cost of the Libor-Libor hedging
is 4 bppa, our total hedging cost will be 6 bppa. The net spread
over Libor on the swap is 10 bppa, and thus we can afford to enter
into the swap at this price if the costs of capital, credit, and
administration are less than 4 bppa.

This demonstrates a strategy for micro hedging a bullet Libor-
Libor cross currency swap with initial exchange and for
determining the contribution of the hedging cost to the price of the
swap.

For greater efficiency swaps should be hedged as part of a
portfolio rather than micro hedged. The analysis above can still
estimate the marginal hedging cost for an additional deal; for
example, if historically the average Libor-Libor cost as calculated

above is 10 bppa, and the actual cost for the portfolio has been 8 bppa, then it is reasonable to price a new deal on the basis that its hedging cost will be the predicted Libor-Libor cost minus 2 bppa. Sophisticated management accounting will be necessary to analyse such costing.

Most cross currency swaps have a fixed interest rate in at least one of the currencies, or have some other complication, but it turns out that the Libor-Libor hedging technique can be extended to cope with any variety of swap. To demonstrate this, four separate variations of the basic cross currency swap are considered below; it is shown how to hedge each, together with how to work out the contribution of the hedging cost to the pricing of the swap.

16.3.1 Fixed to floating cross currency swaps

A fixed to floating cross currency swap is a swap in which the interest in one currency is calculated at a fixed rate while the interest in the other currency is calculated at a floating rate.

For example, we could enter into a swap where we pay fixed interest of 9.56% annually on a Deutschmark principal of DEM20 million, and receive interest semiannually at Libor on a yen principal of JPY1,647 million; the swap will be taken to have an initial exchange of principals, with value in 6 months and maturity 5 years later.

Suppose that the market rate for a 5-year Deutschmark single currency swap 6 months deferred is 9.70%/9.77% for annual interest payments; we could therefore enter into a 5-year swap where we receive 9.70% fixed annually and pay Libor semiannually on DEM20 million.

Consider the effect of entering into this single currency swap together with the proposed cross currency swap described above. The Deutschmark cashflows are:

	Cross currency	Single currency	Net
Year 0.5	Receive principal		Receive principal
Year 1.0		Pay Libor	Pay Libor
Year 1.5	Pay 9.56%	Receive 9.70%	Pay Libor - 14 bp
		Pay Libor	
Year 2.0		Pay Libor	Pay Libor
Year 2.5	Pay 9.56%	Receive 9.70%	Pay Libor - 14 bp
		Pay Libor	
"	"	"	"
Year 5.5	Pay principal	Receive 9.70%	Pay principal
	Pay 9.56%	Pay Libor	Pay Libor -14 bp

The net Deutschmark cashflows are thus the same as the Deutschmark side of a Libor-Libor cross currency swap with an initial exchange, where we pay Deutschmark interest at Libor semiannually, less 14 basis points per annum which we underpay at the end of each year. Since Deutschmark interest rates are about

9.735% for the period, this is approximately equivalent to paying Libor minus 13.7 bppa semiannually. To see this, consider future valuing the first semiannual underpayment of 6.85 basis points from year 1.0 to year 1.5. The interest rate will be approximately 9.735% annually, which gives a scaling factor of 1.0475, giving a future value of 7.18 basis points. Add to this the 6.85 basis points underpayment at year 1.5 to give a total of 14.03 basis points. (Using an approximate method to work out the semiannual equivalent of an annual payment is satisfactory here, since a cross currency swap will not generally be priced as accurately as the nearest 0.1 bppa.)

The yen cashflows are:

Year 0.5	pay principal
semiannually year 1.0 to year 5.0	receive interest at Libor
Year 5.5	receive principal plus interest.

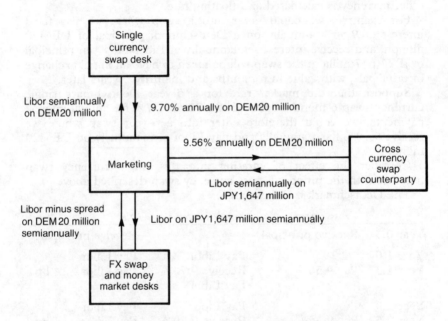

Figure 16.4 Hedging a fixed to floating cross currency swap. This figure illustrates the example discussed in subsection 16.3.1. Interest flows only are shown. As demonstrated in section 16.3, as the spot rate changes the Libor-Libor hedging through a foreign exchange (FX) swap must be supplemented by a placing or taking in one currency. Here the assumption is that the JPY FX swap principal will always be JPY1,647 million; this will necessitate a balancing money market transaction in DEM. The exact spread under Libor in DEM will depend on the rates achievable in the FX swap and money markets.

The combined cashflows of the fixed-floating cross currency swap and the single currency swap are thus equivalent to the cashflows of a Libor-Libor cross currency swap where we receive yen Libor semiannually and pay Deutschmark Libor minus 13.7 bppa semiannually. We can now use the general Libor-Libor method to calculate the total hedging cost from which we shall price the cross currency swap, and if we do enter into the cross currency swap we can hedge it with the single currency swap together with the Libor-Libor hedging described above; this is illustrated in Figure 16.4 on the previous page.

16.3.2 No initial exchange

Suppose a customer wishes to enter into a cross currency swap with us where we would pay interest semiannually at Libor on CHF13 million and receive interest semiannually at Libor plus 10 bppa on US$10 million, where the value date would be in 3 months and the maturity date would be 3 years later, and where there would be no initial exchange of principals. How could we go about hedging such a swap, and hence how would we price it?

If there were to be an initial exchange of principals then we could hedge and price the swap using the Libor-Libor hedging method developed above. Since there is no initial exchange in the swap, in order to use the Libor-Libor hedge method we have to recreate the cashflows of the initial exchange as part of our hedge.

The missing cashflows are, in 3 months' time: we receive CHF13 million, and we pay US$10 million.

Suppose that the 3 months forward US$/CHF exchange rate happens to be 1.3000/10. Then we can go into the forward foreign exchange market and buy CHF13 million and sell US$10 million in 3 months, thus exactly replacing the missing cashflows. From this it can be seen that if the ratio of the two currency principals on the cross currency swap exactly equals the exchange rate to the value date, then the pricing of the swap will be the same whether or not there is an initial exchange. However, if there is no initial exchange, then we have to add an extra hedging transaction which is a forward foreign exchange deal to the value date for the principal amounts.

What happens if the 3-month forward rate is, say, 1.4000/10? In this case we could buy CHF14 million forward against our US$10 million; we would need CHF13 million for hedging the swap, which would leave us with CHF1 million profit. In practice the interest payable on the swap would be adjusted to compensate for the profit on the initial exchange. Conversely, if the forward rate happens to be 1.2000/10, then our forward exchange deal of buying CHF12 million against US$10 million would leave us CHF1 million short for our hedging cashflows, making the swap on the terms given extremely unattractive; the interest payable would therefore have to be adjusted to compensate for the loss on the initial exchange.

To summarise, if a Libor-Libor cross currency swap has no initial exchange, then it can be hedged and priced as a swap with initial exchange plus a forward foreign exchange deal to the value date for the receive-side principal; if the forward exchange deal generates more than the principal on the pay interest side of the swap then this will be a profit to be added into the pricing, and if it generates less than the principal then the shortfall will be a cost to be added into the pricing.

The method is illustrated above by matching the receive-interest principal on the foreign exchange deal; if it is preferable, you can achieve the same effect by matching the pay-interest principal instead.

Note that if a swap is entered into at a ratio of principals which is materially different from the foreign exchange rate to the value date, then the two principal amounts can be expected to be materially different at the start of the swap, increasing the credit exposure of one of the counterparties, and thus potentially increasing the costs of credit and capital for that counterparty; this will be discussed further in the next section.

16.3.3 Accretions and amortisations

Consider a Libor-Libor cross currency swap with initial exchange, with principals as follows:

	CHF millions	US$ millions
Year 0	13	10
Year 0.5	26	20
Year 1.0	13	10
Year 1.5	0	0

The schedule shows the principal at the start of each period, so that, for example, the CHF principal from year 1.0 to year 1.5 is CHF13 million.

Since there is initial exchange of principals, there will be exchanges on each date on which the principal increases; as always, there will also be an exchange on each date on which the principal decreases. If we are paying interest on the CHF, then the principal exchanges will be:

	CHF millions	US$ millions
Year 0	+13	−10
Year 0.5	+13	−10
Year 1.0	−13	+10
Year 1.5	−13	+10

Let us see how this feeds through to the net cashflows of the swap and the Libor-Libor hedging; it is assumed for simplicity that all interest payments, and all interest rates implicit in foreign exchange swap rates, are at Libor, and that the exchange rate turns out to be exactly 1.3000 on each date on which we roll the hedge. (The use of more realistic assumptions would not affect the result but would make the explanation here less clear.)

The cashflow of a series of 6-month CHF takings equivalent to the swap will be, in CHF millions:

Year 0	+13
Year 0.5	−13 − Libor
Year 0.5	+26
Year 1.0	−26 − Libor
Year 1.0	+13
Year 1.5	−13 − Libor

You should check that the net cashflows of these takings are in fact identical to the CHF cashflows of the swap.

If we hedge each taking with an equal and opposite foreign exchange swap, then the cashflows of the swap and the hedge in CHF millions become:

	Swap/takings	Hedge
Year 0	+13	−13
Year 0.5	−13 − Libor	+13 + Libor
Year 0.5	+26	−26
Year 1.0	−26 − Libor	+26 + Libor
Year 1.0	+13	−13
Year 1.5	−13 − Libor	+13 + Libor

Again you should check that the hedge cashflows match a series of foreign exchange swaps for the cross currency swap CHF principal. It is easy to see that the net cashflow on each date is zero.

Following the same process on the dollar side will show that the net dollar cashflow on each date is also zero. By reperforming the original analysis of Libor-Libor hedging for this example, you should be able to check that the effects of changing the spot rate and changing the implied interest rate achievable through foreign exchange swaps are the same for an accreting and amortising currency swap as for a bullet swap.

This demonstrates that the Libor-Libor hedging technique extends in a natural way to accreting and amortising cross currency swaps, and can thus continue to be used for hedging and pricing.

If there is no initial exchange on an accreting swap, then, in general, the forward exchange rate to each accretion date will be different. Hedging such a swap will necessitate entering into a forward foreign exchange deal to each accretion date for the amount of the principal accretion, with a profit or loss being created according to whether the exchange rate is better or worse than the ratio of the two currency principals on the swap.

16.3.4 Offsetting off-market interest in both currencies

Suppose that a cross currency swap where we pay interest on CHF at Libor and receive interest on dollars at Libor plus 10 basis points is priced satisfactorily. If our customer now says that she wants to receive CHF Libor minus 2% per annum instead, what corresponding reduction can we make in the dollar interest rate to keep the same profit in the deal?

As always, pricing follows hedging. We can hedge the cashflows of the original swap through the Libor-Libor method. If we use the same hedging for the new swap, we have residual positive CHF interest payments of 2% per annum. We can hedge these most simply by taking a series of CHF amounts from the spot date to each payment date of the swap, in such a way that the total principal and interest repayment on the takings at each maturity is the 2% per annum residual income on the swap. This will then give us the total taking amount as being a free CHF cashflow on the spot date, with all other CHF cashflows exactly matched. We can then sell this CHF amount spot for dollars, and use the dollar proceeds to subsidise a reduction in the dollar interest rate we receive by making a series of dollar placings, one to each dollar payment date of the swap, in such a way that:

(a) the sum of the placings equals the dollar proceeds of the spot foreign exchange deal described above; and

(b) the total repayment of placing principal and interest at each maturity matches the reduction in dollar interest we receive on the swap.

This sounds complicated, but a numeric example should clarify that what is going on is very similar to the process discussed in Part III for hedging a yield adjustment for a single currency swap.

Suppose that the spot exchange rate is 1.3000 and the swap has value spot and maturity in 5 years, with principals CHF13.5 million and US$10 million, and semiannual payments on both sides. Note that the ratio of principals is not exactly the spot rate. As we have seen, this will not materially affect the pricing of an on-market swap with initial exchange; however, it will have an effect on the off-market interest component, as will be shown below.

It is assumed for simplicity here that CHF and US$ Libors are quoted on a whole year basis; in fact, like most Libors, they are quoted on a 360-day year and calculated on the exact number of days in a period, so that using this calculation in real life would require an adjustment for the basis of the interest rate quotation.

The 2% per annum reduction in CHF payments gives us a net positive CHF cashflow of CHF135,000 every 6 months. We can calculate takings to bring this back to spot as follows:

Calculate the exact taking to the 5-year date such that its principal and interest repayment matches the 5-year CHF135,000 income. If, for example, the interest rate on a taking paying semiannual interest to 5 years is 8%, then a taking of CHF129,808 will have interest plus principal repayment at 5 years of CHF135,000. This taking has interest repayments every 6 months of CHF5,192, which will reduce the available free semiannual cashflow to CHF135,000 minus CHF5,192, which equals CHF129,808.

We can repeat the process to calculate a taking to $4\frac{1}{2}$ years of CHF124,695 if the interest rate to that date is 8.2%, giving a further reduction of free semiannual cashflow available of CHF5,112, and we can continue in the same way back to 6 months to calculate all the CHF takings required.

Suppose that the total of the CHF takings is CHF1,089,540. We can sell this at a spot rate of 1.3 to give US$838,108. Rather than trying to invent a new method to calculate directly the reduction in dollar interest rate which this amount represents, we shall start by repeating for US$ the process by which we worked out the achievable present value of the 2% per annum reduction in CHF interest. That is to say, we work out the series of dollar *placings* which we would have to make today so that the interest and principal repayments of the placings would match a 2% per annum dollar cashflow on the swap principal. A 2% per annum cashflow on the dollar principal equals US$100,000 every 6 months. If, for example, the 5-year dollar placing rate is 6.5% for a placing paying semiannual interest, then a placing of US$96,852 will have interest plus principal repayment at 5 years of US$100,000, and its intermediate interest payments will subtract US$3,148 from the semiannual dollar shortfall on the swap of US$100,000 to leave a shortfall of US$96,852 to be met by further placings. We can continue this process in the same way as for CHF, to give a total of placing principals of, say, US$845,380.

But we know that we have US$838,108 proceeds to pay for the placings, and so we must scale each placing down by the ratio (838,108/845,380) to use up the free dollars we get from the spot foreign exchange deal; this will scale the dollar interest subsidy down by the same ratio to give:

2% per annum times (838,108/845,380)

which equals a reduction of 1.98% in the original swap rate, so that we are happy to enter into a swap where we pay CHF Libor minus 2% and receive dollar Libor minus 1.88%.

If the swap had a ratio of principals equal to the spot rate, then the CHF principal would be CHF13 million, and the total of the CHF takings would be scaled down by a factor of 13/13.5 to give a dollar equivalent of US$807,067. This would reduce the dollar placings proportionately, to give a dollar interest subsidy from the placings of 1.91% per annum, leading to a swap where we pay CHF Libor minus 2% and receive US$ Libor minus 1.81%. You can see from this the effect of a change in the ratio of the swap principals on the price of an off-market-rate swap.

The above discussion is conducted on the basis that you will borrow the francs from the market and deposit your free dollars with the market. In micro hedging in practice, a bank would manage these transactions as far as possible through the foreign exchange swap market and hedge its long term interest rate risk in each currency as an amortising single currency swap. If the bank is able to amalgamate these positions efficiently into the macro hedging of its existing off-balance-sheet positions, then a further potential saving can be made over the rates achievable through the placing and taking market. In either type of hedging the principles of pricing discussed above will still hold, with external placing and taking rates replaced by rates achievable from a dealer internally.

To summarise this section, the price at which a bank will enter into a cross currency swap will be the price at which it can hedge the transaction minus the costs of credit and capital. For a Libor-Libor swap with initial exchange, Libor-Libor hedging matches all the swap cashflows and thus is the only hedging component of the pricing. There are two costs in Libor-Libor hedging, the expected spread in implied interest rates on the foreign exchange swaps, and the expected spread on placing surplus funds either into the market or into the bank's own funding. For cross currency swaps which are not straightforward Libor-Libor swaps, the Libor-Libor hedge process will still form the basis of hedging and pricing, with a combination of other instruments used to meet additional hedging needs. Where a bank hedges on a portfolio basis it may reduce overall costs, but it should still price deals on a marginal cost basis using the techniques discussed above; the portfolio savings can be recognised by reducing the assumed cost of Libor-Libor hedging. Although only four types of swap variants are considered above, the hedge and pricing techniques discussed can be mixed and matched to cover, for example, an amortising swap with a fixed interest rate on both sides and with no initial exchange.

16.4 COST OF CAPITAL AND CREDIT

Section 7.4 looked at the cost of capital and of credit for a single currency interest rate swap. That material is applicable to cross currency swaps also, and so this section need merely signpost the differences between single and cross currency swaps in the construction of the mathematical model to predict credit and capital costs.

The basic difference in the calculation of credit risk is that the credit exposure on a cross currency swap is most sensitive to movements in the spot foreign exchange rates between the two currencies, rather than to a movement in interest rates, although, as will be shown, there will be some sensitivity to interest rate movements also.

The expected credit loss on a cross currency swap is:

*default probability * expected positive value * default %,* where the italicised terms are defined in section 7.4. For a particular class of counterparty, the default probability and the default % will be the same as for a single currency interest rate swap, and thus in amending the model it is necessary to consider only the expected positive value of a cross currency swap.

At any time, the mark-to-market value of a cross currency swap will be the net present value of its future cashflows, where the cashflows in each currency are discounted separately and the present values are then added by converting the one value into the other currency at the prevailing spot rate. (Holdbacks, to be discussed in the next chapter, would be immaterial in the discussion here.)

For a Libor-Libor swap, the present value of the future cashflows in each currency will be close to the principal amount. To see this, use the usual trick of adding cancelling pairs of principal flows at each payment date of the swap. This gives future payments on, say, the pay interest side, as:

next pay date   − principal − interest

next pay date   + principal
next pay date +1   − principal − Libor + spread

next pay date +1   + principal
next pay date +2   − principal − Libor + spread

and so on to the swap maturity.

We know that after the principal plus interest payment on the next pay date, each subsequent pair of cashflows represents a taking at Libor minus a spread; the takings at Libor represent zero present value, while the spread interest represents a small additional present value which can be assumed to be immaterial for the current discussion. The bulk of the present value is thus due to the single payment of principal plus interest at the next payment date. Since the interest is the Libor interest for a calculation period starting before today and the discount factor is based on the Libor for the period from today to the payment date, present value would be expected to be somewhere between the principal amount and, say, 10 per cent over the principal amount, with the higher value possible only when we get close to the payment date. The present value of the receive side will be confined to a similar range, again with the higher values possible only close to the payment date.

Restricting the discussion to swaps with concurrent payments and receipts, since the present value of each side will be within 10% of the currency principal value, with a strong correlation between the ratio of present value to principal in the two currencies, the bulk of the fluctuation in net present value will depend on the spot exchange rate. If the payment period is semiannual on both sides, then it will probably give reasonable accuracy to assume that the net present value is based on the current spot rate times, say, 1.05 times the principals in the two currencies. (For particular currency pairs it might be appropriate to change this figure.)

For Libor-Libor swaps with concurrent payments, therefore, it is possible to calculate the expected positive value using the same binomial tree model as was used for single currency interest rate swaps, where the up and down volatility movements in interest rates in each period are replaced by up and down movements in the spot exchange rate; again an appropriate size for the periodic movements can be selected based on historic volatilities. The mark-to-market value at each node should be the swap principals times 1.05 converted at the projected spot exchange rate.

Following through the same process as for interest rate swaps will then give the expected credit loss from which the cost of credit can be calculated. The same model can be adjusted to give the expected cost of capital, where the BIS risk capital formula for cross currency swaps has an 'add-in factor' of 5% of principal, compared to 0.5% of principal for single currency swaps; the final year has an add-in factor of 1% compared to zero. As a bonus, the same basic model can be further enhanced to output the expected average placing amount needed in Libor-Libor hedging, from which the expected cost of these placings can be determined.

If the pay and receive side of a Libor-Libor swap do not have concurrent payment dates, then the mark-to-market value will alter when interest is paid in one currency and not in the other; the model can be adjusted in a straightforward way to incorporate this calculation.

If the swap is fixed against floating, then the present value of the fixed side can vary substantially from the principal amount. For example, if a swap has 5 years left to run, and we are paying Deutschmark interest annually at a fixed 6% when today's Deutschmark yield curve is flat at 8%, then the present value of the future Deutschmark payments is calculated as:

	Cashflow	Scaling factor	Present value
Year 1	6%	1.080	5.56%
Year 2	6%	1.166	5.14%
Year 3	6%	1.260	4.76%
Year 4	6%	1.360	4.41%
Year 5	106%	1.469	72.14%

giving a total present value of 92.01% of principal.

The value of the future cashflows on the fixed side will depend on the yield curve in the currency of that side of the swap, but the net present value of the swap will depend also on the spot exchange rate. There is no simple way of incorporating movements in these two variables into the binomial tree on which the model is based. A more complex model in which the tree branches in two variables simultaneously (or in three variables if both sides of the swap are fixed) can quickly become unwieldy. Alternatively, a Monte Carlo simulation might be used to calculate the expected values; there is a discussion of this possibility in *Options, Futures, and Other Derivative Securities*. It may be worth while using a two or three variable model or a Monte Carlo simulation when pricing a swap originally, but it will not necessarily be cost effective to use such a model to recalculate exposures regularly on a portfolio; hence a simpler model will be needed.

The best approach may be to increase the volatility of the exchange rate used in the binomial tree by a 'fudge factor', to take account of the extra volatility in the mark-to-market value implied by possible interest rate movements. Luckily, for reasonable values, the output of the model will not be tremendously sensitive to changes in the volatility used, and therefore it is not too difficult to choose a value for volatility which you believe will give, say, 10% accuracy to the final answer compared to the accuracy of the model for Libor-Libor swaps; this will probably be adequate for use on a portfolio of swaps.

As before, the same model which predicts the cost of credit will also predict the cost of capital and the cost of the placings needed as part of Libor-Libor hedging.

You can generally expect a cross currency swap to have a considerably greater cost of capital and credit than a single currency interest rate swap to the same maturity. Moreover, the credit risk of the cross currency swap will be concentrated in the final exchange at the maturity date and thus will not tend to decrease over the swap's life, whereas the credit risk of a single currency interest rate swap will tend to decrease as the number of outstanding payment periods becomes small. Thus the credit risk on a cross currency swap tends to be greater in both amount and tenor than the risk on a single currency swap.

There will also be delivery risk on a cross currency swap on each day on which there is a payment in one currency and a receipt in the other; each delivery risk represents a one day risk only. Delivery risk, as for other sorts of credit risk, should be recorded and managed by a single credit area for each counterparty. If material, the credit area can charge a rent for the creation of the delivery risk in addition to the rent for the overall credit exposure. The delivery risk has no impact on the cost of capital.

Before leaving costing it is worthwhile adding a reminder that the remarks in section 7.5 on the operational costs of single currency interest rate swaps apply equally well to cross currency swaps.

16.5 APPLICATIONS FOR CROSS CURRENCY SWAPS

The introduction to cross currency swaps at the start of this chapter described the major application for cross currency swaps as being that they gave a mechanism to allow borrowers to access the capital market in a foreign currency. In symmetry to this, an investor can use a cross currency swap to convert the cashflow on an asset in one currency into a cashflow in a second currency; the combination of asset and swap is known as a synthetic asset.

Cross currency swaps also have applications in managing revenue streams; for example, a company with a foreign subsidiary might hedge the expected dividend flow for the next 3 years into its home currency using a cross currency swap.

Cross currency swaps can be particularly useful because of the specificity of cashflow which they offer; for example, a swap may allow the hedging of a highly structured private placement of a debt instrument, or may be used to hedge a complex financing transaction. Identifying such opportunities for using cross currency swaps requires good cooperation between the risk management group and other areas of a bank.

It is worthwhile noting that because of the high bid-offer spread on cross currency swaps, and because of the high credit risk inherent in the instrument, their use is becoming more common in shorter maturities.

SUMMARY

This chapter has shown how the cross currency interest rate swap arises as a natural contract for converting a cashstream in one currency into a cashstream with equivalent present value in a second currency. As for single currency swaps, a bank should base its pricing for a cross currency swap on the blended rate of the hedge contracts plus the cost of capital and credit. The basic mechanism for hedging a cross currency swap is to use a succession of foreign exchange swaps to roll the foreign exchange risk from period to period; this will also match any Libor interest flows and will convert the risk of a fixed interest flow into the risk of the equivalent single currency swap. The use of foreign exchange swaps will introduce an extra hedging cost, as will the spread around Libor on funding or investing the large cashflows caused by changes in the spot exchange rate over the life of a swap; these two costs may be reduced if portfolio hedging is used in place of micro hedging. Variations of the techniques developed for single currency swaps will allow the pricing and hedging of complex cross currency swaps. The high credit and capital costs on cross currency swaps makes them less useful as an interbank risk management instrument.

CHAPTER 17

Medium-term foreign exchange

This chapter deals first with *medium-term foreign exchange*, that is to say forward foreign exchange deals beyond 1 year; the focus is on pricing these correctly for their inherent interest rate risk. Two other topics are then addressed to complete the treatment of cross currency interest rate risk management: the statistical basis for measuring interest rate risk in a multicurrency portfolio, and the valuation of transactions and the reporting and measurement of risk in a multicurrency environment.

17.1 MEDIUM-TERM FOREIGN EXCHANGE

A medium-term foreign exchange deal is simply a forward foreign exchange deal beyond the normal maturity boundary of 1 year. Pricing and management of medium-term deals differs from that for normal forwards in two respects: first, such deals tend to be highly illiquid, and secondly, interest rate risk plays a much greater role.

The requirement for medium-term foreign exchange deals comes predominantly from companies with large project-related individual future cashflows denominated in a foreign currency which they need to match with cashflows in their home currency. If such cashflows are more-or-less periodic then they can generally be fitted into the pattern of a fixed-fixed cross currency swap, but if they are irregular then it may be cheaper to hedge them through a medium-term foreign exchange deal. There are examples of such future cashflows in the export of aerospace equipment, where a fixed price contract might involve delivery over a period of several years with payments denominated in a foreign currency; the supply of generating equipment for power stations might follow a similar pattern. Shipbuilding would be another example of an industry with long lead times and fixed prices in foreign currencies. Such contracts can necessitate medium-term foreign exchange deals out to 10 years or beyond, but a maturity of 1-5 years is more common. Since a large number of international contracts are priced in US dollars, suppliers entering into medium-term foreign exchange deals typically wish to sell the dollar and buy their home currency. Purchasers of capital equipment often plan to pay for these out of future revenue; consequently, they will be more likely to borrow funds in a foreign currency or use delayed-start cross currency swaps to hedge their risk. Because of this asymmetry between the needs of suppliers and purchasers, there tends to be a bias among end users of medium term foreign exchange towards selling the US dollar.

Given the illiquidity of medium-term deals, a market maker will expect to offset a position with another foreign exchange deal in a different maturity; as was shown in section 15.2, this will leave him with an interest rate position. Since the forward exchange market up to 1 year is so liquid, it is easy for a dealer to close out any residual foreign exchange position with a relatively short-dated forward, leaving himself with a pure interest rate position to manage; it will be assumed that a dealer will do precisely this, allowing the treatment here to concentrate on interest rate risk management.

The reporting of risk for medium-term foreign exchange is straightforward; the complications lie in pricing risk for quoting bid-offer spreads.

Reporting interest rate risk under the discrete cash gaps methodology consists simply of reporting within each currency the net cashflows on each day. Thus if a bank buys DEM5 million against French francs in year 1.5 and sells DEM6 million against the US dollar in year 3, then its DEM cash gaps report will show:

Year	1.5	3.0
Gap (DEM millions)	5	-6

If the dealer has correctly hedged all the foreign exchange risk, then the present value of the cashflows within each currency, other than the home currency of the organisation, should be zero; this can be checked by listing the net present value of the cashflows within each currency on the cash gaps report.

A market maker in any market will quote a bid-offer spread large enough to recompense him for his costs and risks; competitive pressure from other market makers should keep the spread to where it just covers the costs and risks of the most efficient market participants. The problem for a market maker in medium-term foreign exchange is that he has to manage his position through interest rate instruments, and therefore he has to translate the spread on interest rate transactions into an appropriate spread in forward foreign exchange.

Medium-term exchange rates are constrained by interest rate parity in the same way as forward rates out to 1 year. The difference is that the cash market for zero coupon placings and takings is highly liquid out to 1 year, thus providing tight arbitrage limits on forward rates; beyond 1 year, the market for bullet placings and takings is highly illiquid, making for wide arbitrage limits.

Because of the illiquidity of medium-term zero coupon placings and takings, a dealer wanting to take advantage of a theoretical arbitrage opportunity or wanting to hedge a particular forward foreign exchange would probably have to synthesise the necessary long-dated money market transactions through more liquid instruments. Although in practice a dealer would not actually create the synthetic forward exchange as a hedge, in order to estimate the bid-offer spread needed to reflect the interest rate risk of the forward exchange it is necessary to be able to price the synthetic; this is addressed below.

How should a dealer go about constructing, say, a 3-year zero coupon placing? There do exist placings and takings with maturity 3 years which are reasonably liquid, but they involve paying interest on a regular frequency, say, annually, whereas we want no intermediate interest payments.

One solution would be to place funds for 3 years, and simultaneously to take funds to 2 years and 1 year in order to meet the intermediate placing interest; the combination of placing and takings would synthesise the 3-year zero coupon placing. This would involve suffering the large bid-offer spread for on-balance-sheet instruments, made worse by the reduced liquidity of transactions beyond 1 year.

A cheaper solution is to use single currency interest rate swaps to match the risk characteristics of the placing and takings described above, and to place funds for the first year only; this would involve the reduced spread on off-balance-sheet instruments, with a money market instrument used only in a maturity where it is liquid. In a year's time we would 'roll' the placing for the appropriate amount for the next year at the prevailing market rate, and we would repeat this a year later to roll the placing to the maturity of the synthetic zero coupon transaction.

To see this in action, let us pick some interest rates. Suppose that the 3-year rate for swaps with annual fixed interest is 10%/10.07%, the 2-year swap rate is 8.93%/9%, and the 1-year swap offer is 8%, which equals 1-year Libor. Let us start by receiving fixed at 10% on a 3-year swap with a principal of 100; fixed and floating interest will be on an annual frequency. We can employ the usual trick of adding matching pairs of principal payments and regrouping the swap cashflows to see that the swap is economically equivalent to:

- a placing of 100 where we receive fixed 10% annually; and
- a taking of 100 where we pay floating Libor annually.

Let us anticipate the fact that we are going to neutralise the Libor payments by placing equivalent funds in the market for the same period. Unfortunately, we shall place funds not at Libor but at Libid.

Therefore, in order for these placings to neutralise exactly the floating interest of the swap, we must restate the swap cashflows so that the floating interest is at Libid. Assuming that Libid is consistently 12.5 basis points below Libor as it is in the most liquid currencies, we can restate the swap cashflows as being equivalent to:

- a placing of 100 where we receive fixed 9.875% annually; and
- a taking of 100 where we pay floating Libid annually.

The fixed cashflows are:

Year 0   -100
Year 1   9.875
Year 2   9.875
Year 3   109.875

We need to eliminate the interest payments in years 1 and 2 to produce a zero coupon cashstream.

The way to eliminate the 9.875 receipt at year 2 is to take funds today so that the interest plus principal repayment at year 2 is 9.875. Again a swap is used to create the fixed taking. This time we pay fixed on a 2-year swap at 9% on a principal of p, so that the swap cash flows are economically equivalent to:

- a taking of p where we pay fixed at 8.875% annually; and
- a placing of p where we receive fixed at Libid annually.

Again we shall ignore the floating side for the moment and concentrate on the fixed side. In order for the principal plus interest at 2 years to equal 9.875, we must have 108.875% of p equal to 9.875, which gives p equals 9.070034.

Our two swaps now have fixed cashflows as shown in Table 17.1.

TABLE 17.1 INTERMEDIATE STAGE OF CONSTRUCTION OF SYNTHETIC ZERO COUPON PLACING

	Swap 1	Swap 2	Net
Year 0	−100	+9.070034	−90.929966
Year 1	9.875	−0.804966	9.070034
Year 2	9.875	−9.875	0
Year 3	109.875	0	109.875

We have eliminated the 2-year cashflow, and so we have only to eliminate the 1-year cashflow to be left with the required zero coupon structure. We could use a swap again to eliminate the 1-year cashflow, but if instead we take funds directly we shall avoid a bid-offer spread. We have to take funds at a rate of 8% to achieve a principal plus interest repayment at 1 year of 9.070034; the required taking is thus 9.070034 over 1.08, which equals 8.398180. Adding the cashflows of this taking to the net fixed cashflows above gives net cashflows:

Year 0   -82.53178
Year 3   109.875

which corresponds to a zero coupon placing at 10.0084%.

We still have to show that the floating side of the swaps can be matched by money market placings at Libid. The floating-side cashflows of our two swaps as expanded above are:

	Swap 1	Swap 2	Net
Year 0	+100	−9.07	+90.93
Year 1	−Libid on 100	+Libid on 9.07	−Libid on 90.93
Year 2	−Libid on 100	+9.07	+9.07
		+Libid on 9.07	−Libid on 90.93
Year 3	−100		−100
	−Libid on 100		−Libid on 100

The net cashflows are equivalent to:

Year 0   +90.93
Year 1   −90.93 − Libid on 90.93

Year 1   +90.93
Year 2   −90.93 − Libid on 90.93

Year 2   +100
Year 3   −100   − Libid on 100

and thus can be hedged exactly by three successive 1-year placings at Libid, of 90.93, 90.93, and 100.

Since we can match the swap floating sides with money market placings, we have demonstrated that our set of swaps, takings, and placings gives us the required net 3-year zero coupon cashflows.

In fact, we can improve slightly on the rate of 10.0084% which we obtained above, since our transactions include a 1-year taking at Libor on 8.398180 and a 1-year placing at Libid on 90.93 (more exactly, 90.929966). We can instead net the taking and placing, so that we can effectively use a taking at Libid instead of at Libor to eliminate the 1-year cashflow from Table 17.1. We can calculate the taking as being 9.070034/1.07875, which equals 8.407911. The net placing which we must make in the market is 90.929966 minus 8.407911, which equals 82.522055. The net cashflow at year 0 becomes -90.929966 from Table 17.1 plus the taking of 8.407911, which again equals 82.522055, giving net cashflows:

Year 0   − 82.522055
Year 3   +109.875

which corresponds to a zero coupon placing at 10.0127%, an improvement of 0.43 basis points.

We can similarly work out the swaps and takings necessary to synthesise the cashflows of a 3-year zero coupon taking; in contrast to the situation for placings, there is no need to restate the swap rates since we can take funds at Libor. Try to calculate the figures yourself before examining the answer below.

The swaps are:

- pay fixed on 100 for 3 years at 10.07%; and
- receive fixed on 9.244469 for 2 years at 8.93%.

The three 1-year takings are:

- 82.195837 at 8%;
- 90.755531 at Libor; and
- 100 at Libor.

These give net cashflows of:

Year 0   + 82.195837
Year 3   −110.07

giving a zero coupon taking rate of 10.2232%. This gives a bid-offer spread of 10.0127%/10.2232%, which equals 21.05 basis points; it is pointed out below that it should be possible to reduce this spread by using foreign exchange swaps rather than placing funds directly in the market.

The same process extends to synthesising zero coupon takings or placings in any maturity. It should be noted that it would be more common to have the floating side of the swaps on a semiannual payment frequency because of the greater liquidity available in the shorter maturity; this makes the calculation longer, but does not otherwise increase the complexity.

Suppose now that we are trying to synthesise a medium-term foreign exchange deal; for example, let us consider a 3-year forward dollar/sterling deal where we sell sterling. We can synthesise this by taking sterling for 3 years, selling sterling against dollars in the spot foreign exchange market, and placing dollars for 3 years. Suppose that by the process described above we can achieve 3-year zero coupon rates of 7%/7.21% for the dollar and 11.79%/12% for sterling, and that the spot foreign exchange rate is 1.6520/30; then the synthetic forward rate would be:

$$1.6520 * 1.07^3/1.12^3 = 1.4405.$$

However, in our analysis of synthetic placings and takings, we assumed that we would have to use money market placings at Libid. Where we have placings in one currency and takings in another, we would expect to be able to use foreign exchange swaps to achieve the taking and placing cashflows up to the lower of the two currency principals. This would allow us to improve on our effective placing rate of Libid for that portion of the placing amount; if there were surplus funds to place then we could use the technique described in section 16.3, and swap them into our home currency, where we presumably have a net funding requirement. It should thus be possible to improve on Libid as the short-term placing rate in our synthesis of zero coupon placings; the size of the improvement will depend on the factors discussed in section 16.3. Swapping instead of placing will also reduce a bank's required risk-based capital; the pricing implication of this is discussed below.

Suppose that it is possible to improve the 3-year dollar zero coupon bid rate to 7.08%. Then the synthetic forward rate becomes 1.6520 times $1.0708^3/1.12^3$, which equals 1.4437, representing an improvement of 32 FX points.

Does this mean that we can buy sterling 3 years forward at any rate below 1.4437 and make a riskfree profit by selling through the synthetic transaction at an effective rate of 1.4437? As you might expect, the answer is no, since we also have to take into account the cost of credit and, for a bank, the cost of capital; given the complexity of the synthetic, operational costs could also be material if it is intended to use a synthetic deal to hedge a single forward exchange.

The method of calculating the cost of credit and capital for a cross currency swap described in section 16.4 can be extended to deal with medium-term foreign exchange deals; indeed a medium-term foreign exchange deal is equivalent to a zero coupon fixed-fixed cross currency swap. The risk-based capital formula for a medium-term foreign exchange deal is the same as for a cross currency swap, that is, it is based on the positive mark-to-market value plus 5% of the principal amount (reducing to 1% of the principal in the final year).

Suppose that the model predicts that, for the proposed counterparty, the cost of capital, credit, and operations represents 15 FX points on a 3-year forward foreign exchange deal where we buy sterling and sell dollars. Then we need to buy sterling at a rate below 1.4422 in order to be able to lock in a profit through a synthetic forward deal.

Similarly, we can work out the arbitrage boundary for selling sterling. If the sterling zero coupon bid rate becomes 11.87% when we manage cash through swaps, then the 3-year forward rate at which we can buy sterling through a synthetic deal becomes $1.6530 * 1.0721^3/1.1187^3$, which equals 1.4549. If we assume that the cost of capital, credit, and operations represents 14 FX points on this transaction, then we have to sell sterling at above 1.4563 to be able to lock in an arbitrage profit.

Thus, with reasonable estimates for bid-offer spreads and costs, we obtain a bid-offer spread for the arbitrage limit on the forward exchange rate of 1.4422/1.4563, which is 141 FX points; on a principal of US$10 million this represents US$97,767. Where bid and offer spreads are quoted on medium-term foreign exchange deals they are wide, but, just as for short-term forwards, they will be narrower than the spread implied by the arbitrage limits.

The arbitrage limits achievable through synthetic transactions should give a guide to the bid-offer spread to quote. If a portfolio is managed on a macro hedging basis then the true arbitrage spread achievable may be lower; a market maker will have to estimate the improvement and price accordingly. For example, a market maker might have a policy of always quoting at least the cost of capital and credit plus a fifth of the arbitrage spread net of these costs on his side of the midmarket price. For example, in the example above the arbitrage spread of 1.4422/1.4563 gives a midmarket price of 1.4492. The spread net of capital and credit is 112 FX points, so that the market maker following the rule of thumb described above would quote a minimum price to buy the dollar of 1.4492 plus 22 FX points plus 14 FX points for capital and credit, which equals 1.4528. Since end users are net sellers of the US dollar in medium-term foreign exchange, the banks' prices usually tend towards the arbitrage limit for buying the dollar, and so a bank might well quote a rate higher than 1.4528 in this case.

Typically a bank market maker will be a net buyer of US dollars in the longer maturities and will hedge by selling the dollar in shorter maturities. This will give him an interest rate and foreign exchange risk position which can be calculated from the cash gaps of his position.

It is being assumed that the dealer will keep his foreign exchange position at zero and thus has no foreign exchange risk; it should be noted that it will probably be cheaper to do this through the forward foreign exchange market rather than through the spot market, since use of the forward market will reduce the problem of cash management.

The dealer will have to manage his cash positions through using foreign exchange swaps to create the appropriate synthetic placings and takings. He can then manage the interest rate risk in each currency as part of his general management of his position in that currency. Where foreign exchange or cash is being managed by someone else it will be important to have management accounting in place to split profit and loss accurately between the different dealers. Reporting and position management are considered further in section 17.3 below.

17.2 STATISTICAL BASIS FOR MANAGING CROSS CURRENCY RISK

If an organisation has interest rate risk in two currencies, it will generally not be the case that its overall risk will be the sum of its risk in each of the currencies. For example, if it is long in a Deutschmark swap and short in an equivalent Belgian franc swap, then the overall risk will be lower than if it had entered into the Deutschmark swap only but will still be greater than zero, since there is a strong but not perfect positive correlation between interest rate movements in the two currencies.

In order to quantify such effects, a theoretical framework is needed for describing interest rate movements in each currency. Such a framework would aim to capture as much information as possible about day-to-day yield curve movements in a manageably small number of parameters, say two or three. The analysis in Part I of a yield curve in a single currency suggested fitting a 'best hinged line' to the zero coupon yield curve, where the hinged line would consist of a straight line segment from year 0 to year 1, and a second straight line segment from year 1 to year 10 or beyond, with the constraints that the two segments should meet at year 1 and that the sum of the squares of the distances of each yield curve point from the hinged line should be a minimum. Such a hinged line would be described by three descriptors; the descriptors chosen were the value of the zero coupon rate at year 1 and the slopes of the two straight line segments. It is natural to carry over this model into the analysis of many currencies.

By recording the yield curve daily in each currency and deriving the best hinged line, a database covering an extended period can be built up. This will give the daily change in the three descriptors for each currency; from these daily changes you can work out the standard deviation of the daily change in each descriptor for each currency, and the correlation of daily changes between different currencies. This data should be checked to ensure that the hinged line does give a good approximation to the points on the yield curve; in order to allow the calculation of confidence levels for changes of portfolio value over a period, it will also be necessary to check that the individual daily changes conform to a normal distribution.

If you are given the sensitivity of the present value of your portfolio to changes in each of the three descriptors in each currency, together with the standard deviation of the daily change in each descriptor and the correlation between changes in each pair of descriptors, it is possible to work out the magnitude of the expected daily change in the overall portfolio value. The details of this calculation are not given here, since to do so would involve developing most of the machinery of Modern Portfolio Theory; instead you are directed to any of the excellent textbooks written on the subject of portfolio theory itself, and the treatment here will merely summarise the rules for calculating total risk for three extreme states of correlation. For simplicity, it will be assumed that the total risk is derived from risks associated with just two descriptors.

If the sensitivity to a fixed change in descriptor 1 for currency 1 is s_1, and the standard deviation of the daily change in descriptor 1 is c_1, then the standard deviation of the daily change in portfolio value associated with changes in descriptor 1 will be $s_1 c_1$. Risk is defined as the likely change in the present value of a portfolio over a particular period, and, if one standard deviation is used as the measure of risk, then the expression $s_1 c_1$ will be the daily risk associated with this descriptor for this portfolio.

If s_2 and c_2 are similarly the sensitivity and daily standard deviation for descriptor 2 in currency 2, then the daily risk associated with descriptor 2 for the portfolio is $s_2 c_2$.

Note that s_1 and s_2 may be positive or negative, whereas c_1 and c_2 will always be positive; the total risk will always be taken as positive, but risks associated with specific descriptors used to calculate the total risk may be negative.

If the correlation between descriptor 1 and descriptor 2 is 1, that is, if there is perfect correlation, then the total risk will simply be $s_1 c_1 + s_2 c_2$. It is easy to understand this, since, on each day, if s_1 is positive then s_2 will also be positive and if s_1 is negative then s_2 will also be negative; the change in portfolio value associated with change in the two descriptors will thus always move in step.

If the correlation is -1, that is, if there is perfect negative correlation, then the total risk will be $s_1 c_1 - s_2 c_2$. Again, it is easy to understand this, since on each day s_1 and s_2 must have opposite signs in order to achieve the perfect negative correlation, and hence the total daily change in portfolio value should be the difference between the changes associated with each of the descriptors.

If the correlation is 0, that is if changes in descriptor 1 are totally independent of changes in descriptor 2, then the total risk will be

$$\sqrt{(s_1{}^2 c_1{}^2; + s_2{}^2 c_2{}^2)}.$$

This is far from obvious, but it follows from the well known result in statistics that the variance, the square of the standard deviation, is additive for independent random variables; that is,
variance$(x + y)$ = variance(x) + variance(y).

If there are portfolios in n currencies, then the yield curves will have $3n$ descriptors, giving $(3n * (3n-1)/2)$ correlations between pairs of descriptors to calculate and to use in combining the individual risks. This will involve excessive computation as soon as n becomes larger than 2 or 3, and so it will probably be necessary to use some approximations in order to shorten the calculation; for example, you could assume that correlations between 0.4 and -0.4 were simply zero. This would reduce the complexity of the overall calculation without necessarily producing huge inaccuracy in the result; the validity of the approximation used should be checked.

The framework developed here assumes that there is no foreign exchange risk; this could be achieved by selling or buying into your home currency each day the present value of the future cashflows in each foreign currency. In practice, closing out the foreign exchange position daily in this way would involve high transaction costs, and it may therefore be more practical to close out foreign exchange positions weekly or monthly; this would introduce a small foreign exchange risk, and you will have to review your business to see how material this would be.

The statistical analysis could be extended to include spot foreign exchange rate movements, but the integration of the management of interest rate and foreign exchange risk which this would imply is beyond the scope of this book.

This section has recommended the development of a database of average rate movements and correlations as a risk management tool, but such a database should also have value in trading and marketing. Thus although the procedure described above seems complex and expensive, the resultant data could potentially repay your investment in several different ways.

The framework described above may not be the best method for your particular requirements, but the important point is to realise that any estimation of risk must be based ultimately on some statistical analysis of rate movements.

17.3 REPORTING AND MANAGING CROSS CURRENCY INTEREST RATE RISK

This section briefly discusses the reporting and managing of interest rate risk across many currencies; the points made here will be summarised, and in some cases extended, in Part VII.

The discrete cash gaps methodology developed in Part I to measure interest rate risk in a single currency should also be the basis of reporting interest risk in a multicurrency environment.

In addition, if you use the statistical analysis of yield curves and correlations discussed in the last section, then you should report the sensitivity of your portfolio present value to changes in each of the descriptors of the yield curve in each currency, together with the expected daily change in portfolio value associated with each descriptor and the expected daily change in total portfolio value. Position limits should be set based on expected daily changes in present value, and these should be monitored regularly for compliance. The other major report needed is the daily profit or loss, calculated as the change in portfolio mark-to-market value; this is discussed further below.

Up-to-date software will supply the above reports at the end of each day, and will allow recalculation of reports on an intraday basis, using different yield curves and exchange rates as required.

In addition to recreating the single currency reporting in a multicurrency environment, there are several additional reporting requirements if your positions include cross currency interest rate swaps or medium-term foreign exchange.

First, there has to be a report of foreign exchange risk so that the dealer can check that he has fully hedged his foreign exchange

GUIDE TO INTEREST RATE RISK MANAGEMENT

position; as mentioned above, this can be achieved by the addition in the cash gaps report of the present value of the future cashflows in each currency. As discussed, it may, in fact, be more cost effective for the dealer to allow small foreign exchange positions to run for a few days, and this report will then become an important control.

Secondly, because of cash management requirements, Libor-Libor hedging for cross currency swaps must be carried out as foreign exchange swaps, as must any synthetic placing and taking hedges for medium-term foreign exchange. This requires a reporting structure to advise the dealer in advance of his requirements to enter into foreign exchange swaps, together with a review process to ensure that the swaps are transacted correctly. A sophisticated reporting structure should enable the dealer to identify opportunities for netting different swaps against each other, and should alert him to other possibilities of reducing the cost of hedging.

Thirdly, the pricing of cross currency swaps and medium-term foreign exchange depends critically on assumptions made about the future cost of capital and credit, and on the efficiency of hedging through foreign exchange swaps. In order to allow accurate pricing of these instruments in future, it is vital to review the actual cost of capital and the actual rates relative to Libor achieved on foreign exchange swaps. Credit losses are unlikely to happen regularly enough to submit to useful statistical analysis, but some of the assumptions going into the mathematical model which predicts credit losses could be checked by reviewing the positive mark-to-market exposures on deals over their life in a systematic way. Designing reports to enable analysis of the costs and exposures is not easy, but it is vital to check in retrospect whether you are correctly estimating them when you price deals, so that you can improve your future pricing.

A portfolio of cross currency transactions will contain mainly offsetting buy and sell positions; the starting point for marking cross currency transactions to market should therefore be the present value of cashflows using midmarket zero coupon rates converted to the currency of account of the organisation at the midmarket spot rate. From this present value it will be necessary to subtract allocations for the cost of credit and the cost of capital; these will be income to the credit area and the management account. It will also be necessary to subtract a holdback, as for single currency swaps. For short term foreign exchange swaps or outright forwards the holdback may be ignored as being immaterial, but for medium-term cross currency swaps and medium-term foreign exchange transactions there should be a substantial holdback to cover operations and hedging costs. Since the costs of capital, credit, and hedging will be different for different transactions, a sophisticated reporting mechanism will be required to capture the cost data and to calculate the holdback for each deal.

There is an alternative methodology for marking to market forward foreign exchange deals out to one year; this consists of marking to market each deal as a future cashflow using the midmarket forward rate for that currency to that date and then present valuing using the midmarket zero coupon rate. For example, if you sold £100 and bought US$160 4 months forward, and a month later the midmarket 3-month forward £/US$ rate is 1.75, then the forward valued mark to market of the deal is -US$15; if the 3-month scaling factor in US$ is 1.01, then the present valued mark to market is -US$15/1.1, which is -US$13.64. Interest rate parity should ensure that any difference between mark-to-market values under this methodology and under the methodology described above is small; a difference will correct itself by the time the deal comes into value.

In addition to the requirements discussed above, the management accounting system must be able to allocate income and expense correctly between different foreign exchange and interest rate dealers, so that a proper evaluation of dealer profitability and trading strategy may be made.

The management of multicurrency interest rate risk thus requires sophisticated reporting, which might prove not to be cost effective for less frequent participants in these markets. Therefore, the larger banks, which already have a liquidity advantage in these markets, should be able to afford a management information advantage also.

SUMMARY

This chapter has concluded the treatment of cross-currency interest rate risk by looking at three disparate subjects. An approach to the pricing of medium-term foreign exchange transactions is to look at the most effective way of synthesising zero coupon placings and takings to the required maturity in each currency. The spot exchange together with a placing and a taking synthesises the forward exchange transaction, and so, allowing for the cost of credit and capital, it is possible to establish arbitrage boundaries for the forward exchange rate. Macro hedging may allow reduction of the arbitrage limits for a particular transaction.

Establishing a statistical basis for quantifying multicurrency interest rate risk is complicated by portfolio effects. The yield curve model developed in Part I can cope with the risk within each currency; examining the correlations between currencies within the framework of this model can predict the overall interest rate risk from a multicurrency portfolio.

Management of multicurrency interest rate risk requires the equivalent of cash gaps reporting within each currency; this should be enhanced to predict an overall risk, taking into account correlations between rate movements in different currencies. In addition, there needs to be reporting of foreign exchange risk and Libor-Libor hedging, and the management accounting should be extended to split profitability between dealers and to provide a check for the pricing models.

Self-study questions

Unless otherwise stated, all interest is quoted on an annual basis, and each month should be considered to be an exact twelfth of a year.

6.1 If the XEU is quoted against the US$ at 0.8031/0.8035 by the direct quotation method, how would it be quoted by the inverted quotation method?

If you sold XEU1 million to a market maker for spot delivery, how many dollars would he give you in return?

6.2 A dealer quotes the DEM/US$ exchange rate by the direct quotation method as 1.8130/40. If you sell DEM1 million to a market maker, how many dollars will you receive?

6.3 The spot DEM/US$ exchange rate is 1.8130/40 and the 3-month forward points are 90/87. If you sell US$1 million to a market maker for delivery in 3 months, how many DEM will you receive?

6.4 The spot CHF/US$ rate quoted on the direct basis is 1.5320/30, and the 6-month forward points are 35/37. If you buy US$1 million for delivery in 6 months, how many CHF will you have to deliver?

6.5 The spot £/US$ rate is quoted on the inverted basis as 1.6500, and the 6-month Libors in the two currencies are 10% in sterling and 6% in dollars. Assuming that all bid-offer spreads are zero, what will the 6-month forward £/US$ rate be? If the rate were higher, demonstrate how you could make a profit through a riskfree arbitrage.

6.6 Suppose that the spot JPY/US$ exchange rate is 140.00/140.10, and 3-month Libor is 8% in JPY and 6% in US$; Libid is 0.125% below Libor. What 3-month forward bid-offer spread can be achieved synthetically, and what arbitrage restriction does this imply for the actual 3-month forward exchange rates?

6.7   The spot CHF/US$ rate is 1.4410/20, and the 6-month forward
      points are 52/54. You enter into a 0 v 6 foreign exchange swap
      with a market maker where you buy and sell the CHF; what spot
      and forward rates do you get?

      If the forward US$ amount is US$1 million, what saving do you
      make by using the forward swap rate rather than the outright
      forward rate?

6.8   You have BEF60,000,000 which you want to place on deposit
      for 3 months. Your bank offers you a deposit rate of 10%, which
      is the same as the 3-month sterling deposit rate. The spot BEF/£
      exchange rate is 59.9970/60.0000, quoted as BEF per £1, and
      the 3-month forward points are 10/15. How do you maximise
      the return on your money?

6.9   The following are today's foreign exchange rates:

      spot Swiss franc/dollar   1.4320/30
      3-month forward points   54/57
      6-month forward points   115/119

      Also, the 3 v 6 dollar FRA rate is 7.03%/7.07% and the 3v6
      Swiss franc FRA rate is 8.60%/8.70%.

      How would you create a synthetic CHF 3 v 6 FRA where you
      receive fixed? What effective rate would you obtain? How does
      this compare to the market CHF 3 v 6 rate? What additional
      risks do you run by entering into the synthetic FRA?

6.10 You enter into a transaction with your bank, which is equivalent
      to a back-to-back loan and deposit where both parties have the
      right of offset in the event of a default. You deposit £10,000,000
      with the bank from spot to 3 years, with the bank paying you
      interest at 11% annually. In return, the bank lends you
      US$17,000,000 from spot to 3 years, with you paying interest
      semiannually at 6-month Libor.

      Describe this transaction in the terminology of a cross currency
      swap:

      Effective date:

      Termination date:

      Initial exchange yes/no:

      Currency A:

      Currency B:

      Currency A payer:

      Currency A principal amount:

Currency A payment dates:

Currency A interest rate:

Currency B payer:

Currency B principal amount:

Currency B payment dates:

Currency B interest rate:

6.11 A bank dealer enters into a 5-year cross currency swap starting spot, where she pays interest semiannually on £10 million at 6-month Libor, and receives interest semiannually on US$16 million at 6-month dollar Libor plus 10bppa; there is an initial exchange of principals. Libors are set for the first period as 10.5% in £ and 6.3% in US$, and the spot exchange rate is 1.6000.

What is the dealer's interest rate risk? What is her foreign exchange risk? How should she hedge her risks?

6.12 The dealer has hedged the risks identified for the swap in question 6.11. The swap is now approaching its 6-month payment date, and the spot foreign exchange rate is 1.5000. Before Libor is fixed, what interest rate risk and what foreign exchange risk does the dealer have? When Libor is fixed, what risks does she have? How should she hedge these risks?

6.13 You enter into a cross currency swap with value spot and maturity 7 years, where you pay fixed interest at 11% annually on £10 million, and receive floating interest at 6-month Libor semiannually on US$16 million; the spot rate is 1.6000 and there is no initial exchange. Assuming that Libor has been set today for the first floating side period, what interest rate risks do you have? What foreign exchange risk do you have? How can you hedge these risks?

6.14 A Belgian chocolate company can issue 5-year BEF bonds at par to domestic retail investors at 10% annual interest. The company would have to pay the relatively high rate of 8% annually to borrow dollars, since there is no domestic retail demand for dollar assets and the company is not well known abroad. The market rate for a 5-year BEF single currency interest rate swap is 9.8% for annual interest, and the corresponding US$ swap rate is 7.5%.

A bank advises the company that its costs for credit, capital, administration, and hedging on a 5-year BEF/US$ cross currency swap would be 20 bppa paid annually on the US$ interest rate. Given reasonable assumptions, what would the equivalent cost be in bppa on the BEF rate?

If the bank paid 20 bppa above the BEF market rate on a cross currency swap, approximately how many bppa would it want to receive above the US$ swap rate in return?

How can the company raise funds most cheaply to finance a 5-year investment abroad which will be repaid out of US$ income?

What disadvantages does the cheaper funding have?

6.15 You enter into a 3-year forward foreign exchange deal with a bank where you sell DEM and buy US$. Describe this deal in the terminology of a cross currency swap:

Effective date:

Termination date:

Initial exchange yes/no:

Currency A:

Currency B:

Currency A payer:

Currency A payment dates:

Currency A interest fixed/floating:

Currency B payer:

Currency B payment dates:

Currency B interest fixed/floating:

6.16 You sell 3 years forward DEM16,000,000 and buy US$10,000,000. What types of risk do you have? If DEM interest rates increase do you make a profit or a loss? If the spot DEM/US$ exchange rate increases from 1.80 to 1.81, do you make a profit or a loss? Are DEM interest rates higher or lower than US$ interest rates?

6.17 DEM interest rates are:

| 1-year | Libid 8.875% | Libor 9% |
| 2-year swap with annual payments | | 9.30%/9.37% |

US$ interest rates are:

| 1-year | Libid 6.375% | Libor 6.5% |
| 2-year swap with annual payment | | 7.30%/7.37% |

The spot exchange rate is 1.7990/1.8000.

At what rate can you construct a synthetic 2-year forward transaction where you buy DEM and sell US$? What should you consider in comparing the rate achievable synthetically with the outright forward foreign exchange rate quoted by a dealer?

6.18 A bank dealer enters into a cross currency swap where he pays Libor in DEM and receives Libor plus 15 bppa in US$. He estimates that his Libor-Libor hedge cost will be 6 bppa, and that the credit, capital, and administration costs will be 7 bppa.

The bank marks its cross currency swaps to market at the present value of their future cashflows; administration costs are charged as they are accrued, credit losses are charged when they happen, and each operating unit is charged 14% of the regulatory capital needed to support its outstanding deals each year.

What will be the recorded value of this swap immediately after the initial exchange of principals, if the spot rate is still the ratio of the swap principals? What is the true profit in bppa? By how much is the bank overstating its profits?

If the bank's cross currency swap portfolio grows for 3 years and then stabilises, what do you think will happen to the recorded profitability of the portfolio?

PART VII

MANAGING INTEREST RATE RISK

The ultimate goal of Part VII is to show how the interest rate risk management process can be integrated into the running of an organisation. The key features of such an integration are the setting of objectives and the implementation of controls.

In order to reach this point it is necessary to review and consolidate the reporting of risk identified throughout the book. Part I developed the discrete cash gaps methodology for defining and reporting interest rate risk; Part VII builds on this to show how *convexity* can be incorporated explicitly into cash gaps reporting, and how different methodologies based on cash gaps may be appropriate for particular organisations. The other types of risk reporting identified as necessary throughout the book are also summarised.

Note that the discussion of controls focuses on market and credit risk; this book does not cover the operational control structure which must be imposed over the life of each deal.

CHAPTER 18

Reporting and managing risk

Throughout this book the development of each instrument has covered reporting within the discrete cash gaps methodology developed in Part I; this has tended to concentrate on the micro hedging of individual risk positions. This chapter takes discrete cash gaps as a starting point, and examines how interest rate risk should best be measured and reported to enable management, hedging, and controlled risk taking for a portfolio of positions or for an entire organisation; here the viewpoint is of macro hedging.

The choice of zero coupon curves determines the present values used in the calculation of risk; the chapter therefore begins with a discussion of how best to obtain a representative market zero coupon curve. It is then shown how the reporting of discrete cash gaps can be enhanced to give explicit information on *convexity*. Based on discrete cash gaps two other methodologies for measuring interest rate risk are then defined: *maturity bucket cash gaps* and *funding gaps*. The circumstances in which each of these is appropriate are discussed; this involves a consideration of *asset-liability management* and an examination of the different sources of interest rate risk, which can be classified into financial contracts, operating cashflows, and *economic risk*. As well as the risk measured by cash gaps, the various other types of risk identified throughout the book are summarised.

The final section of the chapter looks at integrating the management of interest rate risk within the running of an organisation. As in any other management process this involves setting objectives, imposing a control structure, and reviewing performance. Considerations of space prevent a detailed treatment of such a complex subject; therefore, the focus is on identifying key issues and on presenting a framework for you to use in analysing your own requirements.

18.1 MEASURING RISK – CHOOSING A YIELD CURVE

Part I showed that the measurement and management of interest rate risk depended on establishing the market zero coupon curve; this section will discuss this process in more detail. Part IV dealt with the riskfree yield curve, and consequently only the interbank curve is covered here.

It is possible to record bid and offer yield curves. However, as discussed previously, for a portfolio of transactions most pay positions will be offset by receive positions, and thus there will be very little net error in using the midmarket zero coupon curve to calculate the scaling factors for establishing the net present value of future cashflows. For instruments with material future operational or hedging costs, holdbacks should be subtracted from the present value to give the market value of the portfolio. It is worth noting that for very illiquid instruments, particularly in minor currencies, there is an argument for subtracting a further holdback to represent the potential cost of closing down the net position of the portfolio.

In order to ensure that a swap at the current midmarket rate has zero present value on its fixed and floating legs, it is necessary to use Libor rates to construct the midmarket zero coupon curve out to 1 year and midmarket swap rates thereafter. The use of Libor out to 1 year is consistent with Libor being a bank's marginal cost of funding.

Since the sensitivities for a portfolio consist of the change in market value for a small change in the zero curve, it is appropriate to use the midmarket zero coupon curve in risk management also. In the calculation of sensitivities the change in holdbacks will generally be immaterial, so that it is possible to compare present values directly.

The market yield curve used in Part I had ten points, which were 1 year Libor and the 2 to 10 year swap rates; we can aim to construct a yield curve which reflects market rates in finer detail, particularly in the shorter maturities.

At the very short end of the yield curve there is no alternative to on-balance-sheet instruments; since the market in interbank placings is extremely liquid in short maturities it makes sense to use Libor to define the yield curve out to, say, 6 months. Appropriate rates might be, for example, overnight, 1 week, 1 month, 2 months, 3 months and 6 months, giving six points on the curve.

From 2 years to 10 years, swaps tend to be the most liquid instrument, and therefore it is sensible to continue to use swap rates for that part of the curve; swap brokers normally quote rates for 2, 3, 4, 5, 7, and 10 years[1], and so these six points can be used to define the curve over this maturity range.

Between 3 months and 2 years it is possible to improve on the bid-offer spread of interbank placings by constructing synthetic placings from short-term placings and FRAs. For example, if 3-month placing rates are 8%/8.125% and the 3 v 6 FRA rate is 7.5%/7.55%, then the rate which you can lock in for a 6-month placing is 7.825%/7.914%. To see this, consider the scaling factors defined by the two instruments. On the bid side, the scaling factor for the first 3 months is 1.02, and for the second

---

[1] In some currencies swaps will not be quoted as far out as 10 years. This does not affect the principle of the discussion.

3 months it is 1.01875; multiplying these gives a 6-month scaling factor of 1.039125 which corresponds to an interest rate of 7.825%. The offer side is calculated similarly. The bid-offer spread of 8.9 basis points is less than the placing bid-offer spread of 12.5 basis points, and therefore the synthetic placing is a more liquid instrument. However, if the 6-month zero coupon rate is not based on 6-month Libor, then a swap floating leg which has just been set at 6-month Libor will have a non-zero present value. For this reason, it might be appropriate to use synthetic placings to define the zero rate only beyond 6 months, say, in maturities of 9, 12, 15, and 18 months, to give an additional four points on the yield curve.

It will be assumed that the yield curve is constructed from the sixteen points defined above. Note that this is not necessarily the best way to construct the curve in any particular currency; for example, it might be better to use Libor all the way out to 1 year, to create an extra point at 21 months, or to use rates derived from futures instead of from FRAs.

Where rates derived from futures contracts are used you should remember that the underlying period of a Eurodeposit future is 3 months, even though successive futures are not exactly 3 months apart. For example, if the June future has underlying dates 22 June to 22 September, the September future may have underlying dates 21 September to 21 December. This means that the futures prices do not translate into an exact strip. This contrasts with the way that FRA rates for, say, 3 v 6, 6 v 9, and 9 v 12 FRAs form an exact strip which can be combined with 3-month Libor to give 6-, 9-, and 12-month zero coupon rates. The futures prices therefore need further adjustment before they can be used in place of FRA rates in generating the zero coupon curve.

Because of the convergence of rates of different instruments due to the possibility of arbitrage, it is possible that provided you use extra points on the yield curve out to 2 years the exact details of the points may be relatively unimportant. The main effect may be to alter slightly the mark-to-market value of the portfolio; this will cause a timing difference in income recognition which will be rectified when the deals in the portfolio come into value.

Now that we have our market yield curve, how do we calculate the zero coupon curve? For the placings and synthetic placings out to 18 months the calculation follows straightforwardly from the results of Part I for converting deposit interest rates into zero coupon rates.

For the rates from 2 years to 10 years, the calculation is more involved. First we have to interpolate the par yield curve to obtain 6-, 8-, and 9-year swap rates; the market convention is to use straight line interpolation. If the swaps are quoted on the basis of annual payments on the fixed side, then you can calculate the zero rates using the formula derived in Part I, remembering first to convert the day basis if necessary. If they are quoted on a semiannual basis, it will be necessary to interpolate the yield curve again to produce swap rates for $2\frac{1}{2}$, $3\frac{1}{2}$, ..., $9\frac{1}{2}$ years, and to use the semiannual equivalent of the formula. If they are quoted on a quarterly basis, it will be necessary to interpolate swap rates for every quarter out to

10 years and to apply the corresponding formula. The good news is that once all of this is set up on a computer it can run automatically.

18.2 CONVEXITY

The discrete cash gaps methodology derived in Part I involved reporting the sensitivities of portfolio value to a parallel shift in the zero curve of, say, 1 bppa, and to rotations of the overnight and 10-year rates around the 1-year rate of the same amount. The logic was that the change in present value for, say, a 14 bppa parallel shift would be about 14 times the change for a 1 bppa shift. As was pointed out in that derivation, an improvement in predicting the sensitivity for larger shifts could be obtained by reporting *convexity* along with the 1 bppa sensitivities. This section will define convexity and will show how calculating and reporting it can improve the accuracy of the methodology. Although the underlying concept being considered is the same as in Appendix D, it should be noted that in that appendix, to conform with the practice of the bond market, convexity is reported in artificial units of time; here convexity will be recorded in a natural way as a cash sensitivity.

The basic idea is as follows. If the sensitivity of portfolio present value is, say, £10 for a rotation of the 10-year zero rate about the 1-year rate of 1 bppa, then the assumption of Part I was that a graph of present value against the size of the rotation would look like the straight line in Figure 18.1.

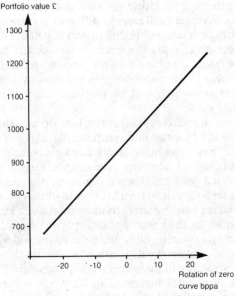

Figure 18.1 Portfolio value against 1-10 year rotation of zero coupon curve under linearity assumption of Part I.

However, it turns out that the graph of value against rotation will be a curved line, represented by one of the two dotted lines in Figure 18.2. Convexity is a measure of how curved the dotted line is, that is, how quickly it deviates from the straight line; the higher the convexity, the faster the deviation, and the poorer the assumption of linearity of Part I. Where the dotted line is above the straight line the convexity is positive, and where it is below the convexity is negative. As shown below, the use of convexity gives a formula with two variables which can better approximate the dotted line of value against movement in the zero curve.

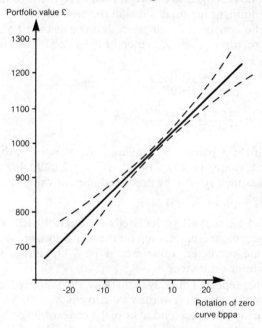

Figure 18.2   Actual portfolio value against 1–10 year rotation of zero curve. Portfolio value will follow one of the dotted lines.

The analysis of convexity below uses a parallel level shift, but the equivalent analysis would hold for either of the rotations. The starting point is to use elementary calculus to express the present value (PV) of a portfolio using a Taylor expansion as:

$$PV = K_0 + (K_1 * delta) + (0.5 * K_2 * delta^2)$$
$$+ \text{ terms in } delta^3 \text{ and higher powers}$$

Equation 18.1

where K_0 =   Value of PV at original position of zero curve

K_1 = $\dfrac{dPV}{dZ}$

K_2 = $\dfrac{d^2PV}{dZ^2}$

delta   =   parallel shift in zero curve

For very small parallel shifts, the value of PV will be close to K_0 plus the term $(K_1 * \text{delta})$; this is the linearity assumption of Part I, with K_1 being the sensitivity calculated there. For larger shifts the term in K_2 will become significant; K_2 is a measure of the non-linearity of the dependence of PV on the level of the zero curve, and convexity is defined here as the value of K_2. By reporting sensitivity and convexity it is possible to use Equation 18.1 to predict more accurately the effect of parallel shifts in the zero curve on the present value. This will be particularly important when the portfolio is hedged so that K_1 is close to zero; the term in K_2 may then become dominant for small shifts in the zero curve.

If the portfolio consists of a single cashflow c at time t and the zero coupon rate to time t is Z_t, then PV is $c/(1+(Z_t/100))^t$, and, differentiating,

$$K_1 = \frac{dPV}{dZ_t} = \frac{-tc/100}{(1 + (Z_t/100))^{t+1}} \qquad \text{and}$$

$$K_2 = \frac{d^2PV}{dZ_t^2} = \frac{t(t+1)c/10,000}{(1 + (Z_t/100))^{t+2}}$$

For example, if t is 3 years, c is 1 million, and Z_t is 10%, then K_0, the current present value, is 751,314.80, K_1 is -20,490.40, and K_2 is 745.11. If Z_t becomes 10.6% the predicted present value is:

$$K_0 + (K_1 * 0.6) + (0.5 * K_2 * 0.6^2),$$

which is 739,154.68; the value calculated directly is 739,153.47. It can be seen that the agreement is close, even for the relatively large shift; without the K_2 term the predicted value would be 739,020.56, which is a substantially poorer estimate.

If K_1 and K_2 are reported directly in this way, then the predicted change in present value for a 1% shift in the zero curve is $K_1 + (0.5 * K_2)$. Since daily changes in interest rates tend to be of the order of single basis points, it may be more natural to report K_1' and K_2', multiples of K_1 and K_2, so that the predicted change for a 1 bppa shift is $K_1' + (0.5 * K_2')$. This can be achieved by setting:

$$K_1' = K_1/100 \qquad \text{and}$$
$$K_2' = K_2/10,000.$$

For the example above, K_1' is -204.9040 and K_2' is 0.074511; the predicted present value for a 60 bppa shift in Z_t is:
$K_0 + (K_1' * 60) + (0.5 * K_2' * 60^2)$, which again equals 739,154.68.

Note that for a rotation the change in Z_t will be a fraction of the maximum movement of the rotation. For example, if the 1-10 year rotation is measured by a 10 bppa shift in the 10-year rate, then this will cause a 4.444 bppa shift in the 5-year rate. For this rotation and cashflow, K_1 should therefore be the first derivative times 0.4444 and K_2 should be the second derivative times 0.4444^2. The 6-month zero coupon rate will not change under a 1-10 year rotation, and therefore K_1 and K_2 for a 6-month cashflow should be zero.

If you are considering the cashflow equivalent of an option, then K_1 will be given by the formula above, but taking the second derivative of the option price will show that K_2 will have an extra term in $\frac{\partial N(x)}{\partial Z}$. If you wish to report convexity exactly for an option portfolio it would therefore be necessary to calculate a formula for the convexity of each type of option. If the delta hedge of an option portfolio is adjusted after small rate movements then the effect of the difference in convexity may not be material. Since there is a tradeoff between transaction costs and risk in adjusting the delta hedge frequently, it may be worthwhile carrying out an exercise to estimate the effect of convexity on your cost of delta hedging.

For a portfolio of cashflows, K_1 and K_2 are simply the sum of the sensitivities and convexities of the individual cashflows. Reporting the sensitivity and convexity for the portfolio for level risk and for both rotations allows dealers and management to calculate the effect of zero curve movements with greater accuracy.

18.3 MATURITY BUCKET CASH GAPS

Each instrument described in this book has been fitted into the discrete cash gaps methodology. For most organisations of any size, the number of cashflows arising from the business and from financial contracts is too great to allow reporting and management at such a detailed level, and so in order to make the reporting manageable it is necessary to consolidate all the cashflows within a series of *maturity buckets*. This means simply that all the gaps within a particular period are added to give a single net gap for that maturity. For example, if you are managing risk out to a horizon of 5 years, you might choose to have quarterly maturity buckets out to 2 years and then annual maturity buckets out to 5 years.

It would be possible simply to take the algebraic sum of all the cashflows in each maturity bucket to give one net cashflow, but it is more accurate to future value each cashflow to the midpoint of the bucket and then to take the sum. This means that it is possible to get an accurate measure of the present value, and a fairly accurate measure of the risk, by discounting the net cashflow in each bucket by the scaling factor to the midpoint of the bucket.

Setting up this reporting system for all the cashflows of an organisation would give a succinct report on a daily or intraday basis showing the zero curve, the cash gaps, the present value of the cash flows, and the three components of interest rate risk identified in Part I: level risk, 0-1 year rotation risk, and 1-10 year rotation risk. Exhibit 18.1 is a sample layout of such a report, using five annual maturity buckets.

Exhibit 18.1 Sample maturity bucket cash gaps report.

	Year 1	Year 2	Year 3	Year 4	Year 5	Total
Net cashflow	-100	-130	120	100	200	NA
Zero coupon	7.55	7.83	7.91	7.99	8.04	NA
Scaling factor	1.0371	1.1197	1.2096	1.3087	1.4162	NA
Present value	-96.43	-116.10	99.20	76.41	141.22	104.31
Sensitivities:						
Level	0.0448	0.1615	-0.2298	-0.2476	-0.5882	-0.8593
0-1 rotation	0.0224					0.0224
1-10 rotation		0.0090	-0.0383	-0.0688	-0.2287	-0.3268
Convexities:						
Level	-0.0001	-0.0004	0.0007	0.0010	0.0030	0.0042
0-1 rotation	0					0
1-10 rotation		0	0	0.0001	0.0005	0.0006
Actual changes for 10 bppa shift						
Level	0.0448	0.1614	-0.2295	-0.2471	-0.5867	-0.8571
0-1 rotation	0.0224					0.0224
1-10 rotation		0.0090	-0.0383	-0.0687	-0.2285	-0.3265

All cash amounts are US$ millions. Level risk is measured against a +10 basis point change in the zero curve. Rotation risks are measured against a +10 basis point change in the overnight or 10-year rate. The best estimate of the change in present value for a shift of delta in any risk is (sensitivity $*$ delta) + (0.5 $*$ convexity $*$ delta^2) where delta is measured in units of 10 bppa.

In Exhibit 18.1 the bottom eleven rows of the table are calculated from the top two rows on the assumption that all cashflows take place at the midpoint of the maturity bucket. In an operational environment, it would be more accurate to calculate the sensitivities and convexities for the individual cashflows within each maturity bucket and then sum them for reporting.

A key feature of this methodology is that it lets you calculate the sensitivity of your portfolio to *any* change in the yield curve, by discounting each cash gap at the new zero rate. It can thus answer 'what if' questions to help manage positions; this capacity will be enhanced if the report is automated in some way, for example by being downloaded to a spreadsheet.

Note that in practice you would want to use smaller maturity buckets, at least out to 2 years, in order to give greater accuracy to the sensitivity calculations.

If it is possible to produce a report such as this, then it will be an excellent tool for managing interest rate risk. Unfortunately, in practice a wide variety of organisations would find it difficult to collate the information for such a report; to see why, it is necessary to look at the problems of obtaining information on cashflows. Two types of organisation will be considered, corporations and banks.

In corporations, future cashflows come from two sources, from the business and from financial contracts. Financial contracts are relatively straightforward to predict, but even with these there can be difficulties, as discussed for banks below. A greater source of difficulty is the operational cashflow to be generated by the business. This will have two sources of uncertainty: first, cashflows may vary because of factors unconnected with interest rates, and secondly they may vary in a way which is correlated with interest rate changes. The second of these possibilities is known as economic risk and it will be examined in more detail in the next section.

Cashflows which are inherently uncertain can still be represented in the cash gaps methodology, but the appropriate discount rate to use in the present value calculation, and hence in the measurement of risk, may be greater than the interbank zero coupon rate. It will therefore be necessary to estimate a spread over the interbank zero curve for present valuing operational cashflows and to report these cashflows as a separate sheet in the cash gaps report. As well as agreeing on reporting, there needs to be a clear decision within an organisation as to how to manage the interest rate risk of operational cashflows.

The cashflows of banks are primarily from financial contracts, but even here the flows are not certain because of credit risks and because the cashflow equivalents of certain complex option products cannot be calculated analytically. However, to a good approximation, large classes of transactions, particularly government bonds, short-term interbank placings, medium-term off-balance-sheet contracts, and the bank's own debt, can be considered to be relatively free of credit risk, and can be managed accurately using the cash gaps methodology. Loans and other direct extensions of credit, however, involve a systematic risk which requires a higher zero coupon rate for discounting. A bank will also have uncertain future fee income and uncertain expenses, and it will therefore not be possible to manage its risk with total accuracy. Moreover, it is a difficult task to produce the cash gaps information for the many possible types of contract and commitment, and the cost of producing the cash gaps for all products may prove prohibitive, especially for smaller banks.

These difficulties do not invalidate the cash gaps methodology; rather they indicate that it should be restricted to areas where the cashflows are reasonably predictable. For example, this could be the risk management portfolio of a bank, or the debt portfolio of a corporation, or the micro-hedging of a particular risk position. For other applications a methodology which is more approximate but easier to apply may prove more useful. Funding gaps provides such a methodology, but before we can examine it we need two further sections. Section 18.4 deals with economic risk, and section 18.5 will set the scene for funding gaps by introducing the concept of asset-liability management.

18.4 ECONOMIC RISK

Economic risk exists where the future operating profits of a company will vary when interest rates vary; this is in distinction to *transaction risk*, where the value of a company changes with changing interest rates because the present value of fixed future cashflows changes. For example, a housebuilding company may see demand for houses decrease when interest rates rise, and this will result in reduced operating profits. Similarly, a manufacturer of engineering components may discover that when interest rates increase its customers take longer to pay it; this will increase its working capital requirement and consequently increase its funding cost.

It is often difficult or impossible to quantify accurately such economic risk. Examination of historic data may give an approximate value for the expected movement in a particular variable (such as house prices or days credit taken) for a given movement in interest rates, and then a calculation based on the company's budget can give the effect on net cashflows. It should be emphasised that there are often difficulties in obtaining an estimate for the expected movement in the chosen variable; such difficulties can include obtaining the data and isolating the effect of interest rate changes. It would be inappropriate to go into this process here, and so in the example of economic risk given below the expected movement in prices for a movement in interest rates is assumed to be given.

The example is based on the housebuilding company mentioned above. Interest rates are currently 10%, and every 1% increase in interest rates causes a 2% drop in house prices. Suppose the company's annual budget, in £ millions, is:

Sales	200
Cost of sales	150
Operating profit	50
Interest	20
Net profit	30

Then if interest rates increase by 1%, sales will decrease by 2% and the interest charge, assuming that there is no hedging in place, will increase by 1% over 10%, giving revised figures:

Sales	196
Cost of sales	150
Operating profit	46
Interest	22
Net profit	24

The economic risk is the change in the operating profit of £4 million for a 1% change in interest levels. (The change in the net profit of £6 million includes a £2 million extra cost on the floating rate debt.) Note that this risk is calculated as a single year's loss, rather than as a present value of the total future effect; given the imprecision of measurement, it is necessary to make some such approximation.

Since the aim of the cash gaps methodology is to calculate risk, it is somewhat perverse to take a risk which we have already calculated and represent it as a cash gap. It makes more sense to present a cash gaps report looking something like this:

Exhibit 18.2 Maturity bucket cash gaps plus economic risk reporting.

Quarter	One	Two	Three	Four	Total
Cashflow	100	-200	300	-500	
1% level risk	-0.25	0.48	-0.71	1.15	0.67
Economic risk					-4.0
Total level risk					-3.33

All cash amounts are in £ millions. Level risk is measured against a +1% change in the zero curve.

This type of hybrid methodology for representing risk will be the basis for the method recommended in section 18.7 below.

If it is required to represent the economic risk within the cash gaps methodology, then it is necessary to work out what amount in which maturity bucket would have a sensitivity of £4 million for a 1% parallel shift in the yield curve. Alternatively we can ignore second order effects and find the cashflows with sensitivity £400,000 for a 0.1% parallel shift; this will match previous calculations of risk and will not involve unreasonable approximations. Suppose we are working with quarterly maturity buckets. Rather than be over sophisticated, we can decide to represent the economic risk by the same sum in each bucket. (An alternative might be to put a sum with the same present value in each bucket.) Suppose we put £10 in each bucket. The total level risk is calculated as:

Quarter	One	Two	Three	Four	Total
Cashflow	10	10	10	10	
PV at 10%	9.8816	9.6489	9.4217	9.1999	
PV at 10.1%	9.8804	9.6456	9.4164	9.1926	
Level risk	-0.0012	-0.0033	-0.0053	-0.0073	-0.0171

If a cashflow of £10 in each quarter has a risk of -£0.0171, then to obtain a risk of -£400,000 requires a cashflow in each quarter of (400,000/0.0171) times £10. This equals a cashflow of £234 million in each quarter.

It can be seen that the implied cashflow from this economic risk will dwarf the real cashflows generated by the business. Because of the size of the economic risk and the imprecision in measuring it, it would not be possible to hedge the overall risk of this company to any accuracy. Luckily, there are often valid reasons for *not* hedging economic risk. This would primarily be the case for quoted companies within a defined industry sector where the risk is recognised across the sector; investors in the sector would be aware of the economic risk and would hedge or not hedge depending on their own needs, and therefore companies within the sector should not hedge the risk themselves. This argument would not apply to companies which were in danger of being in financial distress if economic risk crystallised; such companies might be well advised to hedge economic risk to minimise the danger of their being put out of business. It might also not apply to privately owned companies where the owners could not diversify their risk. For a fuller discussion of this issue see the sources listed in the bibliography.

18.5 ASSET-LIABILITY MANAGEMENT

Cash gaps give theoretically correct results, but, as discussed above, in some circumstances the cashflow information is expensive or cannot be obtained with accuracy. If there is another methodology which is easier to apply, even it is less accurate, then it may prove useful in some applications of risk management. In order to describe such a methodology, it is necessary to explain the concept of asset-liability management.

Consider a bank which engages in only two activities: it takes deposits and makes loans. (For a bank, deposits are the main liability and loans the main asset.) For simplicity, assume that all loans and deposits pay fixed interest annually and that there are no credit risks, capital requirements, or bid-offer spreads. If the bank always takes deposits (borrows) and lends to the same maturity then it will have no interest rate risk, since all future cashflows will net to zero. What happens if it borrows in a shorter maturity than it lends? If the bank lends £100 for 4 years and borrows £100 for 2 years and the yield curve is flat at 10%, then the net cashflows, present value, and level risk will look something like this:

	Cashflow	PV at 10%	PV at 10.1%	Level risk
Year 1	0	0	0	
Year 2	-100	-82.64	-82.49	
Year 3	10	7.51	7.49	
Year 4	110	75.13	74.86	
Total		0.00	-0.14	-0.14

Although the bank is borrowing and lending the same sum it still has interest rate risk because of the different maturities involved; this mismatch can be represented as follows:

Year 1	0
Year 2	0
Year 3	-100
Year 4	-100

This table shows that the bank will be short funded in years 3 and 4 by £100, and so it will have to borrow £100 at the start of year 3 at the then prevailing interest rate. If that rate goes up to 10.1% then the bank will be borrowing at 0.1% more than it is lending, giving a net cashflow for these 2 years of:

Year 3   -0.10
Year 4   -0.10

Present valuing each of these cashflows again gives a total of -0.14. We can thus interpret the level risk shown by the cash gaps methodology as being the *funding risk* when assets and liabilities have different maturities. If instead the bank has more deposits than loans then it will have to reinvest its extra funds at future rates. This gives *reinvestment risk* which is the mirror image of funding risk; the two terms will be used interchangeably below.

Asset-liability management is the process of identifying, measuring, and managing funding risk. It will also involve issues such as cash and liquidity management, but these are outside the scope of this book and will not be discussed further here.

Historically, asset-liability management was first recognised as necessary by banks, but now other organisations with potential maturity mismatches between their funding (liabilities) and their investments (assets) also carry out asset-liability management. The theoretically correct way to manage the mismatch risk is through cash gaps. However, this methodology may have the disadvantage of being difficult to apply and difficult to explain to senior management. Also, for organisations accounting on an *accrual basis*, that is, recognising interest income in a period as net interest received plus the net change in accrued interest, there may be a desire to maximise accrual earnings rather than maximise the present value of the organisation.

The analysis above suggests that in such cases a funding risk methodology for analysing the risk of a portfolio of assets and liabilities could prove more suitable than the cash gaps methodology. We simply construct a table showing the net long or short funding in each year, work out the funding risk in each year for a 10 basis point parallel shift in the zero curve, and present value that risk to give the net present value funding risk corresponding to level risk. A similar process will give the funding risk corresponding to rotation risk. Note that in this methodology any floating loan or deposit should be considered to have maturity of its next repricing date, since the rates in the following periods will be sensitive to future rate changes.

These calculations are shown below for a bank which borrows £100 at 1-year Libor for several years and £200 at a fixed rate for 5 years, and lends £300 at a fixed rate for 3 years.

		<-- - - - - - - - - Cost of funding - - - - - - - - ->		
		<-- 10 bp level shift -->	<--- 10 bp rotation --->	
	Long/short	FValue PValue	FValue PValue	
Year 1	0	0 0	0 0	
Year 2	-100	-0.1 -0.08264	-0.0222 -0.01835	
Year 3	-100	-0.1 -0.07513	-0.0444 -0.03336	
Year 4	200	0.2 0.13660	0.0889 0.09111	
Year 5	200	0.2 0.12418	0.1667 0.11040	
		0.10301	0.14980	

The long/short column shows the net funding position in each year. The next two columns show the future and present values of the reinvestment cost or income in each year for a parallel shift in the yield curve of plus 10 basis points. The last two columns show the corresponding future and present values for a rotation of the 1-10 year yield curve generated by a plus 10 basis point shift in the 10-year rate. A rotation of the yield curve causes a proportionately larger change in the forward 1-year rates used to calculate the reinvestment cost or income; this is explained as follows.

In calculating the level risk, a 10 basis point shift in the yield curve will imply almost exactly a 10 basis point change in the 1-year rate in 1 year's time or in 2, 3, or 4 years' time. However, a rotation which causes, for example, an increase of 2.222 basis points in the 3-year rate, implies a larger increase in the 1-year rate in 2 years' time. To see this, recall from Part I that the forward scaling factor for a period is the ratio of the scaling factor to the end of the period to the scaling factor at the beginning. Applying this here for a +10 bppa rotation of the 10-year zero coupon rate relative to the 1-year rate gives:

	Interest	Scaling factor	Implied 1-year scaling factor	Implied 1-year Libor
Year 1	10	1.1		
Year 2	10.0111	1.210244	1.100222	10.0222
Year 3	10.0222	1.331807	1.100444	10.0444
Year 4	10.0333	1.465875	1.100667	10.0667
Year 5	10.0444	1.613766	1.100889	10.0889

For example, the implied 1-year rate 1 year forward is 10.0222%, and so the reinvestment cost in year 2 is 2.22 basis points of -100, which equals -0.0222 as a future value. All the entries in the fourth column of the funding requirements table are calculated in the same way.

If you use discrete cash gaps to work out the level and 1-10 year rotation risks, you should obtain close to the same values, namely 0.1029 and 0.1497. In order to get such exact agreement it is necessary to take a smaller sensitivity shift in the cash gaps calculation;

this minimises the effect of convexity. Try the calculation yourself before looking at the answer below.

DISCRETE CASH GAPS

Year	One	Two	Three	Four	Five
Cashflow	-100	10	310	-20	-220
Scaling factor	1.1000	1.2100	1.3310	1.4641	1.6105
Present value	-90.9191	8.2645	232.9075	-13.6603	-136.6021
1 bppa level shift					
Scaling factor	1.1001	1.2102	1.3314	1.4646	1.6112
Present value	-90.9008	8.2630	232.8440	-13.6553	-136.5400
Sensitivity	0.0083	-0.0015	-0.0635	0.0050	0.0621
Total sensitivity equals level risk			0.01029		
Level risk for 10 bppa shift			0.1029		
1 bppa 1-10 year rotation					
Interest rate	10	10.00111	10.00222	10.00333	10.00444
Scaling factor		1.21002	1.33108	1.46428	1.61084
Present value		8.2643	232.8934	-13.6586	-136.5745
Sensitivity		-0.0002	-0.0141	0.0017	0.0276
Total sensitivity equals rotation risk			0.01497		
Rotation risk for 10 bppa shift			0.1497		

It seems that we have found a replacement methodology which has all of the accuracy of discrete cash gaps and involves far less work. Unfortunately, the precise agreement between this methodology and cash gaps holds only when all assets and liabilities are on the same payment frequency and are at matching interest rates. This result is not proved here, but you can experiment to see the effect of changing the loan interest rate or frequency in the above example to convince yourself that this methodology loses accuracy in these circumstances.

Because of the lack of precision, it is probably not worthwhile to calculate convexity under the funding risk methodology; this is why the example above concentrated on the sensitivities for representative shifts in the zero curve.

Since asset-liability management generally involves a series of approximations about the future shape of the balance sheet, the imprecision of the funding risk methodology may be acceptable. The imprecision will be reduced if:

(a) All loans and deposits are booked at the prevailing market rate.

(b) All loans and deposits have regular interest payments with at least one payment per year.

(c)   Any loan or deposit with a more complex structure, such as a zero coupon loan, is analysed as the equivalent of a sum of par loans or deposits at the market rate prevailing at the original deal date.

(d)   There is no systematic difference between loans and deposits, such as, for example, all loans being on annual interest and all deposits being on quarterly interest.

(e)   Interest rates change reasonably slowly from year to year.

In order to determine the accuracy of the reinvestment risk methodology for a particular portfolio it is necessary to undertake a detailed analysis, possibly including a simulation of risk under different yield curves; the accuracy obtainable would then have to be compared with the needs of the organisation. It is most appropriate here to state baldly:

Assumption 18.1 The funding risk methodology gives reasonable accuracy for asset-liability management under normal circumstances.

As for interest rate risk management in general, an important part of asset-liability management is deciding on a hedging horizon beyond which risk will be ignored; this is covered further in section 18.7 below.

Asset-liability management is described above for a bank in terms of loans and deposits. For a pension fund the assets would be fixed investments, and the liabilities would be the commitment to pay pensions; the liabilities would have to be predicted on an actuarial basis. For a company, the assets would be projected income from the business, and the liabilities would be debt.

As a further example, consider a brewery which has budgeted net income of £20 million a year before interest charges, and budgeted net borrowing of £100 million per year; its hedging horizon is 5 years. All income is cash, and any net profits after interest will be paid out as dividends.

The assets of the brewery have no sensitivity to interest rate movements. Therefore, assuming that there is currently no fixed borrowing, the funding risk of the brewery can be represented as:

Year	1	2	3	4	5
Funding	-100	-100	-100	-100	-100
Floating borrowing	-100	-100	-100	-100	-100
Funding risk	1	1	1	1	1

(All figures in £ millions. Funding risk is for 1% shift in rates.)

Suppose now that it borrows £40 million at a rate fixed for 4 years. Its funding risk can now be represented as:

Year	1	2	3	4	5
Funding	-100	-100	-100	-100	-100
Fixed borrowing	40	40	40	40	0
Floating borrowing	-60	-60	-60	-60	-100
Funding risk	0.6	0.6	0.6	0.6	1

(All figures in £ millions. Funding risk is for 1% shift in rates.)

Such a report could include any combination of fixed loans. The next section explains the *funding gaps* methodology, which is an extension of funding risk to cover other instruments in addition to loans and deposits; this would allow the incorporation of FRAs, swaps, and other risk management instruments in the reporting here.

In this example the funding requirement is flat and the company's income is not sensitive to interest rates; in practice, the funding requirement could change from year to year especially if there are large differences between accounting income and cashflow, income could be proportional to cumulative inflation which could be correlated with interest rates, and there could be other economic risk. Nevertheless, the methodology here could clearly provide a useful report of interest rate risk even in more complex circumstances, and it could be a good starting point for decision making.

18.6 FUNDING GAPS

The funding gaps methodology extends funding risk in a natural way to deal with other instruments. As for cash gaps, funding gaps are used to define gaps for a series of maturity buckets which are then analysed to give a measure of interest rate risk. The process works as follows:

(a)   Express all financial instruments in terms of *placing equivalents*. A placing equivalent is defined by its principal, its value date, and its maturity. The conversion to placing equivalents is done in a natural way as follows:

Product	Principal	Value date	Maturity
Placing (Loan out)	Loan principal	Loan value date	Loan maturity
Taking (Loan in)	Minus loan principal	Loan value date	Loan maturity
FRA	If past value date then zero, otherwise contract amount; principal is plus if you sell an FRA and minus if you buy an FRA	FRA value date	FRA maturity

Product	Principal	Value date	Maturity
Eurodeposit future	Contract amount multiplied by scaling factor for underlying deposit; principal is plus if you buy future, minus if you sell future	Underlying deposit value date	Underlying deposit maturity
Bullet swap (single or cross currency)			
Fixed side	If receive fixed then plus notional principal; if pay fixed then minus notional principal	Swap value date	Swap maturity
Floating side	If pay floating then minus notional principal if receive floating then plus notional principal. If no floating rate has yet been fixed, then do not include any floating side	Value date of period where floating rate has been fixed	End date of period

Caps, floors, swaptions
As for the equivalent portfolio. A zero coupon placing or taking should be replaced by an equivalent set of par placings and takings with regular interest payments.

If the value date of any placing equivalent is before today, then replace it with today; if the maturity is before today then ignore that placing equivalent.

(b)   In each maturity bucket take the algebraic sum of all placing equivalents overlapping the bucket. If the overlap is not full, then multiply the principal by the fraction of the overlap.

For example, if we are taking annual gaps and we have the following placing equivalents:

Value	Maturity	Principal
Year 0	Year 2	100
Year 0.5	Year 2.5	-50
Year 1.5	Year 3.25	-30

then the interest rate gaps for annual maturity buckets are:

Year 1	75	(100 + (half of -50))
Year 2	35	(100 + (-50) + (half of -30))
Year 3	-55	((half of -50) + (-30))
Year 4	-7.5	(quarter of -30)

The sum of all the placing equivalents is referred to as the gap in each bucket.

(c)   Calculate the reinvestment risk for each bucket as the gap times the *period* of the bucket in years times the implied zero rate *shift* for each risk.

The shift for each risk is the implied movement in the rate for an FRA with value date equal to the start date of the bucket and maturity equal to the end date of the bucket under the yield curve shift used to measure the risk. For level risk, the shift will be very close to the parallel shift in the yield curve used to measure the risk; any difference can be made relatively smaller by taking a smaller level shift. As shown above, for rotation risk the shift will normally be different from the rotation shift in the yield curve at the maturity of the bucket.

(d)   Using the scaling factor to the end of each bucket, present value the reinvestment risks to get the total risk.

It should be clear that this process equates each financial contract to an equivalent placing or set of placings in a natural way, and thus the analysis of risk will work in the same way as for reinvestment risk. The other change from the funding risk methodology is to move from discrete cashflows to maturity buckets; again it should be clear that this will not affect the underlying calculation of risk.

This methodology can be simpler to implement than cash gaps, particularly for relatively unsophisticated organisations. However, if the organisation also has operating cashflows and economic risk, it is not necessarily appropriate to represent these in the funding gap methodology. The best route to reporting and managing risks from all three sources – financial contracts, operating cashflows, and economic risk – may be a hybrid methodology, incorporating elements from cash gaps and funding gaps. This is discussed in the next section.

18.7 SUMMARY OF REPORTING

This is a long chapter, and it would be useful to summarise the conclusions so far.

For an organisation there are three possible sources of interest rate risk:

● financial contracts (including debt);
● operating cashflows; and
● economic risk.

The most appropriate way to report and manage risk will depend on the organisation and the circumstances; a useful scheme might be:

Financial contracts   Report as maturity bucket cash gaps for a sophisticated organisation or as funding gaps for a less sophisticated organisation. If there are very few instruments involved it may be possible to report discrete cash gaps.

Operating cashflows   Report as maturity bucket cash gaps. To the extent
                         that cashflows incorporate systematic risk, the
                         Capital Assets Pricing Model shows that they
                         should be present valued using zero coupon rates
                         higher than the interbank zero curve. Since the
                         calculation of risk is relatively insensitive to the
                         absolute level of the zero curve, a reasonable
                         estimate of the correct zero curve should provide
                         at least an approximation to the risk.

Economic risk   Report   risks   directly   as   calculated.
                         Approximations may be required due to the
                         difficulty of obtaining good data.

An organisation aiming to maximise an accounting profit based on
accrual income, rather than to maximise the present value of its future
cashflows, might find it more appropriate to use funding gaps in place of
cash gaps. Similarly, an organisation trying to minimise its funding costs
on an accrual basis should consider the use of funding gaps on its debt
portfolio. However, in both these cases it is important to use some
method to measure the locked in mark-to-market gain or loss beyond the
current period.

In addition to interest rate risk measured by cash gaps or their
equivalent, various other types of risks and costs have been identified in
different places in the book; for ease of reference these are summarised
here.

Risk	*Chapter*
Short-term repricing risk	4
Basis risk of futures versus FRA	5
Basis risk of futures settlement versus Libor	5
Cost of capital	7
Credit risk and cost of credit	7
Spread risk	9
Basis risk in general	9
Basis risk of interest rate option pricing versus Black formula	13
Vega (Volatility risk)	14
Gamma (Second order interest rate risk on delta hedging)	14
Theta (Option time decay)	14
Foreign exchange risk	15
Delivery risk	15
Basis risk of future Libor-Libor hedging	15, 16
Cost of placings on Libor-Libor hedging	16
Cost of Libor-Libor hedging	17
Risk capital and positive mark-to-market value of swap portfolio	17
Effect of convexity on cost of delta hedging	18

You should consider the materiality of each risk within your organisation
before expending energy in managing it.

For all reporting, consideration should be given to the best means of delivering the information; decisions have to be made regarding format, frequency, and distribution, and there needs to be a strategy for choosing between printed reports and online enquiries. These points are expanded in the next section.

18.8 MANAGING INTEREST RATE RISK WITHIN AN ORGANISATION

All the tools necessary for managing interest rate risk are now assembled and it is possible to consider the management process itself.

Any management process consists of three activities; defining objectives, establishing a structure within which the objectives can be achieved, and periodically reviewing progress and adjusting the structure or objectives accordingly. Each of these activities is considered separately below. To prevent this section being inordinately long, the treatment is necessarily abbreviated; the intention is that the issues raised here should give you a coherent starting point for considering the management process in your own organisation.

18.8.1 Defining objectives

High-level objectives should be set at a high level in the organisation and low-level objectives should be set at a low level. In the context of interest rate risk management (IRRM), setting high-level objectives would include identifying:

(a) Is IRRM a cost or a profit-making activity?

(b) How should the cost or profit be measured?

(c) How should cost or profit targets be set?

(d) What risk is acceptable?

(e) Should IRRM be centralised in one organisational unit?

(f) What is the hedging horizon beyond which IRRM will be ignored?

(g) How should IRRM be integrated with cash and liquidity management?

(h) Should budgeted operational cashflows be considered for the purposes of IRRM?

For example, a bank might decide at board level as follows: all interest rate risk will be centralised in two organisational units, IRRM and Funding. Internal contracts at market rates will be used to transfer risk from other organisational units to IRRM and funding. IRRM is a profit centre, separate from the funding activities of the bank, with profitability being measured on a mark-to-market basis. The profit target is a return on capital employed of 15%, with minimum profit of £20 million this year. A loss of more than £4 million in any quarter would be unacceptable. Funding is a cost centre responsible for cash and liquidity management, with a target cost of funds of 3-month Libor minus 0.10% measured on an accrual basis.

As soon as you consider these objectives you can see that there is a need to clarify certain points. For example, will transfer pricing be at midmarket or at a bid or offer rate, how are complex options to be marked to market, how is marketing income on risk management products to be included, and how is any mark-to-market profit or loss on Funding's books at period end to be taken into account? Such issues will have to be resolved as part of the process of periodic review.

Lower level objectives should aim to translate the high level objectives into 'bite-sized chunks'. These could be set at the level of the manager of the responsible organisational unit (described below as a division) and could include such items as profit targets for individual dealers, maximum size of gaps in each currency, development of new products, and improvement of systems.

Such objectives will raise further questions, which again will have to be resolved through the review process.

18.8.2 Control structure

Control starts with an organisation chart defining clear responsibilities and reporting lines. Large organisations often create a central Asset and Liability Management Committee (ALMC), consisting of senior managers and reporting to the board, which is responsible for creating high-level policy and reviewing performance for interest rate risk management. Responsibilities could include approving aggregate position limits, authorising new products, setting credit policy, and agreeing accounting policies, as well as reviewing the overall risk of the organisation. (In addition, an ALMC would have responsibilities for policy on cash and liquidity management; these are not considered here.) A strong ALMC can be an effective control over the risk management function, especially where it has the expertise and independence to identify risks and to explain them at board level.

Assuming that a suitable organisational structure is in place, the controls necessary for IRRM can be split into:

(a)   Position reporting

(b)   Position limits

(c)   Credit limits

(d)   Management accounting

Position reporting has been discussed at great length in this chapter. It is important to decide which reports are needed to give dealers the information they need to run their positions, and which consolidated reports should be prepared (and on what frequency) for divisional management and for senior management. Reports should contain information understandable by and of use to the recipient and should highlight useful information and exceptions. (If this seems obvious, you might like to wander around your organisation looking at reports and asking people which reports they use out of those they receive.)

Position limits should be set by the manager of the IRRM division, based on an explicit authority from senior management; they should ensure that total risk is compatible with the objectives. Position limits could include, by currency, cash gaps, foreign exchange, volatility, short-term repricing, spreads, and basis risks. Ideally, limits should be expressed in a way which relates to trading activity; for example, cash gap limits could be expressed in terms of level and rotation risk. Where different dealers are involved in the same currency, limits should be split as appropriate. Position limits should be translated into expected risk, using the statistical analysis discussed in this book; this should give management a better idea of potential earnings and risk and should allow a more informed analysis of dealer performance. Remember that where liquidity is lacking, expected risk should be calculated for the time it will take to close out a position, rather than for the time it will take management to instruct the position to be closed.

Credit limits will generally be set outside the IRRM division. However, before any deal is done it is important to ensure that credit authorisation is in place; this will require an independent control structure. This should check before a deal is agreed that there is a credit line available for the counterparty and for the country of risk. The authorisation process should also check that each deal will have no adverse tax consequences, that it is of an authorised transaction type, that there is adequate legal documentation, and that there is regulatory compliance. For example, a bank might not enter into swaps with counterparties in a particular country because of problems with withholding tax, or it might not enter into any risk management transaction with a UK building society because of a fear that such a transaction might be ultra vires for the counterparty. The appropriate credit area should be informed as each deal is done, so that credit records can be kept up to date.

Management accounting should provide information for the review process. For example, it should show profits, risk, and capital employed for each trading portfolio. The management accounting must correctly identify the profit transfer effect of internal deals, either between dealer and dealer or between dealers and some other organisational unit. Where a portfolio of transactions has a surplus or deficit of cash, then interest on the cash should be imputed at current market rates as an income or cost, with the balancing posting going to the funding desk; this should also be done for unrealised mark-to-market gains and losses which are taken into income or expense. In addition, it is important to measure and record the sort of costing information discussed at various points in this book; for example, the actual average positive value of swaps should be compared with the predictions of the models used for calculating credit and capital costs, and for Libor-Libor hedging the actual rates obtained should be compared with the rates predicted. This should enable more accurate costing in future.

18.8.3 Periodic review

The aim of the review process is to confirm that limits and policies are being adhered to, to identify additional controls which are needed, to clarify objectives, and to identify where objectives require amendment. Resources should be focused on reviewing the most material costs and risks. Where appropriate, review functions should be carried out by organisational units independent of the divisional management responsible for IRRM.

The review process should include, but should not be confined to:

(a) Ensuring position and credit limits are adhered to.

(b) A comparison of trading profits and expenses to objectives.

(c) A reconciliation of management accounting to the financial accounts; this will prove that the management accounts provide a valid basis for decision making.

(d) A review of the basis of transfer pricing, either where one dealer deals with another or between a dealer and another organisational unit; this will prove that costs and income are being correctly allocated.

(e) Reviewing earnings for reasonableness and checking that management accounting is accurate.

(f) Reviewing position reports for reasonableness and checking their accuracy.

(g) Checking that all interest rate risk in the organisation has been identified and is being managed by the appropriate organisational unit.

(h) A review of profitability per dealer, with emphasis being placed on the ratio of profitability to risk and profitability to capital employed.

(i) A periodic review of particular risks; for example, the exposure to a major change in the market pricing of option risk.

(j) A periodic review of key assumptions; for example, if budgeted operational cashflows are included in cash gaps, are the cashflows known accurately enough to be useful and is the discount rate used to determine risk appropriate?

(k) A periodic review of the statistical analysis used to quantify risk.

(l) A periodic review of the size of holdbacks.

As part of the periodic review, consideration could also be given to reducing costs and improving performance; for example, consolidating the management of risk in one location for each currency, replacing printed reports by access to an online system, or integrating IRRM marketing with the marketing of other products.

As well as market and credit risk, the management process should also deal with operational risk; this is an important and extensive subject and it is beyond the scope of this book.

This section was chosen to complete the book since it contains the key ideas necessary for you to implement interest rate risk management successfully. Even if you disagree with some of the detail here, you should still consider using the basic framework outlined above to analyse the needs of your organisation.

Afterword

If you have read this far, you must be presumed to be keenly interested in the subject matter. Since you have now reached the end of the book, a reasonable question is: 'Where do you go from here?'

Interest rate risk management is a mature discipline; this means that you can use its techniques to reduce the risk run by your organisation, but it also implies that competitive pressure will prevent a bank from earning super profits simply by selling interest rate risk management products to its customers.

Your goal should be for your organisation to increase its earnings or decrease its costs and risks in risk management; the analysis of this book is that to achieve this you should implement the techniques developed therein and you should also consider:

- investigating the implications of portfolio theory in improving your management of risk.
- if relevant, keeping up to date with research on option pricing.
- reducing your cost base.
- controlling operational risk.
- identifying a business strategy for risk management.
- if you work for a bank, integrating the marketing of risk management products into your general marketing.

It is the hope of the author that this book will encourage you – and will give you some of the tools – to implement such a programme.

Self-study questions

Unless otherwise stated, all interest is quoted on an annual basis, and each month should be considered to be an exact fraction of a year.

7.1 Zero coupon rates are 9.9% to 1 year and 10.1% to 18 months. What is the implied 12 v 18 FRA rate? If you buy such an FRA with a contract amount of 10 million, how do you represent the risk in the discrete cash gaps methodology?

Since the FRA is at the market rate its value is zero. What is the sensitivity and convexity of its value for parallel shifts in the zero curve?

What predicted value does the sensitivity and convexity give for the zero curve moving up by 0.7%? What is the actual value?

7.2 You have the following cashflows and zero coupon yield curve:

Year	Cashflow	Zero coupon
1.1	100	9.3
1.2	-100	9.31
1.5	-90	9.34
1.9	100	9.36

You report risk using maturity bucket cash gaps. How should the above cashflows be represented in the 1-2 year maturity bucket?

What is the sum of the sensitivities of the cashflows to a rotation of the 1-10 year yield curve of 10 bppa in the 10-year rate? What would be the sensitivity predicted by assuming that you had the single cashflow of the 1-2 year gap?

7.3 A retailer has a budget for next year of:

Sales	500
Cost of sales	200
Fixed operating expenses	200
Operating profit	100
Interest	40
Net profit	60

The interest is all short-term interest on a mortgage of the shop premises; the outstanding mortgage is 400. The budget assumes that interest rates are unchanged.

Historically, if short-term interest rates go up 1%, the retailer would expect to see a 3% drop in turnover, with no other change in the cost structure.

If interest rates increase by 1%, what would the retailer's budget become? What is the transaction risk and what is the economic risk, assuming that a 1% up or down movement is to be expected.

What might the retailer do about these risks and what factors might affect the decision?

7.4   In constructing funding gaps, if today is 1 January 1992 and the zero coupon yield curve is flat at 8%, what are the placing equivalents of the following:

(a)   You place 100 from 1 February 1992 to 1 August 1992 at 10%

(b)   You place 100 from 1 February 1992 to 1 August 1992 at Libor.

(c)   You take 100 from 31 March 1991 to 31 March 1992.

(d)   You buy a Eurodeposit future with underlying principal 1,000,000 and underlying period 22 March 1992 to 22 June 1992.

(e)   You pay fixed annually and receive floating semiannually on a swap with a notional principal of 1,000, with value 1 January 1991 and maturity 1 January 1996; the floating side is set on 1 January 1992 at 7.85%.

(f)   You sell a 6 v 12 FRA with contract amount 200.

Using an exact day count, what is the funding gap in the second quarter of 1992?

7.5   A company has a total funding requirement of DEM120 million in 1993; this is budgeted to increase by DEM3 million for each of the following 4 years. It has issued a fixed interest bullet bond for DEM60 million which matures on 30 June 1996. The balance of its funding comes from short-term borrowing based on Libor. It has also entered into a single currency swap maturing 31 December 1995 on which it pays fixed annually and receives Libor semiannually on a notional principal of DEM30 million.

The company's net income after dividends is budgeted to be just sufficient to pay its interest costs at current rates; income is not sensitive to the level of interest rates. Tax can be ignored.

Today is 31 December 1992 and the DEM yield curve is flat at about 8%. Use the funding gap methodology with annual buckets from 1993 to 1997 to estimate the future effect on the funding cost of the company for a 1% parallel shift in the zero curve. If all funding costs are at year end, what is the present value of the incremental funding cost of a 1% shift in the zero curve?

Answers to self-study questions

PART I

1.1 (1.09 - 1) * 100, which equals 9%.

 1.09^3, which equals 1.29503.

 $1.09^{1/4}$, which equals 1.02178.

1.2 $(1.15^{1/2} - 1) * 100$, which is 7.2381%.

1.3 $(1 + (6/100))^{1.5}$, which equals 1.09134.

1.4 $-£10/1.08^{2.5}$, which is $-£8.2497$.

Year 0	$-£10$
Year 1	$+£18.5185$
Year 1.5	$-£26.7292$
Year 2	$+£21.4335$
Total	$+£3.2228$

 The future value is the present value times $1.08^{1/4}$, which equals £3.2854.

1.5 The principal repayment will be the same on the quarterly and annual bond, and the pattern of interest payments will repeat itself annually. Therefore, it is necessary to consider only the first year in equating rates.

 The present value of the 10% interest at the end of the first year is 10%/1.07, which equals 9.34579%.

 If the answer is $4x\%$, then interest of $x\%$ will be paid quarterly; the present value of $x\%$ quarterly can be calculated as:

 Q1 $(x\%/1.07^{0.25})$ +
 Q2 $(x\%/1.07^{0.50})$ +
 Q3 $(x\%/1.07^{0.75})$ +
 Q4 $(x\%/1.07^{1})$

 which equals $x\%$ times 3.83507.

The present value is x times the present value of 4% annual interest paid quarterly. The 4% interest flow can be calculated using the HP12c calculator, setting:

n	4
i	1.70585
PMT	1
FV	0

Press PV to get the value -3.83507, so that the present value is again x% times 3.83507.

Note that i is set to the deposit interest for a 3-month period, which can be calculated from the annualised scaling factor of 1.07 as $(1.07^{0.25}- 1) * 100 = 1.70585$.

By either of the methods above, x% is 9.34579 over 3.83507, which equals 2.43693%, and the annual interest rate is 4 times this, which equals 9.74772%.

1.6   Over a period of 360 days the interest is exactly 10%. If the interest rate on an actual/365 basis is i%, then we have that 10% is i% $* 360/365$, so that i% equals 10% $* (365/360)$, which is 10.139%

1.7   Call the equivalent interest rate on an actual/360 basis i%. A calendar year of 365 days corresponds to 360 days for bond basis. Thus over a year the bond basis interest will be 5% $* (360/360)$ which is exactly 5%. This gives that 5% equals i% $* (365/360)$, so that i% equals 5% $* (360/365)$, which is 4.931507%. You can check that 4.931507% times (365/360) equals 5%. The equivalence is approximate because the ratio of days in a period in the two bases will vary slightly, depending on the exact dates of the period.

The period has 186 days, but for the bond basis it has 182 days. Therefore the bond basis interest is 5% $* (182/360)$, which equals 2.527778%. If the interest rate on an actual/360 basis is i%, then 2.527778% = i% $* (186/360)$, so that
i% = 2.527778% $* (360/186)$, which is 4.892474%

1.8   The 1-year par rate for an annual bond is 10%. Consequently, the par yield curve slopes down; the zero coupon curve will therefore slope down more steeply, so that the 2-year zero coupon rate will be below the 2-year par rate of 9.8%.

We know that the present value of the cashflows of the 2-year par bond is 100%. Therefore, if s is the 2-year scaling factor, $(9.8\%/1.1) + (109.8\%/s) = 100\%$, giving
s = 109.8%/(100% - 8.909091%), which equals 1.205389. The zero coupon rate is $(s^{1/2} - 1) * 100$, which equals 9.7902%.

The estimate of the 21-month zero coupon rate can be obtained by linear interpolation of the 1- and 2-year rates as $((3 * 9.7902\%) + (1 * 10\%))/4 = 9.8427\%$.

(There are other possible approaches to interpolation.)

1.9   If a 1-year par bond pays $x\%$ semiannually, then the present value of its cashflows will be 100%, which equals

6m $(x\% * 0.5/1.07^{0.5}) +$
1y $((100\% + (x\% * 0.5))/1.071)$

giving
$100\% = (x\% * 0.5/1.03441) + 93.37068\% + (x\% * 0.5/1.071)$

so that $6.62932\% = 0.95022 * x\%$, and thus $x\% = 6.97662\%$.

An estimate for the rate for a par 18-month bond can be obtained by linear interpolation as $(6.97662\% + 7\%)/2$, which equals 6.98831%.

The 18-month scaling factor s can be calculated from the present value of the 18-month par bond

  6m $(6.98831\% * 0.5/1.03441) +$
12m $(6.98831\% * 0.5/1.071) +$
18m $(103.49415\%/s)$

equalling 100%. This gives $s = 1.10855$ and the zero coupon rate is $(s^{2/3} - 1) * 100$, which equals 7.11169%.

The 2-year scaling factor can be calculated similarly. The 2-year bond present value is

  6m $(7\% * 0.5/1.03441) +$
12m $(7\% * 0.5/1.071) +$
18m $(7\% * 0.5/1.10855) +$
24m $(103.5\%/s)$

which equals 100%, giving $s = 1.14756$; hence the zero coupon rate equals $(s^{0.5} - 1) * 100$, which is 7.12423%.

The computation could be reduced by accumulating totals, as was done in deriving zero coupon rates from par bonds rates in Chapter 2.

Note that the assumptions above, while being reasonable, are inconsistent with the zero curve from 1 to 2 years being a straight line. Assuming that the zero curve is a straight line would give slightly different values for the 18-month and 2-year zero coupon rates.

1.10 The computation can be laid out as

Year	Zero rate	Cashflow	Scaling factor	Present value
0	6%			
0.5	6.25%	4%	1.030776	3.880570%
1	6.5%	4%	1.065000	3.755869%
1.5	6.65%	4%	1.101390	3.631773%
2	6.8%	4%	1.140624	3.506852%
2.5	6.9%	4%	1.181529	3.385445%
3	7.0%	4%	1.225043	3.265192%
3.5	7.05%	4%	1.269268	3.151423%
4	7.1%	4%	1.315703	3.040200%
4.5	7.15%	4%	1.364473	2.931536%
5	7.2%	104%	1.415709	73.461436%

giving a total present value of 104.010296% of principal.

Note that we have to use linear interpolation to calculate the zero coupon rates at each half year.

1.11 *Case A*

Its expected pre-tax profit is (50% of £100) + (50% of £200) which equals £150. £100 pre tax is £70 post tax, and £200 pre tax is £140 post tax, so that its expected post-tax profit is (50% of £70) + (50% of £140), which equals £105.

Case B

Its expected pre-tax profit is (50% of -£200) + (50% of £500), which equals £150. Minus £200 pre tax is minus £200 post tax, while £500 pre tax is £350 post tax, so that its expected post-tax profit is (50% of -£200) + (50% of £350) = £75.

From the facts given there is no reason to hedge the risk in Case A, although there might be reasons not included in the wording of the question. However, in Case B the company would be advised to hedge its risk, at least to the point where its lower income expectation was zero, since this would increase its expected post-tax income, provided that the upper income expectation was not reduced too far. For example, if it could hedge its risk to make its possible pre-tax earnings £0 and £290, then its expected pre-tax profit would be £145, and its expected post-tax profit would be £101.5, an increase of £26.5.

If the company is sure of making future profits then it may be more willing to risk losses this year, although the offset to the losses will have a reduced present value since it will not happen this year.

1.12

Year	Bond C/f	Scaling Zero	C/f factor	Shifted PV	Scaling Zero	C/f factor	PV
1	10000	10%	1.1	9091	10.01%	1.1001	9090
2	10000	10.3%	1.21661	8220	10.31%	1.21683	8218
3	10000	10.5%	1.34923	7412	10.51%	1.34960	7410
4	10000	10.6%	1.49631	6683	10.61%	1.49685	6681
5	110000	10.6%	1.65491	66469	10.61%	1.65566	66439
Total				97875			97838

Sensitivity is -£37 for a 1 basis point movement.

Year	Bond C/f	Scaling Zero	C/f factor	Shifted PV	Scaling Zero	C/f factor	PV
1	3000	10%	1.1	2727	10.01%	1.1001	2727
2	3000	10.3%	1.21661	2466	10.31%	1.21683	2465
3	3000	10.5%	1.34923	2223	10.51%	1.34960	2223
4	3000	10.6%	1.49631	2005	10.61%	1.49685	2004
5	103000	10.6%	1.65491	62239	10.61%	1.65566	62211
Total				71660			71630

Sensitivity is -£30 for a 1 basis point movement.

The 10% bond has ratio of sensitivity to value of 37/97,875, which equals 0.00038. The corresponding ratio for the 3% bond is 30/71,660, which equals 0.00042.

For a 5-year zero coupon bond, the ratio of sensitivity to value can be seen from the second table above to be 28/62,239, which equals 0.00045. In general, the lower the coupon of a bond the higher its sensitivity as a fraction of its value; this means that the greatest leverage can be obtained with a zero coupon bond.

1.13 From question 1.12, the original present value of the 10% bond is £97,875, and the original present value of the 3% bond is £71,660. Under rotation of the zero curve, the present values can be calculated as:

Year	Bond C/f	Shifted Zero	Scaling factor	C/f PV
1	10000	10%	1.1	9091
2	10000	10.325%	1.21716	8216
3	10000	10.55%	1.35106	7402
4	10000	10.675%	1.50037	6665
5	110000	10.7%	1.66241	66169
Total				97543

Sensitivity is -£332 for a + 10 basis point rotation.

Year	Bond C/f	Shifted Zero	Scaling factor	C/f PV
1	10000	10%	1.1	9091
2	10000	10.275%	1.21606	8223
3	10000	10.45%	1.34740	7422
4	10000	10.525%	1.49225	6701
5	110000	10.5%	1.64745	66770
Total				98207

Sensitivity is +£332 for a -10 basis point rotation.

Year	Bond C/f	Shifted Zero	Scaling factor	C/f PV
1	3000	10%	1.1	2727
2	3000	10.325%	1.21716	2465
3	3000	10.55%	1.35106	2220
4	3000	10.675%	1.50037	2000
5	103000	10.7%	1.66241	61958
Total				71370

Sensitivity is -£290 for a +10 basis point rotation.

The ratio of sensitivity to present value is 0.00339 for the 10% bond and 0.00405 for the 3% bond; again the 3% bond has the higher proportional sensitivity.

Examining the tables for the 3% bond shows that the ratio for a 5-year zero coupon bond is 281/62,239, which equals 0.00451; again the zero coupon bond is the most sensitive.

1.14 From questions 1.12 and 1.13 we have:

Level sensitivity:
3% bond £30 for £71,660 value, £100,000 face value;
10% bond £37 for £97,875 value, £100,000 face value.

Rotation sensitivity:
3% bond £290 for £71,660 value, £100,000 face value;
10% bond £332 for £97,875 value, £100,000 face value.

You have issued £100,000 face value of the 10% bond which has level sensitivity +£37. To neutralise this, you must buy (37/30) times £71,660 value of the 3% bond, which is a value of £88,381 for a face value of £123,334.

The sensitivity for a plus rotation of the 10% bond is +£332, and the sensitivity of the 3% bond is (88,381/71,660) times -£290, which equals -£358. Therefore, the net rotation sensitivity is -£26 for a 10 basis point rotation of the 5-year rate about the 1-year rate.

Answers to self-study questions

PART II

2.1 The scaling factor to 6 months is $1.07^{0.5}$, which equals 1.034408.

The scaling factor to 9 months is $1.071^{0.75}$, which is 1.052791.

Therefore, the implied 3-month scaling factor in 6 months' time is 1.052791/1.034408, which is 1.017772. This gives the implied Libor as $(1.017772 - 1) * 4 * 100$, which is 7.1088%.

2.2 The scaling factor to 1 year is 1.08.

The scaling factor to 18 months is $1.078^{1.5}$, which equals 1.119253.

Therefore, the implied 6-month scaling factor in 1 year is 1.119253/1.08, which is 1.036345.

This gives the implied Libor as $(1.036345 - 1) * 2 * 100$, which equals 7.2690%.

2.3 Fixed payer: bank

Floating payer: you

Contract amount: £123,456,789

Contract period: 3-9 months

Contract rate: 12%

Reference rate: 6-month £ Libor

The bank is buying the FRA and is 'long funded'.

2.4 The 6 v 9 FRA has value in 6 months and maturity in 9 months, so that its contract period is 23 July to 23 October. If the spot date convention is being used, then the spot date is Tuesday 27 January, and the contract period is 27 July to 27 October.

For the FRA over the 15th, the 3-month date is 23 April, and so the FRA value date is in the month beginning then. Therefore, the contract period is 15 May to 15 August.

2.5   The contract period 25 April to 25 October has 183 days, and so the fixed interest equivalent for cash gaps is

US\$10,000,000 * 6 * 183/36,000 = US\$305,000.

The FRA is therefore equivalent in cash gaps to:
25 April you receive US\$10,000,000; and
25 October you pay US\$10,305,000.

The contract period 12 June to 12 September has 92 days, and so the fixed interest equivalent for the cash gaps is

US\$20,000,000 * 8 * 92/36,000 = US\$408,889.

On 1 February, the FRA is therefore equivalent to:
12 June you pay US\$20,000,000; and
12 September you receive US\$20,408,889.

An FRA in US\$ will generally be for spot settlement, so that settlement will be agreed based on the 3-month Libor on 10 June. Therefore, on 11 June, the FRA will be equivalent in cash gap terms to a single cashflow of the settlement amount on 12 June. Since the settlement rate is 7%, you will receive net 1% interest discounted by the scaling factor

$(1 + (7 * 92/36,000))$,

which is US\$51,111/1.017889, which equals US\$50,213. The cash gap will therefore be the single figure of US\$50,213 on 12 June.

2.6   From 1 March to 1 June is 92 days, from 1 June to 1 September is 92 days, and from 1 March to 1 September is 184 days. The fixed interest on the FRA is £10,000,000 * 10 * 92/36,500, which equals £252,055. The FRA is therefore equivalent in cash gaps to a cashflow of plus £10,000,000 on 1 June and minus £10,252,055 on 1 September. This lets us calculate the level risk:

Days	Cash	Zero	Scaling factor	PV	Zero	Scaling factor	PV
92	10,000,000	9%	1.021959	9785128	9.01	1.021983	9784899
184	-10,252,055	9.1%	1.044883	-9811677	9.11	1.044932	-9811217
Total				-26549			-26318

The sensitivity to a 1 basis point level shift is £231.

The scaling factor for 92 days for a zero coupon rate of 9% is calculated as $1.09^{92/365}$, which equals 1.021959; the other scaling factors are calculated similarly.

If the 'zero-day' zero coupon rate moves by 1 basis point relative to the 1-year zero coupon rate, then the 92-day zero coupon rate will move by (365-92)/365 basis points, which is 0.748 basis points.

Similarly, the 184 day rate will move by (365-184)/365 basis points, which equals 0.496 basis points. This lets us calculate the rotation risk:

Days	Cash	Zero	Scaling factor	PV	Zero	Scaling factor	PV
92	10,000,000	9%	1.021959	9785128	9.00748	1.021977	9784956
184	-10,252,055	9.1%	1.044883	-9811677	9.10496	1.044907	-9811452
Total				-26549			-26496

The sensitivity to a 1 basis point rotation is £53.

Over 25 days the standard deviation of a normally distributed variable will be the daily standard deviation times the squareroot of 25, that is the daily standard deviation times 5. This gives one standard deviation:

level shift   35 basis points and
rotation   15 basis points.

Multiplying these by the sensitivities calculated above gives one standard deviation movements in the FRA value of:

level shift   £8,085 and
rotation   £ 795.

Assuming that the two risks are uncorrelated, the square of the total risk is the sum of the squares of the individual risks, giving the total risk as £8,124. This should be approximately the standard deviation of the distribution of FRA values after a 25 day period.

A bid-offer spread of 8 basis points per annum equals a future value cost at 1 September of £10,000,000 ∗ 0.08 ∗ 92/36,500, which equals £2,016, giving a present value of £1,929.

It can be argued that the cost of a single FRA is half this, that is £965, since you would lose the full bid-offer spread by hedging with one FRA and reversing the hedge with another.

2.7 The future value cost 3 months later is

£100,000,000 ∗ 0.1 ∗ 0.25/100 = £25,000.

The present value would be this divided by the 3-month scaling factor of about 1.03, which is £24,272.

The cost of an FRA spread of 2.5 basis points per annum would be (£100,000,000 ∗ 0.025 ∗ 0.25/100)/1.03 = £6,068.

2.8 You must pay the initial margin of US$750, plus the variation margin of US$25 per 01 for two 01s, giving a total of US$800.

The next day you receive the variation margin on three 01s of US$75.

On the last day you receive back the initial margin of US$750, plus the variation margin of US$25 on one 01, giving a total of US$775.

Your net receipt is US$50. Your funding cost at 6.2% is
$(6.2\% * US\$800/365) + (6.2\% * US\$725/365) = US\$0.26$.

2.9   The market maker has bought an FRA, so that he is paying fixed at an effective rate of 6.37%; therefore, on his hedge he wants to receive fixed on the future, and so he will buy futures at 93.62. This corresponds to receiving fixed on an FRA at 6.38% net of the costs of margining.

There are 275 days to 22 December; the scaling factor to 22 December is therefore $1.065238^{275/365}$, which is 1.048767.

Since there are 91 days in the contract period, the FRA settlement formula future valued to 22 December is interest differential $* US\$25$ million $* 91/36,000$.

An interest differential of 1% on the FRA will therefore cause a settlement of US$63,194 valued at 22 December. Present valuing this at a scaling factor of 1.048767 gives US$60,256, valued at 22 March.

The same interest differential on 25 futures contracts would cause a settlement of $25 * 100 * US\$25$, which equals US$62,500, valued at 22 March.

In order to equate the sensitivity of the value of the futures to the value of the FRA, it is therefore necessary to buy $25 * 60,256/62,500$ futures, which is 24.1024; since only whole contracts can be traded, the market maker will buy 24 contracts.

If the market maker expects that the price of the future will change by 0.50 during the time that he holds the position, then his unhedged risk is

$(24.1024 - 24) * 50 * US\$25 = US\$128$.

The basis risk is half the cost of an 01 per contract, that is 24 times US$12.50, which is US$300.

2.10 The scaling factor to the FRA maturity date is $1.07^{21/12}$, which equals 1.1257. Therefore, the number of future contracts to sell is $100/1.1257$, which is 88.8336, so that you will sell 89 contracts.

You will adjust your hedge when the scaling factor to the FRA maturity date reduces enough to make the contracts required greater than 89.5, that is, when the scaling factor is less than 100 over 89.5, which equals 1.1173. If the time to maturity is t years, then we shall have equality when $1.07^t = 1.1173$; taking natural logarithms of both sides gives $t * (\log 1.07) = (\log 1.1173)$, which gives $t = 0.110915/0.067659 = 1.6393$.

The elapsed time to the date at which the hedge has to be changed is thus 1.75 minus 1.6393, which is 0.1107 years or about 40 days.

As a check, $1.07^{1.6393}$ equals 1.1173, giving a hedge requirement of 100/1.1173 equals 89.501 contracts.

If the 21-month zero coupon rate decreases to Z, then the scaling factor will become $(1 + (Z/100))^{1.75}$. As before, we shall have to change the hedge when the scaling factor becomes 1.1173, corresponding to $(1 + (Z/100))$ being $1.1173^{1/1.75}$, which gives Z equals 6.5432%.

In practice, you will have to change your hedge for a combination of reasons involving the passage of time, the changing of rates, and the changing of positions held.

2.11 The contract period of the FRA is 21 April to 21 July. The scaling factor to 21 July is $1.068^{0.5}$, which equals 1.0334, giving a total hedge requirement of 97 contracts. Of these, some will be March contracts and some will be June contracts. Assume that the yield curve for implied 3 month Libor is straight between March and June, and denote the rates for 3-month FRAs as:

m_{3v6} for contract period starting on 21 April,

m_{2v5} for contract period starting 21 March, and

m_{5v8} for contract period starting 21 June.

Then $m_{3v6} = ((2 * m_{2v5}) + m_{5v8})/3$.

This comes from the general formula for linear interpolation, which states that if a straight line in the x-y plane is described by the function $y = f(x)$, then $f(x_3)$ equals

$$\frac{(f(x_1) * (x_2 - x_3)) + (f(x_2) * (x_3 - x_1))}{(x_2 - x_1)}$$

Since the desired FRA rate is this linear combination of the FRA rates corresponding to the March and June futures, the hedge should be the same combination of futures, giving:

March contracts - 2/3 * 97 = 65; and
June contracts   - 1/3 * 97 = 32.

You should check that the sensitivity of the value of the hedge to rigid movements in the yield curve is approximately the same as the sensitivity of the original FRA.

Answers to self-study questions

PART III

3.1 Value date: 1 July 1992

Termination date: 1 July 1997

Notional principal: FRF200,000,000

Fixed payer: XYZ plc

Fixed interest rate: 10%

Fixed payment frequency: annual

Floating payer: You

Reference rate: 6-month FRF Libor

Floating payment frequency: Semiannual

3.2 Libor for the first period is set two business days before 1 July 1992, that is, on 29 June 1992. The first settlement will be on 1 January 1993, when you will pay FRF9 million.

The second settlement will be on 1 July 1993. You will be due to pay FRF11 million, and XYZ plc will be due to pay FRF20 million; since the payments are concurrent they will be netted, resulting in a single payment of FRF9 million by XYZ plc.

3.3 The company is paying fixed interest on the bond, and so it would wish to receive fixed interest on a swap. Therefore it will enter into a 5-year swap on a notional principal of XEU50 million, where it receives fixed annually at 10.33%, and pays Libor semiannually.

Its net cashflows will be:
semiannually pay Libor; and in addition
annually pay 67 basis points.

Its residual risks will be the credit risk on the swap together with the interest rate risk on each 6-month Libor payment and on the annual fixed payments. In comparison with borrowing floating funds its risk will be the difference between paying 67 basis points per annum (bppa) annually and paying 70 bppa semiannually; since the annual payment will always have a lower present value than the semiannual payment, the interest rate risk can be seen to be immaterial.

Since the 5-year swap rate is 10.33%, the average 6-month scaling factor over the life of the swap is about $1.1033^{0.5}$, which equals 1.0504. A payment of 70 bppa semiannually can thus be future valued to the end of the year as 35 basis points plus (35 basis points times 1.0504), which equals 71.76 basis points. Thus the cost of the swapped fixed debt is about 4.76 bppa less than the cost of the floating debt, with the provisos that the associated swap has a credit risk and that the exact value of the difference in costs will fluctuate slightly with changing interest rates.

Apart from costs, a company might choose to borrow through a bond in order to lock in funding over a period (compared to short-term floating borrowing) or to diversify its source of funds (to protect itself against a bank calling in a loan) or to obtain funds with fewer restrictive covenants than might be required from a bank loan. It can thus be seen that interest rate risk management cannot be totally divorced from other concerns of the corporate treasurer.

3.4   The present value can be calculated as:

	FV	Zero rate	Scaling factor	PV US$
Year 1	1	10.000	1.100000	909,091
Year 2	2	10.210	1.214624	1,646,600
Year 3	1	10.318	1.342577	744,836
Year 4	3	10.430	1.487128	2,017,311
Year 5	2	10.548	1.651028	1,211,366
Total present value				6,529,204

If the zero curve shifts upwards by 10 basis points, then the present value becomes:

	FV	Zero rate	Scaling factor	PV US$
Year 1	1	10.100	1.101000	908,265
Year 2	2	10.310	1.216830	1,643,615
Year 3	1	10.418	1.346231	742,815
Year 4	3	10.530	1.492522	2,010,021
Year 5	2	10.648	1.658509	1,205,902
Total present value				6,510,618

This gives a change in present value of minus US$18,586.

The company can protect itself against this risk by entering into a series of takings such that the interest plus principal repayments on the takings are equal and opposite to the dividend receipts. Since a pay-fixed bullet swap is equivalent economically to a fixed taking together with a strip of floating placings, the company can hedge using swaps with the same fixed side as the proposed takings. As will be shown, this will leave a risk at year 1 which will have to be hedged by a 1-year taking.

The actual swaps to transact are calculated as follows:

The 5-year swap rate which it will pay is 10.5%, and the 5-year fixed payment which it has to pay is US$2,000,000. Therefore, considering the fixed side of the swap as a taking, the principal plus interest repayment at maturity is 110.5% of principal, so that the principal must be US$2,000,000 divided by 1.105, which is US$1,809,955. This swap will require a payment of US$190,045 in each year, leaving residual payments of:

Year 1   US$ 809,955
Year 2   US$1,809,955
Year 3   US$ 809,955
Year 4   US$2,809,955

The process can be repeated to fix the 4-year swap as the company pays fixed at 10.4% on US$2,809,955 over 1.104, which equals US$2,545,249. This gives a US$264,706 payment at each year, giving a residual of:

Year 1   US$ 545,249
Year 2   US$1,545,249
Year 3   US$ 545,249

The year 3 swap will have to match the residual year 3 cashflow, giving the swap as the company pays fixed at 10.3% on US$494,333. This gives an annual payment of US$50,916, resulting in residual flows of:

Year 1   US$ 494,333
Year 2   US$1,494,333

The final swap is to pay fixed at 10.2% on US$1,356,019 to 2 years, giving a residual cashflow at year 1 of US$356,019. It can hedge this exactly by taking US$323,654 for 1 year at 10% to match the residual 1-year cashflow.

The four swaps and the taking will maintain the present value of the future dividends and will remove the interest rate risk; to remove the risk in a year's time it will be necessary to take funds at Libor for 1 year, and similarly at years 2, 3, and 4.

This analysis assumes zero bid-offer spreads on swaps and takings; the effect of spreads will be to reduce the present value of the swapped cashflows, but this may be acceptable given the reduction in risk.

3.5   The market maker will receive fixed at 7.28%. Therefore the marketing officer should quote 7.29% to build in a 1 point spread income.

3.6   He should widen his quote to 10.28%/10.44%.

3.7   The profile of the swap is as shown, with the simple swaps as defined below.

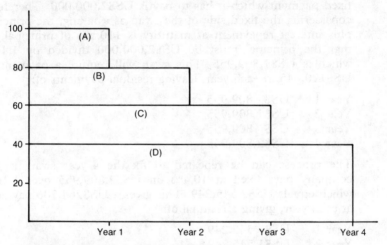

Swap (A): principal 20 maturity 1 year
Swap (B): principal 20 maturity 2 years
Swap (C): principal 20 maturity 3 years
Swap (D): principal 40 maturity 4 years

It should be clear from the diagram that the total notional principal of the four swaps at each maturity equals the notional principal of the required amortising swap.

3.8   The 1-year zero coupon rate is taken as the same as the 1-year Libor of 9%, giving a 1-year scaling factor of 1.09.

The 2-year zero coupon rate Z_2 is worked out from the present value of the fixed side of a 2-year swap being zero. The fixed cashflows as percentages of principal are:

Year 0   -100   present value -100
Year 1   8.8   present value 8.8/1.09
Year 2   108.8   present value 108.8/s_2

where s_2 is the 2-year scaling factor.

This gives s_2 equals 1.183553. Since s_2 is $(1 + (Z_2/100))^2$, this gives the 2-year zero coupon rate as 8.7912%.

The 3-year zero coupon rate is worked out similarly. The fixed cashflows of a 3-year swap are:

Year 0	-100	present value -100
Year 1	8.6	present value 8.6/1.09
Year 2	8.6	present value 8.6/1.183553
Year 3	108.6	present value 108.6/s_3, where s_3 is the 3-year scaling factor.

This gives s_3 = 1.279999, giving Z_3 = 8.5767%.

For the 4-year swap, the fixed cashflows are:

Year 0	-100	present value -100
Year 1	8.5	present value 8.5/1.09
Year 2	8.5	present value 8.5/1.183553
Year 3	8.5	present value 8.5/1.279999
Year 4	108.5	present value 108.5/s_4, where s_4 is the 4-year scaling factor.

This gives s_4 = 1.384292, giving the 4-year zero coupon rate Z_4 equal to 8.4693%.

To summarise:

	Swap rate	Zero coupon	Scaling factor
Year 1	9.0	9.0	1.09
Year 2	8.8	8.7912	1.183553
Year 3	8.6	8.5767	1.279999
Year 4	8.5	8.4693	1.384292

3.9 Swap bid rates are:

Year 1	9.00%
Year 2	8.76%
Year 3	8.56%
Year 4	8.45%

Using midmarket zero coupon rates we can calculate *PV*s of 1% for the swaps of each maturity as:

Year 1	0.917431%
Year 2	1.762345%
Year 3	2.543596%
Year 4	3.265987%.

This gives a *PV* of 1% for the blended amortising swap:

(20 * 0.917431%) +
(20 * 1.762345%) +
(20 * 2.543596%) +
(40 * 3.265987%)

which equals 2.351069.

The total present values of the simple swaps to each maturity are:

Year 1   20 * 0.917431% * 9.0 = 1.651376
Year 2   20 * 1.762345% * 8.76 = 3.087628
Year 3   20 * 2.543596% * 8.56 = 4.354636
Year 4   40 * 3.265987% * 8.45 = 11.039036

giving a total present value of 20.132676.

This gives a blended rate of:

$$\frac{\text{total present value of fixed sides of four simple swaps}}{\text{PV of 1\% over amortising swap}}$$

which equals 20.132676 over 2.351069, which is 8.5632%.

3.10 The differences in cashflow between the blended rate of 8.56% and the simple swap rates are shown below. Differences in interest rate and annual payment amount are given as positive if there is a positive cashflow from the point of view of the marketing officer.

| | <------- Simple swap -------> | | <-----Difference-----> | |
Maturity	Rate	Principal	Rate	Payment
Year 1	9.00%	20	0.44	0.0880
Year 2	8.76%	20	0.20	0.0400
Year 3	8.56%	20	0.00	0
Year 4	8.45%	40	-0.11	-0.0440

This gives total differential cashflows in each year of:

Year 1   0.084
Year 2   -0.004
Year 3   -0.044
Year 4   -0.044

3.11 The capital cost for a bank counterparty is 40% of the capital cost for a corporate counterparty; therefore the capital cost for a corporate counterparty is 1 bppa. This means that each of the bid and offer rates has to be moved by (1.5 bppa + 1 bppa) - (0.5 bppa + 0.4 bppa), which equals 1.6 bppa, to include the greater cost of the corporate counterparty. In addition the requirement of a spread income of 1 bppa necessitates moving each rate by a further 1 bppa, for a total of 2.6 bppa, giving:

bid   12.274%
offer   12.396%.

Since it is unusual to quote rates to less than half a basis point, it is likely that in practice these quotes would be rounded.

3.12 The scaling factors to each maturity are shown below, assuming that the zero rates are interpolated by straight lining to give the half yearly factors.

	Zero coupon	Scaling factor
Year 0.5	9.4116	1.046
Year 1	9.0	1.09
Year 1.5	8.8956	1.136359
Year 2	8.7912	1.183553
Year 2.5	8.6840	1.231442
Year 3	8.5767	1.280000
Year 3.5	8.5230	1.331454
Year 4	8.4693	1.384291

If the 3½-year rate is $f\%$, then the fixed side cashflows on a principal of 100, considering the swap as economically equivalent to a fixed placing together with a floating taking, are:

		Present value
Year 0	-100	-100
Year 0.5	$f * 0.5$	$f * 0.5/1.046$
Year 1.5	f	$f/1.136359$
Year 2.5	f	$f/1.231442$
Year 3.5	$100 + f$	$(100/1.331454) + (f/1.331454)$

Since the net present value of the fixed side cashflows must be zero, we have:

$24.894138 = f * 2.921130$, giving the swap rate $f = 8.5221\%$.

3.13 Let us assume that the swap is being priced by the marketing desk, which will enter into the deferred swap with the counterparty and hedge its cashflows with simple swaps with the trading desk. The simple swaps will be:

the trading desk receives fixed on a 5-year swap; and
the trading desk pays fixed on a 2-year swap.

The rates on these swaps are given in the table below. As explained in Chapter 8, the rate on the short swap is given net of capital and credit costs, while the rate on the long swap is inclusive of these costs; this means that the calculated deferred swap rate includes approximately the correct amount for capital and credit costs.

	Rate	PV of 1%	Total fixed interest PV
2 year	8.705	1.76682	15.38017
5 year	9.08	3.89895	35.40247

By subtraction, the PV of 1% of the deferred swap is 2.13213. The rate on the deferred swap is thus

$$\frac{35.40247 - 15.38017}{2.13213}$$

which equals 9.391%. The marketing desk would probably round this rate up to 9.395% or 9.40%.

You can check that the present value of the fixed interest flows on the deferred swap is equal and opposite to the net present value of the two simple swaps.

To use the same process to calculate the rate for a corporate counterparty, we need simply adjust the 5-year offer rate by subtracting the interbank costs of (0.5 bppa + 0.6 bppa) and adding the costs for the corporate of (1.25 bppa + 1.75 bppa), thus giving a 5-year offer rate of 9.099%. This lets us recreate the above table as:

	Rate	PV of 1%	Total fixed interest PV
2 year	8.705	1.76682	15.38017
5 year	9.099	3.89895	35.47655

giving the deferred swap rate as

$$\frac{35.47655 - 15.38017}{2.13213}$$

which equals 9.425%.

Note that the deferred swap rate to the corporate is 3.4 bppa above the rate to a bank, although the increase in capital and credit costs for a corporate is only 1.9 bppa on a 5-year swap; this is partly because of the approximations we are making, and partly because the bank has to make its extra revenue over 3 years rather than over 5 years.

3.14 The profile is as shown:

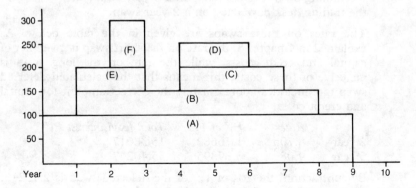

This gives swapsicles as marked:

	Value	Maturity	Principal
(A)	Year 0	Year 9	100
(B)	Year 1	Year 8	50
(C)	Year 4	Year 7	50
(D)	Year 4	Year 6	50
(E)	Year 1	Year 3	50
(F)	Year 2	Year 3	100

Answers to self-study questions

PART IV

4.1 The clean price is 98.765% of DEM20 million, which is DEM19,753,000. The dirty price is the clean price plus accrued interest. The accrued interest is 8% * DEM20 million * 2/12, which is DEM266,667, so that the dirty price is DEM20,019,667. The dirty price is also the value of the bond, since it is the cash amount which could be exchanged for it.

4.2 Scaling factors can be derived by observing that the value of each bond is the present value of its future cashflows.

For the 0.5-year bond, $100.123 = 104.15/s_{0.5}$, giving $s_{0.5}$ as 1.04022.

For the 1.0-year bond, $100.028 = 4.12/s_{0.5} + 104.12/s_{1.0}$, giving $s_{1.0}$ as 1.08382.

For the 1.5-year bond, $99.986 = 4.03/s_{0.5} + 4.03/s_{1.0} + 104.03/s_{1.5}$, giving $s_{1.5}$ as 1.12595.

For the 2.0-year bond, $99.954 = 4.005/s_{0.5} + 4.005/s_{1.0} + 4.005/s_{1.5} + 104.005/s_{2.0}$, giving $s_{2.0}$ as 1.17055.

Alternatively, using the method of section 9.2 and accumulating A_t gives:

Year	m	v	A	s	Zero coupon rate
0.5	8.30	100.123	0	1.04022	8.206
1.0	8.24	100.028	0.48067	1.08382	8.382
1.5	8.06	99.986	0.94200	1.12595	8.230
2.0	8.01	99.954	1.38607	1.17055	8.192

4.3 The accrued interest is 8% for half a year, which is 4%. The dirty price is therefore 103.023. This makes the cashflows on a face value of 100 of the bond:

Year	Cashflow
0	-103.023
0.5	8
1.5	8
2.5	108

Successive estimates of the flat zero coupon rate give:

		<- - - - - - *Present value for flat zero rate*- - - - - ->				
Year	*Cashflow*	*8%*	*8.1%*	*8.4%*	*8.41%*	*8.412%*
0	-103.023	-103.023	-103.023	-103.023	-103.023	-103.023
0.5	8	7.698	7.694	7.684	7.683	7.683
1.5	8	7.128	7.118	7.088	7.087	7.087
2.5	108	89.097	88.891	88.278	88.257	88.253
Net present value		0.900	0.680	0.027	0.004	0.000

(Note that each guess uses the change between the previous two guesses to predict a more accurate rate. For example, the change from 8% to 8.1% causes a change of 0.220 in the present value. To cause an additional change of 0.680 to bring the present value to zero should therefore require about three times as great a change in the zero rate; hence the next estimate of 8.4%. A more sophisticated version of this approach can obtain great accuracy with relatively few iterations.)

The table shows that a flat zero coupon rate of 8.412% makes the dirty price almost the same as the present value of the future cashflows of the bond.

The yield to maturity is the zero coupon rate of 8.412% converted to a semiannual rate. The 6-month scaling factor is $1.08412^{0.5}$, which equals 1.04121; this equates to a deposit interest rate of 8.242%, which is thus the semiannual equivalent rate. The yield to maturity is thus 8.242%, and the swap rate is a spread of 52 basis points over this, which equals 8.762%.

4.4   If spreads widen then swap rates will increase relative to bond rates. If bond rates stay the same, then your swap will increase in value while the bond maintains the same value. If swap rates and bond rates both change with the spread increasing, then you would still expect to make money; however, you are exposed to risk since the two positions will not exactly hedge each other. The other risks you have include the interest rate risk due to the imperfect nature of the hedge, together with credit risk on the swap.

4.5   (a) The bond value will be unchanged, and the Libor funding of the bond will match the first Libor period of the swap. Therefore the change in value will affect the fixed side of the swap only. The effect will be:

Year	Cashflow	Zero rate	PV	Shifted zero	PV
0	10000000		10000000		10000000
0.5	-325000	4.040	-318627	4.050	-318612
1.0	-325000	4.500	-311005	4.510	-310975
1.5	-325000	4.791	-302968	4.801	-302925
2.0	-325000	5.082	-294325	5.092	-294269
2.5	-325000	5.352	-285283	5.362	-285216
3.0	-325000	5.621	-275824	5.631	-275746
3.5	-325000	5.900	-265918	5.910	-265830
4.0	-325000	6.178	-255709	6.188	-255612
4.5	-325000	6.469	-245120	6.479	-245017
5.0	-10325000	6.759	-7445049	6.769	-7441563
Total present value			172		4235

The change in value is thus +US\$4,063 for a 1 bppa shift in spread.

(b) The riskfree and interbank zero rates will increase by 1 bppa in every maturity. The swap will increase in value by US\$4,063 from the calculation in (a), the Libor side of the swap will match the Libor funding of the bond, and thus it is necessary to calculate the sensitivity only of the value of the bond.

Year	Cashflow	Zero rate	PV	Shifted zero	PV
0.5	292500	3.836	287046	3.846	287032
1.0	292500	4.100	280980	4.110	280953
1.5	292500	4.332	274473	4.342	274434
2.0	292500	4.564	267523	4.574	267472
2.5	292500	4.778	260286	4.788	260224
3.0	292500	4.991	252737	5.001	252665
3.5	292500	5.268	244393	5.278	244312
4.0	292500	5.544	235717	5.554	235628
4.5	292500	5.802	226936	5.812	226840
5.0	10292500	6.059	7669786	6.069	7666171
Total present value			9999877		9995731

The change in value of the bond is thus -US\$4,146 for a 1 bppa level shift in the riskfree zero curve.

The change in value of the portfolio for a 1 bppa parallel shift of both zero curves is US\$4,063 minus US\$4,146, which is a net movement of -US\$83. Although this change is small it is not zero, demonstrating that the swap is not an exact hedge for the bond.

4.6 The value of the bond can be calculated by discounting its future cashflows:

Year	Cashflow	Zero rate	Present value
0.5	7.5	7.1	7.247
1.5	7.5	7.3	6.748
2.5	7.5	7.5	6.260
3.5	107.5	7.7	82.919
			103.174

Duration and convexity can be calculated from the formulae in Appendix D.

Modified duration is given in Formula D.3 as

$$\frac{1}{PV} \sum_i \frac{t_i * C_i}{(1 + (Z_i/100))^{t_i + 1}}$$

The sum can be calculated as:

Year	Top line	Bottom line	Full term
0.5	3.750	1.1084	3.383
1.5	11.250	1.1926	9.433
2.5	18.750	1.2880	14.557
3.5	376.250	1.3963	269.462
Total			296.835

Dividing the total of 296.835 by the present value (PV) of 103.174 gives a modified duration of 2.877 years.

The convexity is given in Formula D.4 as

$$\frac{1}{PV} \sum_i \frac{t_i * (t_i + 1) * C_i}{(1 + (Z_i/100))^{t_i + 2}} .$$

The sum can be calculated as:

Year	Top line	Bottom line	Full term
0.5	5.625	1.1871	4.738
1.5	28.125	1.2797	21.978
2.5	65.625	1.3846	47.396
3.5	1693.125	1.5038	1125.898
Total			1200.010

Dividing the total of 1200.010 by the PV of 103.174 gives a convexity of 11.631 years.

If there is a parallel shift of 0.1% of the zero curve, Equation D.1 together with the subsequent definitions predicts that the change in the present value will be:

(- modified duration $*$ PV $*$ 0.1) +
(0.5 $*$ convexity $*$ PV $*$ 0.1^2),
which is (-2.877 $*$ 103.174 $*$ 0.1%) +
(0.5 $*$ 11.631 $*$ 103.174 $*$ $0.1\%^2$), which equals -0.296,
giving a new present value of 102.878.

The actual present value for the shifted zero curve can be calculated as:

Year	Cashflow	Zero rate	Present value
0.5	7.5	7.2	7.244
1.5	7.5	7.4	6.738
2.5	7.5	7.6	6.245
3.5	107.5	7.8	82.650
			102.877

Duration and convexity thus give a good prediction for the bond's value under a parallel shift in the zero curve. However, they do not give any prediction for the effect of rotations of the zero curve or any other change in shape, and they cannot be extended in a natural way to cope with options.

Answers to self-study questions

PART V

5.1 Buyer: You

Writer: Your bank

Premium: US$1,000

Exercise period: The one day in 6 months' time

Option period: Today to 6 months

Maturity date: 6 months

Underlying contract: You buy 200 ounces of gold at US$370 per ounce

The option is European, since it can be exercised only on one day.

It is a call option since you have the right to buy an asset at a fixed price.

The strike price is US$370 per ounce, which equals US$74,000.

5.2 The option is a put option on the same terms as the call option in question 5.1; it can be priced using put-call parity. The formula for put-call parity is $P = C - S + Kr^{-t}$

In this case we have:

C US$ 1,000
S US$70,000 (US$350 * 200)
K US$74,000 (US$370 * 200)
t 0.5

Also we have r^t equals the 6-month scaling factor of 1.035.

This gives the value of the put option as
$P = $ US$1,000 - US$70,000 + (US$74,000/1.035),
which equals US$2,498.

Note that 6-month Libor has been used as a reasonable approximation to the 6-month riskfree interest rate.

5.3   You can make a riskfree profit provided that you can sell gold
      short. Sell 200 ounces of gold short today at US$73,000 and pay
      out US$1,000 to buy the option. Your net cashflow in is
      US$72,000; you put this on deposit at Libor to realise
      US$74,520 in 6 months' time. In 6 months, if the price of gold
      is below US$370 then buy 200 ounces at less than US$74,000,
      or else exercise the option and buy 200 ounces at US$74,000.
      Use the gold you have bought to deliver on the short sale, thus
      realising a profit of at least US$520.

      The assumptions you have made are:
      (a) You can sell gold short and deliver in 6 months without
           penalty.
      (b) You can invest money at Libor.
      (c) There is no bid-offer spread on the price of gold.
      (d) There is no credit risk in depositing money in a bank.
      (e) There is no credit risk on the option contract with the bank.

5.4   Buy the asset and sell the call option. Your net cashflow is
      positive today and cannot be negative in future, since the worst
      that can happen is that the buyer will exercise the option, pay
      you the strike price, and take the asset. The assumption is that it
      does not cost you to hold the asset. This is untrue for physical
      assets which need to be stored and insured.

5.5   (B) allows arbitrage, since you can buy a call option at a strike of
      10 and sell an option at a strike of 12.

      (C) allows arbitrage, since you can sell a call at a strike of 10 and
      buy a call at a strike of 12.

      (F) allows arbitrage, since you can write two calls at a strike of
      12 and buy a call at a strike of 10 and a call at 14. Your total
      cashflow is +0.5 today, which is positive. At maturity there are
      four cases, all with positive or zero cashflow:

      (1) S^* less than 10
           No option is exercised and so your cashflow is 0

      (2) 10 less than or equal to S^* less than 12
           You exercise your call at 10 realising a profit; no other
           option is exercised.

      (3) 12 less than or equal to S^* less than 14
           You exercise your option at 10, realising a profit of $S^* - 10$.
           The two options at 12 are exercised against you, giving you
           a loss of
           $24 - (2 * S^*)$. Your net cashflow is thus $14 - S^*$, which
           must be positive, since S^* is less than 14.

(4) 14 less than or equal to $S^\star$
All the options are exercised, giving you cashflows of $(S^\star - 10)$, $(24 - (2 * S^\star))$, and $(S^\star - 14)$, for a total cashflow of zero.

5.6 Sell the 3-month call and buy the 6-month call, giving you a net positive cashflow today of £10. In 3 months, if the option is not exercised you have definitely made a profit. If the option is exercised, receive the strike price but do not deliver the share until 6 months. At 6 months you can buy the share for the strike price or less, thus guaranteeing yourself a positive cashflow.

The key assumptions are that you can borrow the share and that there are no dividends between the 3- and 6-month date, since otherwise you would have to pay the dividend amount yourself. In fact, provided the dividend is less than £10 you will still definitely make a profit; if you analyse the example carefully taking into account the time value of money, you can increase this allowed dividend amount.

5.7 The option can be priced using the single period binomial model of Chapter 11, although it is something of an act of faith to assume that the detailed assumptions of the model are satisfied.

The possible upward movement in price is u equal to 2.5, while the possible downward movement is d equal to 0.5. The riskfree scaling factor $\check{r}$ is 1.12. The future value of the call option if the price goes up is C_u, which equals £5 million, while if the price goes down it will be C_d equal to zero.

Plugging these values into Equation 11.3 gives the value of the option today as C equal to

$$\frac{(\check{r} - d) * C_u}{\check{r} * (u - d)}$$

which is

$$\frac{(1.12 - 0.5) * £5 \text{ million}}{1.12 * (2.5 - 0.5)}$$

which equals £1,383,929.

To construct a portfolio equal in risk to the option we need to buy a fraction of Δ of the horse today and buy £B of Treasury bills. We then have next year:

(a) The horse wins
$(\Delta * 10 \text{ million}) + (1.12 * B) = C_u$, which is 5 million.

(b) The horse loses
$(\Delta * 2 \text{ million}) + (1.12 * B) = C_d$, which is 0.

This gives $\Delta = 0.625$ and $B = -1,116,071$.

The value of this portfolio today is £2,500,000 minus £1,116,071, which equals £1,383,929. This agrees with the value of the option as calculated by the formula above.

As noted above, the delta is 0.625.

5.8   An annual interest rate of 12.551% corresponds to a quarterly scaling factor of 1.03; this becomes $\check{r}$ in the multiple period binomial pricing model.

The binomial pricing formula is
$$C = S\Phi(a; n, p') - K\check{r}^{-n}\Phi(a; n, p)$$

where $p = (\check{r} - d)/(u - d)$
         $p' = p * (u/\check{r})$
         a is the smallest whole number $> \log(K/Sd^n)/\log(u/d)$

We have $n = 4$
         $\check{r} = 1.03$
         $u = 1.1$
         $d = 0.9$
         $S = 100$
         $K = 100$

giving $p = 0.65$
         $p' = 0.694175$ and
         $$\frac{\log(K/Sd^n)}{\log(u/d)} = 2.1,$$
so that $a = 3$

(You can also observe that a is the minimum number of up movements necessary to give the option positive value at exercise; it is then obvious that a equals 3.)

The formula then is
$C = (100 * \Phi(3; 4, 0.694175)) - ((100/1.12551) * \Phi(3; 4, 0.65))$
$= (100 * \Phi(3; 4, 0.694175)) - (88.8486 * \Phi(3; 4, 0.65))$

$\Phi(3; 4, p)$ is the probability that a sequence of 4 ups and downs, where each up has a probability of p, will have at least 3 ups.

A little thought will show you that is the sum of the probabilities of five possible sequences:

uuuu;
uuud;
uudu;
uduu; and
duuu.

The first of these has probability p^4, while each of the others has probability $p^3 * (1 - p)$. Adding these together gives a total probability of $4p^3 - 3p^4$. This gives $\Phi(3; 4, 0.65) = 0.562981$ and $\Phi(3; 4, 0.694175) = 0.641411$.

Substituting these in the formula for C above gives
$C = (100 * 0.641411) - (88.8486 * 0.562981)$, giving the value of the call option as £14.12.

If there are four up movements the price of the share will be £146.41, and the value of the option will be £46.41. If there are three ups and a down the price of the share will be £119.79, and the value of the option will be £19.79.

After three periods with up movements, the value of the option will be

$(1/\check{r}) * (pC_u + (1 - p)C_d)$

where p has the same meaning as before and is 0.65
$\check{r}$ is again 1.03
C_u is £46.41
C_d is £19.79

giving the value of the option as $0.970874 * (30.1665 + 6.9265)$, which equals £36.01.

The same process can be repeated to find the value of the call at any possible price at 9 months, and then for any possible price at 6 months, and then for 3 months, and finally for today. The price derived by this method should equal the price of £14.12 derived directly above.

5.9   The option can be priced using the Black Scholes formula, which gives the price of a call option as:

$C = SN(x) - Kr^{-t}N(x - \sigma\sqrt{t})$

where $x = \dfrac{\log(S/Kr^{-t})}{\sigma\sqrt{t}} + \dfrac{1}{2}\,\sigma\sqrt{t}$

We have $S = 100$
$K = 100$
$r = 1.1255$
$t = 1$
$\sigma = 0.19$

giving $x = (\log(1.1255)/0.19) + (0.5 * 0.19)$
$= 0.622249 + 0.095$
$= 0.717249$

and $x - \sigma\sqrt{t} = 0.527249$

From the table at the head of the questions:
N(0.717249) = 0.7634
N(0.527249) = 0.7010

giving the price of the call option as C equal to
(100 * 0.7634) - (100 * 0.8885 * 0.7010) = £14.06.

5.10 An interest rate option is the right, but not the obligation, to earn a profit or to enter into a profitable transaction when a particular combination of interest rates occurs at a particular time. The following have embedded interest rate options:

(C) If Libor is, say 10% at the start of a period, and drops to, say, 9% 5 days later, then the issuer can call the note, pay 5 days' interest at 11% and borrow elsewhere for the rest of the period at 10%, thus saving himself 1% interest for the remaining 85 days of the quarter. Thus the right to call is an option on a particular combination of short-term interest rates.

This assumes that the issuer can borrow consistently at Libor plus 1%, and that transaction costs are immaterial. The calculation ignores the small increase in present value caused by the 5 days' interest being paid today, rather than in 85 days' time.

(F) Assuming that the credit quality of the issuer remains unchanged, the value of the bond at any time will depend only on market interest rates. If interest rates decrease then the bond value will increase, and if the value rises sufficiently above 101 it will pay the issuer to call the bonds and to reissue at a higher price. If the value of the bond depends only on interest rates, the right to call is equivalent economically to an option on a swap to the bond maturity.

(G) If market rates for a mortgage to the 6-year date drop sufficiently below 13%, the borrower can make a present-value profit by redeeming the mortgage at 105% and taking out a new fixed mortgage.

(H) If the borrower can borrow at below 8% elsewhere he will not extend the loan; otherwise he can obtain cheap funding by extending.

(I) The note is equivalent to the investor:
receiving Libor; and
receiving the differential if Libor is below 8%.
It thus incorporates an option element.

Other embedded options are:

(B) If the issuer's credit quality improves so that he can borrow below Libor plus 1%, then he can call the note and issue a new note at a lower rate.

(C) The note also includes an option on credit quality, as in (B) above.

(E) If the covenant is breached the investor will have the option to redeem.

(F) Again there is an option on credit quality, since if interest rates remain static but the issuer's credit status improves, then the value of the bond may exceed 101 and it will pay the issuer to call and reissue.

(H) If the borrower's credit quality deteriorates so that he has to pay a higher spread over government bonds, the ability to borrow at 8% may be worthwhile, even if interest rates are unchanged.

The question illustrates the interplay between interest rate risk and credit risk.

5.11 In the first contract you have bought a sterling cap.

Buyer	you
Writer	bank
Premium	£90,000
Value date	6 months
Maturity date	5 years 6 months
Payment date	every 6 months
Notional principal	£10 million
Strike rate	12%
Reference rate	6-month sterling Libor

In the second contract, you have sold a sterling floor.

Buyer	bank
Writer	you
Premium	£45,000
Value date	6 months
Maturity date	5 years 6 months
Payment date	every 6 months
Notional principal	£10 million
Strike rate	7%
Reference rate	6-month sterling Libor

In the combined contract you have bought a sterling collar.

5.12 The payoff diagram for the combined contract at the 1-year date against 6-month Libor at the 6-month date is as shown below.

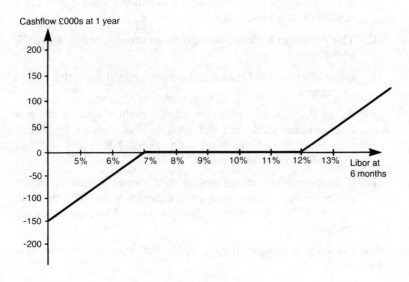

5.13 You pay the exchange 34 times US$25, which equals US$850.

If the futures price is 93.50 then the option expires worthless and there is no settlement; if the price is 94.20 then you receive 20 times US$25, which equals US$500.

You have bought an option which is approximately equivalent to a floor on a 3-month calculation period starting in June on a principal of about US$1 million. The strike rate is 6%, since your option will have value at expiry provided that the futures price is above 94.00, that is, provided that 3-month Libor is below 6%. The principal is about US$1 million, since the value of a 1 bppa shift in rates is US$25; in fact the equivalent principal is greater than US$1 million by the 3-month scaling factor, since the US$25 is a present value whereas the floor payment would be future valued.

A floor is a European option, whereas the traded call is American. In extreme circumstances, where the futures price becomes close to 100, it may be worthwhile exercising the option early. The traded option should thus be worth marginally more than the floor, but in practice the effect will be very small.

5.14 You do have a credit risk, since if the option is exercised you will have to enter into a swap which will carry a credit risk; there would be no credit risk if the swaption were for cash settlement, since you would never receive any payment from the counterparty after the initial payment of premium.

Selling a receiver's swaption is giving the right to the counterparty to receive fixed and pay floating; this most resembles selling a floor.

5.15 The 6-month scaling factor is the squareroot of 1.1, which equals 1.048809, giving the 6 v 12 FRA rate, or in the case of a flat yield curve any 6-month rate, as 9.7618%.

The price of the floor is given by put-call parity as:
the cap price minus
the present value of FRA Libor interest plus
the present value of the strike rate on the FRA terms.

Cashflows over the FRA terms are valued as at 1 year, so they can be present valued by dividing by the 1-year scaling factor of 1.1; the present value of the Libor interest on the FRA is the same as the present value of the fixed interest, since there are no spreads.

This gives the floor price as a percentage of the principal as:
0.05% - (9.7618% * 0.5/1.1) + (11% * 0.5/1.1) = 0.6128% of principal.

For the 12 v 18 floor, the scaling factor to value the FRA cashflows is the 18-month scaling factor of 1.15369, giving the floor price as:
0.13% - (9.7618% * 0.5/1.15369) + (11% * 0.5/1.15369) = 0.6666% of principal.

5.16 The 6-month riskfree scaling factor is 1.05, and so the forward price should be 1.05 * £100, which is £105.

If the forward price is less, say £103, then you can buy a share forward at £103, sell a share today for £100, and invest the money to return £105 in 6 months' time, giving you a riskfree future profit of £2.

If the forward price is more, say £108, then you can buy a share today at £100, sell it forward at £108, and borrow the £100 for 6 months, repaying £105 for a profit of £3.

The assumption that you can borrow at the riskfree rate is consistent with theory but is not usually achievable in practice. However, the difference this makes will not change the essence of the argument, but will simply translate into a small possible spread on the forward price.

5.17 First sort out the FRA rates which the market maker will use to price her bid and offer. Her bid could result in her effectively paying fixed on an FRA, and thus it should be based on the FRA bid rate, which is where she would pay fixed on the FRA directly; an easy way to remember this is that the bid should be the lower price, and so she should base it on the lower FRA rate. A similar argument shows that she should base the cap offer on the FRA offer.

Z_v equals 10.97% for both bid and offer. For the offer price, Z_m can be calculated from the 15-month offer side scaling factor s_{15}, which is the product of the 12-month and 12 v 15 offer side scaling factors, giving: $s_{15} = 1.1097 * 1.027525$, which is 1.140244, which gives $Z_m = 11.070\%$.

Similarly, for the bid quote she will use Z_v of 10.97% to 1 year and Z_m of 11.055%, based on a 15-month scaling factor of 1.140050.

In pricing her bid she will use the bid volatility of 11%, and in pricing the offer she will use the offer volatility of 13%.

The cap pricing formula is

$$C = r_m^{-t_m}(S'N(x) - KN(x - \sigma\sqrt{t_v}))$$

where $x = \dfrac{\log(S'/K)}{\sigma\sqrt{t_v}} + \dfrac{1}{2}\sigma\sqrt{t_v}$

This gives us the list of variables to price the cap, following the computation laid out in Chapter 13.

	bid	offer
t_v	1	1
t_m	1.25	1.25
Z_v	10.97	10.97
Z_m	11.0555	11.070
$K\%$	11	11
σ	0.11	0.13
f	500,000	500,000
r_v	1.1097	1.1097
r_m	1.11055	1.11070
m	10.94	11.01
S'	5,470,000	5,505,000
K	5,500,000	5,500,000
$\text{Log}(S'/K)$	-0.005469	0.000909

	bid	offer
$\sigma\sqrt{t_v}$	0.11	0.13
x	0.005282	0.071992
$x - \sigma\sqrt{t_v}$	-0.104718	-0.058008
$N(x)$	0.5021	0.5287
$N(x - \sigma\sqrt{t_v})$	0.4583	0.4769
Cap price	£198,095	£252,178

The market maker may alter her quote if her perception of rates or volatilities differs from the market, if she believes that the counterparty will definitely be a particular way round and is only interested in the other side of the quote in order to check the spread, or if she is keen to take one side of the transaction only.

5.18 The floor can be priced using put-call parity. The maximum spread is given by:

$$P_{offer} = C_{offer} - r_m^{-t_m}(S'_{bid} - K)$$
$$P_{bid} = C_{bid} - r_m^{-t_m}(S'_{offer} - K)$$

Remember that S'(bid) is based on the FRA bid rate, and is therefore given in the cap bid column in the worked answer to question 5.17; similarly, S'(offer) is in the cap offer column.

Taking r_m as the midpoint 1.110625% gives

$$P_{offer} = £252,178 - (0.877083 * (£5,470,000 - £5,500,000))$$
$$= £278,490.$$

$$P_{bid} = £198,095 - (0.877083 * (£5,505,000 - £5,500,000))$$
$$= £193,710.$$

This is the maximum spread which the market maker can quote without allowing arbitrage; she might well quote a narrower spread.

5.19 A single period cap price is determined by:

t_v The time to the value date
t_m The time to the maturity date
r_m The zero coupon rate to the maturity date expressed as an annualised scaling factor
S' The future value at maturity of the floating interest on an FRA on the same terms as the cap
K The future value at maturity of fixed interest at the strike rate on an FRA on the same terms as the cap
σ Volatility

Of these, K will not change after the cap contract is agreed. Also, after the cap is agreed, t_v and t_m will change only in step, so that they can both be considered as functions of a single variable, which we can call t.

Thus, after a cap is agreed, its value will depend on four independent variables, S', r_m, t, and σ. The variable r_m is a function of the zero coupon rate to maturity Z_m, and S' will depend on the FRA rate, which is a function of Z_m and Z_v, the zero rate to the cap value date. Z_v and Z_m have the advantage of both being zero coupon interest rates; it is thus possible to consolidate information on both of them in the same report and to add information in a natural way to risk management reports on non-option products.

It might thus be best to replace the four variables above by the more useful variables for risk management: Z_v, Z_m, σ, and t. A dealer managing a position containing caps will have to consider possible movements in all of these variables.

5.20 The FRA rate is defined by the 15 v 18 scaling factor, which is given by the 18-month scaling factor over the 15-month scaling factor, that is

$$\frac{1.168667}{1.138058} = 1.026896,$$

giving the FRA rate as 10.7584%.

When Z_m increases to 10.97%, the 15 v 18 scaling factor becomes

$$\frac{1.168983}{1.138058} = 1.027173,$$

giving the new FRA rate as 10.8692%

The price of the caps can be calculated as:

	Z_m=10.95%	Z_m=10.97%
$t_v =$	1.25	1.25
$t_m =$	1.50	1.50
$Z_v =$	10.9%	10.9%
$Z_m =$	10.95%	10.97%
$K\% =$	11%	11%
$\sigma =$	0.14	0.14
$f =$	250,000	250,000
$r_m =$	1.1095	1.1097
$m =$	10.7584	10.8692
$S' =$	£2,689,600	£2,717,300
$K =$	£2,750,000	£2,750,000
$\log(S'/K) =$	-0.022208	-0.011962
$\sigma\sqrt{t_v} =$	0.156525	0.156525
$x =$	-0.063618	0.001840
$x - \sigma\sqrt{t_v} =$	-0.220144	-0.154685
$N(x) =$	0.4747	0.5007

$N(x - \sigma\sqrt{t})$ $=$ 0.4128 0.4385
$S'N(x)$ $=$ £1,276,753 £1,360,552
$KN(x - \sigma\sqrt{t_v})$ $=$ £1,135,200 £1,205,875
Cap price $=$ £121,123 £132,318

The change in the cap price is +£11,195

From Chapter 14, the partial derivative

$$\left.\frac{\partial C}{\partial Z_m}\right|_{Z_v} \text{ is } \frac{Ft_m N(x)}{100 r_m r_v^{t_v}} - \frac{t_m C}{100 r_m}$$

which can be calculated as follows:

F $=$ £100,000,000

t_m $=$ 1.5

t_v $=$ 1.25

$N(x)$ $=$ 0.4747

Z_m $=$ 10.95

Z_v $=$ 10.9

C $=$ £121,123

$Ft_m N(x)$ $=$ £71,205,000

$100 r_m r_v^{t_v}$ $=$ 126.2675

$\dfrac{t_m C}{100 r_m}$ $=$ £1,637.53

giving the partial derivative as £562,284 per % change in Z_m.

The change in Z_m is 0.02%; multiplying this by the partial derivative gives a predicted change of £11,246, which is very close to the actual value.

5.21 Overnight you would expect to see a change in level of the order of the standard deviation of 7 bppa; this would cause a change in portfolio value of about RUR7,000. Over 256 days, you would expect a change in level of the order of (the squareroot of 256) times 7 basis points, that is 112 basis points, which would cause a change in value of about RUR112,000.

The expected daily change in the slope is about 3 bppa, causing a change of approximately RUR15,000 in the value of the portfolio. Over a year, change in slope should be increased by about the squareroot of 256, giving a 48 bppa change in slope and a RUR240,000 change in value.

The expected weekly change in volatility is about 0.25%, so that the consequent change in value is approximately RUR50,000. Over a year of 49 weeks, these changes should be multiplied by the squareroot of 49 to give a change in volatility of about 1.75% and a change in value of about RUR350,000.

The standard deviation of volatility changes over one week is 0.25%. Therefore two standard deviations is 0.5%, and a change of this magnitude would cause a change of about RUR100,000 in the portfolio value. You would not expect to see a loss of greater than this amount in more than 2.3% of weeks, that is not more than about once a year. (Symmetrically, you would not expect to see a profit of more than this amount more than 2.3% of weeks.)

The main limitation of reporting risk in this way is that the value of the portfolio may have different sensitivities to movements of different rates or volatilities along the yield curve. For example, the RUR1,000 sensitivity to changes in the level of the yield curve could be the sum of a sensitivity of +RUR5,000 to a 1 bppa movement in the 1-year rate and a -RUR4,000 sensitivity to a 1 bppa movement in the 4-year rate. Therefore, to be effective, a reporting methodology must break down the total sensitivity of the portfolio to a particular variable into 'maturity buckets', that is, it must give the sensitivity to changes in value of interest rates and volatilities separately for each maturity band in the yield curve.

The statistics should also be reviewed to see if there is any correlation between changes in the different variables. This information is needed in order to determine the best estimate of the total risk from the individual risks. Knowledge of correlations may also allow you to achieve particular risk positions more cheaply.

5.22 If you are convinced that volatility is too high then you should sell the option, wait for volatility to decrease, and then buy back the option at a profit.

The problem with this is that you are at risk from any change in the price of the underlying future, since the price of the option is dependent on the price of the future as well as on the volatility.

The solution is to sell the option and simultaneously to sell delta futures. Then for any small change in the futures price, the option price will change in the opposite direction by the same amount multiplied by delta. The value of the whole portfolio would then be unchanged for small changes in the value of the future.

Since delta equals 0.53, an appropriate combination would be to sell 100 puts and sell 53 futures. If volatility decreased by 2%, you would expect to make 100 times US$88, which equals US$8,800, less your spread costs of 53 times US$25 for the futures plus 100 times US$25 for the options, for a net profit of US$4,975.

If volatility does not decrease, then you will lose at least the bid-offer spread of US$3,825 on closing out the 153 contracts.

If the option position is held for a relatively long time then the option price will reduce due to time decay. Gains on your short option position should be balanced by losses on delta hedging, but, if you are right about volatility, your delta hedging should be cheaper than implied by the 16% volatility priced into the option. However, you will have spread costs on the delta hedging which are not incorporated into the theoretical price.

Small volatility changes will not materially change the delta. However, you are at risk from discontinuous changes in the volatility or in the futures price.

Expected margin costs increase the longer a position is held.

Remember that a future is roughly equivalent to an FRA with a notional principal greater than the underlying principal of the future by the scaling factor from today to the FRA maturity date, and a traded option is roughly equivalent to a cap or floor with a notional principal greater than the future principal by the scaling factor from value date to maturity date. Interest rates are a little over 6%, and thus the position you have set up is more or less equivalent to selling a cap at 6.50% on about US$102 million, and buying an FRA (paying fixed) on about US$56 million.

Your potential profit is greatly reduced by the spread costs; a futures and options market maker might be able to carry out the same trade with markedly lower spread costs.

Answers to self-study questions

PART VI

6.1   The inverted quote (which is the normal method for XEU) would be 1.2446/1.2452. If you sold XEU1 million to a market maker he would give you dollars at the lower rate of 1.2446, that is US$1,244,600.

6.2   You will receive the lower amount of dollars; since the dollar amount is the DEM amount divided by the exchange rate, this will mean the market maker using the higher right-hand-side exchange rate of 1.8140, to give a dollar amount of US$551,268.

6.3   The forward points must be subtracted to give the forward rate, since otherwise the forward spread will be less than the spot spread. Therefore, the forward price is 1.8040/1.8053. If you sell US$1 million, the market maker will give you DEM at the lower left-hand-side rate of 1.8040, that is he will give DEM1,804,000.

6.4   The forward points must be added to widen the spread, giving a forward rate of 1.5355/1.5367. If you buy US$1 million, you must deliver CHF at the higher right-hand-side rate, that is you deliver CHF1,536,700.

6.5   The 6-month scaling factor in sterling is 1.05, and in dollars is 1.03. We have that at spot £1 equals US$1.65, so in 6 months we have £1 * 1.05 = US$1.65 * 1.03
giving an exchange rate of £1 = US$1.6186.

Equivalently, you can use the interest rate parity formula, which is derived from the same economic argument.

If the rate is higher, say at 1.63, then the forward £ is overvalued relative to the spot £. You can therefore make a profit by buying £ spot and selling £ forward. If you buy spot £1 you can deposit it to have £1.05 in 6 months, which you can sell for US$1.7115. The spot £1 will cost you US$1.65, which you can borrow for 6 months repaying the future value amount US$1.6995 out of the proceeds of the forward foreign exchange, to give yourself a profit of US$0.012.

6.6   You can create a synthetic forward purchase of JPY as follows:

borrow US$ at 6%;
buy JPY spot at 140.00; and
deposit JPY at 7.875%.

If the spot exchange is sell US$1, buy JPY140, then the 3-month cashflows are pay US$1.015, receive JPY142.7563, giving a forward exchange rate of 140.6466.

Similarly, you can create a synthetic forward sale of JPY as follows:

borrow JPY at 8%;
sell JPY spot at 140.10; and
deposit US$ at 5.875%.

If the spot exchange is sell JPY140.10, buy US$1, then the 3-month cashflows are receive US$1.014688, pay JPY142.902, giving a forward exchange rate of 140.8334.

The bid-offer spread achievable synthetically is thus 140.6466/140.8334. The actual forward rate cannot allow arbitrage against the synthetic rate, and thus the forward left-hand-side rate cannot be higher than 140.8334, while the right-hand-side cannot be lower than 140.6466.

6.7   You buy the CHF spot at the market maker's normal left-hand-side rate of 1.4410. Because the transaction is a swap, you sell the CHF forward at the right-hand-side forward points of 54 added to the left-hand-side spot rate of 1.4410, giving a forward rate of 1.4464.

If the forward US$ amount is US$1 million, the CHF amount will be CHF1,446,400, instead of CHF1,447,400 as it would be with an outright forward; the forward swap rate has thus saved you CHF1,000 compared with the outright forward rate.

6.8   If you deposit your BEF at 10% you will receive back BEF61,500,000 at 3 months. However, if you sell and buy the BEF in a foreign exchange swap, and deposit the £ which you then have for 3 months, then your transactions and cashflows are:

spot: sell BEF60,000,000 at 60, buy £1,000,000
                  deposit £1,000,000

3 months: deposit matures £1,025,000
                  sell £1,025,000 at 60.0010,
                  buy BEF61,501,025

Your net 3-month cashflow under the swap and £ deposit is BEF61,501,025, which is BEF1,025 better than the straight BEF deposit.

6.9 An FRA in CHF where you receive fixed is equivalent in risk to a placing of CHF from month 3 to 6. You can synthesise such a placing by selling CHF at month 3 and simultaneously buying them back at month 6. This gives you a pay fixed position in US$, which you can neutralise by receiving fixed on a US$ FRA. The placing and taking would have initial cashflow of principal and final cashflow of principal plus interest, and so your foreign exchange swap would have to duplicate these cashflows.

Thus the component transactions of your synthetic FRA are:

(a) A 3 v 6 dollar FRA where you receive fixed at 7.03% on a principal of, say, US$10,000,000. This has the same interest rate risk as a placing, and hence has the same risk as a cashflow of US$10,000,000 out at month 3 and US$10,175,750 in at month 6.

(b) A foreign exchange swap from month 3 to 6, where you sell and buy CHF. The 3-month rate will be the normal rate at which you could sell CHF to a market maker, that is the right-hand-side rate of 1.4387. The 6-month rate will be the swap rate of the left-hand-side 6 months forward points applied to the right-hand-side spot rate, that is 1.4445. You need to sell CHF14,387,000 at 3 months to match the US$ principal amount of US$10,000,000, and you need to buy back CHF14,698,871 at 6 months to match the 6-month cashflow of the dollar FRA.

This gives you net cashflows economically equivalent to zero in US$, and net cashflows in CHF of CHF14,387,000 out at 3 months and CHF14,698,871 in at 6 months. The CHF cashflows correspond to a placing of CHF14,387,000 for 3 months at 8.67%, which is equivalent in risk to a 3 v 6 CHF FRA where you receive fixed at 8.67% on CHF14,387,000.

If you received fixed on a 3 v 6 CHF FRA from a market maker you would receive 8.60%; you are thus receiving 7 basis points per annum better through the synthetic FRA.

With the synthetic you are running the additional risks:

(a) when you close out the floating side of the FRA with a 0 v 3 swap in 3 months, you may get implied interest rates worse than Libor in one or both currencies, thus giving you an additional cost; and

(b) with more transactions you have more credit risk and more administration costs.

6.10 Effective date: spot

   Termination date: 3 years

   Initial exchange yes/no: yes

   Currency A: £

   Currency B: US$

   Currency A payer: bank

   Currency A principal amount: £10,000,000

   Currency A payment dates: annually

   Currency A interest rate: 11%

   Currency B payer: you

   Currency B principal amount: US$17,000,000

   Currency B payment dates: semiannually

   Currency B interest rate: 6-month US$ Libor

6.11 Her interest rate risk in £ is equivalent to a 5-year taking in £ where she pays interest semiannually at 6-month Libor. Since the interest rate risk of a future taking or placing at the then prevailing Libor is zero, the £ interest rate risk comes only from the current period where the Libor has been set at 10.5%.

In US$, the interest rate is slightly above Libor, but part of this margin is needed to cover future costs as they arise, and the balance representing profit is probably too small to worry about for risk management purposes. Therefore, the dollar interest rate risk can be considered to arise purely from the current period where the Libor has been set at 6.3%.

The interest rate risk is thus equivalent to a 6-month £10 million taking at 10.5%, and a 6-month dollar placing at 6.4%.

The foreign exchange risk is effectively zero, since the net present value of the £ cashflows is zero, and the net present value of the US$ cashflows is close to zero. (The US$ present value is positive because of the extra 10 bppa interest; the effect is small enough to ignore here, but might be material in a large portfolio.)

The dealer could hedge her interest rate risk by placing £ and taking US$, but this would mean putting a £10 million asset on the books, probably at Libid. It would therefore be cheaper to enter into a 0 v 6 foreign exchange swap, selling and buying £, to match closely the cashflows of the cross currency swap in its first period, thus removing the interest rate risk.

6.12 Before Libor is fixed, interest rate and foreign exchange risks are zero. Interest rate risk is zero because it is zero for the future Libor placings and takings, and because the cashflows are completely matched in the current 6-month period. Foreign exchange rate risk is zero because it is zero on the cross currency swap, and it is separately zero on the 0 v 6 foreign exchange swap.

After Libors are set, the foreign exchange risk is still zero, but there is now an interest rate risk in the second 6-month period equivalent to a fixed taking in £ and a fixed placing in US$.

The interest rate risk can again be hedged by entering into a 6-month swap where the dealer sells and buys £. However, this time she will sell £10 million and buy US$15 million at the prevailing spot rate, so that she will succeed in hedging the £ position fully, but will leave unhedged US$1 million of the US$ position. She can correct this by taking US$1 million for 6 months at Libor, to completely match the US$ position also.

6.13 Your £ interest rate risk is equivalent to a 7-year £10 taking where you pay interest of 11% annually. (The risk is slightly different from a taking, since there is no receipt of principal at the spot date, but the difference is small and will, in fact, be corrected by the foreign exchange hedging below.) The US$ interest rate risk is equivalent to a placing of US$16 million for 6 months; as usual, the future floating periods carry no risk. (Again the risk is marginally altered by the absence of the initial payment of principal, and again this will be corrected by the foreign exchange hedging.)

If the swap did have an initial exchange, then the net present value of the US$ cashflows would be zero, since the present value of a Libor placing is zero. Also, if 11% is close to the market rate for a 7-year £ swap paying fixed annually, the net present value of the £ cashflows would be close to zero; this is because a single currency interest rate swap is equivalent to a fixed taking back to back with a strip of Libor placings, and since the present value of the Libor placings is zero, the present value of the fixed taking at the market swap rate must also be zero.

Since an equivalent swap with an initial exchange would have zero present value of cashflows within each currency, the present value of the cashflows within each currency on your swap must be equal and opposite to the cashflows of the initial exchange, that is, they must be equal and opposite to the swap principals. Thus the present value of the cashflows, and hence your foreign exchange risk in each currency, must be

-£10,000,000 and
+US$16,000,000.

Let us look at hedging the foreign exchange risk first. This can be done simply by entering into a spot transaction with another counterparty, where you receive £10,000,000 and pay US$16,000,000; this is simply a spot foreign exchange deal at the market rate, and you can look on it as replacing in the market the swap cashflows which are not present in your swap transaction.

You can hedge your £ interest rate risk by receiving fixed annually and paying semiannually at Libor on a 7-year single currency swap with a notional principal of £10 million. This matches your 7-year risk, but gives you a 6-month risk on the first Libor period of the single currency swap, since the Libor will have been set for this period.

Your residual interest rate risk is thus the same as a 6-month taking at Libor in £ and a 6-month placing at Libor in US$; this is the same as the risk of a Libor-Libor swap discussed in question 6.11, and it can be hedged in the same way by entering into a 0 v 6 foreign exchange swap where you sell and buy £.

6.14 Five-year BEF swap rates are 9.8% for annual interest, and 5-year US$ rates are 7.5% for annual interest; the average zero coupon rates out to 5 years should be at about these levels. The bank expresses its costs as 20 bppa in US$; present valuing at a conservative rate, from the viewpoint of the bank, of 7.4%, gives a present value of 81.13 basis points on the principal. If the swap principal exchange is at the market spot rate, then this should have the same present value as basis points on the BEF principal; future valuing this at the conservative BEF interest rate of 9.9%, gives an annual payment of 21.35 bppa. Thus the bank should be willing to receive about 21.35 bppa annually in BEF instead of 20 bppa in US$.

This calculation can be done easily using the HP12c calculator. Set:

n	5
i	7.4
PMT	20
FV	0

and press PV to get the present value 81.13. Now set

i	9.9

and press PMT to get the annual payment 21.35 basis points.

If the bank pays 20 bppa above the BEF swap rate it would present value the cashstream at a conservative rate of say 9.7%. This would give a present value of 76.40 basis points. Future valuing this at the conservative US$ rate of 7.6% gives a required US$ income above the swap rate of 18.93 bppa. Again the calculation is simple using the HP12c.

If the company borrows directly in US$ it will pay 8%. If instead it borrows in BEF and enters into a cross currency swap, where it receives fixed at the BEF swap rate plus 20 bppa, and pays fixed at the US$ swap rate of 7.5% plus 18.93 bppa to balance the BEF off-market rate plus the bank's costs of 20 bppa, its transactions will be:

Bond: Receive BEF principal spot, pay BEF interest at 10% annually for 5 years, repay BEF principal at 5 years.

Swap: Pay BEF principal and receive US$ principal spot, receive 10% BEF interest and pay 7.8893% US$ interest annually for 5 years, and receive BEF principal and repay US$ principal at 5 years.

The net cashflows of the BEF bond and cross currency swap will be the cashflows of a US$ bond at 7.8893%, thus representing a saving of just over 11 bppa on the US$ bond rate.

Disadvantages of the swap route are that it gives the company a credit risk on its bank, and the additional bid-offer spreads on terminating the swap would make it more expensive to call the bond early. There might also be tax considerations regarding the treatment of cross currency swaps relative to bonds.

6.15

Effective date:	spot (or any date before 3 years)
Termination date:	3 years
Initial exchange yes/no:	no
Currency A:	DEM
Currency B:	US$
Currency A payer:	you
Currency A payment dates:	3-year date only
Currency A interest fixed/ floating:	fixed
Currency B payer:	bank
Currency B payment dates:	3-year date only
Currency B interest fixed/ floating:	fixed

6.16 You have a spot exchange risk on the present value of minus DEM16 million and on the present value of plus US$10 million. You also have interest rate risk in each currency, since the present value of the 3-year cashflow depends on the 3-year zero coupon rate. As with any such transaction, you also have a credit risk on your counterparty.

If DEM interest rates increase, the present value of your future DEM payment decreases, and so you make a profit. If the spot rate moves from 1.80 to 1.81, the US$ present value you receive becomes worth more relative to the DEM present value you pay, and again you make a profit. Since the forward rate is 1.60 and the spot rate is 1.80, the US$ is worth relatively less against the DEM forward compared with spot, and thus DEM interest rates are lower.

6.17 To construct a synthetic 2-year forward purchase of DEM it is necessary to:

borrow US$ on a bullet taking for 2 years;
sell US$ spot and buy DEM; and
invest the DEM in a bullet placing for 2 years.

The spot transaction will be at the left-hand-side rate of 1.7990. We shall now look at constructing the bullet taking and placing.

In US$, you can synthesise a bullet taking by taking funds for 1 year at Libor and entering into a 2-year interest rate swap to pay fixed and receive Libor; at the end of the first year you can borrow funds at Libor for the second year. Suppose that the swap has notional principal US$100. Then the fixed rate is 7.37%, and the fixed cashflows, considered as a taking, are 7.37 at 1 year and 107.37 at 2 years. In order to create the zero coupon cashflow it is necessary to eliminate the 1-year fixed cashflow of pay 7.37. You can do this by placing funds for 1 year so as to receive interest plus principal of 7.37. In fact, instead of placing funds you can net funds against your 1-year Libor taking, and thus the interest rate you can achieve is the Libor rate of 6.5%. The 'placing' principal is thus 7.37 over 1.065, which equals 6.920188, and this will be netted against your 1-year US$100 taking, to give you a net taking of US$93.079812. Thus your cashflows become:

Spot   receive 93.079812
2 years   pay 107.37

giving a scaling factor in US$ of 1.153526, which equates to a zero coupon rate of 7.4023%.

In DEM, you will similarly place funds for a year at Libid, swap into fixed for 2 years, and place funds in a year's time for the second year. A complication this time is that we have to express the swap rate against Libid, in order to be able to net the placing interest against the swap floating side. Since the differential between Libid and Libor is 0.125%, you can receive fixed on a 2-year swap against Libid at 9.175%. Assume again that the swap principal is 100. Your fixed cashflows this time are receive 9.175 at 1 year and receive 109.175 at 2 years. To eliminate the 1-year cashflow you must take DEM for 1 year so that the principal plus interest repayment equals 9.175. The taking can be netted against your placing, allowing you to achieve an interest rate of 8.875%, so that the 'taking' principal should be 9.175 over 1.08875, which equals 8.427095. This will be netted against your placing of DEM100 at Libid to give you a net placing of DEM91.572905. Thus your DEM cashflows become:

Spot   pay 91.572905
2 years   receive 109.175

giving a scaling factor in DEM of 1.192219, which corresponds to a zero coupon rate of 9.1888%.

Putting these together, if you start with US$1 in 2 years, its value spot in US$ is

(1/1.153526) = DEM (1/1.153526) * 1.7990,

which in 2 years equals

DEM (1/1.153526) * 1.7990 * 1.192219,

which equals DEM1.8593.

The forward rate achievable through the synthetic transaction is thus 1.8593.

However, because you are simultaneously placing DEM and taking US$, you should be able to improve on the Libid-Libor spread by using a foreign exchange swap instead of the placings and takings themselves; this should let you improve slightly on the rate quoted.

You should consider that the synthetic transaction will have a greater credit risk and will involve a greater transaction cost than the actual forward foreign exchange deal.

6.18 The recorded value will be minus the principal in DEM and in US$ it will be plus the principal plus the present value of 15 bppa; the net of these will be the present value of 15 bppa on the US$ principal.

The true profit is 2 bppa, which is 15 bppa minus 6 bppa for hedging minus 7 bppa for credit, capital, and administration. The bank is overstating its profit on this deal by a factor of 7.5.

As the portfolio grows the bank will overstate the profits on new deals. As each deal progresses, the bank will suffer expenses which will reduce the original profit recorded. (In the example above, it will record the present value of 15 bppa up front and then suffer costs at 13 bppa for the life of the swap.) So long as the portfolio grows, it is likely that the initial overstatement of profits will dominate and the bank will record large gains, but eventually, and certainly when the portfolio stabilises after 3 years, the bank will start recording large losses. Provided all deals are done at a mark-to-market profit, the excess profits will eventually be written off and a small but steady income will be reported.

Answers to self-study questions

PART VII

7.1 The 12 v 18 scaling factor is 1.155263/1.099, which is 1.051195; this gives an FRA rate of 10.2390%. The FRA would therefore be represented in cash gaps as:

year 1   +10,000,000
year 1.5   -10,511,950.

The sensitivity of the present value of a single cashflow c is given as:

$$\frac{dPV}{dZ} = \frac{-tc/100}{(1 + (Z/100))^{t+1}}$$

and the convexity is given as:

$$\frac{d^2PV}{dZ^2} = \frac{t(t + 1)c/10,000}{(1 + (Z/100))^{t+2}}$$

This gives:

	Sensitivity	Convexity
year 1	-82,795	1,507
year 1.5	123,967	-2,815
Total	41,172	-1,308

The predicted present value following a 0.7% level shift of the zero curve is given by Equation 18.1 as:

$$0 + \left(\frac{dPV}{dZ} * 0.7\right) + \left(0.5 * \frac{d^2PV}{dZ^2} * 0.7^2\right) = 28,500.$$

The actual present value following a 0.7% shift in the zero curve will be:

$(10,000,000/1.106^1) - (10,511,950/1.108^{1.5}) = 28,503.$

The agreement is thus excellent, even for a relatively large shift in the zero curve.

7.2   The cashflows should be reported at their net future value at 1.5 years; this equals the present value times the scaling factor to 1.5 years of 1.143322. The present value is:

Year	Cashflow	Zero coupon	Present value
1.1	100	9.30	90.681318
1.2	-100	9.31	-89.868631
1.5	-90	9.34	-78.717973
1.9	100	9.36	84.366270
Total			6.460984

Giving a future value of 7.386985, which should be the gap reported.

If the zero curve rotates around the 1-year point with a 10 bppa movement of the 10-year rate, then the changes in the rate to each date are as shown in the table below. The sensitivity of each rate to a 10 bppa rotation should be the absolute sensitivity times the ratio of the actual change to 10 bppa; this ratio is shown in the next column. The absolute sensitivity of each cashflow to a 1% change in the zero rate is calculated using the same formula as in question 7.1, and the relative sensitivity is the absolute sensitivity times the ratio. The relative sensitivity has to be divided by 10 to be in the correct units for a 10 bppa shift.

Year	Zero shift bppa	Ratio	Cashflow	Absolute sensitivity	Relative sensitivity
1.1	0.11111	0.011111	100	-0.912621	-0.0101401
1.2	0.22222	0.022222	-100	0.986574	0.0219236
1.5	0.55556	0.055556	-90	1.079906	0.0599953
1.9	1.00000	0.100000	100	-1.465764	-0.1465764
Total					-0.0747976

The sensitivity in the present value predicted for a 10 bppa rotation is thus -0.0074798. Repeating the same calculation for the single cashflow reported in the cash gaps gives:

1.5   0.55556   0.055556   7.386985   -0.0886361 -0.0049243

giving a sensitivity of -0.0004924 for a 10 bppa rotation.

The difference in the two predicted values demonstrates the importance of calculating the sensitivities reported in the cash gaps from the underlying cashflows, and not from the gaps themselves.

If there is a 10 bppa rotation, then the zero curve and present values will be:

Year	Zero	Cashflow	Present value
1.1	9.301111	100	90.680304
1.2	9.312222	-100	-89.866439
1.5	9.345556	-90	-78.711974
1.9	9.370000	100	84.351614
Total			6.453505

The present value predicted by the sensitivity is

6.460984 - (0.0747976 * 0.10) = 6.453504.

The agreement is excellent, provided that the sensitivity is calculated from the individual cashflows.

7.3 Since the interest on a mortgage of 400 is 40, interest rates must currently be around 10%. If the interest rate increases to 11%, then the mortgage interest will become 44 and the turnover will drop by 3% to 485. Presumably the cost of sales will also drop by 3% to 194, while other operating expenses will stay fixed. This will give a budget of:

Sales	485
Cost of sales	194
Fixed operating expenses	200
Operating profit	91
Interest	44
Net profit	47

The cost of the mortgage has increased from 40 to 4, giving a transaction risk of 4, while the operating profit has decreased from 100 to 91, giving an economic risk of 9.

The retailer might choose to reduce its transaction risk by buying FRAs or paying fixed on a swap to lock in a fixed rate on its floating rate mortgage repayments; alternatively it might buy an interest rate cap. If necessary, it could hedge its economic risk similarly.

The disadvantage of hedging risk is that the retailer will pay a transaction cost (disguised as a bid-offer spread) and will not benefit so greatly from any downturn in rates. The decision as to whether to hedge will therefore depend on factors such as economic predictions of future levels of interest rates, whether possible rate movements could cause financial distress, the retailer's tax position, the competitive structure of the retailer's business, and the risk preference of the management and owners.

7.4

	Principal	Value date	Maturity
(a)	100	1 Feb 1992	1 Aug 1992
(b)	0		
(c)	-100	1 Jan 1992	31 Mar 1992
(d)	1,020,000	22 Mar 1992	22 Jun 1992
(e)	-1,000	1 Jul 1992	1 Jan 1996
(f)	200	1 Jul 1992	1 Jan 1993

A placing to be set at some future Libor does not contribute to the gaps. The futures contract principal is scaled up by the scaling factor of its underlying period to make it equivalent in sensitivity to a placing over the same period. The currently set floating side of the swap is netted against the fixed side of the swap.

The second quarter of 1992 has 91 days. Of the placing equivalents (a) overlaps the quarter completely, and (d) overlaps it by 83 days. The placing equivalent in the quarter is, therefore,

$$100 + (1,020,000 * 83/91) = 930,430.$$

7.5   The funding risk of the company can be represented as:

Year	1993	1994	1995	1996	1997
Funding	-120	-123	-126	-129	-132
Fixed borrowing	60	60	60	30	
Hedges	-15	-30	-30		
Net floating funding	-75	-93	-96	-99	-132
Funding risk	0.75	0.93	0.96	0.99	1.32

All figures are in DEM millions. Funding risk is future value for 1% shift in rates.

The bond overlaps half of 1996 and thus half its principal counts in that year. The floating side of the swap is already set and so it offsets the fixed side in the first half of 1993.

The present value of the funding risk is:

$(0.75/1.08) + (0.93/1.08^2) + (0.96/1.08^3) + (0.99/1.08^4) + (1.32/1.08^5),$

which is DEM3.88 million.

Bibliography

This is a brief and eclectic list of source documentation and further reading; it contains works which the author has found useful in particular areas and which incorporate material which may be of interest to the reader of this book. The intention is to *recommend* works; therefore, not every subject covered in the text is represented below.

For each work cited, a description of *relevant* contents is given; in most cases, the work also includes additional material. References to current academic research can be found in works marked with an asterisk (*).

BACKGROUND

Brealey, Richard A. and Stewart C. Myers, *Principles of Corporate Finance*, McGraw-Hill, 1990. *

Corporate finance, a good basic introduction to Modern Portfolio Theory and the Capital Asset Pricing Model, present valuing after-tax cashflows, a good discussion of efficient markets.

Elton, Edwin J. and Martin J. Gruber, *Modern Portfolio Theory and Investment Analysis*, John Wiley & Sons, Inc, 1991. *

A thorough guide to modern portfolio theory and its ramifications, including the Capital Asset Pricing Model and Arbitrage Pricing Theory.

Katz, Ian, *Managing Financial Risk*, Euromoney, 1991.

This explicitly ignores market risk and instead looks at the control structure necessary to manage derivative products over their lifetime. While the price is astronomic and some details of the approach are not to this author's taste, there does not seem to be any other extensive treatment of the subject.

Ritter, Lawrence S. and William L. Silber, *Principles of Money, Banking, and Financial Markets*, Basic Books Inc., 1989. ★

Macroeconomics as it affects the determination of interest rates, and the role of a central bank. Deals only with the USA, but is nevertheless a valuable exposition of these two topics for the non-specialist.

Smith Jr, Clifford W., Charles W. Smithson and D. Sykes Wilford, *Managing Financial Risk*, Harper & Row Publishers, New York, 1990. ★

A readable exposition of the economics and instruments of risk management.

OPTIONS

Cox, John C. and Mark Rubinstein, *Options Markets*, Prentice-Hall, 1985. ★

The standard textbook on option theory and practice. Although it contains little material explicitly on interest rates, it is still required reading for anyone seriously studying options.

Hull, John, *Options, Futures, and Other Derivative Securities*, Prentice-Hall International, 1989. ★

A much more concise and mathematical treatment of option theory. Difficult but necessary reading for anyone wishing to go beyond Black Scholes in pricing and managing options. It builds on the theory of stochastic processes to price general derivative products, including options. There is a chapter devoted to interest rate products.

Press, William H., Brian P. Flannery, Saul A. Teukolsky, and William T. Vetterling, *Numerical Recipes in C — The Art of Scientific Computing*, Cambridge University Press, 1988. ★

Not bedtime reading, but an invaluable sourcebook for methods of mathematical programming. Also available in versions for Fortran and Pascal.

OTHER INSTRUMENTS

Credit Suisse First Boston, *The CSFB Guide to Yield Calculations in the International Bond & Money Markets*, Probus Publishing Company, Chicago, 1988.

Details of various national bond markets plus specification of different yield and yield-related calculations for bonds.

Rivett, Phil and Peter Speak (eds), *The Financial Jungle — A Guide to Financial Instruments*, IFR Books for Coopers & Lybrand, 1991.

An extensive review of debt, asset backed, equity, and hedging instruments, giving high-level discussion of risk; particularly useful for discussing accounting and tax treatment for each class of instrument in eighteen European countries.

In addition, the futures and options exchanges produce brochures explaining their various contracts. Addresses are given in Appendix C.

STANDARD CONTRACTS AND REGULATIONS

Forward Rate Agreements ('FRABBA' terms), British Bankers' Association, 10 Lombard Street, London EC3 V9EL, UK, telephone +44 (71) 623 4001.

Standard market terms for FRAs.

1991 ISDA Definitions, International Swap Dealers Association, Inc., 1270 Avenue of the Americas, Rockefeller Center, Suite 2118, New York, NY 10020, USA, telephone +1 (212) 332 1200.

Standard market terms for single and cross currency swaps and interest rate options; also a useful source document for definition of different interest bases.

Notice to institutions authorised under the Banking Act 1987: Implementation in the United Kingdom of the Solvency Ratio Directive, Number BSD/1990/3 December 1990, Bank of England, Banking Supervisory Division, Threadneedle Street, London EC2R 8AH, UK, telephone +44 (71) 601 4444.

The BIS risk-based capital rules for banks as implemented in the UK. An equivalent publication should be available from each national bank regulator.

PERIODICALS

In order to keep up with market developments it is important to read the trade press. Obvious sources of information are the major business newspapers, in particular the *Financial Times* and *The Wall Street Journal*. More specialist publications include:

Euromoney, Euromoney Publications PLC, Nestor House, Playhouse Yard, London, EC4V 5EX, UK, telephone +44 (71) 779 8888.

The house magazine of the capital markets; important monthly reading.

International Financing Review, IFR Publishing, South Quay Plaza 11, 183 Marsh Wall, London E14 9FU, UK, telephone +44 (71) 538 5384.

Essential reading to keep up to date on the capital markets on a weekly basis.

Risk, Risk Magazine Ltd, 104-112 Marylebone Lane, London W1M 5FU, UK, telephone +44 (71) 487 5326.

Technical articles on new risk management products and markets; probably the most read specialist publication among risk management professionals.

Swaps Monitor, Suite 705, 648 Broadway, New York, NY 10012, USA, telephone +1 (212) 254 9500.

A pricey newsletter; although much of its material will also be in *International Financing Review*, it is a particularly good source for early warning of legal or credit issues affecting the swaps markets.

Glossary of symbols

The following are the symbols used in more than one part of the text. Symbols used in one place only are defined where used and are not included below.

A_t	Variable accumulated in calculation of zero coupon yield curve
c	Convexity
C	Present value of call option
d	Downward movement of asset price in single period of binomial option pricing model
d	Duration
delta	Sensitivity of option price to asset price
d_m	Modified duration
e	Basis of natural logarithms; equals 2.718281828459...
f	Cap or floor notional principal times period in years over 100
f	Forward foreign exchange rate
F	Cap, floor, or swaption notional principal
gamma	Sensitivity of delta to asset price, sensitivity of interest rate option delta hedge ratio to zero coupon rates
$i\%$	Deposit interest rate
K	Future valued strike price
$K\%$	Strike rate
K_i	Fixed cashflow at payment date i on underlying swap of swaption
$L\%$	Libor interest rate
L_t	Libor at time t
$m\%$	Par interest rate on bond, market rate on FRA
$\max(a,b)$	Larger of a and b
n	Number of periods in binomial option pricing model
$N'(z)$	Normal density function, $\dfrac{1}{\sqrt{2\pi}}\, e^{-\frac{z^2}{2}}$
$N(x)$	Normal distribution function, $\displaystyle\int_{-\infty}^{x} N'(z)dz$

p	Variable used in binomial option pricing model; equals $(\check{r}\text{-}d)/(u\text{-}d)$
p'	Variable used in binomial option pricing model; equals $u * p/\check{r}$
P	Present value of put option
PV	Present value
$PV1\%$	Present value of a 1% interest flow over a given swap profile
q	Probability of upward movement in single period of binomial option pricing model
r	Annualised scaling factor
$\check{r}$	Scaling factor for single period of binomial model
r_i	Annualised scaling factor to payment date i on underlying swap of swaption
r_m	Annualised scaling factor to maturity of cap, floor, or swaption
r_v	Annualised scaling factor to value date of cap, floor, or swaption
s	Scaling factor
S	Current price for asset
S'	Forward price of asset
$S^\star$	Asset price at option exercise date
t	Time in years; for options, time to exercise date
t_i	Time in years to payment date i on underlying swap of swaption
t_m	Time in years to maturity of an FRA, cap, floor, or swaption
t_v	Time in years to value date of an FRA, cap, floor, or swaption
theta	Minus sensitivity of option price to time
u	Upward movement of asset price in single period of binomial option pricing model
vega	Sensitivity of option price to volatility
x	Term in Black Scholes or Black option pricing formula
x	Spot foreign exchange rate
$Z\%$	Zero coupon interest rate
Z_i	Zero coupon rate to payment date i on underlying swap of swaption
Z_m	Zero coupon rate to maturity date of an FRA, cap, floor, or swaption
Z_v	Zero coupon rate to value date of an FRA, cap, floor, or swaption
σ	Volatility (sigma)
ϕ	Complementary binomial distribution function (phi)

Index